Jossey-Bass Teacher

Jossey-Bass Teacher provides educators with practical knowledge and tools to create a positive and lifelong impact on student learning. We offer classroom-tested and research-based teaching resources for a variety of grade levels and subject areas. Whether you are an aspiring, new, or veteran teacher, we want to help you make every teaching day your best.

From ready-to-use classroom activities to the latest teaching framework, our value-packed books provide insightful, practical, and comprehensive materials on the topics that matter most to K–12 teachers. We hope to become your trusted source for the best ideas from the most experienced and respected experts in the field.

THE CLASSROOM TEACHER'S SURVIVAL GUIDE

Practical Strategies, Management
Techniques, and Reproducibles
for New and Experienced Teachers

Third Edition

Ronald L. Partin

Foreword by
Stephen G. Barkley

JOSSEY-BASS
A Wiley Imprint
www.josseybass.com

CONTENTS

FOREWORD BY STEPHEN G. BARKLEY   xiii

ABOUT THE AUTHOR   xv

ACKNOWLEDGMENTS   xvii

I THE BASIC TEACHER TOOLKIT

1 CREATING A SUPPORTIVE LEARNING ENVIRONMENT
FROM DAY ONE   1

The First Day of School   2

Arranging Successful Classrooms   2

Students' Desks   3

Seat Assignments   4

Keeping Desks Clean   5

The Teacher's Desk   5

Basic Classroom Supplies   6

Seventeen Tips for Making Outstanding Bulletin Boards   6

Helping English Language Learners   8

The Room Environment   9

Noisy Classrooms Impede Learning   10

Greeting Your Students   11

Getting to Know Your Students   12

Welcoming New Students   13

The Importance of Relationship Building   14

Resources to Help in Relationship Building   16

Clarifying Expectations   16

Tasks to Accomplish   17

First-Day-of-School Checklist   18

Additional Suggestions   18

Creating an Inviting School Climate   19

2 NURTURING POSITIVE STUDENT BEHAVIOR   29

Proactive Classroom Management   30

Establishing Rules   30

Thirty Hot Tips for Managing Classroom Behavior   32

What Do You Want?   36

Positive Reinforcement of Good Behavior   36

The Reward Hierarchy   37

Tips on Using Positive Reinforcement in the Classroom   37

Potential Classroom Rewards   38

Tangible (Physical) Reinforcers   38

Activity Reinforcers   39

Help the Teacher   39

Rental Privileges as Potential Activity Reinforcers   40

Social Reinforcers   40

Recognition   40

Intrinsic (Internal) Reinforcers   41

Creative Self-Expression   41

Positive Referrals: Recognition That Works   41

Helpful Resources   42

Cell Phones and Text Messaging in Class   42

Corporal Punishment   44

The Case Against Corporal Punishment   45

Additional Information on Corporal Punishment   46

Time-outs   46

Dos of Using Time-outs   46

Don'ts of Using Time-outs   47

Bullying in Schools   48

Why Students Bully   48

Successful Interventions   48

"Fight, Fight!": Intervention Strategies   49

Motivating the Unmotivated   50

The Teacher as a Skilled Helper   51

What Good Listening Is Not   52

Reflection of Feelings   53

Twenty-three More Tips for Becoming a Better Listener   54

3 TIME MANAGEMENT AND ORGANIZATIONAL STRATEGIES   73

The Erosion of School Time   74

The School Calendar   74

Instructional Time   75

Teacher Time-on-Task   76

The Pace of Instruction   77

Student Time-on-Task   77

Conclusion   79

References   79

Prisoners of Time   80

Block Scheduling   80

Advantages of Block Scheduling   81

Disadvantages of Block Scheduling   82

For More Information   83

Eleven Tips for Minimizing Classroom Interruptions   83

Teacher Time Robbers   84

Full-Time Teachers' Workweek   85

Classroom Routines   85

Taking Attendance or Lunch Count   87

Distributing and Collecting Materials   88

Regaining Students' Attention   89

Seeking Permission to Leave the Room   90

Seeking Help   91

Students' Tools   92

Assignments and Homework   92

Storage Solutions   93

The Challenge of Paperwork   93

Causes of the Paper Deluge   94

Thirty-four Tips for Handling Paperwork   95

Communications   98

Teacher Time Log   99

To-Do List   100

Assessing Student Time-on-Task   101

Conquer Procrastination Now!   102

Procrastination Payoffs   104

Attacking Procrastination   106

Tips on Getting Organized   107

Know What You Want   107

Plan for Success   107

Discover Your Prime Time   107

Keep a Personal Calendar   108

Lead a Balanced Life   108

Finding Time for a Really Important Task   110

Been to a Good Meeting Lately?   110

Look for Alternatives to a Meeting   111

Have an Agenda   111

Begin on Time   111

Include Only Necessary People   112

Select a Conducive Environment   112

Keep the Meeting on Task   113

Record Progress 114
End on Time 114
Student Help 114

II ESSENTIALS FOR EFFECTIVE TEACHING AND LEARNING

4 CREATING SUCCESSFUL LESSONS 133

Planning Effective Lessons 134
Beginning a Class 136
Action Verbs for Writing Instructional Objectives 138
Learner-Centered Lessons 140
For More Information 141
Planning Units of Instruction 141
For More Information 141
Thirty-eight Hot Tips for Maintaining Interest 142
Seven Cardinal Rules for Effective Visuals 147
Additional Tips for Using Overhead Transparencies 148
Storyboarding 148
For More Information 149
Internet Resources 149
Review Techniques 150
Mind Maps 150
For More Information 151
Mind Mapping Software 151
Nineteen Tips for Closing a Lesson 151
Differentiating Instruction 154
Multiple Intelligences 154
Emotional Intelligence 157
Preferred Learning Modalities 160
Teaching to Students' Strengths: Homework That Helps 161
Interesting Homework 163
Making Assignments 165
The Internet and Homework 166
Collecting and Grading Homework 166
Handling Makeup Work 166
Putting More Pizzazz in Your Presentations 168
Voice 168
Nonverbal Communication 169
Improving Your Speaking Effectiveness 170
Humor in the Classroom 171
Tips on Using Humor in Your Classroom 171
For More Information 173
Seeking Student Feedback 174

Guidelines for Fair Use of Copyrighted Educational Materials   175
   Public Domain   176
   Seeking Permission to Use Copyrighted Material   176
   Protecting Your Creative Works   177

5 INTERACTIVE TEACHING AND LEARNING STRATEGIES

183

Question and Answer   184
Twenty-two Hot Tips for Asking Effective Questions   185
Inquiry Learning   187
   For More Information   188
Brainstorming   188
Creativity Crunchers   190
Brainwriting   192
List Making   192
Class Discussions   193
Fishbowls   194
Artwork   195
Music   196
Guided Imagery   197
Journal Keeping   198
Field Trips   200
   Ideas for Potential Field Trips   202
   Field Trip Sypply List   203
   Field Trip Follow-up Activities   204
   Virtual Field Trips   204
Guest Speakers and Panels   205
Debates   208
   For More Information   209
Videos and DVDs   209
Podcasts   211
   For More Information   212
   Internet Resources   212
Blogs   212
Interactive Technology in the Classroom   214
   For More Information   214
Video Recording   214
   For More Information   216
Designing Effective PowerPoint Presentations   217
   Free PowerPoint Lessons   217
   Sources for Free Images and Sounds   217
Dyadic Encounters   218
Demonstrations   219
Board Work and Whiteboards   219

Action Research **220**

Interviews **221**

Construction **222**

Card Sorts **222**

Surveys and Questionnaires **223**

Oral Presentations **223**

Role Playing **224**

Dramatization **227**

Games and Simulations **228**

Helpful Resources **230**

Cooperative Learning **231**

For More Information **233**

6 ASSESSMENT AND TESTING TOOLS 241

Assessing Student Performance **242**

Formative versus Summative Assessment **242**

Monitoring Student Progress **243**

Variability in Assessment **244**

Grading Student Performance **245**

Twenty Tips for Making Grading as Painless as Possible **246**

Tests and Quizzes **247**

Grade Contracts **249**

The Multiple-Option Grade Contract **249**

Authentic Assessments **251**

Portfolio Assessments **252**

Performance Assessments **254**

Self-Assessment **254**

Designing Rubrics **255**

Sample Generic Rubric **255**

Thirty Alternative Assessments **256**

For More Information **256**

Interpreting Standardized Test Scores **257**

High-Stakes Testing **258**

Arguments for High-Stakes Testing **259**

Arguments Against High-Stakes Testing **260**

For More Information **260**

III STRIVING FOR EXCELLENCE

7 BUILDING A LEARNING COMMUNITY 269

Twenty-four Hot Tips for Working with Other Teachers **270**

Working with a Mentor **272**

Telementoring **274**

For More Information **274**

Guidelines for Collaborative Teams   **274**

Suggestions for Effective Action Planning Teams   **277**

  Helpful Resources   **278**

Working with Your Principal   **278**

Improving Parent-Teacher Relations   **280**

Parent or Guardian Conferences   **282**

The Successful Open House   **285**

Tips for Helping Substitute Teachers   **286**

Working with Support Staff   **288**

Working with Volunteers and Aides   **289**

8 STAYING ON TOP OF YOUR GAME   297

Twenty-two Tips for Becoming an Effective Teacher   **298**

  Suggested Reading on Effective Teaching   **300**

Teacher Expectations Revisited   **301**

  For More Information   **301**

Are You an Effective Teacher?   **302**

Twenty-seven Mistakes Teachers Commonly Make   **305**

Thirty-two Strategies for Nurturing Peak Performance in Others   **305**

Effective Schools   **307**

  For More Information   **308**

Indicators of Quality   **308**

National Teaching Standards   **310**

Professional Development   **312**

National Board Certification   **316**

Educational Research   **317**

  The Scientific Method   **318**

  Types of Research   **318**

  Common Flaws in Research Articles   **319**

  The Importance of Statistics   **321**

  Basic Research and Statistics Glossary   **321**

  For More Information   **322**

Learning What Works: Action Research   **325**

  For More Information   **326**

Professional Organizations   **326**

Education Journals   **330**

  General Education Periodicals   **330**

  Research Journals   **331**

  Subject Specialty Journals   **331**

  Online Education Journals   **332**

Stress and Burnout in the Classroom   **333**

  Stress Management in the Classroom   **334**

  For More Information   **336**

  Stress Busters and Sanity Savers   **336**

Famous Americans Who Also Taught School   341
Ten Inspirational Teacher Movies   342

9 HELPFUL RESOURCES FOR TEACHERS 347

Scrounging for Supplies   348
   Potential Sources for Teaching Supplies   349
   Suppliers of Instructional Materials   350
   Sources of Rubber Stamps   353
The Internet as a Learning Resource   353
   E-mail   355
   Electronic Discussion Groups   356
   Some Popular Online Education Discussion Groups   357
   Online Resources for Beginning Teachers   357
   Online Lesson Plan Archives   358
   Online Collaborative Learning Resources   360
   Educational Search Engines   360
   Useful Online Databases   361
   Online Directories   363
   Helpful Books on Using the Internet in the Classroom   363
   Organizations Supporting Educational Use of the Internet   363
Computer Software for Improving Teacher Productivity   364

FOREWORD

I guess it's to be expected that a man as multifaceted as Dr. Ron Partin would likewise create a multifaceted book filled with strategies, techniques, and useful materials for beginning and veteran teachers alike. An educator, guidance counselor, scholar, and consultant—among other interests and avocations ranging from bluegrass music to genealogy—Ron is best known to me as providing the backbone to multiple graduate courses developed by Performance Learning Systems, Inc., for over thirty years.

Ron conducts research in all facets of education, guiding the legitimacy and credibility of PLS courses internationally. He has coauthored graduate courses and penned many rich articles to benefit teachers. First and foremost, Ron's intention is to assist the classroom teacher to impart knowledge to students.

This third edition of *The Classroom Teacher's Survival Guide* provides a rich recipe book or, depending on your generation, a drop-down menu of multiple options for teachers to use immediately and with tremendous success. It's a virtual bible for K–12 educators, parents, home schools, administrators, coaches, and others. I have been known to use some of the techniques in my own instruction of teachers!

Beginning teachers, in particular, will find *The Classroom Teacher's Survival Guide* a life raft of support as they navigate their first years of school, as it is comprehensive, user-friendly, and provides practical strategies and tips for the everyday problems of organizing and managing a classroom. It's no wonder that some districts in this country consistently order *The Classroom Teacher's Survival Guide* for all their beginning teachers. Nothing could get them off to a better start.

Veteran educators will find these cutting-edge concepts and practical ideas a stimulus to meeting new challenges and finding more enjoyment and satisfaction in their teaching, as this third edition taps into the newest research and trends toward technology, globalization, and multicultural teaching.

Turn to any chapter or any page in this book and you will find ideas, activities, tips for successful teaching, checklists, forms, certificates, and, of course, substantiating research. Ron has included books, online resources, and Internet sites for virtual field trips, as well as advice, suggestions, and encouragement in a wide range of topics, including parent conferences, cooperative learning, alternatives to lecturing, homework ideas, learning modalities, and how to use action verbs in developing lesson plans. And that is just for starters.

Because Ron is so well versed in the current research about teaching, learning, and education now and in the future, his approach incorporates many real-life, interactive, and technology-based exercises for students that are also filled with fun and that are reality based, enriching, and empowering for students.

As I travel around the country—and now internationally—presenting and instructing on behalf of good teaching, coaching, and sound learning, I am constantly met with educators seeking creative ideas to use with their students. Passionate and dedicated to teaching, these educators thrill at resources or suggestions for activities or lessons they can readily and immediately adapt to their classroom. Ron's book answers these needs and then some.

Mentors, coaches, staff developers, and supervisors can also find ideas, suggestions, and creative options for the educators they support. Oftentimes the coaching relationship calls for a teacher or administrator to observe his or her peers on whatever the person being coached wants to focus on, whether delivery, classroom management, reading, or other topics. To have a lesson or teaching tips at the ready augments this process and allows more in-depth time for feedback and coaching.

Written with humor, peppered with quotes, current in its examples, research, and references, *The Classroom Teacher's Survival Guide* belongs in every new and veteran educator's classroom or office.

—Stephen G. Barkley
Executive Vice President, Performance Learning Systems, Inc.

ABOUT THE AUTHOR

Ronald L. Partin, professor emeritus and former coordinator of the graduate guidance and counseling program at Bowling Green State University, holds a Ph.D. in educational psychology and counseling and has more than thirty years' experience as an educator, scholar, and consultant. As a counselor educator, he taught courses in counseling, educational consultation, group dynamics, and learning psychology. A former high school teacher and coach, Ron is in frequent demand as a speaker, trainer, and consultant. He uses his classroom experiences to teach and motivate, with his everyday examples and ready-to-implement techniques.

Ron is the author of numerous journal articles in the areas of time management, goal setting, creative problem solving, stress management, and effective teaching skills. He is the coauthor of Classroom Management: Orchestrating a Community of Learners®, a graduate training program completed by over fifty thousand teachers nationwide.

Ron is the coauthor of *The Social Studies Teacher's Survival Kit* (Prentice Hall, 1992) and author of *The Prentice Hall Directory of Online Social Studies Resources* (Prentice Hall, 1998) and *The Social Studies Teacher's Book of Lists* (Jossey-Bass, 2nd ed., 2003).

Ron serves as research editor for Performance Learning Systems, an educational services company. Ron is known for facilitating fun, interactive workshops and has been invited to present programs to over four hundred schools, businesses, and professional organizations.

Ron and his wife, Jan, are now enjoying their second adulthoods as residents amid the mountains of western North Carolina. Their twin sons are both gainfully employed and are excellent parents. Ron collects hobbies: woodworking, genealogy, golf, square dancing, bluegrass music, gardening, stained glass, and travel. His overwhelming passion continues to be helping teachers thrive in the classroom. He may be contacted at rpartin@bgsu.edu.

Dedicated with love and pride to our grandchildren,
Braedon, Jacob, Brooke, Aaron, and Drew

ACKNOWLEDGMENTS

The greatest source of ideas for this book were the hundreds of teachers who participated in my workshops and classes over the past thirty-five years. Where known, the original or published sources are credited for any ideas used. This project would have been much more difficult without the emotional support and encouragement of my wife, Jan.

The selection of clip art in this book is from a variety of electronic sources, including the following: clipart.com and iclipart.com subscription services, DeskTop Art by Dynamic Graphics, Desk Gallery by Zedcor Corporation, Digit Art from Image Club Graphics, Metro ImageBase, Click Art from T/Maker Company, Image Club, Images With Impact!, School Clip Art from Quality Computers, and Volk Clip Art from Dynamic Graphics.

Articles originally published in *Heart of Teaching* newsletters, © 2001–2005 Performance Learning Systems, Inc.®, an educational services company located in Allentown, PA, and on the World Wide Web at wws.plsweb.com. Used with permission. All rights reserved.

The diligent efforts of Marjorie McAneny, senior editor, K–12 Education for Jossey-Bass, Justin Frahm, production editor, and the rest of the editorial staff at Jossey-Bass greatly contributed to the successful completion of this book. Special gratitude is extended to Steve Barkley of Performance Learning Systems for his support and kind words expressed in his foreword to this book.

Creating a Supportive Learning Environment from Day One

1

THE FIRST DAY OF SCHOOL

The foundation for a successful school year is laid on the first day of school. Everything you do on that day sets the tone for the rest of the year. Spending time planning and organizing the first day's activities is one of the most valuable investments you can make as a teacher.

Your three primary objectives for the first day of school are to get acquainted, establish your expectations, and stimulate enthusiasm and interest in what you will be teaching. The best advice for the first day is "Be prepared." You want to convey to your students that you are organized, are in control, and know what you are doing. It is wise to develop a checklist of items to cover the first day. (See the sample checklist at the end of this section.)

This chapter will address the key things you can do to assure the first day gets the year off to a positive beginning.

ARRANGING SUCCESSFUL CLASSROOMS

Before the first day of school, spend time organizing your classroom for maximum efficiency. The physical arrangement of your classroom can influence your students' behavior and learning. The placement of desks, bookshelves, pencil sharpeners, and cabinets can influence traffic flow, student interaction, as well as noise, attention, or disruption levels. The impact of the room arrangement is too important to leave to chance.

Plan the classroom learning environment before the beginning of the school year. Your goals for the class must guide your choices. Whether you wish to maximize group interaction with lots of small-group activities or lecture most of the time, the physical arrangement can help or hinder. Students get a pretty good picture of what their year is going to be like from the decor and arrangement of the classroom as they enter for the first time.

More than creating aesthetic appeal, each piece of furniture redefines a part of the classroom space, directing attention, pupil interaction, or traffic flow. Overlooking the importance of even casual rearrangements within the classroom is easy. Something as simple as the placement of a new pencil sharpener, a new bookshelf, or an area rug can have a significant impact on the learning events of your classroom.

The environment you see may be quite different from what your students perceive, especially younger ones. When no one else is around, crouch down to the children's eye level and view your room as they see it. Waddle around the room to see how the furniture directs your attention and movement.

Draw your current classroom arrangement to scale on graph paper. Include all the furniture, windows, doors, bulletin boards, electrical plugs, cabinets, wastebasket, and pencil sharpener. Observe your class for a day, noting on your drawing the traffic patterns. Indicate any bottlenecks. Are there any areas that invite students to stop and talk? Does the present arrangement direct students through work centers or group activities? Are there dead spaces that no one ever enters? Be sure to place electrical equipment so that students cannot trip over the cords.

Arrange any special areas in the room. Some teachers have reading areas, perhaps with stuffed furniture, a rug, or pillows. Have the necessary supplies and materials sorted and organized for any learning centers, art area, writing area, labs, and so on.

Give special attention to minimizing unnecessary noise in your classroom. Where possible, use soft, quiet, sound-absorbing materials: carpeting, rubber, sponge, cardboard, and cork.

STUDENTS' DESKS

The single most important decision influencing the physical classroom environment is the students' seating arrangement. Ideally, the arrangement of students' desks should not be permanent, except for large lecture halls or laboratories. The purpose of the learning activity should dictate the most favorable seating pattern. Unless furniture is bolted to the floor, it can be moved during the day as the lesson dictates. The custodial staff's ease of cleaning should play only a minor role in such decisions. What to do:

- Traditional seating in rows has endured because it is very functional for many classroom purposes. Particularly early in the year, seating students in rows enables you to observe behavior more easily and minimizes distractions. Research has shown that row seating produces higher levels of on-task behavior in elementary classrooms.

- The greater the distance between students, the less they will distract each other. However, theater or row seating can facilitate independent seatwork, lecture, movies, and tests.

- If your class uses several seating arrangements regularly, teach your students how to move from one to another as quickly and quietly as possible. You may want smaller children to help each other carry desks without dragging them across the floor.

- Seating students in clusters or around a table facilitates group interaction. This arrangement enhances small-group discussions and cooperative learning, but it also invites chatting and socializing.

- Whole-class discussion is facilitated with a circular, semicircular, or open-ended rectangular seating arrangement. Traditional rows are probably least supportive of student-to-student interaction.

- Performance classes, labs, and special activities such as story time might dictate atypical seating choices or even no seats at all. The important thing is to monitor your seating pattern's effects. Don't be afraid to experiment with different arrangements to achieve different results.

- After a few weeks, experiment with other seating arrangements. Simply changing the seating patterns, even which direction the seats face, will influence your group's dynamics.

- To minimize the tendency to look primarily at the students in the front and center of a classroom, make a conscious attempt to scan the back corners, where the more disruptive students tend to cluster. It is often wise to move such students to the front center, as that is the natural region of most eye contact. Interestingly, some researchers have discovered that students' test scores increase after they move to the front center. However, avoid seating two troublesome students next to each other.

- Give careful consideration to the direction students normally face in your chosen seating arrangement. As they will attend most to whatever is in their direct line of sight, try to arrange for students to face away from windows and doors to minimize distractions. Facing windows or bright lights creates excessive glare, causing eye-strain.

If you have several learning centers or areas in your room, separate noisy from quiet areas. Plan your seating so that you can move freely among students when providing individual assistance. Avoid seating arrangements that hide some students behind bookshelves or cabinets. Avoid creating mazes that force students into long, winding traffic patterns to reach the pencil sharpener or wastebasket.

SEAT ASSIGNMENTS

You must decide before school begins whether to assign students to specific seats or to allow them to select their seats. Most teachers prefer to assign seats at first. It is best to announce that the initial seating assignments will be temporary. After having learned their names, established behavioral control, and taught students your desired procedures and routines, you might allow them to choose (or assign them) different seats. However, if you have several difficult students, it is best to maintain control over the seating pattern, separating troublemakers from one another and keeping them where you can easily monitor their behavior. You need not single them out or draw attention to the fact that you are putting them where you want them. Whatever seating pattern you select, always be sensitive to the special needs of hearing- or visually impaired students.

If you use printed seating charts, use a pencil to fill them in, as they will change. Keep any seating charts current in case a substitute must use them in your absence.

Hot Tip for a Seating Chart

Becky Laabs, a veteran art teacher at Bowling Green City Schools (Ohio), devised a creative and handy seating chart that you can make too. On the outside of a manila folder, sketch your classroom-seating layout, with a small rectangle to represent each student's seat. Cut out small pieces of cardstock and print a different student's name on each one.

Attach each name to its appropriate spot with Velcro. Future changes in assigned seats will be easy to make, simply by switching the removable rectangles. Make a different colored folder for each class, if you have more than one.

Store daily lesson plans, papers to be returned, or other items inside the folder for easy access. The folder will prove especially valuable to any substitute teachers during the year.

Another option is to tape or staple a clear transparency over the master seating chart. Names can be easily changed using an erasable marker on the transparency film.

KEEPING DESKS CLEAN

Some students' desks begin to resemble an attic, hiding assorted old papers, tattered books, pencil stubs, broken crayons, pens, and miscellaneous treasures. Teachers have resorted to a range of tactics for encouraging students to keep their desks tidy, from spot checks to formal inspections with checksheets. Some choose to ignore the mess and allow students to suffer the consequences.

One strategy that many teachers adopt is to institute visits by a desk fairy, a mythical creature that visits their desks after school. If the desk is orderly, the fairy leaves a special surprise such as a certificate, sticker, or ribbon.

THE TEACHER'S DESK

Not all teachers require a desk. If your room is crowded and you spend little time at your desk, consider removing it or replacing it with a small table and a filing cabinet. Some prefer an old-fashioned writing desk, which makes monitoring students easier. A high stool eases the burden on the feet.

If you do have a desk, the next choice is where to place it. It does not have to be at the front center of the classroom. If you do not usually sit at your desk during class, place it in a front corner or even at the back of the classroom. It is best not to place it near the door, thus inviting people to grab things off it as they leave the room or to interrupt or distract you as you work there. Make sure your desk does not block any student's view of the chalkboard.

Germs at Your Fingertips

A study by University of Arizona microbiologist Chuck Gerba revealed that the average desktop has four hundred times more bacteria than the average toilet seat. And the office telephone is even worse.

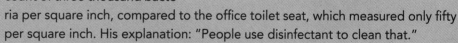

After collecting seven thousand bacteria samples from a variety of office building surfaces, Gerba found that bathrooms had the lowest levels of germs of all. The average keyboard had a count of three thousand bacteria per square inch, compared to the office toilet seat, which measured only fifty per square inch. His explanation: "People use disinfectant to clean that."

The telephone had the highest bacteria counts, closely followed by the desktop itself and the computer keyboard. Water fountain knobs and microwave oven door handles also harbored high levels of germs. The report concluded: "The oily grime that collects on keys and headsets becomes a breeding ground for bacteria, increasing the risk of colds and other infections spreading through an office. They get this contaminated because they're rarely cleaned."

The area where you rest your hand on your desk contains some ten million bacteria! While the research examined business offices, it is unlikely that cleaning patterns are any better in schools.

Gerba suggested that regularly cleaning the desktop greatly reduces the number of germs. Daily use of disinfecting wipes decreased the bacteria count by 99 percent.

Other teachers have an open-desk policy, inviting students to help themselves to staplers, tape, and other materials. Of course, a locked drawer or closet might be reserved for private belongings or confidential records. Whichever practice you adopt, communicate your expectations to your students at the beginning of the year.

Source: Gerba, C. (2002). Office germ study. Available from www.shinytech.co.il/en/news/office_study.pdf.

This article was originally published in the *Heart of Teaching* newsletters, © 2001–2005 Performance Learning Systems, Inc.®, an educational services company located in Allentown, PA, and on the World Wide Web at www.plsweb.com. Used with permission.

Note to the reader: This book intentionally omits the standard http:// prefix from all Web site addresses. Most Internet browsers do not require users to type that prefix into the address bar.

Teachers have different perspectives on the ownership of their desks. Some prefer to define their desks as private territory, off-limits to students. They may even arrange bookshelves and filing cabinets to create barriers from others' intrusions.

BASIC CLASSROOM SUPPLIES

Address book
Attendance forms
Chalk
Cleaning rags
Clock
Desk calendar
Dictionary
Disposable tissues
Eraser
Extension cord
Felt pens
File folders
First-aid kit
Glue
Grade book
Hole punch

Note cards
Old towels
Paper
Paper clips
Paper towels
Rubber bands
Rulers
Stapler
Staples
Tape
Tardy slips
Teacher's manuals for texts
Thumbtacks
Tool kit
Whistle
Yardstick

SEVENTEEN TIPS FOR MAKING OUTSTANDING BULLETIN BOARDS

Well-designed bulletin boards can be effective learning and motivational tools. Their value as an instructional device should not be overlooked or left to chance. Preparing bulletin boards can be time-consuming. Enlist others' help. Occasionally allow students or parent volunteers to help create attractive bulletin boards.

Don't assume that attractive bulletin boards are for elementary classrooms only. They are just as effective with middle and high school students. For inspiration and ideas, check Web sites and professional journals. Here are some tips for constructing great bulletin boards:

1. From a roll of colored paper, tear a piece to the approximate size of the bulletin board to make a cover. Mold this to the bulletin board by hand and temporarily pin it to the board. With a small pin or razor knife, tear or cut along edges to remove the excess paper. You are ready to place objects and letters on the board.

2. Make two to three covers for bulletin boards at once, placing one on top of the other. When it is time to change displays, simply pull off the top display, revealing the next one beneath it.

3. Rather than repeatedly correcting students for the same errors, create a bulletin board display explaining the error and the correct procedures.

4. You need not decorate every bulletin board. Use blank ones for announcements, posters, student work, newspapers, magazine articles, and so on. Use some class time to have students brainstorm ideas for bulletin boards.

5. Generate graphics and letters with computers. Special software is readily available in most schools for printing banners and posters. Use letters of various sizes. Large ones grab the students' attention and get them to read the rest.

6. Give your students time and materials to cut out bulletin board letters of various styles and sizes. Store these in envelopes for future use.

7. Project coloring-book images onto large sheets of paper taped to the wall. Trace and color the images to make large characters to include in your bulletin boards.

8. Use some bulletin boards to teach or reinforce a skill or concept. Make them interactive, engaging students in tactile or kinesthetic learning.

9. Reserve one section of a bulletin board for students to use to post interesting articles, invitations, unusual quotations, pictures, cartoons, and other items of interest.

10. At the end of the school year, whenever students have some free time, let them create a bulletin board for you. It will be ready for the fall, welcoming the new class back to school. You might want to have them cover it with newspaper to protect it during the summer.

11. Develop interactive bulletin boards. Use pockets and flaps to hide answers to questions displayed on the board. Post a daily question, riddle, or puzzle for students to explore when they enter the room. Some displays might pose a question to which students write their answers or estimate in a block on the bulletin board. These are especially valuable if they relate to a topic to be studied that day.

12. Hang a clothesline across one wall of your room. Attach students' papers to the line with clothespins.

13. Velcro or flannel boards can be incorporated into manipulative boards that invite students to experiment. Bulletin boards can be dynamic, inviting students to interact

Internet Sources for Bulletin Board Ideas

Bulletin Board Ideas from Teacher Vision
www.teachervision.fen.com/bulletin-board/
curriculum-planning/6515.html

Bulletin Boards Across the World
www.gigglepotz.com/bulletin.htm

Bulletin Boards and Tips for the K–3 Teacher
www.teachingheart.net/bboard.html

Classroom Displays and Bulletin Boards
http://my.att.net/p/s/community.dll?ep=16
&groupid=20303&ck=

Interactive Bulletin Boards for Secondary School
Mathematics
http://faculty.kutztown.edu/schaeffe/
BulletinBoards/bbs.html

and reform the display. Self-checking questions can be displayed, with answers covered by flaps.

14. Shop fabric stores after holidays to purchase inexpensive fabrics with holiday themes. These make excellent backgrounds for seasonal bulletin boards and can easily be reused for many years.

15. Think of creative materials and ideas to incorporate into unique borders. Discarded fabric, game pieces, silk flowers, ribbons, leaves, greeting cards, or photographs can all be incorporated into attractive borders.

16. Go 3-D, attaching objects to your bulletin board display. Objects such as feathers, dried flowers, discarded ties, masks, hats, and costume jewelry can all be incorporated into your bulletin boards. Strive to use multiple textures to make the bulletin boards more attractive.

17. To help maintain interest, alter some part of a bulletin board every day or once a week. Changing a featured quotation or startling statistic each day keeps the students motivated to keep looking at it. Remember, a bulletin board is more than just wall decoration. It can be a great motivational device and instructional aid.

HELPING ENGLISH LANGUAGE LEARNERS

An ever-growing number of classrooms include students for whom English is their second language. Many of these English language learners (ELLs) may struggle with their schoolwork. Teachers can make a difference in easing their transition.

Here are some tips successful teachers have implemented to help their English language learners:

- Pair ELL students with native English speakers for some learning experiences. Assure that the ELL students have access to translation dictionaries.

- The first few weeks, allow ELLs to work with selected buddies. You might use older students for limited tutoring with younger students.

- Use parent volunteers to help students improve their English skills.

- Use as much visual communication (for example, props, cues, and text) as possible to reinforce your verbal content.

- Allow students to record your oral presentations to review later.

- Simplify your language in explaining abstract concepts.

- Try to avoid using slang.

- Idioms particularly create problems for ELLs. Check out the Pocket English Idioms Web site (www.goenglish. com/ Idioms.asp) for examples of common English idioms. When you do use idioms, clarify for your students what they mean.

- Use gestures and visual expression to reinforce your speaking.

- Nurture an atmosphere of acceptance. Model appropriate behavior and do not tolerate disrespectful treatment of any students. Encourage empathy in the rest of your students.

Go Green: Eco-Friendly Classrooms

Strive to model good environmental stewardship in your classroom.

- Provide bins for recycling paper, aluminum cans, and plastic.
- Create a tray for used papers that have a blank side. Encourage students to use the old paper whenever feasible.
- Minimize paper use as much as possible. For example, allow students to submit some assignments or projects electronically.
- Include environmental issues related to the subjects you teach.
- If relevant to your subject, help students do a classroom energy audit.
- Turn off lights and electronic equipment when not needed.
- Decorate your room with plants.
- Have students brainstorm energy-saving ideas for use in the classroom.
- Recycle printer ink cartridges.
- Use non-toxic cleaning supplies.
- Use rechargeable batteries where possible.
- Use acid-free glue.
- Open the windows when possible.
- Use school supplies made of recycled materials.
- Check out Live Green Teacher Grants at http://livegreen.discoveryeducation.com/ for funds to support your eco-friendly projects.
- Dispose of old computers through the Dell and Goodwill's Reconnect electronics recovery program. See www.reconnectpartnership.com/ for more information.
- Encourage your students to get involved with the Student Environmental Action Coalition (SEAC), a "grassroots coalition of student and youth environmental groups, working together to protect our planet and our future." See www.seac.org/ for more information.

- Be sure ELLs can see your face when talking.

- Be sure to enunciate clearly, yet naturally, when speaking. Avoid speaking louder. That doesn't help.

- Offer encouragement and praise as much as possible.

THE ROOM ENVIRONMENT

Your classroom's physical arrangement can minimize off-task behavior and invite learning. Experiment with changing your room setup, including the arrangement of students' desks, making it a regular part of your preparation. It pays dividends.

- Be creative in arranging your room. You need not be bound by the traditional configurations, with everything arranged in a rectangle. Filing cabinets or bookshelves do not have to be placed against the walls. Placed at right angles to the wall, they create study areas or redirect traffic.

- Plan the traffic patterns you wish to create. Keep high-traffic areas, such as the pencil sharpener, clear of obstructions. If a student's desk is immediately in front of the pencil sharpener, a disturbance is inevitable when other students use the sharpener. Avoid patterns that create congestion by funneling many students through a small path.

- When working with small groups, place their chairs so that the students face away from the rest of the class. This prevents their being distracted by the rest of the class, and it allows you to monitor all students. If an aide is working with small groups, you may use a portable chalkboard to screen the small-group activity from the rest of the class.

- Keep the room tidy. Before allowing a class to leave the room, have students pick up litter around their desks. A cluttered and dirty environment invites further abuse. Similarly, have any graffiti removed immediately. Research has shown that graffiti's presence serves as a stimulus for more graffiti. Removal may involve some additional effort at first but saves time and damage later. Avoid creating an impression that abuse of the room is acceptable.

- Use posters, decorations, banners, signs, artifacts, and displays to create an inviting atmosphere. Changing them periodically to reflect the topic your class is studying is especially effective.

- Before school begins inspect your classroom to identify any broken, dirty, or unsightly clutter. Broken windows, hinges, desks, shades, or locks should be repaired or replaced. It may take time, but see your principal about how to get these things done. Don't give up easily if you encounter delays. Doing some smaller tasks yourself may be easier.

Suggestions for Improving Classroom Acoustics

- Close the classroom door to eliminate ambient hallway noise.
- Keep windows closed if possible.
- Cover hard surfaces with sound-absorbing materials (acoustic tiling, carpeting, cork, or cloth).
- Ideally, floors should be carpeted and windows curtained.
- If floors are not carpeted, cover chair feet with slit tennis balls.
- Use felt or cork pads on desk lids to minimize noise from opening and closing.
- Turn off computers and printers when not in use.
- From the beginning of the year, set noise rules: indoor voices only, no slamming books or doors.
- Get every student's attention before talking.
- At the beginning of the year, establish a nonverbal cue to signal that students are to stop talking and listen.

Source: Originally published in the *Heart of Teaching* newsletters, © 2001–2005 Performance Learning Systems, Inc.®, an educational services company located in Allentown, PA, and on the World Wide Web at www. plsweb.com. Used with permission.

NOISY CLASSROOMS IMPEDE LEARNING

A series of research studies by University of Florida professors Gary Siebein and Carl Crandell revealed that noisy classrooms seriously impair students' learning. Observations in forty-seven Florida elementary, middle, and high schools revealed that most had background noise levels between forty and fifty-five decibels. Most people have difficulty hearing once background noise reaches fifty decibels.

The research revealed that students seated more than twelve feet away from the teacher in noisy classrooms hear less than 5 percent of what their teachers say when addressing the whole class. Research also shows that between 10 percent and 30 percent of students possess some kind of moderate to mild hearing impairment. Noisy classrooms further impede the learning of students with attention deficit disorder.

Source: Most classrooms are too noisy for learning. *University of Florida News,* December 5, 2001.

GREETING YOUR STUDENTS

On the first day, greet all students at the door with a smile and tell them where to sit. You might have a seating chart on the overhead with their names placed on their assigned seats. Some elementary teachers have name tents already at each student's desk. It is wise to direct them to begin work on a specific task as soon as they take their seats: completing a word puzzle, filling in a personal information survey, or scanning their textbook's table of contents. You are creating an expectation that learning begins as soon as your students enter the classroom, not necessarily when the bell rings.

The first day of school is likely the single most important day of the school year. Expectations are created; the foundations of routines and procedures are established; and first impressions are formed. You should be better organized and better prepared for the first day than any other of the year. Recovering from a bad start will take a long time.

Post your name and room number beside your door. That will help students avoid the embarrassment of discovering ten minutes into the class that they are in the wrong room.

The first five to ten minutes of the first day's contact with your students is probably the most important segment of time the entire school year. Consider carefully what you want to accomplish these first few minutes and the most effective means of doing so. Choose your words carefully.

Your goal is to create a warm yet businesslike atmosphere. You must convey that you know what you are doing, have confidence in yourself, and expect appropriate behavior and effort from your students.

Don't waste the most precious minutes of the year taking roll. That can wait. First, introduce yourself. Have your name printed on the board. Clearly and slowly pronounce it for your students and tell them how you expect to be addressed. If you have an aide in the room, introduce him or her. Spend a couple of minutes telling the class a little about yourself and your background. Share a bit of your life: family, hobbies, pets, interests, where you went to school, or experiences. If you are just beginning your teaching career, it is best not to emphasize your inexperience. Don't overdo the introduction; a couple of minutes are sufficient. Some teachers allow students to ask them questions. Other teachers construct a biographical display or bulletin board. How much you choose to share about yourself and when are matters of personal comfort and judgment.

If you are particularly skilled in some aspect of what you will be teaching, you might exhibit your skill by demonstrating something students will be learning. Show them you are a pro; it helps establish respect and credibility.

During these first few minutes, your students are sizing you up. Who are you? How will you treat them? What are the boundaries of what they can do in your classroom? It is wise to convey positive expectations and enthusiasm. You aren't going to get them very excited about your class if you don't seem too enthusiastic yourself. Put some energy into your opening. Also use your most poised, assertive body language. If possible, stand, scan the class with your eyes, and don't be afraid to smile.

GETTING TO KNOW YOUR STUDENTS

Spending time getting to know your students is one of the most valuable investments you can make. Establishing rapport helps build mutual respect and minimize classroom behavior problems. A deeper understanding of your students' needs, problems, and interests will enable you to plan instruction that succeeds. Here are some tips for getting to know your students:

- Some teachers prefer to look at each student's cumulative folder before school begins. This gives them a sense of their class's special talents and problems. Of course, this may not be feasible for high school teachers with over a hundred students.

- Allow some time the first day to get acquainted with your students. A fun icebreaker activity, particularly if it can relate to your subject area, can be helpful. One way to learn a bit more about your students is to call the class roll this way: instead of replying "here," have them respond by naming their favorite hobby or sport. The next day you could have them answer with their favorite song or food.

- The first day may be the only time you actually call the roll. The main purposes are to clarify the pronunciation of students' names and identify what they prefer to be called. One of the best ways you can show respect for your students and earn their respect and trust is to learn their names. This should be a prime objective for the first week of school. Make a special effort to use a student's name any time you address a specific individual the first week. Many effective teachers use name tags or name tents to help learn students' names.

- Have students create name tents. A sample is found at the end of this chapter and additional ones can be found at the *Classroom Teacher's Survival Guide* Web site josseybass.com/go/classroomteacher. Print the blank templates on card stock. Give a printed name tent to each student, and instruct them to print their names in bold letters on one side. Students fold them, so the tent stands by itself.

- If you really want to impress your students, end the first day by having them remove their name tags or name tents. Then proceed around the room, identifying each student by name. You don't have to hit 100 percent; they will be impressed that you even tried. It doesn't take a great memory, just a focused, determined effort. If you accomplished little else that day, the year would be off to a good start. Knowing and using a student's name communicates that you regard that person as more than an anonymous face among a group of students. Some have suggested that a person's favorite word to hear is his or her own name.

- To help in remembering names, attempt to connect a student's name with another person of the same name. For example, if you have a student named Brett and that is also your son's name, try to visualize the two playing together. If you don't know anyone by that name, associate that person with a famous person of the same name.

Visualize a new student named George with a powdered wig like George Washington's. As you make a mental connection, consciously use that student's name every time you talk to or call on him or her for the next week. Stand by the door and greet each one by name to reinforce your name awareness.

- Take photographs of students the first week and attach their names and cutouts of their faces on a master seating chart.

- If you have a printed roster the first day, be sure it is accurate. Make any corrections, but do not write your class roster in the grade book the first week. It will change. Indeed, assume that no matter when you finally write your class roll into your grade book, a new student will show up the next day!

- Make a special effort to welcome students new to the school or area. Try to pair them up with a returning student and make sure they are included in some of the student groups during lunch and recess.

- Some kindergarten and first-grade teachers send notes to their students inviting them to come to school in small groups a couple of days prior to the beginning of the school year. They might invite students to bring a favorite toy to share. This provides an opportunity for the teacher to get to know their students before school begins; and the students get a chance to meet their teacher and a few of the other students in a safe, inviting environment.

- Give students a chance to get to know you. One option is to let the group interview you for a few minutes.

Who Is Your Teacher?

Create a "Who Is Your Teacher?" bulletin board to welcome students the first week. You might include photos of your family and samples or photos of you enjoying your favorite activities. Share your interests, travels, and hobbies.

WELCOMING NEW STUDENTS

Arriving in a new school the very first day is a stressful event for most students. They may be filled with anxiety about whether they will be accepted, whether they will be academically competitive with their new classmates, and how their new teachers will treat them. Make a special effort to make new students feel welcome.

- In elementary classrooms invite the rest of the class to brainstorm things they might do to make a new student feel welcome. This is especially helpful if you know ahead of time that a new student will be joining the class.

- Spend a few minutes getting to know a little about the student's background. Ask to meet with him or her a few minutes during the day to chat informally.

- Some teachers develop a brief questionnaire for new students to complete, detailing family information, interests, extracurricular activities, and past coursework.

> The dream begins with a teacher who believes in you, who tugs and pushes and leads you to the next plateau, sometimes poking you with a sharp stick called "truth."
>
> **—Dan Rather**

- Consider pairing the new person with a reliable student buddy or guide who can teach your routines and procedures. The buddy can show the new student around the school and introduce him or her to schoolmates.

- Give the new student some time to get acclimated before calling a lot of attention to him or her. If the student appears shy, don't publicly make too big an issue of his or her arrival. If the student seems comfortable after a few days, you might spend a few minutes letting the student tell the class a little about his or her background, interests, and family.

- Consider calling the parent(s) or guardian of a new student to introduce yourself and to learn a little more about their child. Invite them to visit the school for a conference.

- Have several welcome folders prepared to immediately give any new students. Besides classroom and school rules and routines, include a personal note or letter welcoming the new student.

- To help the new student feel more comfortable with the class, find something to praise or acknowledge.

- Some teachers have everyone wear name tags during the week following a new student's arrival.

THE IMPORTANCE OF RELATIONSHIP BUILDING

Positive teacher-student relationships provide the foundation for effective instruction and constructive classroom management. For example, research by psychologists Jan Hughes and Timothy Cavell indicated that a close, warm relationship between students who are at risk for behavioral problems and their teachers diminishes the chances of aggressive behavior in the future.

Your goal is not to become your students' friend, although many students may attempt to craft such a connection. There is a boundary.

Too frequently headlines have reported sensational stories about teachers who have engaged in inappropriate behavior with their students, often costing them their jobs, and leading to imprisonment. Use common sense in maintaining appropriate boundaries and avoiding compromising situations with students.

- Avoid being alone with one student behind closed doors.
- Never use double entendres with any students.

- Do not allow students to touch you.

- Maintain a comfortable professional boundary.

- Avoid engaging in sexually explicit conversations with students.

Here are a few habits that successful teachers adopt in striving to build positive relationships with their students:

- Always remain sensitive to the influence you have in your students' lives. Your choice of words, disapproving nonverbal messages, harsh tonality, ignoring, or sarcasm can have long and profound effects on your students' self-esteem.

- Treat students decently. Treat them as you would have wished to be treated as a student, not necessarily as you were treated.

- Strive to catch the student being good. Too often we ignore students until they misbehave. Then we reprimand or punish them. Acknowledging what they are doing right is more helpful than only giving criticism of what they do wrong.

- Never use sarcasm or ridicule when talking to students. It accomplishes nothing permanently positive. Once used, it is hard to retract and erodes the teacher-student relationship. When reprimanding a student for misbehavior, condemn the behavior, not the person.

- Always try to convey an attitude of acceptance toward all students. This does not mean you must approve of everything they do; but when you must condemn an unacceptable behavior, do so without rejecting the child.

- Develop the habit of saying "please" whenever you make a request of a student. Convey respect by responding with "thank you" whenever a student complies with a request, no matter how grudgingly he or she may do so. Strengthen the appreciation by also using the student's name.

- Remember the adage "Praise publicly, criticize privately." Even when reprimanding or criticizing students' behavior, do so in a style that leaves their dignity intact. If at all possible, never cause a student to lose face in front of his or her peers. It achieves nothing positive in the long run.

- Aim to talk with each student every day, even if it is only a smile and greeting as they leave or enter the classroom. Attempt to get to know your students better during these mini-conversations. This will help you build rapport as well as discover the frustrations, challenges, disappointments, and conflicts facing your students.

> One looks back with appreciation to the brilliant teachers, but with gratitude to those who touched our human feelings. The curriculum is so much necessary raw material, but warmth is the vital element for the growing plant and for the soul of the child.
>
> —Carl Jung

> A student never forgets an encouraging private word, when it is given with sincere respect and admiration.
>
> —William Lyon Phelps

RESOURCES TO HELP IN RELATIONSHIP BUILDING

Adams, C. (2007). Not getting along? *Instructor, 116*(7), 47–50.

Johnson, L. P. (2008). *The caring teacher: Tips to motivate student learning.* Lanham, MD: Rowman & Littlefield.

Noguera, P. A. (2007). How listening to students can help schools to improve. *Theory into Practice, 46*(3), 205–211.

Ryan, M. (2008). *Ask the teacher: A practitioner's guide to teaching and learning in the diverse classroom* (2nd ed.). Boston: Pearson/Allyn and Bacon.

Witmer, M. M. (2005). The fourth R in education: Relationships. *Clearing House: A Journal of Educational Strategies, Issues and Ideas, 78*(5), 224.

CLARIFYING EXPECTATIONS

Establishing your hopes, expectations, rules, and routines is an essential first-day goal. Clearly explain, demonstrate, and allow time for students to practice the routines that will help get things done smoothly throughout the year. Clarify specific procedures for taking attendance, beginning work each day, turning in assignments, requesting help, going to the bathroom, and other reoccurring classroom routines. It is not essential to introduce every routine the first day but certainly do focus on each as the need arises. (See Chapter Three for successful teachers' suggestions on how to manage these routines.)

In communicating your hopes for the class, you might say something like, "I don't expect you to be perfect. I do hope you will strive for excellence and work to improve. We all will make mistakes. The important thing is to learn from those mistakes."

Students' Psychological Needs

Students enter a new classroom experiencing common psychological needs that can be expressed in the following questions:

- Will I feel accepted?
- Will I be safe?
- What will be expected?
- How comfortable will I be?
- Will the class content be helpful to me?

TASKS TO ACCOMPLISH

There are several important tasks to accomplish during the first week, if not the first day. Be sure to include the following items:

- Explain the rules. A few rules (ideally, no more than five) are preferable to a long list. Some teachers prefer to hold a class meeting, allowing students to provide input into the norms that should be enforced. Beyond giving them some influence in their school lives, it also provides practice in the process of democracy.

- Discuss emergency procedures. Clarify and perhaps practice the drills for fire, tornadoes, or other emergencies. Be sure everyone knows which exits to use in the event of an evacuation.

- Distribute books and other materials. This provides a good opportunity to practice routines for distributing materials. Be sure to have students complete the necessary records for end-of-the-year collections of signed-out materials.

- Assign lockers or drawers. If combination locks are provided, be sure to keep a master list for those who forget their combinations.

- Clarify what materials and supplies students will need for your class. What items will the students be expected to bring every day? Which will they need tomorrow? Will you need to collect any fees? It is generally best to distribute a written list they can take home.

- Discuss your grading procedures. Many (but not all) students want to know this: "What do I have to do to get an A in this class?" or at least to pass it. Clarify what their academic responsibilities will be, what criteria you will be using to evaluate their performance, and how you will allot grades. Clarity and fairness here can eliminate a lot of arguments and protestations at the end of the term.

- Many teachers distribute a handout detailing their class expectations and grading scheme. Clarify what constitutes acceptable work. Explain any rubrics that you might be using in evaluating work.

- Explain the schedule that your class will typically follow. At least the first day, having the day's activities listed on the board is a good idea.

- In laboratory or shop classes and in elementary classrooms, a tour of the classroom will be helpful in orienting students to the various stations and features they will be using during the year.

- Set the tone for the year. Creating an inviting, warm class environment gets the year off to a good start.

FIRST-DAY-OF-SCHOOL CHECKLIST

Before School Begins

_____ Become familiar with the building.

_____ Post your name, grade level or subject, and room number beside your door.

_____ Have name tags or name tents and markers available.

_____ Write your name on the chalkboard.

_____ Have a sufficient number of textbooks available (remember the teacher's edition).

_____ Write the day's class schedule on the board.

_____ Double-check the day's school schedule (recess, lunch, class changes).

_____ Have the class roster readily accessible.

_____ Have all teaching materials ready for the first day's lesson.

_____ Know the school rules and policies.

_____ Complete the first day's lesson plans.

_____ Arrange desks in the desired pattern.

_____ Create an inviting atmosphere (bulletin boards, posters).

_____ Set up CD player and any music to play.

_____ Have "sponge" activities available.

Opening Day

_____ Greet students at the door—smile!

_____ Assign temporary seats.

_____ Begin learning students' names (check pronunciation).

_____ Establish rules.

_____ Get students started on learning.

_____ Specify supplies and fees that students must provide.

_____ Make any assignments for the next class.

_____ Begin training routines and procedures.

_____ Show enthusiasm for your subject!

ADDITIONAL SUGGESTIONS

Be an early bird. Arrive early the first morning, allowing ample time to tend to any last-minute details. Be available to greet students as they enter the room. You cannot do that if you are in the office waiting for the copy machine. Also, students are less likely to engage in mischief if you are in the room when they arrive.

Expect the unexpected. The first day is always a bit hectic. Murphy's Law will rule: anything that can go wrong will. Students will show up in the middle of the class because they have been sitting in the wrong class. There may not be enough textbooks, desks, or supplies. Strive to remain calm and flexible. Remember, students are assessing your mettle the first day. If you are easily flustered, it will undermine your credibility and respect. A true professional can handle any situation, even when things don't go as planned. Be patient.

Overplan the first day. It is better to have too much to do than to have a class of students sitting idly or for you to aimlessly wing it.

Dress your best the first day. This is part of creating a professional image and establishing credibility. It also communicates that you value your students enough that you will make a special effort to look your best for them. We also tend to be more confident when we are well groomed.

Set your standards from the very beginning. Classroom management style is very much established the first day. Be fair yet firm in enforcing your classroom rules. Once you tolerate a behavior, changing it later is difficult.

Show that you have a sense of humor. Don't try to be a stand-up comedian, but allow yourself to laugh with—not at—your students. An amusing cartoon on the door or overhead helps create a warm, inviting atmosphere.

Don't hesitate to ask your principal or colleagues questions if you don't understand something. If you are new, be sure to explore the building and meet some of your colleagues before the first day. Also read the policy manual.

CREATING AN INVITING SCHOOL CLIMATE

For all too many students, school has become something to avoid. Many see it as a boring, depersonalized, irrelevant institution. Fortunately, school doesn't have to be a dreaded experience. Some classrooms and schools, even in the most impoverished of environments, remain inviting and nurturing. Schools that maintain a positive school climate are marked with a high degree of cohesiveness and high level of morale, among students as well as staff. Research provides evidence that school climate is related to the level of academic achievement.

Interestingly, research reveals that students' self-esteem increases immediately on dropping out of school. The students' former environment daily communicated that they were losers, incompetent, and slower than everyone else. When they stop going to school, they suddenly escape those degrading messages and begin to accept themselves more. (Unfortunately, that gain in self-acceptance may later erode as they face the challenge of surviving in the economic world without a diploma.) Positive school climates occur when students believe they have a shared responsibility in developing and maintaining a warm and supportive environment. The following tips will help you do just that:

- Always remember the adage "Students do not care how much you know until they know how much you care." We earn respect only by showing respect; we gain trust by trusting. Develop a student-centered rather than subject-centered classroom.

- Schools are most likely to be successful when students experience a sense of ownership and belonging. Both are nurtured when students have some degree of choice and control in their daily experience. Involving students in classroom decisions, valuing student contributions, and respecting individual differences help meet these needs.

- Make a conscious effort to get to know the good things about your students. Publicly and privately acknowledge their achievements outside of your class.

- Treat all students fairly. While it is natural for teachers to enjoy teaching some students more than others, overt favoritism can create a divisive and resentful climate.

- Strive to be consistent in your enforcement of rules, grading, and treatment of students. Although we all have our good days and bad days, students' inability to predict a teacher's expectations and responses is poisonous to an atmosphere of trust and respect.

- Take time to listen to your students. Not only does this convey your respect for them, but you may also receive feedback that might help you become a better teacher. Solicit their opinions about how they perceive your class. Occasionally invite them to complete open-ended sentences anonymously, such as "The thing I enjoy most about this class is . . ." or "I would enjoy this class more if . . ."

- Communicate your expectations clearly, both for academic tasks as well as behavioral norms. Don't make students guess what you want.

- Inviting teachers communicate that they expect all students to succeed. Every day, both verbally and nonverbally, inviting teachers genuinely communicate that each student is capable, unique, and valued.

- Provide opportunities for choice. The ability to have control over one's life is a basic human need. Though many school tasks are not optional, there are ample opportunities to allow students a degree of freedom. For example, offering a choice of learning activities or homework assignments may not only give students a greater sense of freedom but may actually enhance their learning as well.

- Consider holding periodic classroom meetings in which students can openly discuss their views on the class procedures and climate. Of course, to succeed you must convey to your students that you are genuinely interested in their views. The best way to communicate this is to listen nonjudgmentally.

- Plan lessons that offer more instructional techniques than the talking head in front of the classroom. Teacher talk is still the dominant instructional

> A teacher who is attempting to teach without inspiring the pupil with a desire to learn is hammering on cold iron.
>
> **—Horace Mann**

mode in many of our schools. Education has become a very passive endeavor. Strive to actively involve students in meaningful learning activities. Construct lessons with ample student interaction, challenging content, and a variety of instructional approaches.

- Pay attention to your classroom's physical environment. The seating arrangement, wall decorations, bulletin boards, special reading areas, learning centers, and posters all contribute to your classroom's emotional tone.

- Recognize, encourage, and reinforce positive behaviors and achievements. Especially express your appreciation for deeds that contribute to a positive class climate: cooperation, helpful behaviors, caring, and inclusion. Reward direction, not perfection. Acknowledge small gains.

- Become an inveterate note writer. Keep a stack of notepaper. Make a commitment to recognize the good deeds of students, colleagues, custodians, secretaries, administrators, librarians, aides, parents, or volunteers. Five minutes each day spent sending a couple of thoughtful notes will pay dividends and contribute to making your school a more pleasant place.

- Pay attention to the students in the middle of the normal curve—those who neither lag nor excel. For the most part, the academically average student is ignored in our classrooms. Recognize and encourage their small successes and progress.

- Don't be afraid to smile. A gentle smile conveys warmth, acceptance, and caring. Avoid the perpetual wide, toothy pseudosmile. A genuine smile is conveyed with the eyes as well as the mouth. If smiling is not a natural behavior for you, practice in front of a mirror (privately, of course!).

- Avoid developing a highly competitive classroom climate. While some argue that competition prepares students for the real world, a great deal of evidence shows that it is destructive and unnecessary. Even corporate America is teaching its employees to work in cooperative teams and strive for win-win solutions to conflict.

- Empathize with the students who are always at the bottom of the normal curve—in academic achievement, athletic ability, popularity, or physical development. Consider ways in which you might help make them feel included and valued. Emphasize growth over perfection or being the best. No matter how hard they try, most students will never be at the top of the class.

- Pay attention to multicultural and gender inclusiveness in all your teaching activities. Use examples and visuals that include persons of a variety of cultural and ethnic backgrounds and of both genders. Do not tolerate bigoted behavior in your classroom.

- Remain sensitive to the fact that your students come from a variety of religious backgrounds. Avoid imposing your religious views on your students. Holidays, especially religious ones such as Christmas or Hanukkah, may not hold the same meaning for some of your students. Respect their freedom of religion and avoid activities that clearly endorse one particular religion to the exclusion of others (unless you teach in a parochial school).

- When a student is ill for any extended period of time, send a "Get Well Soon" message from the entire class. If feasible, let the group use its creative talents to create the message, perhaps on a DVD.

- Recognize birthdays and other special occasions. The first day of school, have your students enter their birth dates on a personal information sheet. Transfer all their birth dates to your calendar. You might make birthday cards for each student. Computer software, such as Greeting Card Factory or Print Shop, makes this quick and inexpensive.

- In the primary grades, you might want to designate a birthday chair and extend special privileges (for example, being first in line) to the honoree. Sing "Happy Birthday."

- Send birthday messages to the other adults in the building as well. Secretaries and custodial staff will appreciate being included. It will pay dividends!

- Find special occasions to celebrate: athletic or quiz-bowl team victories, change of seasons, holidays, or individual student achievements. Let students decorate a bulletin board in recognition of the occasion.

- Don't be afraid to make learning fun. Dress-up days, field trips, skits, songs, demonstrations, and learning games can break up the predictable, dull, passive approach to instruction that many students experience.

- Bring in a camera to take pictures of each student in your class the first week. Post the pictures along with their names on a bulletin board display. It will help you learn your students' names. Take informal shots of various learning activities throughout the year. Display these on a bulletin board for two to three weeks, and then let the students have the pictures.

- Develop a repertoire of anecdotes and amusing stories related to your academic content. Search for cartoons that you can incorporate into lessons.

- Be creative in planning your teaching activities. Challenge yourself to invent new, more interesting ways to help your students learn. Learn from successful teachers through workshops, books, and magazines. Keep an idea notebook with you at all times to jot down interesting possibilities—anecdotes, examples, quotations—anything that might be of use in one of your classes. Part of being a professional is seeking continual improvement in your skills and curriculum.

- Convey your own enthusiasm for the topic you are teaching. Getting your students excited about a topic will be nearly impossible if you are unenthusiastic.

- Publicize your students' successes to the parents and the community. Use local newspaper articles, school assemblies, school and class newsletters, local television stations, parent-teacher associations, and open houses to showcase your students' accomplishments. This has multiple beneficial effects for your students as well as the school.

Note to the Reader

A variety of sample templates, letters, handouts, and other items that may be of value in your teaching are included at the end of each chapter. Additional ones are available for free download from the *Classroom Teacher's Survival Guide* Web site josseybass.com/go/classroomteacher. Check back at the site periodically as new templates, letters, and handouts will be added.

Sample Letter to Welcome Students Before School Starts

Einstein Elementary School
203 Gibson Ave.
Hendersonville, NC 28729

(Date)

Greetings,

In less than two weeks, school will begin. As you probably know by now, I will be your fifth-grade teacher. This is my sixth year of teaching at Einstein Elementary School. I love teaching and very much enjoy the students at Einstein. I always look forward to meeting my new class each year.

I hope you have had an enjoyable summer and look forward to hearing about what you did. My family spent a week camping in a national forest. I'll be showing some of the slides in our geography class this year.

School begins at 8:00 A.M. Tuesday, September 3. You should come directly to room 78. I do expect all students to be on time every day. I think most students find my classes to be fun, although we also work hard. We do a lot of cooperative work in groups. Most nights you can expect to have thirty to forty-five minutes of homework.

I have enclosed a list of supplies you will need. The only ones you definitely need the first day are the pen, spiral notepad, and glue. The rest of the items you should have by Monday, September 9. If you or your parents have any questions, I can be reached at home at 646-3371. It will be easiest to reach me between five and nine in the evening.

Best wishes for a most successful year!

Sincerely,

Mr. Green

Getting to Know You

Directions: Please complete the following sentences. There are no right or wrong answers.

Name _____

1. During the summers I most enjoy _____
   _____

2. I wish I could _____
   _____

3. What I like to do most is _____
   _____

4. The thing I enjoy best about school is _____
   _____

5. I am happiest when _____
   _____

6. My favorite television program is _____
   _____

7. I learn best when _____
   _____

8. My favorite sports are _____
   _____

9. One thing I do well is _____
   _____

10. One thing I would like to do better is _____
    _____

11. I dislike school when _____
    _____

12. When I grow up, I hope to be _____
    _____

Get-Acquainted Bingo

Directions: Find a person who fulfills each of these categories. Collect their signatures in the appropriate boxes. Write your favorite activity, sport, or hobby in the middle box. Try to get as many different signatures as you can.

Is left-handed	Loves to dance	Never wears a watch	Has a birthday this month	Has a cat
Is wearing blue socks	Reads biographies	Walked to school today	Likes broccoli	Has two sisters
Has written a poem	Loves the beach	**FREE**	Plays a musical instrument	Keeps a diary
Owns red shoes	Has lived on a farm	Owns a dog	Has been on a subway	Visited Canada
Enjoys fishing	Is an only child	Likes to cook	Has seen the Grand Canyon	Has ridden a horse

Student Personal Record

Name _____

Street Address _____

City _____

State _____ ZIP _____ Home Phone _____

Parent(s) or guardian(s): _____

_____

Brothers' and sisters' names and ages: _____

_____

_____

_____

Your favorite sports, hobbies, activities: _____

_____

_____

_____

_____

_____

_____

_____

_____

_____

_____

_____

_____

_____

Back-to-School Word Search

```
P Y K A B T R E H C A E T
A R S R N O T E B O O K L
P O I T E E O M T U B E O
E T E N U T P K U N S N O
R S H G C D U N S S N D H
Q I L C D I E P O E I N C
U H E M N E P N M L D C S
I C A L C U L A T O R M E
Z T R D I M L W L R C O D
H G N I D A E R O G M P A
N L I B R A R Y S N E Y R
L N N H O M E W O R K Y G
I H G N I T I R W G I I I
```

BOOKS	CALCULATOR	COMPUTER
COUNSELOR	DESK	GRADES
GYM	HISTORY	HOMEWORK
KNOWLEDGE	LEARNING	LESSON
LIBRARY	LUNCH	MATH
MUSIC	NOTEBOOK	PAPER
PEN	PRINCIPAL	QUIZ
READING	SCHOOL	STUDENT
TEACHER	WRITING	

Sample Letter to Parents at Beginning of School Year

(Date)

Greetings:

Do you have a special talent? Do you enjoy an interesting hobby or activity? What skills do you use in your work? Have you traveled to an interesting or exciting place? Have you had a significant life experience from which young people might learn something? Please consider sharing any of these special abilities or events with my class sometime during the school year.

If you will complete and return the section below, I will contact you to arrange a mutually convenient time when you might visit my class. This is a valuable opportunity to become a part of the school community and to show your child you are interested in his/her education.

Sincerely,

(Your name)

- ✂

Name _____

Phone _____

E-mail address _____

Address _____

_____

What talent, experiences, or hobby would you be willing to share with my students?

_____

_____

_____

_____

_____

_____

_____

Nurturing Positive Student Behavior

PROACTIVE CLASSROOM MANAGEMENT

Dealing with student misbehavior is one of the most daunting challenges facing today's teachers. It is ultimately the key to improving students' academic performance.

Positive classroom management cannot be left to chance. It pays great dividends to be proactive from the very first day, investing the time and energy in building positive relationships with your students. You have a personal "psychological bank account" with each student. You cannot make withdrawals if you don't make deposits (which we do when we do the little things that create personal relationships).

Teachers do influence the behaviors of the students—both positively and negatively. Some teachers are more effective at positive classroom management than others. Think of those teachers from your early schooling whom you fondly remembered. What were they doing right? We can learn much from these exemplary teachers.

There is more to effective classroom management than merely bullying or intimidating students into reluctant compliance. After all, you expect students to behave properly even when you are not standing over them. We want to teach responsibility that transfers beyond the classroom door.

Nothing helps nurture positive student behavior better than an engaging and meaningful lesson. Students are certainly more attentive, motivated, and helpful when they perceive the content to somehow relate to their lives. Certainly we must deal with inappropriate behavior, but we can do so in a manner that treats our students with decency and respect.

This chapter features practical strategies that successful teachers have employed in teaching students at all grade levels.

> Theories and goals of education don't matter a whit if you do not consider your students to be human beings.
>
> —Lou Ann Walker

ESTABLISHING RULES

Research suggests that effective teachers are in control of their classrooms but not obsessed with the idea of control. A necessary (though not sufficient) first step in establishing standards of acceptable behavior in a classroom is to set some norms or rules of conduct.

- Some teachers prefer to involve students in the rule-setting process the first day of class. The class meeting as advocated by William Glasser, founder of control theory and reality therapy, can be an effective device for involving students and gaining their commitment to the rules they set.

- Most effective teachers establish a few, positively stated rules, for example:
  - Keep your hands to yourself.
  - Ask permission before using others' things.
  - Bring your materials and books to class.
  - Only one person should talk at a time.

- Always be on time.

- Complete and turn in all assignments.

- Respect others' rights.

- The maximum number of enforceable rules seems to be around five to seven. Many classrooms function very well with only three or four rules.

- It is important to establish your own set of rules, based on your needs and experience, your students' maturity, and the school climate.

- Don't try to cover every possible unacceptable behavior; you aren't writing a penal code. On the other hand, don't be so vague that no one really knows what the rule means.

- Motivation to comply with rules seems highest when they are stated positively. When possible, convey what you do want to happen rather than trying to list all the possible unacceptable behaviors.

- It is essential the first day not to let behaviors slide that are clear violations. Enforcing a higher standard once you have tolerated a lower standard of behavior becomes very difficult. It is easier to start out a bit firm and ease up later.

- Early in the year, hold a class discussion on students' rights in your classroom. Solicit ideas from your students as to what is a right and which ought to be accorded all students. Examples might include the right to make mistakes or the right to express one's opinion. Focus the discussion on the responsibilities that must accompany any right (for example, the responsibility to learn from our mistakes).

- Construct or let a student volunteer construct a poster listing the class rules. Display it prominently to remind students of the rules. It is imperative that every student know your rules.

- It does little good to establish rules if you have no plan for enforcing them. Your plan should in some fashion provide encouragement and reinforcement for students complying with the rules as well as some penalty or consequence for those who choose to violate the class rules.

- If you find it necessary to add a new rule later in the year, do so. Dr. Harry Wong, an expert on classroom management, suggests replacing an old rule with the new one. The old one can become an unwritten rule or expectation.

- Of course, honor school or district rules beyond those established for your classroom (for example, restrictions on drug use, weapons in the school, attendance policies). You are responsible for knowing and enforcing these. If you don't know them, ask for a copy of the teacher or student handbook. Post these rules and assure that all students know them. You can be held legally liable if you fail to enforce them.

- There is no substitute for consistently and fairly enforcing your class rules. Doing so assures some predictability in the students' learning environment.

- Allow students to role play scenarios in which rules might be violated. Present several hypothetical situations for small groups or individuals to role play. Encourage them to resolve the dilemma by practicing a behavior that does not break the rules. They learn by seeing others model appropriate responses and also by practicing responsible behaviors. Examples might include the following:

- ○ Brenda asks to copy your homework to hand in as hers.
- ○ Jake trips and accidentally pushes you from behind.
- ○ Brooke slips on a wet spot and falls while returning from the pencil sharpener. Other students begin to laugh at him and call him names.
- ○ Shoving breaks out between two students arguing over who was first in line.
- ○ The student seated behind you pokes you with a pencil.

- The classroom routines and procedures you establish at the beginning of the year convey your standards and expectations. They help you get things done in an orderly manner. Such informal rules or expectations complement your formal rules.

THIRTY HOT TIPS FOR MANAGING CLASSROOM BEHAVIOR

The ability to manage students' behavior is the number one concern of beginning teachers, and it is near the top for most experienced teachers. Indeed, the ability to develop harmonious, mutually respectful relationships with students is one of the best predictors of who will survive in the teaching profession. The inability to effectively manage students' behavior accounts for more teacher dismissals than any other cause, including lack of knowledge of subject matter. Here are some tips on effective classroom management gleaned from research and observations of effective teachers.

1. Invest in relationship building from the beginning, nurturing in your "psychological bank account" with your students. Remember the adage "They don't care how much you know until they know how much you care." This does not mean you should try to be their buddy. It does mean treating each student with dignity and respect. Show interest in their lives as you chat before and after class. Sure, it takes time; but much of the success of outstanding teachers, such as Jaime Escalante, the celebrated real-life model for the film *Stand and Deliver,* can be understood in terms of the caring relationship they developed with their students. It is a case of "You can pay me now or pay me later": you'll either spend time now building a mutually respectful relationship or spend it later in a classroom power struggle. If you've made regular deposits to the psychological bank account, you can make withdrawals later when you ask students to comply with your demands. They'll also be more likely to forgive your mistakes than to capitalize on them.

2. Expect some students to test you to determine the boundaries of acceptable behavior and your competency to respond. Although such tests are usually minor infractions (whispering, note passing, and so on), they constitute a challenge to your classroom control. It is essential to react immediately, calmly, and appropriately to these infractions; but it is vital not to overreact.

3. Preserve your classroom momentum at all costs. Momentum means that every student is on task and the lesson is rolling along smoothly. Most discipline problems do not occur during periods of momentum but rather during those periods of chaos—when something has broken the lesson's momentum. These classroom interruptions may sometimes be beyond your direct control: announcements over the P.A., a knock at the door, a fire engine passing the building, or the custodian riding by the window on a power mower. However, sometimes teachers may unwittingly break their own

momentum: by not having the necessary audiovisual equipment ready, by hunting for misplaced items in the middle of the lesson, or by stopping to reprimand an offending student. Note what happens when momentum is lost: the class goes from 95 or 100 percent on-task behavior to 0 percent on task. Now the teacher faces the challenge of refocusing everyone's attention and getting all students back on task. Pay special attention to making smooth, orderly transitions from one activity to another.

4. It may sound cliché, but the best way to prevent classroom misbehavior is to deliver interesting, fast-paced, organized learning experiences, particularly ones that actively engage students in the lesson. A dull lesson is an invitation to misbehave. Much student acting out is simply a reaction to boredom. Though even the best, well-prepared teachers occasionally have behavioral infractions in their classroom, they are less frequent and less severe. Additionally, recapturing students' attention and getting them back on task is less difficult in a fast-paced classroom.

5. Be sure your rules and expectations are clear. Some teachers haven't given much thought to what they do want but only to what they don't want. Such negative focusing is inefficient. Don't assume students will correctly guess what you expect of them. Develop high expectations of your students for their academic performance, as well as their classroom conduct.

6. It is also better to have a few rather than many rules. Remember that you have to enforce them. You have a right to be in control of your classroom, but do not become obsessed with control. Rules should also be conspicuously displayed in the room.

7. Avoid causing students to lose face in front of their peers. Avoid needless public confrontations. You will almost always lose in the long run; kids can, and do, get even. Whenever possible, reprimand privately; avoid giving your perpetrator an audience.

8. Keep your eyes moving. Eye contact is your most powerful tool in maintaining classroom control. Probably 80 percent of potential classroom misbehaviors can be nipped in the bud through timely, direct eye contact. Keep your eyes moving to scan the entire room at least once every minute or less. You actually don't have direct eye contact with every single student every minute but rather focus on clusters of four or five students at a time. Hold that gaze for four or five seconds and then move on to another group. Remember that most teachers have less eye contact with students sitting in the farthest corners of the room, and that is exactly where most troublemakers choose to sit!

9. Continually monitor what is happening in your classroom. Some researchers refer to this as having eyes in the back of your head. Always know what's going on in your classroom. Avoid standing or sitting with your back to the class. For example, when working in a small group, sit so that you are facing the rest of the class. It is also difficult to monitor all of the class if you are sitting at your desk in front of the room. It is generally better to pace around the room during whole-class instruction. Effective teachers seem to develop a sixth sense in anticipating potential problems and appropriately intervening to nip them in the bud.

10. Practice the principle of escalation. This means you don't go after a fly with a baseball bat; if you have a small problem, use a small tool. If your initial strategy doesn't work, you can always escalate to a more potent strategy. You can always go up, but you can never effectively go down to a lower-level strategy if a more confrontational one does not work. Direct eye contact might be the lowest level of challenge. If the student does not correct his or her behavior, then escalate, perhaps by moving into his or her body space,

> Nine-tenths of education is encouragement.
>
> **—Anatole France**

standing near his or her desk. All of this can occur while you are still teaching the rest of the class, without directing everyone's attention toward the transgressing student. You've not broken your own momentum.

11. Use the power of silence. Follow your behavioral directives with a pause while maintaining direct eye contact. Silence is power; use it constructively. After giving each behavioral directive, pause and take two slow, deep breaths. Not only does this give the student time to comply, but the breathing also helps you to remain calm. You don't want to convey either fear or hostility. If you must escalate to the next level of confrontation, pause again for two deep breaths. Say no more than is absolutely necessary. Avoid haranguing or degrading the student. You'll only fuel resentment and create sympathy for the offender among the rest of the class. You don't need to get drawn into a power struggle.

12. Don't overreact. When you lose your composure in front of the class, they, not you, are in control of your behavior. Some students will test you to discover your "hot buttons," the behaviors that cause you to lose control. Also remember that most of the things students do in our classrooms to annoy us are not evil, dastardly deeds. They are simply inappropriate, not acceptable in that situation. Of course, if a student's misbehavior is potentially harmful to others or destructive of property, then we must employ the necessary strategy to deter that behavior. This might mean getting immediate help from other adults. When you correct a student's behavior, don't dwell excessively. Nagging will only alienate the student.

13. Develop selective hearing. Learn to ignore some minor infractions, particularly when you suspect that the student's motive is to bait you into a confrontation. Of course, potentially harmful or disruptive outbursts must be handled. Even things that are ignored during class can be dealt with after class. This also is a way to buy time if you're not sure what to do about a behavior.

14. Divide and conquer. If you have two or three people who sit next to each other and frequently collude to disrupt the classroom, rearrange the classroom seating arrangement to separate the offenders. Sometimes this can be done subtly without revealing your true intent. For example, in forming groups you can count off so that the perpetrators are in different groups. As you assign groups to different areas of the room, you can assure that the troublesome ones are seated as far apart as possible.

15. Never argue with a student in front of the class. Decline to argue the issue now, but offer to discuss it privately with the student later. Public arguments inevitably lead to one of you losing face in front of the class. Either way, you lose! Students who lose face in front of their peers do get even.

16. Quiet reprimands are much more effective than loud ones. Indeed, some research suggests that loud reprimands are actually more disruptive. Avoid shouting at students! It reveals your loss of control. However, your tonality and nonverbal cues must be congruent. If your body language is too nonassertive, students will receive a mixed message that you aren't really serious.

17. When you do discuss a student's misbehavior, make it clear that you find the behavior, not the student, unacceptable. Remain firm yet compassionate. If possible, praise what they do well, but encourage improvement in their erroneous ways.

18. Understand the school's student behavior code. What disciplinary measures are to be taken for serious infractions (for example, fighting, drugs, alcohol, truancy)? What is the procedure for reporting such problems? Is in-school suspension or detention used? If so, how? How are parents involved in correcting misbehavior?

19. Early in the year, develop classroom routines. Carefully explain how students are to handle the details of daily classroom activities: taking attendance, procedures for making up missed work, distributing and collecting materials, going to the bathroom, leaving for lunch, and so on.

20. Be cautious of touching students when they are very angry. This can stimulate a violent response in some students.

21. Be aware of students' occasional concealment (for example, covering their mouths when whispering, hiding behind their desks, standing books on edge to hide other reading material). Moving about the classroom discourages such strategies.

22. Avoid branding a student a failure because of one mistake. Help your students recognize that we all make mistakes but also have a responsibility to learn from our mistakes.

23. Avoid punishing the whole class for one student's misbehavior. It is simply unfair, and the innocent students will perceive it that way. It will only turn the whole class (and probably their parents) against you.

24. Try to find acceptable means for students to receive the attention and approval they often seek through misbehavior. Provide an opportunity for them to earn the spotlight through appropriate behavior.

25. Always have a couple of "sponge" activities (for example, small-group brainstorm, word puzzle, or review game) available to use when the unexpected happens (the projector bulb burns out, a visitor comes to the door, or a student becomes ill in class) or when some students complete seatwork or tests ahead of others.

26. Don't be too quick to send students to the principal's office or to call their parents. If done too frequently, this suggests that you have a problem with classroom management. Involve others only for serious or persistent misbehavior.

27. Don't send students out into the hallway as a punishment. Aside from potential liability problems, many students find the hall a pretty exciting place to be, especially if the class is boring.

28. For persistent, serious problems with a student, use the private teacher-student conference. Explain without blaming exactly what behaviors you find inappropriate and why. Avoid verbally attacking the student, and do listen to his or her view. Push the student for a plan for correcting the behavior in the future and making a commitment to follow through with that plan.

29. If you feel overwhelmed by a student's challenging behavior, don't be afraid to consult other professionals: your principal, experienced teachers, school psychologist, or counselor. They have likely confronted the same problems. Ask several persons for a variety of opinions. Allow yourself to learn from their mistakes and successes. A secondary benefit is that they will probably be flattered that you came to them for advice.

30. There are a few nationally marketed programs on effective classroom management. Performance Learning Systems' Classroom Management course (www.plsweb.com/) is an excellent example. If you are having difficulty managing student behavior, find one of these courses being offered locally, often for graduate credit.

WHAT DO YOU WANT?

A goal-oriented problem focus requires that teachers know what they want to have happen in their classroom as well as what they don't want. If an auto mechanic is confronted with a car that will not run, the goal is quite apparent: to get the car to start. In dealing with students, it is equally important, though not always easy, to clarify what you want to have happen. We often give students lots of information about what they should not do but very little about what we expect them to do.

An objective is incompatible with the problem behavior. It is impossible for both to occur at the same time. Hence, in focusing on any problem, it is important not only to attempt to decrease the undesirable behavior but also to emphasize what we do expect from the student.

PROBLEM	OBJECTIVE
Brooke is out of her seat during class.	Brooke will remain in her chair through class.
Jake doesn't do his homework.	Jake completes his homework.
Braedon hits the other kids.	Braedon keeps his hands to himself.

Remember, success in decreasing an undesirable behavior will be enhanced if you emphasize what you do want.

POSITIVE REINFORCEMENT OF GOOD BEHAVIOR

If consumers shopping at a new department store are pleased with the service and goods received, they will likely continue to shop at that store in the future. Behaviors that have desirable consequences will likely continue. Pleasant or desirable consequences that cause a behavior to be repeated are called rewards or positive reinforcement. Note that any consequence functions as a reward only if the behavior it follows is maintained or increased.

Some might ask: "Isn't rewarding students for good behavior just a form of bribery?" Definitely not. A bribe is payment in kind or value for the commission of an immoral or illegal act. Hopefully, what you are asking of your students is neither immoral nor illegal. Second, a bribe is usually paid before commission of the requested action, whereas a reward should always follow the completion of the desired behavior.

THE REWARD HIERARCHY

Rewards (positive reinforcers) can be extrinsic or intrinsic. The ideal would be for each student to enter the classroom intrinsically motivated and eager to devour the wisdom you have to share. Unfortunately, I have met few self-actualized, self-motivated third graders (or high school or college students, for that matter). My advice is to take students at the level they are and help them move to the next higher level of motivation.

A word of caution: there are few universal rewards. An incentive that may work with most students may not influence the behavior of others. For example, public praise from the teacher would serve many students as a pleasant consequence and positively motivate their behavior. However, for a small portion of students (for example, some adolescent males), public praise from a teacher may backfire, becoming a source of derision from their peers.

Students often enter the classroom with little internal motivation for the virtue of studying Shakespeare, Roman history, or quadratic equations. They might like it once we get them to give it a try, but they may well need some external incentive to entice them into taking that first step. External incentives are not inherently evil. Certainly, they can be misused and overused. Few adults disdain the paychecks they receive for their labors. People of all ages strive for appreciation and approval.

It helps to view rewards as falling into a hierarchy. The reward hierarchy includes four levels of positive reinforcers. At the lowest level are *tangibles*, physical items that the recipient can hold, touch, and taste. These would include stickers, posters, or food.

The next higher level are *activities*, privileges that might include computer time, recess, or being first in line. For younger students particularly, helping the teacher (for example, collecting papers or running an errand) may function as a reward.

Social rewards are next up the hierarchy. These tend to convey appreciation, recognition, or approval. Examples include praise, smiles, or pats on the back.

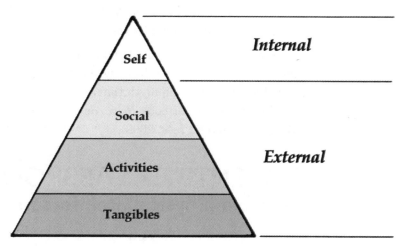

The Hierarchy of Rewards

Intrinsic (or internal) *reinforcements* are at the pinnacle of the reward hierarchy. These are autonomous, arising from within.

TIPS ON USING POSITIVE REINFORCEMENT IN THE CLASSROOM

- A teacher's goal in using positive reinforcement in the classroom should ultimately be to move students up the reward hierarchy from external motivation to internal control. It is best to use the highest level of reinforcement that will motivate a student to put forth the effort toward the desired behavior. If a student is already intrinsically motivated to do a task, don't attempt to offer lower-level reinforcers. Use social reinforcers, such as praise or a smile, if they provide sufficient encouragement for the student to maintain a behavior.

- Reinforce positive behaviors. A great many students go through school generally being ignored, as long as they don't step out of line. They may not be the greatest students, but they don't usually create trouble. They may receive little of the teacher's time or attention. Find ways to show recognition and appreciation of their gains, even the small ones. Reward appropriate behavior; don't ignore it. "Catch the student being good," some teachers say. This involves a different kind of attitude, a new, more positive outlook on the world.

- Use praise effectively. Though verbal praise can be effective in encouraging positive behaviors, it is often used ineffectively. To be most constructive, praise should be specific rather than general. Instead of saying "Good job," offer specific information on what you liked about the student's work: "Excellent paragraph transitions" or "Your use of color in this picture was very unique." Also be aware that public praise does not work for everyone. It may backfire when used with some adolescents, whose peers may rib them mercilessly. However, private encouragement still might be influential with such students.

- Use group contracting to reward good performance, both behavioral and academic. This can be done informally (for example, "As soon as we all have put away the art supplies, we'll go out for recess") or in a more structured, formal contract. It allows the students to earn a group reward, which might be free time to play an educational game, no homework for a night, a field trip, or other special treat.

- When you use rewards, vary them to be effective. The same reward used over and over quickly satiates, losing its value to motivate. Variety and novelty are powerful reinforcers.

Dr. Judy Cameron and Dr. David Pierce, University of Alberta professors, systematically and thoroughly reviewed the body of research on the use of praise and other rewards. Their work has debunked the myth that rewards stifle students' intrinsic motivation. For more information, see their book *Rewards and Intrinsic Motivation: Resolving the Controversy* (Bergin & Garvey Press, 2002).

POTENTIAL CLASSROOM REWARDS
Tangible (Physical) Reinforcers

Popcorn	Computer software
T-shirts	Posters
Pretzels	Music CDs
Bumper stickers	Stickers
Fruit	Scented crayons
Pencils	Ribbons
Pizza	Plaques
Notebooks	Food coupons
Cookies	Trophies
Books	Trinkets
Lemonade	Gift certificates

Activity Reinforcers

Choose seats

Sharpen pencils

Breaks, recess

Use learning center

Lunch with teacher or principal

Independent study activity

Reserved parking space

Receive "no homework" pass

Teacher tells personal story

Work in "quiet" corner

Be first in line

Extra locker space

Hold class outdoors

Computer time

Feed the class pet

Free time to . . .

Reserved seat at sports events

Play games

Hall passes

Play sports

Parties

Cook

Display work

Watch movies or videos

Picnics

Attend concerts

Do artwork

Be on safety patrol

Field trips

Sing

Learn a magic trick

Floor hockey in gym

Teacher reads a story

Early dismissal

Parties

Make videos

Preferred seating

Work with younger students

Assemblies

Take pictures

Go to library

Play musical instrument

Drawing or crafts

Do puzzles

Exercise

Watch TV

Dress-up days

Play with pets

Help the Teacher

Construct bulletin boards

Do research on the Internet

Pass out materials

Collect papers

Be line leader

Design Web pages

Tutor other students

Take attendance

Design a class Web site

Photocopy materials

Help with experiments

Work in office

Arrange furniture

Clean the classroom

Run audiovisual equipment

Use the computer

Edit the newsletter

Take pictures or movies

Rental Privileges as Potential Activity Reinforcers

Games	Musical instruments
Magic Markers	Paints
Hand puppets	Baseball mitts
Calculator	Weights
Chalk	Punching bag
Video camera	Books
Funny hats	Blocks
Laptop computer	Scented markers
Football	Videos
Computer software	Jump rope
Computer	Magazines
Table toys	Colored pencils
Computer games	CDs, DVDs
Sports and playground equipment	Special hat, costume

Social Reinforcers

Grades	Approval
Applause	Drum rolls
Smiles, nods, hugs	Athletic letters
Positive nonverbal gestures	Awards
Certificates of merit	Peer approval
Compliments	Check marks
Winks, eye contact	Encouragement
Acceptance in honor societies	Mysterious warm-and-fuzzy notes
Honor rolls	Positive comments on papers
Drawings on papers, smiley faces	Principal's signature on good papers
Stickers	Standing ovations
Pats on the back	Being asked opinions, advice

Recognition

Name mentioned in assembly	Photograph in paper
Student of the week	Name in paper
Letter to parents	Trophies, stars
Work displayed	Honor roll
Phone call to parents	Photograph on bulletin board

Intrinsic (Internal) Reinforcers

Fun	Having options, alternatives
Success	Relaxation, tranquility, serenity
Meeting goals	Playfulness
Enjoyment of beauty	Meaningfulness
Learning (for the sake of learning)	Self-awareness
Improvement	Novelty, surprises
Self-sufficiency	Constructive feedback
Openness	Self-satisfaction
Philosophical humor	Achievement

Creative Self-Expression

Arts and crafts

Poetry

Painting

Music

Gardening

Dancing

Athletics

Writing

Cooking

Designing

Positive Referrals: Recognition That Works

The adage "The squeaky wheels get the grease" too often holds true in schools. In many schools misbehaving students get the bulk of the staff's attention. In such a climate, educators can easily overlook students' positive behaviors. To assure that didn't happen at Olympia High School in Orlando, Florida, the staff initiated the Positive Referrals Program.

Students gain special recognition when they do something positive—in or out of the classroom—that benefits the school or community. Any student, teacher, administrator, parent, or staff member may fill out a referral form reporting a student's positive behavior. The positive referral forms go to the grade-level administrator, who gives the student a certificate of recognition and calls the parents.

The program was a response to feedback from students that more recognition should be given for positive behaviors. The criteria for behaviors worthy of positive referral are open-ended to allow as many as possible to be recognized.

One student was referred for finding a wallet with $60 and returning it to the owner. The student said it was simply the right thing to do. Another student received recognition for earning a perfect score on a very difficult midterm exam.

Assistant principal David Christiansen believes that "it is a great way to recognize the little things that happen every day that help make a great environment." He reports that the students, staff, and parents have shown an overwhelmingly positive response to the program.

Source: Interview with David Christiansen, assistant principal at Olympia High School in Orlando, Florida. Originally published in Heart of Teaching *newsletters, © 2001–2005 Performance Learning Systems, Inc.®, an educational services company located in Allentown, PA, and on the World Wide Web at www.plsweb.com. Used with permission.*

HELPFUL RESOURCES

Bloom, L. A. (2009). *Classroom management: Creating positive outcomes for all students.* Upper Saddle River, NJ: Merrill/Pearson.

Edwards, C. H. (2008). *Classroom discipline and management* (5th ed.). Hoboken, NJ: Wiley.

Nissman, B. S. (2009). *Teacher-tested classroom management strategies* (3rd ed.). Boston: Pearson.

Palumbo, A., & Sanacore, J. (2007). Classroom management: Help for the beginning secondary school teacher. *Clearing House: A Journal of Educational Strategies, Issues and Ideas, 80*(2), 67–70.

Pedota, P. (2007). Strategies for effective classroom management in the secondary setting. *Clearing House: A Journal of Educational Strategies, Issues and Ideas, 80*(4), 163–166.

Sousa, D. A. (2009). *How the brain influences behavior: Management strategies for every classroom.* Thousand Oaks, CA: Corwin.

Ways to Discourage Students

- Set unrealistically high standards; demand perfection.
- Focus on mistakes to motivate.
- Make pessimistic interpretations.
- Compare people.
- Dominate by being too helpful.

Source: Evans, T. D. (1996). Encouragement: The key to reforming classrooms. *Educational Leadership, 54,* 1, 81–85.

CELL PHONES AND TEXT MESSAGING IN CLASS

The use of cell phones, particularly text messaging in school, has become a major challenge to teachers. Most schools have set rules regulating their usage, although there is great disparity in regulations among school buildings and districts.

Of course, the temptations of cheating via text messaging and photo taking are great. Students have been caught taking photos of their exams and forwarding to friends who will be taking the same test later. For this reason, some schools ban any phones that have cameras. Others ban students from bringing phones to school. Cell phones offer a great deal of temptation for mischief. "Turned off and out of sight" has become the most ubiquitous rule. (Some schools or teachers expand the rule to include all electronic devices, including iPods.)

Some schools allow students to have cell phones in their backpacks or lockers, but they are not allowed to be on or used during school hours. Some allow usage only outdoors or during their lunch period. Most allow phone use only for emergencies.

Students caught violating these rules typically have their phones confiscated. With the first offense, the teacher may return the phone at the end of the day. Later violations result in longer confiscations and often a required visit to the principal by a parent or guardian to retrieve the phone. Many schools suspend students, even for the first offense. Cell phones have created the biggest discipline challenge for many teachers.

Inappropriate photos and video clips taken in bathrooms and locker rooms have been circulated, sometimes appearing on the Internet. Text messaging has replaced smoking as the major subversive activity of restroom visits.

The issue is complicated by the fact that since 9/11 and Columbine many parents are adamant about wanting their children to have cell phones with them at all times. About two-thirds of all teens have cell phones. As a sign of the times, there are Web sites offering students detailed directions on how to use cell phones in school without getting caught!

Some teachers have taken a more benevolent view of cell phones and propose incorporating their use into lessons, for example, text messaging assignment reminders. Others have argued for a fair use policy that allows students to use cell phones in responsible ways.

Here are a few tips that might help you deal with this issue in your classroom:

- Make sure the students and their parents know exactly what the cell phone rules are from the first day of school. Post the rules on a bulletin board and on any class or school Web sites. Some teachers distribute a handout to students clarifying the rules and consequences of cell phone abuse.

- Communicate clearly to the parents why the rules are necessary. Stress the disruptive nature of phone use in class and the potential for cheating, both of which can interfere with their children's learning.

- Where phones are allowed in schools, some teachers require students to check them as they enter the classroom. It might be wise to put them in a locked box. Require that students' names be on their phones. They are returned at the end of the class. This option is probably easier to enforce with elementary school students. Strictly and consistently enforce whatever policies you and your school have announced. It is probably best not to give out your cell phone number. This can be an invitation for prank messages at all hours of the day. There are many other avenues for communicating with you.

CORPORAL PUNISHMENT

The practices of whipping, flogging, paddling, thumping, birching, whacking, caning, and otherwise inflicting physical pain on students is embedded in the history of American education. The Puritans' writings frequently refer to the use of the rod to "beat the devil out of" misbehaving students. The use of corporal punishment is seldom discussed dispassionately; it evokes heated arguments from both its proponents and opponents.

In *Reading, Writing, and the Hickory Stick,* a thorough examination of the use of corporal punishment in schools, Irwin Hyman reviewed studies documenting the following practices:

- Corporal punishment occurs more frequently at the primary and intermediate levels.
- Boys are paddled much more frequently than girls.
- Minority and poor white children receive corporal punishment four to five times more frequently than middle- and upper-class white children.
- Corporal punishment is used least in schools in the Northeast.
- It is a myth that corporal punishment is used as a last resort. Studies suggest corporal punishment is frequently the first punishment for minor and nonviolent misbehaviors.
- There is evidence that corporal punishment is one of the causes of school vandalism.
- Corporal punishment is forbidden in the schools of Europe, Japan, Israel, Ireland, Russia, China, Turkey, Iceland, Puerto Rico, twenty-eight U.S. states, and many U.S. metropolitan areas. The United States and Canada remain the only industrialized nations tolerating corporal punishment in their schools.
- Teachers who frequently paddle tend to be authoritarian, dogmatic, relatively inexperienced, impulsive, and neurotic, as compared with their peers.
- Generally, teachers who do not paddle were rarely, if ever, spanked or paddled as children. This modeling effect has been repeatedly demonstrated. The more teachers were hit as children, the more they tend to hit their students.
- Schools with high rates of corporal punishment also have high rates of suspensions and are generally more punitive in all discipline responses than are schools with low rates of corporal punishment.

Some states now restrict the use of corporal punishment, mandating that a witness be present and that paddling not be done in front of other students; in some locations such punishment can take place only after a parent has granted consent. Some areas continue to permit spanking by the hand but prohibit the use of paddles or other objects. Many organizations, including the National Education Association, the American Civil Liberties Union, the American Academy of Pediatrics, the National Committee on the Prevention of Child Abuse, the Association of Childhood Education International, the American Medical Association, the Children's Defense Fund, the National Association of Social Workers, and the Parent Teacher Association have lobbied to restrict or ban the use of corporal punishment in schools.

The majority of states now ban the use of corporal punishment; others restrict its use. Although reliance on corporal punishment has declined, data from the U.S. Department of Education indicated over 233,000 students were paddled during the 2006–07 school year.

The arguments that paddling develops character or reforms errant behavior simply are not supported by any objective examination of the research data. Indeed, evidence suggests that corporal punishment is counterproductive, degrading to both teachers and students, and increases violence.

The Case Against Corporal Punishment

- Corporal punishment does not extinguish undesirable behaviors. It merely temporarily suppresses them.

- Physical punishment models aggression and violence as appropriate means of getting what you want.

- All child abuse begins as punishment. There is a relationship between how severely and frequently children experienced physical punishment and their propensity toward violence later in life. Researchers estimate between 20,000 and 150,000 children each year require medical treatment as a result of corporal punishment received at school. Circulatory and nervous system problems, paralysis, broken bones, knocked-out teeth, brain damage, and post-traumatic stress disorder have all been documented in instances of school-administered corporal punishment.

- There is an inherent unfairness in who gets punished. Paddling is not distributed equally, even for similar offenses. Race, gender, and socioeconomic level influence whether a particular student will experience corporal punishment.

- Paddling in schools can lead to stress reactions, such as school phobias, nightmares, loss of appetite, bed-wetting, and nervousness.

- Punishing situations tend to be avoided. Schools that rely heavily on corporal punishment also experience higher rates of absenteeism, truancy, and dropping out.

- Paddling poisons the teacher-student relationship. It breeds mistrust. Fear is not the equivalent of respect.

- In instances where paddling was banned, the amount of student misbehavior did not increase. Indeed, in at least one instance, vandalism actually decreased.

- There is increased risk today of being sued or charged with child abuse for paddling students.

Despite overwhelming evidence that corporal punishment has detrimental effects on students as well as teachers, and virtually no evidence that it has any long-term benefits, the practice has its supporters, including some administrators, parents, and teachers. The long-term effects cannot be justified by any short-term gains the teacher may reap from this sadistic behavior. Yet teaching remains the sole profession that is permitted to beat its clients. The beating of criminals or animals is forbidden, yet many states still legally sanction the paddling of students.

There is substantial evidence that corporal punishment is not essential to maintaining decorum and obedience in today's schools. See the earlier section "Thirty Hot Tips for Managing Classroom Behavior" for alternatives to the use of corporal punishment.

Additional Information on Corporal Punishment

Aucoin, K. J., Frick, P. J., & Bodin, S. D. (2006). Corporal punishment and child adjustment. *Journal of Applied Developmental Psychology, 6,* 527–541.

Bitensky, S. H. (2006). *Corporal punishment of children: A human rights violation.* Ardsley, NY: Transnational.

Hart, S. N., Durrant, J., Newell, P., & Power, F. C. (Eds.). (2005). *Eliminating corporal punishment: The way forward to constructive child discipline.* Paris: UNESCO.

Human Rights Watch. (2008). *A violent education: Corporal punishment of children in U.S. public schools.* New York: American Civil Liberties Union.

> A teacher does best armed only with knowledge. Corporal punishment is a cruel and obsolete weapon. The battle for children's minds should not be waged on their behinds.
>
> —**USA Today editorial, August 22, 1990**

TIME-OUTS

Sometimes students do break class rules, behaving in ways that are inappropriate, disruptive, and unacceptable. Usually such misbehaviors are not severe, but they must be discouraged. Maybe the teacher has unsuccessfully tried smaller interventions, such as warning the student or correcting the unacceptable behavior, but to no avail. What's a teacher to do? Many teachers have had excellent success through the use of time-out procedures.

Time-out is not painful. It doesn't hurt. Nor should it humiliate the child. It may be a bit boring. Children would generally prefer to be engaged and participating in anything rather than sitting quietly. Time-out involves isolating the student for a relatively brief period of time. It is quite similar to the cartoons of Dennis the Menace sitting in the corner in his chair.

Time-outs are also designed to allow students time to calm down and to reflect on why their behavior is inappropriate.

Dos of Using Time-outs

- Be sure to check with your principal on any state or local school restrictions on the use of time-outs.

- Generally, it is best to offer a single warning prior to resorting to a time-out.

- Instruct the student in a calm, nonhostile tone to go to the designated time-out area. It should ideally be an area within your classroom where you can clearly see the student but he or she cannot see the rest of the class. A chair off to the side partitioned with a bookcase or filing cabinet may be sufficient.

- Clearly specify the amount of time the student will be in time-out. A relatively brief amount of time is generally sufficient. The younger the child, the shorter the time. Experts typically suggest a maximum of fifteen minutes. A good rule of thumb is to assign one minute of time-out for each year of the student's age.

- Some teachers use a kitchen timer to keep track of the time-out so that everyone knows when the time-out is over.

- Any outbursts require that the time-out interval be restarted.

- Modify time-outs for older students. After-school detentions are a form of time-out.

- Time-outs should be used in conjunction with positive discipline procedures. Technically, time-out is a form of punishment.

- It is a good idea to document in writing any use of time-out, noting the transgression, amount of time, time-out location, and any observed consequences.

- Train students early in the year about time-out procedures. Clarify the behaviors that may result in time-outs.

- Use common sense. Putting a child in a locked or dark closet is inexcusable. One teacher was fired after he put a student in a refrigerator carton, cut holes in the sides, and encouraged the rest of the students to make faces and ridicule the student inside. You are running a classroom, not a marine boot camp.

Don'ts in Using Time-outs

Time-outs can backfire if used foolishly. Here are pitfalls to avoid:

- Never just send the student out into the hall. Big mistake! I know this one from experience: I spent a lot of time standing in hallways as a child, usually for talking too much. It isn't that bad a place to be, especially if the class is boring. You get to chat with everyone who comes down the hallway, make funny faces in the door window, and find other mischief.

- Avoid sending students to the principal's office if at all possible. Done regularly, it communicates that you can't handle your class. And often the principal isn't there, so the secretary is stuck with the problem. One of my former graduate students had one male student who started misbehaving regularly, and she would send him to the principal's office. None of the other teachers seemed to ever have problems with this lad. His motivation was unveiled when she discovered that his girlfriend was an office assistant during that class period. What we think is a punishment may not always be so.

- Don't harangue the child. No shouting. A time-out is more apt to succeed when the teacher uses it without condemnation, instead communicating that he or she cares but cannot accept the behavior. Avoid a public argument. Being firm but fair is the key.

- Avoid allowing the student to garner extra attention from the rest of the class. Ordering the student to stand along the wall (or even worse, behind the teacher) gives the student a free audience.

- Don't overdo it; use time-outs sparingly. Time-out rooms used in some schools are somewhat controversial, as students end up missing too much schoolwork by being out of the classroom.

- Time-outs do not work with all children. Particularly for shy or withdrawn children, time-outs may actually serve as a reward and generally not as a deterrent. Time-outs will not work if they are more rewarding than class.

A True Story

When I was in elementary school, I had a problem: I talked too much. Actually, the way my teachers reported it on my grade cards was "Ronnie has a voice that carries," meaning that even when everyone else was talking, the teachers would always hear me above the rest of the students.

One day my fourth-grade teacher just lost it. She ranted and shouted and then ordered: "Go up to the teachers' workroom, and don't you come out until I tell you." As commanded, I left the classroom and climbed the six steps up to the teachers' workroom. It was a tiny space: a desk, three chairs, and a small window."

I sat quietly looking out the window. In ten minutes I was quite bored. "Come on, let me go back. I'll be quiet. This is dull."

I stirred. I paced the room. I looked out the window. I saw all the kids go home. I sat. I pouted. I saw all the teachers go home.

I don't plead innocence. I knew exactly where this was headed. "Now, let's see. You said, 'Stay there until I tell you to come out.' Hmm. We'll see!"

About five o'clock the school matriarch, a third-grade teacher, entered the room. "What are you doing in here?" she demanded. In my whiniest voice I mumbled, "My teacher made me come in."

"Go on. Go home," she uttered.

The next morning when I returned to school, my teacher said, "Now, Ronnie, you know you could have gone home, don't you?" I just sheepishly peered back up at her. That night I found out through the grapevine that my teacher had really been called on the carpet by her principal.

The moral of the story is this: if you use time-out, don't forget where you put the kid!

BULLYING IN SCHOOLS

Students bullying other students is not a new phenomenon, but the risks of allowing bullying to continue have increased. The level of violence in schools has risen, with kids behaving more aggressively at younger ages and having increased accessibility to guns.

Why Students Bully

Bullying may consist of teasing, taunting, threatening, hitting, or stealing. Students who bully others appear to have a need to feel powerful and in control. They gain satisfaction from inflicting injury and suffering on others, feel little empathy for their victims, and rationalize their actions by claiming that their victims provoked them in some way.

Research suggests that bullies are often raised in homes where physical punishment is used, parental involvement and warmth are missing, and children are encouraged to handle problems by striking back. Contrary to prevailing myths, bullies appear to have little anxiety and to possess strong self-esteem. Young bullies may grow up to be big bullies.

Students who are victims of bullying exhibit anxiety, insecurity, caution, and low self-esteem. Victims are frequently socially isolated, lacking friends or social skills. They tend to be close to their parents, who are often overprotective. Researchers estimate that seven percent of America's eighth graders stay home at least once a month to avoid bullies.

Successful Interventions

The most effective interventions involve the entire school community rather than focusing only on the perpetrators. Experts recommend the following strategies:

- Survey students and adults. The questionnaire helps the school community to become aware of the extent of the problem, gains support for intervention efforts, and provides baseline data for measuring the success of interventions.

- Conduct a parental awareness campaign during parent-teacher conference days, through school newsletters, and parent organization meetings. Distribute survey results as part of this campaign.

- Develop rules against bullying. Role-playing exercises and related assignments can teach alternative coping skills to student bullies and their victims. Other students can learn to assist victims and discuss how everyone can work together to create a school climate where bullying is unacceptable.

- Employ individualized interventions with the bullies and victims, use cooperative learning activities to minimize social isolation, and increase adult supervision during recess or lunch.

- Teach conflict resolution. Research shows that conflict mediation programs do work. If your school doesn't have one, teach your students basic conflict resolution skills.

Sources: Bullying in Schools, *ERIC Digest, by Ron Banks;* The Bully-Free Classroom *by Allan L. Beane (Minneapolis: Free Spirit Publishing, 1999). The above section was originally published in* Heart of Teaching *newsletters, © 2001–2005 Performance Learning Systems, Inc.®, an educational services company located in Allentown, PA, and on the World Wide Web at www.plsweb.com. Used with permission.*

"FIGHT, FIGHT!": INTERVENTION STRATEGIES

Student altercations are among the most stressful events for teachers, but knowing how to safely and efficiently intervene can minimize the risks of escalation to more serious violence. Chandra Hawley of Indiana University's Center for Adolescent Studies offers this advice on intervening in a fight.

- The teacher's top priority must be to avoid getting hurt! Immediately send a student—preferably one you know—for help: "Alice, please go to the office and ask Mr. Gomez to come immediately. Tell him there is a fight in room 122."

- Break up the crowd. With direct eye contact, sternly, but without screaming, direct students to leave the area. Use names of students you know. "Matt, Kelly, all of you, go directly to the cafeteria. Wait there for me."

- After the crowd has moved away and help is coming, you can attend to the fight. Usually, one person quickly dominates the fight. Assertively address the other person, by name if you know it, "Allen, that's enough! Move back now!" If necessary, make a loud noise, such as clapping your hands. Avoid moving into the midst of swinging fists.

Sources: *Chandra Hawley,* Teacher Talk *(Bloomington: Indiana University, Center for Adolescent Studies, 1997). Reprinted with permission from* The Heart of Teaching *newsletter, Performance Learning Systems.*

MOTIVATING THE UNMOTIVATED

Wouldn't life be easy if every student appeared in school eager to learn! Many teachers bemoan that students just aren't as motivated as they used to be. Whether that phenomenon is true or not, the reality is that the students in your classroom are the ones *you* have to teach.

In every classroom, there have always been some students who seem unmotivated to learn—at least to learn the things you have to teach. The challenge is to improve the odds of engaging them in your classroom lessons.

There is no magic potion to sprinkle or secret phrase you can whisper to suddenly convert reluctant learners into passionate seekers of knowledge. However, we can learn from those truly outstanding teachers who have achieved some degree of success in capturing their students' interest and getting them to participate in class.

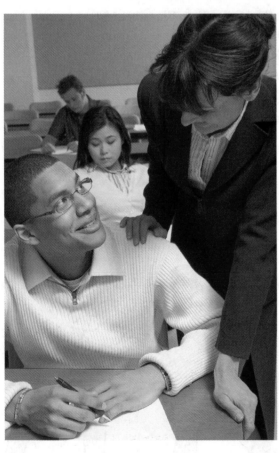

Here are strategies that research shows that successful teachers use to help motivate their unmotivated students:

- Individualize instruction as much as possible.

- Allow students structured freedom. When feasible, offer options in assignments, projects, or assessments. Give them some control.

- Strive to be clear and concise in your explanations. Use good examples. Those that connect with their daily experiences are most helpful.

- Link your content to your students' personal lives and interests whenever possible. There is no sin in making learning fun when possible.

- Find a way to tap their unique talents in special projects or assignments. Build on their strengths.

- Use hands-on learning activities with real-world problems as much as possible.

- Challenge them to stretch themselves. Seldom do you get more than you expect from your students.

- Show genuine enthusiasm for what you are teaching. It is difficult to generate interest if you are just going through the motions. Great teachers exude passion for what they are teaching.

- Just be real. Don't hide behind a role. You can't be your students' best friend but do treat them with respect and sincerity.

- Show students you care about them as individuals. Express interest in their lives and challenges.

- Offer patience and understanding. Put yourself in the shoes of your slowest students. Some students will always take longer to learn any subject.

- A sense of humor is an asset. Lighten up a little but don't try to be a comedian.

- Break up the talk. Few adults can tolerate sitting and listening to someone else talk for hours. Don't expect students to enjoy it any more than you would. Get students actively engaged in the learning experience by not talking more than eight minutes without some student participation.

- Use visual learning aids—props, costumes, demonstrations, images, manipulatives, charts, or graphs.

- Offer compassionate support and encouragement. Reward progress and effort. Don't wait for perfection before giving positive feedback.

- Vary the routine. The element of surprise generates interest. Use a variety of instructional technique—small-group activities, video, role playing, simulation games, debates, and guest speakers. See Chapter Five for at least thirty things to do besides lecturing.

- Give students a chance to move around occasionally. Revive the energy level when it starts to sag.

- Don't give up on your students. Showing that you believe they can ultimately succeed will often pay off in the long run. Each day you are planting seeds. It is a percentage game. The more seeds you plant, the greater the chance of some taking hold and growing.

Check out the following sources for more detailed suggestions:

Bowman, R. F. (2007). How can students be motivated: A misplaced question? *Clearing House: A Journal of Educational Strategies, Issues and Ideas, 2,* 81–86.

Marshall, J. C. (2008). *Overcoming student apathy: Motivating students for academic success.* Lanham, MD: Rowman & Littlefield.

Riggs, E. G., & Gholar, C. R. (2009). *Strategies that promote student engagement: Unleashing the desire to learn.* Thousand Oaks, CA: Corwin.

THE TEACHER AS A SKILLED HELPER

It is not uncommon for students to turn to teachers for help in times of stress, disappointment, frustration, and loss. Almost daily every teacher has the opportunity to respond to at least one student's emotional turmoil. In the course of a year, some students in your class very likely may experience the death or disability of a family member or classmate, their parents' divorce, a parent's unemployment, the loss of pets, moving to new schools, academic failure, or rejection by classmates or sweethearts.

All compassionate teachers should have some high-yield, low-risk listening skills in their repertoire. They are high-yield skills because if they are done well, these basic counseling tools have the potential to make a large difference in students' lives. They are low

risk because as long as teachers stick to these skills and don't venture off into amateur psychotherapy, no harm is likely to occur. No one has ever been hurt by being listened to, and a great many people have been helped.

The skills described here are the basic attending skills that every beginning counselor learns, often termed active listening skills. Passive listening is the kind of listening that occurs when students are staring at you during a lecture. Maybe they even occasionally nod their heads to signal that they are still awake, but you have no idea whether they are actually hearing a word you have said. Passive listening is one way. Active listening, on the other hand, is a two-way process; it involves a true dialogue. What one person is saying is clearly and directly related to what the other has said. The listener must actively prove that he or she has heard the speaker.

Become a good listener, and the world will beat a path to your door. Truly good listeners are all too rare; they stand out. Effective listeners have mastered the fine art of inviting people to talk about themselves; they also seem genuinely interested in what others have to say. Listening is one of the most precious gifts you can give to your students. You may be the only adult in their lives who truly takes time to listen.

> Too often we underestimate the power of a touch, a smile, a kind word, a listening ear, an honest compliment, or the smallest act of caring, all of which have the potential to turn a life around.
>
> **—Leo Buscaglia**

Becoming a skilled helper does not mean having to sit down with a student and become involved in a long tearful conversation. Every day in every classroom, students are struggling with emotional pain and conflict. One compassionate moment of listening can let the child know he or she has been heard, that you care. It may indeed take less than ten seconds. And that student may remember the brief encounter for the rest of his or her life.

What Good Listening Is Not

Good listening is not advice giving. Indeed, giving advice to others is tempting, especially when the solutions to their problems are so obvious to us. Take a moment to recall the last time someone freely offered you advice, especially if it was unsolicited. Chances are it fell on deaf ears. We tend to reject unsolicited advice, no matter what the source. Though it may not be the giver's intent, advice subtly communicates, "I can run your life better than you can"—not a message most people are eager to hear.

Even if the student asks for advice, giving it is not necessarily the best thing to do. There is an old Chinese proverb: "Give me a fish and I eat for a day; teach me to fish and I eat forever." We should be more interested in teaching people how to fish, not in giving fish away. It is far more important to equip our students with the skills needed to face and solve life's challenges than to ease their short-term discomfort. When we prematurely give advice, we rob students of a valuable learning experience. Further, we, not the student, have assumed responsibility for the problem.

Embedded in the use of active listening is the assumption that students can work out the solutions to their problems given support and time. (Of course, advice giving is appropriate if you are in the role of an academic adviser. We are referring here to discussion of students' personal, not academic, problems.)

Reflection of Feelings

Reflection of feelings is a powerful tool that almost every counselor uses. It appears on the surface to be a simple skill. Do not be deceived: it is very difficult to do well and genuinely. The aim is to practice reflections of feeling until they become reflexive, so that the next time you are sitting with a person in pain, you automatically respond with such a response.

The basic structure of a reflection of feeling is "You feel . . ." filling in the blank with a feeling word that accurately reflects the feeling the student is experiencing at that moment. After you have mastered the technique, experiment with putting it into your own phrasing, such as "You seem . . ."; "It sounds like you are . . ."; or "You are . . ." The key ingredient is that you must include the feeling word in your observation. Later you might also add the source of the perceived feeling, "You feel . . . about (or because of) . . ."

Reflection of feeling is one of several perception-checking devices. They are used to verify what we think we have heard. They develop a crucial helping condition called empathy. Empathy (not sympathy) is the ability to communicate to other persons that you are trying to understand what it is like to be them. That is why "I know how you feel" is an inadequate response. Maybe you know; maybe you don't. Only when you test your hypothesis with a reflection of feeling ("You seem pretty discouraged") do you really prove that you heard what the student has said. You are striving for a deeper level of understanding.

The beauty of a reflection of feeling is that you gain either way. If you are accurate in your perception, the student will almost always respond, "Yes," and then will elaborate. They will almost never stop at yes, unless you have raised your tonality at the end of your observation, making your statement into a closed-ended question. If you are off in your observation, the student will almost always reply, "Well, no, it's not so much discouraged [or another feeling] as it is . . . ", giving you more accurate feedback. Either way, you gain.

Reflections of feeling are always offered tentatively. The goal is to check out what you perceive their feelings to be. The fact is that you can never know with absolute certainty what another human being is feeling. You can project how you would feel; you can guess how they feel; but you can never know with 100 percent certainty. Take the risk of checking out your perceptions.

As a skilled helper, it is important to listen more to the feelings a student expresses than the surface content. People, including students, seldom say all that they mean and seldom mean all that they say. It is critical to learn to listen between the lines. Sometimes a student may mean exactly the opposite of what he or she really says (for example, "I don't need your help!"). By listening to students' feelings, we help them move to a deeper level of understanding than if we focus only on the content, which tends to stay at an intellectual level. Students perceive that teachers who listen empathically by using reflections of feeling are more caring.

> *The most basic of all human needs is the need to understand and be understood. The best way to understand people is to listen to them.*
>
> **—Ralph Nichols**

Listening to students' feelings prevents them from bottling up their emotions and ultimately erupting in aggressive and destructive acts. Good active listening helps defuse stress and tension.

There are very practical reasons for using reflections of feeling in working with your students. David Aspy and Flo Roebuck reported in their book *Kids Don't Learn from Teachers They Don't Like* (Human Resource Development Press, 1977) that students of teachers using such active listening skills scored higher on academic achievement tests, attendance, and measures of self-esteem. Good listening does make a difference.

Twenty-three More Tips for Becoming a Better Listener

1. To be a successful listener, you must be genuinely interested in what the student has to say. If you don't have time at the moment, offer to talk with the student later.

2. In a counseling role, listen nonjudgmentally, achieving what psychologist Carl Rogers terms unconditional positive regard. By the time students come to their teachers with a problem, they have probably had advice and lectures from others. They often just need someone who cares enough to listen for a few minutes. Nothing nips trust like critical judgment and negative labeling. Beware of conveying disapproval through your tonality, leading questions, or nonverbal responses.

3. The next time you have a student sitting knee-to-knee in front of you with tears streaming down his or her cheeks, resist the urge to give advice or sugarcoated reassurance. Just take time to listen compassionately. Follow the adage "Talk a little less; listen a little more."

4. Become comfortable with silence in a counseling relationship. These pauses can create valuable reflection time for students.

5. Use a variety of listening skills. Restate a student's comment in your own words. This tends not to include the reference to feelings that are included in reflections of feeling. Good clarifying questions, used sparingly, can be most helpful in students

to examine the causes and possible solutions to their problems.

6. Be sure your nonverbal messages are congruent with your verbal ones. Unless the student's culture forbids it, offer the student direct eye contact while he or she is talking. This helps establish trust and communicates interest. Leaning forward is also interpreted as an expression of concern and interest.

7. Brief responses such as "Mm-hmm" or "I see" or "Go on" are useful in communicating that you are still with the speaker. Occasional nods also encourage the student to continue.

8. Avoid finishing others' statements. Besides being rude, it also communicates impatience and a lack of interest. More important, it's lazy listening. Sometimes you will just be wrong in your interpretation. It's also generally best not to interrupt the speakers unless they begin to ramble. Then you might inject a clarifying phrase or question.

9. Invest in building rapport with your students by listening to them when they don't have serious problems. Acknowledge and validate their positive feelings as well as the negative ones (for example, "You're really excited about making the team" or "You must be very proud of your award.") An example of validating a negative emotion would be "You are really disappointed you didn't do better on the test."

10. Study outstanding listeners in your daily life and in the public media. Larry King and Charlie Rose are good models to observe. Note their nonverbal posture and the quality of their open-ended questions.

11. Reflective listening is also a valuable technique to employ with angry students or adults. You are not getting into the blame game. You are neither saying "You're wrong!" nor "I'm wrong." By listening to their feelings (for example, "You're pretty upset with the way your child has been treated") you are simply communicating that you are listening to them at the deepest level. It is like verbal judo. Instead of meeting force with force, you are letting their anger dissipate into the wind. Once the angry person has vented his or her feelings and you refuse to get caught up in a shouting match, the person will begin to calm down.

12. Avoid the "Have you tried . . .?" trap. Most students will respond with "I tried that" or "It won't work because . . ." They will wait for you to suggest one more solution so that they can chop it down. It creates a no-win game.

13. *Why* questions tend to put a student on the defensive, asking them to justify their actions or feelings. It is preferable to ask what and how questions.

14. Feelings are neither good nor bad. They just exist. What counts is how we handle those emotions. Don't say, "I wish you didn't feel that way." Now the student may feel guilty about the emotions he or she is experiencing. Accept and help the students explore the feelings they are experiencing.

15. A particularly helpful question is "What would you like to have happen?" It encourages the student to focus on a goal.

> ## Comments That Do More Harm Than Good
>
> What you'd better do is . . .
> What's wrong with you?
> I wish you didn't feel that way.
> Others have problems worse than yours.
> Don't worry; everything is going to turn out just fine.
> Here's what I'd do if I were you: . . .
> Why do you feel that way?
> Everyone feels that way.
> Why don't you . . . ?

16. Be cautious of projecting your own issues onto the student. If racial or sexual harassment is an issue in your life, don't assume your students are wrestling with the same issue.

17. It is often helpful to help students explore the potential long- and short-term consequences of their anticipated actions in resolving a problem. They often fail to anticipate the unintended effects of their actions.

18. Respect your students' confidentiality. Of course, you must report instances of suspected child abuse or threatened harm to another or themselves, but don't gossip with other faculty about things students tell you in private.

> *Never give advice unasked.*
>
> **—German proverb**

19. Do be aware of when a student needs professional help. Offer to go to the school psychologist's or counselor's office with the student to make an appointment. Do communicate that you are concerned but that the student needs someone else with specific training in counseling to help with the problem. A classroom teacher will seldom have the time or training to engage in long-term, in-depth counseling relationships with students.

20. Pay attention to what the student is not saying. Are any obvious pieces of information or concerns not mentioned? That does not mean you must force the issue, but do make a mental note of what the student is avoiding.

21. Conclude a helping session with a summary of the main points discussed and any action the student might be planning to take to deal with the issue. Try to end on a hopeful, encouraging note.

22. One of the most valuable things you can give a student is hope, an expectation that things can and will eventually get better. Some students come from deplorable home environments. You have limited power to change the world the student returns to at the end of the day, but knowing that someone genuinely cares can make a tremendous difference.

23. Keep a phone list of various support services, both within the school system and the greater community, to which you might choose to refer parents. It is much easier if you have the information readily at your grasp rather than having to hunt for it and then get back to the parent later. The kinds of information you might want to accumulate could include the following:

   ○ Sources of children's health services

   ○ Emergency food, housing, and clothing assistance

   ○ Sources of scholarship funds

   ○ Counseling services for individuals and families

Barriers to Effective Communication

- Giving unsolicited advice
- Overuse of closed-ended questions
- Criticizing and labeling
- Becoming distracted
- Daydreaming
- Sugarcoated reassurance
- Preaching or moralizing
- Interrupting
- Fixing other people's problems
- Listening only to content, not hearing feelings
- Not attending to nonverbal cues
- Finishing another person's sentences
- Prejudging the speaker
- Jumping to conclusions
- Talking, not listening
- Asking leading questions
- Interpreting, diagnosing
- Incongruent body language

- Tutoring programs
- Child protective services

Teachers become significant persons in many of their students' lives. If you were to list the ten most significant persons in your life, chances are at least one teacher would be on that list. Do you think that teacher realizes how important he or she was in your life? Probably not. It is indeed a joy when former students return years later to let us know how dramatically we shaped their lives, but it is all too rare. Yet it is a certainty we must accept on faith. You never know how much impact you are having. Teachers plant seeds and do everything they can to nurture them. Unfortunately, we aren't always around for the harvest.

Education is the ability to listen to almost anything without losing your temper or your self-confidence.

—**Robert Frost**

Note: Remember that many of the sample templates, letters, handouts for this chapter are available for download from the *Classroom Teacher's Survival Guide* Web site josseybass.com/go/classroomteacher.

Problem Behavior Checklist

Indicate the frequency with which each of the following behaviors occurs in your classroom:

	Frequently	Occasionally	Rarely	Never
Hitting, fighting				
Shouting, loud talking				
Calling out				
Students talking with each other in class				
Stealing				
Cheating on tests, quizzes, homework				
Tardiness to class				
Name-calling				
Use of obscenities				
Handing in assignments late				
Not bringing necessary materials to class				
Not completing homework				
Leaving room without permission				
Wearing hats in the classroom				
Students out of their seats without permission				
Classroom vandalism				
Chewing gum in class				
Bullying others				
Weapons at school				
Violations of school dress code				
Non-compliance with teacher's requests				
Rude comments to others				
Littering				
Whining				
Tattling				
Abuse of books, equipment				
Incessant talking				
Truancy				
Non-participation, apathy				
Sexual harassment of other students				
Doing work for other classes in your class				
Playing dumb				
Excessive messiness				
Teasing other students				
Other:				

Documented Interventions

Student's name _____

Parents' names _____

Parent's daytime phone(s) _____

Teacher _____ Subject/grade_____

Intervention	Date	Comments
Discuss problem with student	_____	_____
Clarify rules	_____	_____
Change seats	_____	_____
Telephone parents/guardian	_____	_____
Parent conference	_____	_____
Peer tutoring	_____	_____
Extra help after school	_____	_____
Adapt assignments	_____	_____
Refer to counselor	_____	_____
Student contract	_____	_____
Time-out	_____	_____
Home/school daily or weekly notes	_____	_____
Individual conference with student	_____	_____
Refer to principal	_____	_____
Refer to counselor	_____	_____
Refer to school psychologist	_____	_____
Refer to specialist: _____	_____	_____
Conference with parent and student	_____	_____
Home visit	_____	_____
Team conference	_____	_____

Notes:

_____

_____

_____

Proficiency Notice

Date _____

To: _____

From: _____

I am most pleased to report that the performance of _____
in my class has been noteworthy and deserving of recognition. In particular, I wanted to bring
to your attention the following success:

_____

_____

_____

I hope we can both encourage this progress to continue. Please feel free to contact me if you

have any questions or concerns.

Teaching is the art of
assisting discovery.

—Mark Van Doren

Hurray!

Well done!

BRAVO!

Excellent!!

Super!   *Fantastic!*

We're very proud of your
accomplishment of

_____

Best wishes for continued success.

_____   _____

Date   Teacher

Wow!

I'm excited for you.

_____

_____

_____

_____

Keep up the good work!

_____   _____
Date   Teacher

Acts of Kindness Citation

was found on this day to have committed one or more acts of kindness, helping make our school a friendlier, more caring community.

_____
Witness

_____
Date

Outstanding Student of the Week

awarded to

_____

for a high level of effort and performance.

_____
Date

_____
Teacher

You're on target!

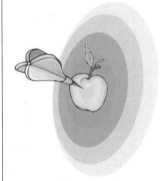

Presented to_____

for outstanding progress in

_____

_____

Way to Go!

Date _____

Congratulations to _____

for _____

_____

Let's Make A Deal!

If _____ can

_____

_____ by

_____

then the teacher will _____

_____

_____

_____ Teacher

_____ Student

_____ Date

Official Seal

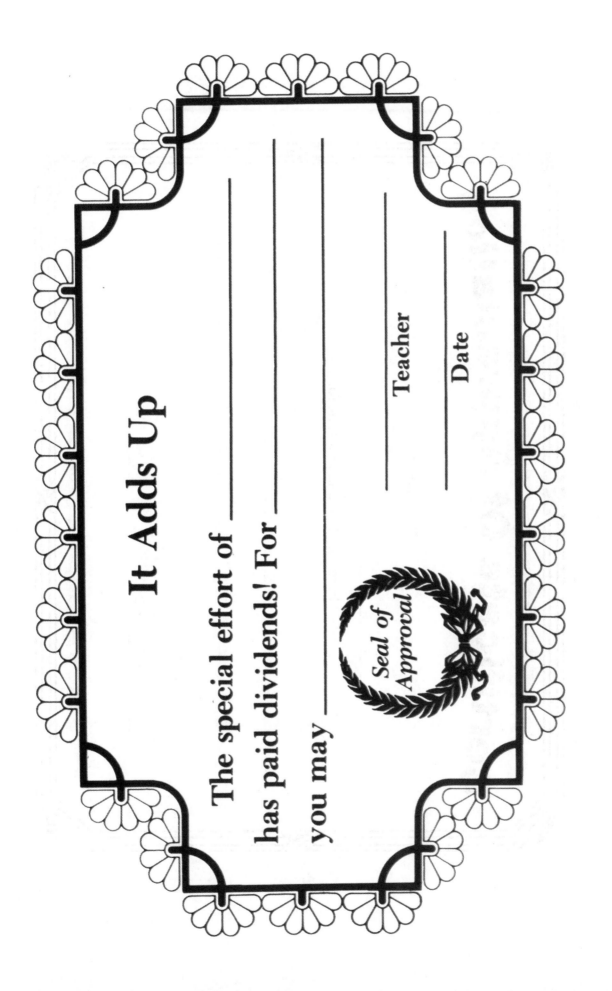

It Adds Up

The special effort of

_____

has paid dividends! For

_____

you may

_____

Seal of Approval

_____
Teacher

_____
Date

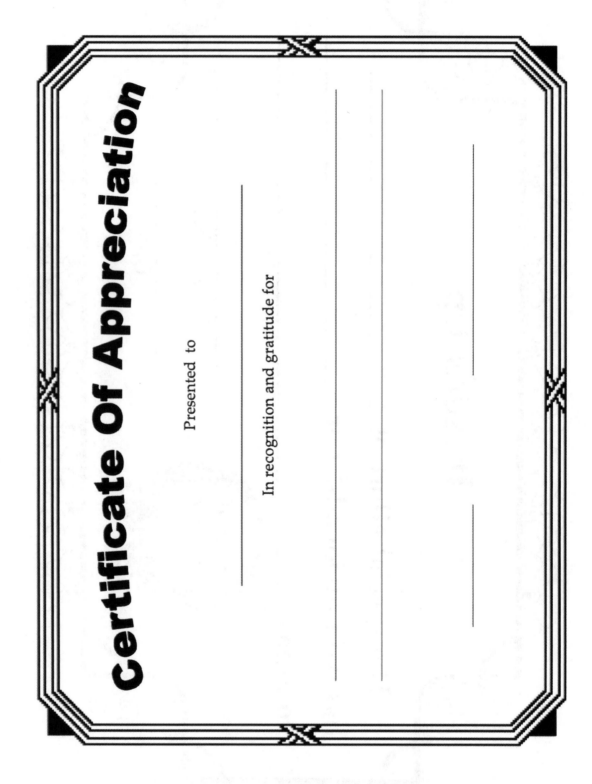

Certificate Of Appreciation

Presented to

In recognition and gratitude for

Outstanding Job

Presented to

_____

Your hard work greatly
improved your achievement!

_____

Thanks for your help!

It really is appreciated.

Homework Pass

Awarded to _____

for _____

This certificate entitles the above person to one free night of no homework. Turn in this pass on the day the assignment is due.

_____ _____
Date   Teacher

Hard Worker Award
To

_____

for

_____

_____
Teacher

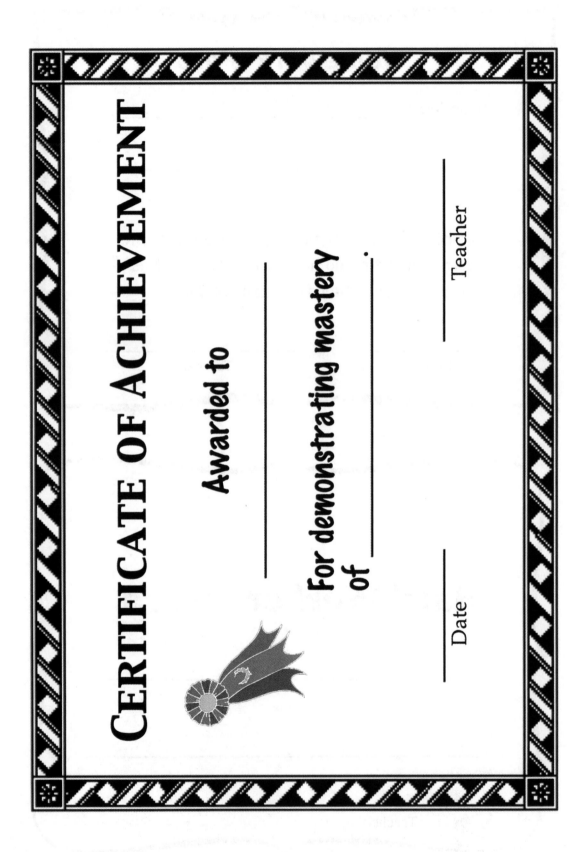

CERTIFICATE OF ACHIEVEMENT

Awarded to

_____

For demonstrating mastery of

_____ .

_____
Teacher

_____
Date

Time Management and Organizational Strategies 3

THE EROSION OF SCHOOL TIME

In the past century, schools have been charged with ever-growing responsibilities. Each time society faces a new problem, schools are expected to become part of the solution, creating a perpetual add-on curriculum. We have added consumer education, drug education, sex education, moral education, character education, driver education, and career education. Schools are expected to turn out students who are good citizens, have positive self-esteem, have mastered the basics, have employable skills, and can act as mature and responsible adults. In short, we expect a lot of our schools.

> Expanding Academic Learning Time is critical to student achievement; just squeezing more content into less time can reduce understanding. Allocating more time is only part of the solution; using it well is equally crucial.
>
> **—Elizabeth Rangel, Time to Learn, Research Points, 2007**

Reports such as *A Nation at Risk* (National Commission on Excellence in Education, 1983), *Educating Americans for the 21st Century* (National Science Board Commission on Precollege Education in Mathematics, Science, and Technology, 1983), and *Prisoners of Time* (National Education Commission on Time and Learning, 1994) suggested that even more must be demanded of our schools, urging a longer school day and extended school year. Proponents of the standards-based and high-stakes testing trend have focused attention on the most precious of resources in the education of youth: time.

With an ever-growing spectrum of goals competing for time in the curriculum, the necessity of using it wisely is paramount. Because time is a finite resource, each wasted minute decreases the amount available for higher-priority goals.

To increase learning time, we are faced with two alternatives or some combination of the two. We can increase the number of hours of schooling by lengthening the school day, at a considerable expense—estimated in the billions. Beyond the financial restraints are the social and psychological impacts on children and their families. Such a move is a policy decision that legislators and educators are debating. That debate is likely to continue for some time.

A more immediate alternative is to use the presently scheduled school day more effectively. Research has found that as little as 50 percent of the scheduled school minutes are actually used for academic instruction.

Teachers vary greatly in their ability to manage classroom time. The ability to use time wisely in pursuing curricular goals is perhaps the most valuable teaching skill. Time-management skills are essential for survival in the classroom. Where else in modern society do we place thirty people in one room with a single leader for six hours a day and expect constant, productive activity?

The School Calendar

The upper limits of academic learning are set by the length of the school year. The average U.S. school year is 180 days (almost one-half of the days in a year). A 2006 report by the Council of Chief State School Officers found that only three states mandated a school year exceeding 180 days. This compares with 243 days in Germany and 240 days in Japan. However, in Sweden, whose students have done fairly well on the Trends in International Mathematics and Science Study (TIMSS) tests, the academic year is only 170 days.

In the United States, the average school day is approximately six hours long, yielding an annual scheduled school calendar of 1,080 hours. However, no school is ever in session the total hours scheduled (Rangel, 2007). Schools close for snowstorms, fog, windstorms, ice, floods, and water shortages. Some buildings have been closed for fuel shortages, broken water lines, bomb threats, vandalism, funerals, or flu epidemics. Work stoppages by faculty or other school employees have caused some schools to close. A few school systems have a history of periodic strikes interrupting the school year. Schools have canceled sessions because their basketball team was competing in the state championship. In recent years many have shut the doors for weeks because they ran out of money. On days that schools are closed, teachers cannot teach and students do not receive supervised instruction. Most school closings are unavoidable, but they yield vastly different amounts of exposure to instruction among schools.

More time is lost for delays of one or two hours because of inclement weather. In some areas frequent fog may force schools to delay opening more than ten or fifteen mornings per year. Impending storms occasionally force early dismissals. Some systems excuse students early for faculty meetings or parent conferences. Others have shortened the school day by moving to double shifts to alleviate overcrowding.

Even when school is in session, students are not always there. Absenteeism may severely limit some students' academic exposure. Certainly, legitimate illnesses keep some students at home. Religious holidays or deaths in the family are also viewed as excused absences. Some parents keep their children home to baby-sit, go on early vacations, or help with work. Parents still schedule doctors' and dentists' appointments during school hours. In many rural schools, it is not unusual for boys to miss school the first day of hunting season. Some students still play hooky. Indeed for many schools, especially in the inner city, it is not unusual for as many as one-half of the students to be absent. This represents a serious loss of learning time.

Schemes for rearranging the way time is distributed (most notably, block scheduling and year-round schools) have gained in popularity. However, these innovations do not necessarily increase the total number of hours spent in the classroom.

Instructional Time

Even when school is in session and the student attends, not all time is available for classroom instruction. Transitions, recesses, and assorted scheduled activities erode available instructional time.

The time allocated to academic classes varies widely from school to school and even within the same building (Rangel, 2007). The power to allocate school time among the various content areas is a most significant tool in determining school effectiveness—one that unfortunately has been abused in some instances. Differences as large as sevenfold have been observed in the amount of time spent on content areas such as math or reading, even within the same school system.

The obvious explanation for such wide variation in time allocated to instructional areas is that the needs of students vary, demanding individualization. But little evidence suggests that this is the reason. The data thus far suggest that students are exposed to large differences in content coverage merely because of the school they happen to attend or the teacher they are assigned. For example, one teacher reported that she spent very little time teaching fractions because she didn't like them. Her students will pay for such preferences later. Indeed, in the Beginning Teacher Evaluation Study, the amount of time allocated to reading and mathematics instruction and achievement test scores were significantly correlated.

Scheduled events such as standardized testing, school pictures, assemblies, fire or tornado drills, or pep rallies cut into the time scheduled for instruction. Individual students are often absent from the room for school-sanctioned activities, such as visits to the counselor's office, special pull-out programs, in-school suspensions, or athletic events. In the spring many high school classrooms may have a third of the students excused early to travel to athletic contests. Teachers may be reluctant to introduce any new material to the remaining students, virtually eliminating the last period of the school day.

Teacher Time-on-Task

Not all regularly scheduled class time is devoted to academic instruction. Most teachers lose time for clerical tasks such as collecting milk money, taking attendance, collecting and distributing papers and materials, counting books, reading announcements, or writing passes—all tasks that do not require a college degree.

Classroom research studies have observed that an average of 18 percent of class time is consumed by discipline matters. The simplest reprimand may further consume time by creating a break in the lesson's momentum, causing the whole class to go off task. That momentum must be regained. Most time is used in managing student behavior; for example, giving students permission to go to the restroom or sharpen pencils eats away at class time.

Beginning the class a few minutes after the scheduled starting time or stopping the lesson a few minutes before dismissal robs more learning time, as much as ten minutes of the class period. Through poor preparation and planning, a teacher can consume more time on noninstructional activities, such as hunting for misplaced papers and materials, clarifying directions, or setting up audiovisual equipment.

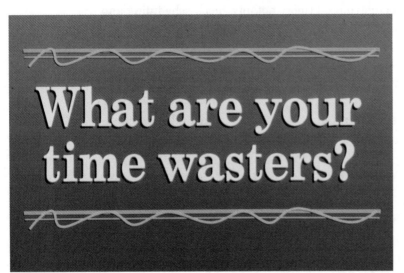

Additional class time is absorbed by a variety of interruptions: students arriving late, drop-in visitors, telephone calls, outside noises and distractions, equipment breakdowns, or ill students.

Transitions from one activity to another consume many minutes over the course of a year. Some teachers have been guilty of using class time poorly by reviewing the previous week's big game, making the class wait while one student is helped, or excessively chatting about personal stories that are irrelevant to the lesson.

Though the individual time robbers may vary from room to room, all schools lose a large proportion of time to noninstructional activities. Indeed, several research studies have found that less than 50 percent of the school day is actually spent in academic instruction! That is 540 hours of the 1,080 allotted to schools to teach the basics, develop minimal competencies, and meet all the other assorted objectives that society imposes on schools.

The Pace of Instruction

The pace of instruction represents how fast a teacher covers the content during the time allotted to a content area. In the same span of time, two teachers may cover different amounts of content.

The guiding principle in pacing instruction is to aim for appropriateness. Too fast a pace and the student is left behind. The teacher is moving on to new material for which the student has not yet mastered prerequisite skills. Instruction paced too slowly becomes inefficient, producing boredom, repetition, and lack of interest.

Not all students require the same amount of time to learn. Research suggests that most concepts and skills learning in schools can be mastered by 80 to 95 percent of all students if given an appropriate amount of time.

The lockstep pacing of the traditional classroom moves everyone at the same pace, some before they are ready, others long after. Observational studies have found that teachers typically move on when approximately 80 percent of the class has grasped the concept or skill. Of course, conscientious teachers have always made attempts to provide remedial instruction to the lagging 20 percent through individual tutoring, small-group instruction, or homework assignments. Indeed, totally individualizing the pace of instruction remains a challenge to the most dedicated of teachers.

With varying degrees of success, teachers have sought to individualize pacing through programmed instruction, peer tutoring, computer-assisted instruction, contract learning, enrichment activities, learning centers, and ability grouping. Matching the time provided with the time required for learning is the key to improving learning gains for all students but benefits low achievers the most.

We must continue to experiment with new techniques that provide the appropriate level of pacing. Part of the key is freeing teachers from routine clerical and noninstructional tasks to provide the optimal instructional time for each student. Computer technologies show great promise in helping to make this a reality.

Student Time-on-Task

Just because teachers are teaching doesn't mean that students are learning. Educational efficiency is eroded further by student inattention and ineffective instruction. Two teachers may allocate the same amount of time to instruction, but their students may be engaged in that instruction at vastly different rates. The percentage of time-on-task or engagement rate has come under increasing scrutiny as a contributor to learning effectiveness. The percentage of time-on-task has been reported to range from 50 to 90 percent, with an average engagement rate of 70 percent of the available instructional time. But remember that 50 percent of the day may already be lost to noninstructional activity; therefore, the student time-on-task may be less than 70 percent of 50 percent, or 350 hours out of the original 1,080 hours per year!

Wide variations in student engagement rates have been observed. Higher on-task rates are observed for girls, high-ability students, and good readers. The highest engagement rates are typically found in music, social studies, and foreign languages. The lowest on-task rates occur in mathematics, language arts, and reading (ironically, the subjects generally allocated the largest block of time). Students are also more attentive to those classes in which they are actively involved in activities, such as music and social studies.

The teaching format also influences time-on-task. Teacher-led discussions tend to elicit greater student involvement than do lectures, audiovisual presentations, or seatwork. Croll and Moses (1988) found that the more time the teacher spends working with the whole class, the greater the percentage of time students spend on a task, even when they are working independently. Small-group activities and seatwork tend to provide the lowest levels of on-task behavior. This does not mean that instructional activities with lower engagement rates should not be used. The benefits gained from a seatwork assignment or small-group project may justify its use.

Student attention to lessons is also influenced by the weather, season, and time of the day. Students experience the highest involvement at the beginning of the morning, but involvement decreases as the day passes. Days right before or after a major holiday or special event usually suffer lower attentiveness.

Not all engaged time is productive learning time. If students are attending to instruction that is ineffective, too easy, or too difficult, they are gaining little. The goal must be to seek high engagement in appropriate learning tasks.

Research shows that increasing the amount of time spent in learning benefits low-ability students more than it does the more capable students. Increased time-on-task shows the greatest benefit in highly structured courses, for example, math and foreign languages.

Out-of-school-time strategies, such as after-school or weekend programs, have been found to be effective in enhancing some students' academic achievement. Students in the early elementary grades seemed to profit most from out-of-school work in reading, while high school students gained the most from extra work in math. One-on-one tutoring in reading was found to be particularly helpful in improving reading skills.

Though proposals to lengthen the school day or add days to the school calendar have an intuitive appeal, careful data analyses indicate that to have a significant impact, the number of instructional hours would have to be extensive. After reviewing related research,

Cotton and Wikelund (2002) concluded that the costs of extending the school day or year are not justifiable. Others caution that increasing time spent in school does little good if the instruction offered is ineffective.

Conclusion

Before the school year is lengthened or the school day is extended, it is imperative to make every effort to ensure that the current available time is being used as effectively as possible. Teachers must create an environment that demonstrates that school time is to be safeguarded. Setting the expectations and standards on the effective use of time must be done the first week of school. Well-prepared, organized lessons are more likely to maximize student time-on-task. Beginning class on time and teaching until the end of the class period are two ways of gaining additional class time.

The educational community must work to assure that learning time is protected. Every effort must be made to free teachers from noninstructional clerical tasks and to minimize interruptions and other time robbers. A humane and fun yet businesslike learning climate should be sought.

References

Bloom, B. S. (1976). *Human characteristics and school learning.* New York: McGraw-Hill.

Cotton, K., & Wikelund, K. R. (2002). *Educational time factors. School Improvement Research Series.* Portland, OR: Northwest Regional Educational Laboratory.

Croll, P., & Moses, D. (1988). Teaching methods and time on task in junior classrooms. *Educational Research, 30,* 90–97.

Davidson, J. L., & Holley, F. M. (1979). Your students might be spending only half of the school day receiving instruction. *American School Board Journal, 161*(3), 40–41.

Ebmeir, H. H., & Zoimek, R. L. (1982, March). *Engagement rates as a function of subject area, grade level and time of day.* Paper presented at the American Educational Research Association, New York.

Fisher, C. W., Berliner, D. C., Filby, N. N., et al. (1980). *Teaching behaviors, academic learning time, and student achievement: An overview.* In C. Denham & A. Lieberman (Eds.), *Time to Learn* (pp. 7–32). Washington, DC: National Institute of Education.

Goodlad, J. I. (1985). *A place called school.* New York: McGraw-Hill.

Harnischfeger, A. (1984, April). *School time and changing curricular goals.* Paper delivered at the American Educational Research Association, New Orleans, LA.

Hiatt, D. B. (1979). Time allocation in the classroom: Is instruction being shortchanged? *Phi Delta Kappan, 61,* 289–290.

Karweit, N. L. (1973). *Time on task: A research review.* Baltimore: Johns Hopkins University, Center for Social Organization of Schools.

Karweit, N. L., & Slavin, R. E. (1981). Measurement and modeling choices in studies of time and learning. *American Educational Research Journal, 18,* 157–171.

Lauer, P. A., Akiba, M., Wilkerson, S. B., et al. (2003). *The effectiveness of out-of-school-time strategies in assisting low-achieving students in reading and mathematics: A research synthesis.* Aurora, CO: Mid-Continent Research for Education and Learning.

Lowe, R., & Gervais, R. (1988). Increasing instructional time in today's classroom. *NASSP Bulletin, 72,* 19–22.

Murphy, J. (1992). Instructional leadership: Focus on time to learn. *NASSP Bulletin, 76*(542), 19–26.

National Commission on Excellence in Education. (1983). *A nation at risk: The imperative for educational reform.* Washington, DC: U.S. Government Printing Office.

National Education Commission on Time and Learning. (1994). *Prisoners of time.* Washington, DC: U.S. Government Printing Office.

National Science Board Commission on Precollege Education in Mathematics, Science, and Technology. (1983). *Educating Americans for the 21st century: A plan of action for improving mathematics, science and technology education.* Washington, DC: Education for All.

Rangel, E. S. (2007). Time to learn. *Research Points, 5*(2), 1–4.

Note: *An earlier version of this section appeared in* American Secondary Education, *17(4), 1989, 6–11. Reprinted with permission from* American Secondary Education.

PRISONERS OF TIME

In April of 1994 the National Education Commission on Time and Learning issued its report, *Prisoners of Time,* which examined the relationship between time and learning in the nation's schools. The commission concluded that schools were very much controlled by the clock and that true school reform must reexamine the allocation and use of time in the schools. Its report labeled school time as the rudder of school reform. The commission issued eight recommendations:

1. Reinvent schools around learning, not time.
2. Fix the design flaw: use time in new and better ways.
3. Establish an academic day.
4. Keep schools open longer to meet the needs of children and communities.
5. Give teachers the time they need.
6. Invest in technology.
7. Develop local action plans to transform schools.
8. Share the responsibility: finger-pointing and evasion must end.

BLOCK SCHEDULING

The trend toward block scheduling in middle and high schools mushroomed during the 1990s. Block scheduling roughly doubles the length of class periods. For example, instead of teaching six classes of forty-five minutes each day, a teacher might have three eighty- or ninety-minute classes per day. An estimated 40 to 50 percent of all high schools use some form of block scheduling, which has gained more support in some states than in others. A 2003 *Christian Science Monitor* article reported that 90 percent of North Carolina high schools are using block schedules.

Many schools have adopted a 4 × 4 block schedule. Under this plan students take four rather than six classes each quarter. What previously were yearlong classes now meet for only two quarters. Courses that met for a semester under the traditional calendar now meet for only one quarter. Many schools have adopted schedules that are variations or combinations of block schedules and traditional schedules.

4×4 Semester Block Schedule

Period		First Semester	Second Semester
	1	Class 1	Class 5
	2		
	3	Class 2	Class 6
	4		
	5	Class 3	Class 7
	6		
	7	Class 4	Class 8
	8		

To address some of the major criticisms of the 4×4 schedule, a variation known as the A-B-A-B or alternating system has emerged. Students attend four extended class periods the first day. The next day they attend four different classes. Students alternate daily between the two daily schedules through the entire year.

Alternative Day Block Schedule for Six Courses

		Monday A Day 1	Tuesday B Day 2	Wednesday A Day 1	Thursday B Day 2	Friday A Day 1	Monday B Day 2
Days	Period	1	2	1	2	1	2
		1	2	1	2	1	2
		3	4	3	4	3	4
		3	4	3	4	3	4
		5	6	5	6	5	6
		5	6	5	6	5	6

A major advantage of the block schedule is that longer periods allow more opportunity for more active learning activities. However, there is no guarantee of the outcome. Many teachers continue to lecture as they have before, perhaps tacking on a study period the last half-hour.

Advantages of Block Scheduling

- Extra time supports more project-based learning.
- Teachers see fewer students each day.
- Time permits more cooperative and small-group learning.
- Greater depth and breadth of content is possible.

- Teacher has the opportunity to change role to facilitator.
- Less time spent in between-class transitions.
- Opportunity to vary instructional approaches.
- Blocks allow time for more one-on-one teaching and evaluation.
- Interdisciplinary teaching is easier to accomplish.
- Common teacher planning time is more feasible.
- Blocks allow opportunity for more hands-on learning.
- Students have less homework each weekday.
- Blocks allow time for integrating technology into instruction.
- Teachers may have longer planning periods.
- Instruction is less hurried.

Disadvantages of Block Scheduling

- Teachers face the challenge of holding students' attention.
- Subjects don't meet every day.
- Teachers must have a variety of instructional skills.
- Teachers have to spend more time with exasperating classes.
- Students lack daily reinforcement of content.
- Students find it harder to catch up after absences.
- Impact on achievement is still questionable.
- Substitutes have more difficulty making good use of time.
- Teachers may end up teaching more courses in a year.
- Student transfers between schools are more difficult to handle.
- Blocks may decrease participation in music programs (largely due to schedule conflicts with academic courses).

The wisdom of moving to the "block" is still being debated. Some teachers love it; others hate it. Block scheduling presents special challenges for teachers of special subjects, like music and gym. The semester format and longer class periods do not allow the daily reinforcement of skills.

Research on the effects of block scheduling is mixed and so far inconclusive. Much depends on the quality of the instruction offered. Research tends to find that students like the block-schedule format, particularly with teachers who are able to do more than lecture for the entire period. At least one study reported increased stress for teachers, at least initially, when moving to the block schedule. Other studies have found less use of lecture by teachers in block-schedule schools.

Research suggests that the longer teachers teach under block scheduling, the more they like it. Some evidence suggests that teachers' acceptance is related to how the decision to move to block scheduling was made, with earlier and active involvement correlating with more positive attitudes. Several studies have reported that after two to four years under block scheduling, 65 to 90 percent of teachers, students, and parents felt block schedules were effective and worth continuing.

Studies seem to consistently report decreased behavior problems and increased attendance rates for schools moving to block schedules. The benefits of block scheduling appear to be most pronounced for at-risk students. The main exception is mathematics achievement, which seems to suffer across the board under block scheduling.

For More Information

Frank, M. (2002). Thinking outside the block: An innovative alternative to 4 × 4 block scheduling. *Science Teacher, 69*(2), 38–41.

Mowen, G. G., & Mowen, C. (2004). To block-schedule or not? *Education Digest: Essential Readings Condensed for Quick Review, 69*(8), 50–53.

Queen, J. A. (2003). *The block scheduling handbook.* Thousand Oaks, CA: Corwin.

Waggoner, C., & Cline, L. (2006). Extending student learning opportunities in a 6–8 middle school. *Middle School Journal, 37*(5), 16–20.

Zepeda, S. J., & Mayers, S. (2006). An analysis of research on block scheduling. *Review of Educational Research, 76*(1), 137–170.

ELEVEN TIPS FOR MINIMIZING CLASSROOM INTERRUPTIONS

Interruptions are the bane of every classroom teacher. Not only is precious class time lost but so is something even more essential: momentum. A class that is 100 percent on task suddenly becomes 100 percent off task as the interruption disrupts everyone's attention. The teacher must then refocus everyone's attention back onto the topic at hand. While many interruptions are beyond teachers' direct control (for example, fire engines, P.A. announcements, or drop-in visitors), some interruptions are created by the teachers (stopping a lesson to hunt for materials or to reprimand a student). Here are some suggestions for minimizing the impact of interruptions.

1. To assess the amount of time that interruptions consume, carry a stopwatch for a day or week. Each time you are interrupted, start the watch. When the interruption ends, stop the watch. At the end of the day, record how much time has elapsed. An alternative is to ask a student to do the timekeeping for you.

2. Let the world know that intrusions are not welcome. Many interruptions occur simply because the offender is not aware that his or her behavior is disruptive. Open doors invite interruptions.

3. Outside their doors, many teachers hang a sign such as "Important Learning in Progress" (or use the "Please Do Not Disturb: Learning in Progress" sign included in this chapter). Tape a note pad and hang a pencil beside the door for messages.

4. Negotiate with the principal for custodians to schedule distracting work, such as mowing beside windows, before or after school. It may not always be possible, but let it be known that such activity detracts from learning.

5. If doors or windows provide too many visual distractions to students, rearrange the furniture to face away from the distraction.

6. Let other teachers know that sending students to borrow supplies during class is not welcome. Be tactful but assertive. Conversely, you have a responsibility to respect your fellow teachers' time. Do not send student messengers to their rooms during classes except in emergencies.

7. The best way to prevent interruptions is to conduct a well-planned, organized lesson. Have the necessary materials and equipment ready before class begins. Stopping a lesson to thread a movie projector or hunt for a book is usually an avoidable distraction. Not only does it use precious class time, but also it invites student misbehavior.

8. When an interruption does occur, your aims are to keep it as brief as possible, minimize the impact on the learning activity, and assure that the same interruption will not occur again. If you are interrupted by a telephone call, get to the point immediately. Be brief and assertive. If the call is going to take too long, give the caller a more convenient time to talk or volunteer to call back.

9. Most principals have discovered the potential abuses of the P.A., restricting announcements to the first and last five minutes of the day. If your school has not implemented such a policy, suggest that it do so. Some have stopped using the P.A. system for routine morning announcements; instead, teachers read them to their classes.

10. People who walk in unannounced cause many classroom interruptions. If someone comes to your door, stand in the doorway so that you can talk with the visitor yet face the class. Try to avoid leaving the room unattended. As much as possible, discourage drop-in visitors.

11. At the beginning of the year, when it is best to establish classroom routines, tell your students what they should do during such interruptions.

TEACHER TIME ROBBERS

The following list contains the activities that teachers most frequently cite as keeping them from doing their job better:

- Filling out forms, paperwork
- Repeating directions
- Dealing with unplanned interruptions
- Doing clerical tasks, photocopying
- Handling classroom behavior
- Grading student work
- Attending meetings, in-service programs
- Cleaning the classroom
- Supervising the playground, the lunchroom
- Keeping track of money
- Doing bus duty
- Taking attendance

FULL-TIME TEACHERS' WORKWEEK

	AVERAGE HOURS PER WEEK REQUIRED TO BE AT SCHOOL	AVERAGE HOURS PER WEEK SPENT OUTSIDE OF REGULAR SCHOOL HOURS IN SCHOOL-RELATED ACTIVITIES INVOLVING STUDENTS[1]	AVERAGE HOURS PER WEEK SPENT OUTSIDE OF REGULAR SCHOOL HOURS IN SCHOOL-RELATED AC-TIVITIES NOT INVOLVING STUDENTS[2]
Public	37.8	3.2	8.7
Elementary	37.6	2.1	8.9
Secondary	38.1	5.2	8.4
Private	38.2	3.1	8.6

[1] *School-related activities involving student interaction include coaching, field trips, tutoring, or transporting students.*

[2] *School-related activities not involving students include preparation, grading papers, parent conferences, or attending meetings.*

Note: *Data did not include public charter schools.*

SOURCE: *National Center for Educational Statistics. (2002). Schools and staffing survey, 1999–2000: Overview of the data for public, private, public charter, and Bureau of Indian Affairs elementary and secondary schools. Available online at nces.ed.gov/pubsearch.*

CLASSROOM ROUTINES

Effective teachers have learned the importance of establishing classroom routines the first week of school. Many daily classroom events and tasks must be accomplished with a minimum of direction and must flow smoothly using the least amount of time possible.

Don't assume students know what you want; train them the first week of school. As each task arises the first time, explain carefully exactly how you would like it to be done. It helps to carefully explain why the routine is helpful in getting things done. Invite questions from students to clarify the procedure. For some you might want to put the directions in writing. Review these routines occasionally if

students begin to deviate from them. Research suggests it generally takes about a month to establish a new habit. Possible tasks for which you might wish to establish routines include the following:

- Beginning the day
- Taking attendance
- What to do when the student arrives late
- Making up missed assignments when returning from an absence
- Making up missed tests
- Taking lunch count
- Seeking help
- Signaling when to stop talking
- Turning in homework papers
- Information to be included on student papers (where they should write their name, period, date, and so on)
- What to do when they finish a test or seatwork early
- Leaving the room (restroom privileges, library, office, and so on)
- What to do when a visitor comes to the door
- Distributing and collecting materials, assignments, and so on
- What to do if they don't bring pencils, paper, and other supplies
- Appropriate responses to emergencies (fire, tornado, earthquake)
- Beginning class
- Leaving and returning from recess
- Signing out materials, tools, books, equipment, and so on
- Seating arrangement
- Using learning centers
- Procedures for moving about the building as a group
- Attending assemblies
- Cleanup
- Obtaining permission for field trips
- Transitions from one activity to another
- Leaving the room at the end of the day

Merely establishing a routine or procedure will not make it happen. You must clearly explain it to your students. If possible, demonstrate it or have a model for them to study. Then provide opportunities for your students to practice the routine. Walk them through it step-by-step if necessary. Reinforce them for complying with your routines. Show students you appreciate their cooperation.

Once the routines are explained, consider posting them on the wall. When a new student enrolls in your class, it is often helpful to appoint a partner who is responsible for teaching the new student the various routines. Here are some specific routines some teachers find helpful in running their classrooms' daily activities.

Taking Attendance or Lunch Count

Taking attendance is one of the necessary tasks of any teacher. There is no one way to take the class roll. Your school policy, the number of students, their grade level and maturity all influence the form of your attendance-taking routine. The important thing is to adopt a procedure that is least disruptive.

- Many teachers prefer to get their students to work immediately and then to unobtrusively take the roll. Generally, after the first week of school, few teachers waste class time calling the roll aloud. Some have been ingenious in subtle ways to take attendance with little disruption and minimal time.

- Attach a library-book pocket for each student to a poster board that hangs on the wall near the door. Put the students' names on these pockets. Attach a separate one in which you insert brightly colored cards. As students enter the room, they pull out a blank card and insert it in the pocket with their name.

- To make an attendance or lunch-count board, you need a board approximately fourteen by eighteen inches, spring-type clothespins (one for each student), a box or can to store the clothespins, a calendar, and attendance slips. Decorate the board and box if desired. Print each student's first and last name on the clothespins. Store the clothespins in the box or can on a small table or desk. Have the calendar and attendance slips handy. After students hang up their coats, they go to the table, get their clothespins, and place them on the board in the appropriate slot to indicate that they are present or that they will be buying lunch. When school actually starts, a volunteer student goes to the desk and fills out the date, teacher's name, counts those buying lunch, and records the number on the slip. Any clothespins left in the box or can indicate students who are absent. The volunteer records these on the slip and takes the list to the teacher for approval. The volunteer then takes the slip to the office or clips it to the door, whichever is your school policy. When the student returns to the room, he or she is responsible for removing the clothespins from the board and putting them back in the box, ready for tomorrow. An alternative is to hang the pins around the rim of a bucket and have the students drop their clothespins into the bucket as they enter.

- If not required, don't begin every class by taking attendance or reading the roll. Jump right into the subject matter. Students most remember the first and last things you do in the class. You can quietly take attendance while they are busy with independent work later in the period. Other teachers have an assignment written on the board. As soon as students enter the room, they are to go directly to their seats and begin work on the day's assignment. Once everyone has begun work, the teacher can quietly take attendance using the seating chart.

- Have each student record his or her name on a three-by-five-inch index card. Different colors can be used for each class or grade level. Keep the cards in one small file box. When students are absent without being excused, their cards are turned sideways in the box and left there until the teacher receives a call or note. It is very easy to check who has not returned an approved absence slip.

- Keep a stack of brightly colored cards in a pocket attached to the wall near the door. Instead of having to take a lunch count, have the children be responsible for their own. Clip two folders (labeled "buy" and "pack") on the bulletin board, next to the folder containing the colored cards. Each day as students enter the room, they get a card and drop it in the "buy" pocket or "pack" pocket. A student volunteer can quickly count the number of cards in each folder, place the cards back in the original holding folder, and turn in the lunch count.

- For elementary school, record each student's name on a paper animal cutout. Hang these with a short string to a poster. As the students enter the classroom, they turn their tags over. Those students whose names still show are absent. At the end of the day, a student helper can turn them all back over to reveal the names again. (Source: Contributed by Janet Smith)

- On the left side of an 8½-by-11-inch paper sheet of paper, type your class roster in a column, listing your name, room number, and the period at the top of the column. Copy or type the same information onto the right-hand side of the paper, giving you two identical lists of the class roster. Duplicate, cut, and staple these into pads of attendance rosters for each class. At the beginning of the class, all you need do is circle the names of the absent students on the top sheet and tear it off. The pads can also be used for field trips, lunch counts, and so on. The office staff will be most appreciative, especially if your hurried handwriting is illegible.

- Some teachers use a loose-leaf notebook to maintain attendance records. Create a section for each class, separating them by tabs. Within each section arrange sheets alphabetically by students' last names. At the top of each student's sheet, have them enter basic information, such as locker number, home address, phone number, parents' names, student identification number, and book number. Note each day when a student is absent, tardy, or fails to bring homework. If disruptive behavior occurs, note it on that student's sheet. You will be able to handle later problems much more smoothly with such documentation.

- Have students who are buying lunch stand up and count off. You have a quick head count. This also reinforces number skills for younger children.

Distributing and Collecting Materials

Getting tools, books, papers, and other materials distributed to students can be a time-absorbing, chaotic, stressful event if you don't develop a smooth routine. Here's what you can do:

- Don't distribute too many things at once, and distribute them in the order in which students will need them.

- Assign a weekly monitor whose job is to assist you in distributing any materials.

- Don't count papers when distributing them in class. Instruct the person at the end of the row to pass them to one corner where a student puts extras in a neat pile for you.

- If students are working in groups, you can unobtrusively place papers or supplies that they will need beneath one person's seat in each group. At the appropriate time, you can direct them to gather from beneath their seats the materials for their group.

- Delegate one student from each group to come pick up the materials the group needs.

- When collecting papers, have students pass them across the rows to one side of the room rather than down the front. There is less poking people in the back, and it is easier to monitor student behavior.

Regaining Students' Attention

Quieting a class to gain its attention is a challenge to many teachers. It is perhaps the first routine that should be taught the first day of school. Most successful teachers develop some form of signal or cue that tells students to stop what they are doing, be quiet, and focus their attention on the teacher. Here are some strategies that many teachers use:

- Use a bell, chord on the piano, or chime to signal that it is time to stop talking and give the teacher attention. Some teachers have collected an assortment of bells, whistles, and other novelty sound instruments that they use for this purpose.

- Use hand signals to cue students to stop talking. Raise your hand palm up or hold up two or three fingers. Don't say anything until you have everyone's attention. Some teachers have their students join the teacher in raising their hands.

- Another commonly used cue to quiet a group is to hold your index finger vertically across your lips.

- Others signal it is time to give the teacher attention by standing in a designated spot in the room.

- Slowly clap your hands together three times. When students hear the first clap, they are to join in on the second clap. This grabs the attention of everyone who didn't hear the first one. Typically, the whole class offers the third clap simultaneously. Now the room is silent, and attention is focused on the teacher.

- Another strategy is to write a cue word (for example, STOP or QUIET) on the chalkboard. On seeing the teacher writing that word on the board, all students are to comply immediately.

- A different signal can be used to cue the class that group activities are becoming too noisy and should be brought down to a lower level. It might be helpful to have all students pause for fifteen to thirty seconds before resuming their activities. Some teachers flick the light switch. This tends to work if used sparingly.

- Some teachers have constructed a flashing red light that they switch on when it is time for students to stop talking.

- A useful way of indicating the time remaining without interrupting small-group discussion activities is to construct a picture of a traffic light, either on a poster or as an overhead transparency. When the discussion begins, show the light with a green light. When one minute is left, reveal the yellow light. That is the cue for students to wind up their discussion. When time is up, reveal the red light. This serves as a signal for everyone to stop talking. (See the transparency master at the end of the chapter. You can create three overlaying transparencies and color the three lights appropriately.)

Seeking Permission to Leave the Room

The first week of school, clarify whatever system you wish to use to handle restroom visits.

- *Restroom pass:* Rather than have students raise their hands to ask to use the restroom, hang a sign from a string that has GO printed on one side and STOP printed on the other. If everyone is in the room, the sign is on GO. If someone needs to use the restroom, he or she turns the sign to STOP (meaning that no one else can leave the room because someone is out). When the person comes back, he or she must turn the sign back to GO, and someone else may go out. Of course, if this privilege is abused, you need to restrict it.

- *Nonverbal signals:* At the beginning of the school year, teach your students the following signals: raise an index finger to indicate a need to use the restroom; raise a pencil if it needs sharpening. Make eye contact with the student, and simply nod your head or raise your hand to indicate that the activity may be done. Using these signals avoids needless interruptions. Other nonverbal cues for signaling that students should be quiet and give you their attention might include holding up an interesting object; pointing toward the clock; flipping the light switch once; gesturing across the throat with your index finger; using chimes, slide whistles, or other noisemakers; holding your finger up to your lips; going to a specified spot in the room; or turning on a colored light.

- Laminate two pictures on cards—one for boys, one for girls. Add a string to hang the cards on a hook or nail beside the teacher's desk. When a student needs to use the restroom, he or she takes the card from the nail and shows the teacher without talking. The teacher sees the student and nods to give permission. The student places the picture on a hook by the door. When he returns, he puts the picture back on the hook beside the teacher's desk. Because neither student nor teacher talks aloud, there is no interruption of class.

- Save time when using written hall passes (such as those included at the end of this chapter). Have the student fill out all the information except your signature.

- Instead of using written passes, many teachers have one made of wood. It is best to make it large enough not to fit into the students' pockets. Paint your name and room number on it. You might choose to decorate it in an interesting way (or delegate the task to a student). By having only one pass, you assure that only one student at a time is out of the room.

Seeking Help

During seatwork students will occasionally need help from the teacher. It is important to let students know the procedure you expect them to follow to get help. If the teacher is not busy with other students, the simplest procedure is for the student to raise his or her hand until acknowledged by the teacher. (Teaching students to raise two fingers would help differentiate seeking help from wanting to use the restroom, which students might signal with just the index finger.) The teacher either comes to the student's desk or nods permission for the student to approach the teacher. With reasonably well-behaved students, some teachers permit students needing help to come to the teacher's desk without first having to gain the teacher's consent. A greater problem occurs when the teacher is busy working with another student or group. A signal or cue needs to be established to let the teacher know that help is needed whenever the teacher has a chance to assist the student.

- Some teachers have a colored card taped to the front of each student's desk. When students need help, they flip the card down over the front of the desk. Another option is to have each student construct a stand-up placard by folding an 8½-by-11-inch sheet of card stock in half. They should print "I Need Help" on the face of the card. To signal the teacher, the student turns his or her card up so that it is visible to the teacher.

- Teacher educator Harry Wong suggests using a toilet paper tube with one end covered with red construction paper and the other with green. A student needing help turns the tube with the red end up and continues to work until the teacher comes to help.

- To avoid being disturbed while working with a group, use a see-me chair. If a student working independently has a question about his or her work that a classmate cannot answer, the student must sit in the see-me chair to ask for help. Check with the student when you have time.

- A signal that many teachers use is for students to turn their textbook up on edge when they need the teacher's help.

Students' Tools

For smooth operation of day-to-day instruction, students should know which supplies and tools they must provide, when they need them, and where to store them. The first week you should clearly specify all the materials they are required to provide. A written list works best.

It is important early in the year to clarify which items in the room are for student use and which are only for teacher use. Also clarify which items students can use with and without permission.

- Keep a store of pencils that students can buy with cash or class points earned. Some teachers lend out pencils, but students must leave collateral (such as a dime or a shoe), which they redeem when they return the pencils.

- If they come without a pen or pencil, lend students a crayon. Some teachers scrounge vacated lockers the last day of school to collect all the leftover pencils. These become loaners the following year. Some break them in half, sharpen both stubs, and lend these. Students are less likely to depend on the teacher for writing instruments if they are not too attractive.

- Let students know when they may use the pencil sharpener. Some teachers let students sharpen pencils only before class and warn them to always bring two. Some teachers do not require students to seek permission to use the pencil sharpener as long as students do not abuse the privilege. Other teachers have students signal when they need to use the sharpener, usually by holding their pencil in the air. In either case it is wise to only allow one student at a time at the pencil sharpener.

- Must assignments be completed in pencil or pen? Let students know your expectations. At first it might even be a good idea to note on the top of the assignment sheet "Complete in pen only." That minimizes debate later about whether a student knew he or she was to use a pen.

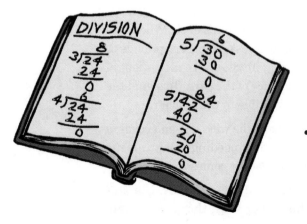

Assignments and Homework

Procedures for completing assignments, turning them in, and returning them need to be established the first week of school. Here are some procedures that must be clarified.

- How will students be given each day's assignment? Will it be posted on the board each day when they enter the room? Will it be given at the beginning or end of class? Are they required to carry an assignment notepad? Will deadlines be announced?

- How do you want them to complete it? Where does the student's name go on the assignment? How and when should it be turned in? As students enter the class? Do they pass assignments in or place them in a basket or box at a designated time? Should the assignment be folded in any specific way?

- How should a student make up work after an absence? How do students find out the assignments? How long do they have to get caught up?

STORAGE SOLUTIONS

It is easier to maintain an organized classroom if sufficient storage facilities are provided. This includes cabinets, shelves, and furniture, as well as ample, accessible storage containers. Use an assortment of resealable, plastic sandwich and freezer storage bags to store game parts, bulletin board letters, crayons, art supplies, and any other small items that need to be kept together.

- Small hardware storage bins are ideal for storing many small items and supplies. Shoeboxes, especially the clear, plastic ones, are great storage containers for many items. Dishpans, wire or plastic baskets, and coffee cans also are handy and inexpensive containers. Though harder to find today, cigar boxes are still some of the finest storage bins available. Parents or garage sales are inexpensive sources for many storage containers.

- Obtaining and organizing adequate storage solutions is only the first step. You must train your students to put materials back in their designated places. It is much easier to teach everyone to put things back where they belong than for you to spend time sorting and shelving misplaced items.

- As much as possible, color code items and storage compartments to facilitate putting things back where they belong. Clearly label all storage containers and cupboards. This task could be delegated to a student volunteer or aide.

- Assign a student to be the postal clerk, librarian, or stock supervisor. The student's job is to see that everything is put back where it belongs that day. You might develop a checklist to facilitate the task. This can be especially helpful in laboratory or shop classes.

THE CHALLENGE OF PAPERWORK

Two and a half trillion pages of paper are generated in the United States each year. According to a study by Partners for Environmental Progress, paper consumes 45 percent of the available landfill space.

Another researcher found that 95 percent of all the pieces of paper that go into filing cabinets in America today will never come out again. To estimate how long a person has been in education, count the number of filing cabinets in his or her room and multiply by five. We seldom purge our cabinets. They simply fill up, and about every five years we requisition another one! Author Tom Parker estimated that each day Americans buy 426 bushels of paper clips—approximately thirty-five million!

Teachers consistently rate paperwork as their biggest time-management problem. Though some paperwork is inevitable in any profession, most teachers probably accumulate much more paper than they really need. Imagine how many pieces of paper you handle on a typical school day: magazines, quizzes, tests, attendance forms, grade records, requisitions, books, letters, forms, memos, mail, and meeting notices and minutes. Then multiply that figure by 180 school days. These reams and reams of paper we swap, hoard, file, and stack consume vast amounts of storage space; they also devour a significant proportion of our lives.

Causes of the Paper Deluge

Paper abounds for many reasons. Governmental, technological, and cultural forces interact to inundate us with paper. Psychological weaknesses often make it difficult for us to rid ourselves of paper once we have it. Here are some of the more pervasive causes of the paper deluge:

- Knowledge grows exponentially. The number of publications has exploded. In 1800 there were approximately one hundred scientific journals; today there are close to one hundred thousand. The number of nonscientific publications has increased as dramatically.

- In this age of litigation, many people are concerned with documenting anything that might possibly be the subject of dispute in the future. This environment feeds insecurity, prompting some—especially administrators—to hoard paper to protect their backsides. Certain disciplinary decisions, personnel dismissals or sanctions, and financial transactions should of course be carefully recorded. Keep only what is absolutely necessary, and file it so that you can find it when you need it. Purge these files after a reasonable time; if you haven't used a paper in the past two years, toss it in the recycling bin.

- Governmental red tape has proliferated. Additional state and federal mandates and standards require massive documentation, consuming not only the mounds of paper that this generates but also the valuable time of the school employees charged with tabulating, assembling, and submitting these documents. Every new educational program funded also creates a paper trail of accountability.

- The copy machine has abetted the paper explosion. Making ten copies is just as easy as making one, so we end up with nine more copies of everything just in case. And the photocopier makes it easy for others to send us copies of their paper collection.

- The computer, which does have the potential of saving time and paper, has thus far failed to create the paperless society. Indeed, many argue that it actually makes generating more paperwork easier. With computers accessible to virtually everyone, the mass of form letters, targeted mailing lists, and databases abounds. In additional, those of us who grew up before computers often don't trust hard drives and CDs to hold our valuable information. We want papers we can touch, file, and carry.

Thirty-four Tips for Handling Paperwork

1. When in doubt, throw it out (or better yet, recycle it). Ask yourself, "What's the worst thing that would happen if I didn't have this piece of paper?" Few papers are totally impossible to replace if necessary.

2. Never save papers simply because you might need them someday. Rather, ask yourself, "If I need this at some time in the future, where will I be able to find it?" Chances are that nine other copies are filed around the school system.

3. Set aside one day a year (perhaps during the summer) to purge all your files of any piece of paper you don't need. If you haven't used it in the last three years, you probably don't need it.

4. Time-management experts advise that we strive to handle each piece of paper only once. This is not always possible, but the less we shuffle papers back and forth from our briefcase to our desk and back, the more effective we are likely to be in controlling the paper plague.

5. Label a basket or folder "To be filed." Set aside a few minutes every week to file papers. Don't let them accumulate longer.

6. Label twelve file folders with the names of the months. Keep this in a convenient file drawer near your desk. As you receive pieces of paper that you will need at some time later during the year, file them under the month they will be needed. At the first of each new month, pull out the corresponding file.

7. Tape or glue to your desk blotter important or frequently used lists, numbers, rosters, or schedules.

8. Save only one copy of papers you need in the future. Be sure to save one clean master (or a computer file) of handouts and letters you use each year.

9. In your desk or at the front of your file drawer, keep three folders; label the first Correspondence, the second Schedules, and the third Forms. Place master copies in these so you won't have to redo them the next time.

10. Keep a colored manila folder in your briefcase or book bag labeled To Do. Keep your to-do list in that folder as well as any memos, letters, forms, or other items you'll need

> Never stack paper; to stack is to stay!
>
> —**Don Ashlett, *Not for Packrats Only***

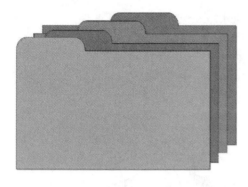

in order to accomplish the tasks on your list. Keep it in your briefcase so that it is always with you.

11. Use colored folders or labels when you file papers. Use a different color for each subject you teach or for each period of the day. (If possible, match the color of your textbook. This minimizes the possibility of misfiling the folder in the wrong drawer.)

12. When file folders get too fat, split them into smaller categories or move all the papers to a large three-ring binder. The same principle holds for accumulating files on your computer hard drive.

13. Develop a test-question bank on note cards or on the computer. Several excellent test-generation programs are available from computer software suppliers (see the list in Chapter Nine). This makes construction of tests and quizzes much easier.

14. For each class you teach, keep a three-ring binder in which you file all lesson plans, handouts, assignments, samples, problems, and other items you want to have available when you teach the class again. It is helpful to have a different colored notebook for each class.

15. Plan to make photocopies at times when there is no line. Right before school in the morning is probably the busiest time.

16. Set aside a specific spot on your desk at school where you place items to go to the office. As you think of such items, always place them in that spot. Whenever you have to make a trip to the office, take those items with you. You should do the same thing with items you plan to take home each night. Strive to make every trip count.

> *Half of our life is spent trying to find something to do with the time we have rushed through life trying to save.*
>
> —**Will Rogers, *The Autobiography of Will Rogers***

17. Organize your work area at home with all the necessary supplies at hand (pens, paper, envelopes, stamps, paper clips, stapler, scissors, and so on).

18. Probably the hardest things for teachers to discard are books, no matter how outdated, unused, or duplicative. This is doubly difficult for hardcover books. If it is not a much-used reference book, ask yourself, "Will I ever read this book?" If the answer is not a definite yes, then donate it to a book sale or library or give it to a student. Put a bunch of discarded books in a box labeled FREE for your students to pick the ones they want.

19. If you have forms you must complete for many students, complete one form with all the basic information that is the same for all students (for example, your name, date, school building, signature). Photocopy the necessary number of forms and complete by hand only the necessary individual information.

20. If professional journals accumulate unread for more than three months, give them away or cut out and file the most promising articles for future reference. Do not feel guilty if you do not read every publication cover to cover. They might contain only one or two articles really of interest to you.

21. If it is your magazine, cut out the articles you want to read later. Save these in a file folder to read in your free time. Some keep this file in their briefcase or take it with them when they are likely to be waiting, such as at the doctor's office or the airport.

22. You might put a blank label on the front cover of a magazine. As you read it, jot down the page numbers you would like to copy. Another way is to keep small strips of scrap paper handy and mark the page numbers on these slips, and then insert them as page markers.

23. Cancel subscriptions to publications you don't have time to read or that really don't meet your needs. Avoid renewing simply out of habit. Set yourself a goal to reduce the volume of paper crossing your path.

24. Set limits on how long you will save various types of papers (for example, two years for professional magazines, six months for memos to parents, three years for grade books, two weeks for meeting minutes). Whenever you run across a piece of paper whose time line has expired, discard it.

25. Use three-ring notebooks to preserve masters of tests and handouts for copying. Keep your masters sequential and easy to find. Use a separate notebook for each subject area. Be sure to back up to external hard drives or CDs all computer files that contain your lessons and handouts.

26. Keep a file box or drawer beside your desk for all the worksheets and homework sheets you will use in all your classes that week. In the box place manila file folders labeled by subject and day (for example, Science—Mon.; Science—Tues.; and so on). Duplicate all materials you're going to use on Friday and fill up your box. (Obviously, not every subject has a handout for every day.) This makes it very easy for the rest of the week. If handouts are used for that day, they are easily found. If you are absent, you don't have to worry about a substitute finding the handouts to use.

27. Always carry three-by-five-inch note cards in your purse or pocket to record ideas and facts as you think of them to use in class and on tests. Also list home needs and class needs on these cards. An ideal time to use them is when you are waiting for an appointment or meeting to begin.

28. Whenever possible, develop individualized form letters you can use for repeated correspondence. Also keep a file of letters you must send out every year so that you do not have to redraft them each time. This is even easier if you maintain these as a computer file.

> Junk mail in the U.S. alone consumes one hundred million trees each year.
>
> **—Native Forest Network**

29. Quickly sort your mail into four stacks: NEVER, which you throw out unread; NOW, which receives top attention because some degree of urgency or importance is attached to it; LATER, which deserves attention but is not urgent; MAYBE, which may get a cursory glance sometime but probably isn't important or urgent (for example, catalogs, general notices, and newsletters).

30. For routine interoffice mail and school memos, jot your response on the same piece of paper and return to the sender immediately. Of course, don't do that with important pieces of correspondence, such as job offers.

31. As you read a piece of correspondence that will require a response, jot down a few notes in the margin to remind yourself of what you want to say. It is quicker to use postcards or e-mail rather than letters whenever possible.

32. If you spend lots of time commuting to and from school, keep an audio recorder in your car. You can dictate into it as you drive. It is a great way to create letters, to-do lists, quiz questions, teaching ideas, and so on.

33. Eliminate junk mail by contacting the Direct Mail Marketing Association online at www.the-dma.org. You can complete their Mail Preference Service Form to be placed on their suppression list.

34. A computer has the potential to help with all kinds of paperwork chores. You can get software to handle addresses, phone numbers, grades, to-do lists, and calendars. However, don't rush to put everything on a computer just because you can. Keeping your calendar on the computer may become an extra chore if you also have to carry a pocket calendar with you, duplicating the effort.

COMMUNICATIONS

A teacher's job entails hundreds of communications each day. In addition to traditional oral and paper exchanges, technology innovations like voice mail and e-mail greatly expand the opportunity to give and receive messages. These additional communication channels can be a mixed blessing. Used effectively, they can make us more productive. Poorly used, they can become time robbers. Here are some helpful tips gleaned from other teachers:

- Leave notes for teachers, administrators, or students—rather than taking the time to wait for someone. The recipient can write a short response and leave it in your mailbox or on your desk. Both of you save time as there is little opportunity for idle conversation.

- Buy a Rolodex file that holds three-by-five-inch cards. Record not only names and postal addresses but also phone and fax numbers and e-mail addresses if available. File any numbers you have to look up more than twice. You can also note in the file special information about the individuals, such as birthdates, spouses' and children's names, or interests. The file is also a useful place to record membership or subscription numbers, lock combinations, directions to places, and other miscellaneous bits of information that are easy to misplace.

- If you hate to write, try writing postcards. Or better yet, make your own postcard by cutting 8½-by-11-inch card stock in half, yielding two 5½-by-8½-inch cards. Fold these in half to make inexpensive note cards.

- Use a carbon-backed form for parent conferences. It gives a record of what was discussed, comments, and so on. You can give the parent a copy and keep one for your class file. If necessary, you can send a copy to the guidance office or principal.

- Develop form letters to handle routine and repetitive correspondence. Storing your form letters as template computer files saves much time in written communications. Where available, transmit electronic text messages to colleagues and others with access to e-mail.

TEACHER TIME LOG

Keep a daily time log for three or four school days to get a more accurate picture of how your time is consumed. Enter the data on the time log form from the time you get up until the time you go to bed. It is important to accurately record what you are really doing during these small segments to get a good reflection of where your time really goes. It does no good to enter what you could have done, should have done, or would have done. You must be honest for the time log to have any meaning.

Record the specific activity for each fifteen-minute block of time. You need not actually stop what you are doing every fifteen minutes to enter your information. A useful procedure is to carry a three-by-five-inch card with you and take fifteen to twenty seconds each hour to briefly note what you were doing in each of the previous fifteen-minute segments.

At the end of the day, enter the information onto your time log form. At that time also enter comments reflecting on specific activities. What were your most frequent interruptions? Were there any patterns? Which activities would you like to increase? Which

You've Got Mail: Coping with E-mail Overload

- Send fewer and shorter e-mail messages.
- Create an "action" folder for those items needing immediate action.
- Check e-mail less often, perhaps only once or twice each day.
- Use filters to screen out spam and low-priority messages.
- Create different templates for routine, repetitive responses.
- Unsubscribe from blogs or newsletters you don't need.
- Delete unread most jokes, political commentary, and other forwarded messages.
- Set up logical folders to file received and sent messages for future reference.
- Create mailboxes to organize your outgoing and incoming e-mail messages. Once messages have been read, move them into a mailbox folder based on subject areas (for example, parents, students, professional development, and courses).
- Use signatures. Rather than retyping your name and contact information at the end of each message, use a signature file with the relevant information. Your e-mail program will automatically append your signature file to the end of every outgoing message. Most e-mail software allows the user to have several different signatures to use with different groups (for example, friends, colleagues, parents, and students).
- Delete outdated e-mail messages and other unnecessary files from your computer.

would you like to decrease? In the priority column, assign a value to each activity: A is for important activities that contribute to your essential life goals; B for activities that are urgent but not particularly important to fulfilling your life goals; C for maintenance activities, routine chores, not especially important.

Analyze the log at the end of the week. The following questions may be helpful in analyzing your record:

- What percent of your total time did you spend on A, B, and C items?
- What were your major interruptions? Was there a pattern (time of day, in person, activity)? How can you decrease them in the future?
- What activities would you like to eliminate or decrease?
- Which would you like to increase?
- What strategies will help you spend more time doing higher-priority items?

TO-DO LIST

As the cartoon character Ziggy exclaimed, "I made a mental note of it, but I lost it." That's exactly what happens to many of our mental notes—we lose them. A simple written reminder or to-do list can effectively help teachers complete the many little tasks that make up the profession of teaching.

- The trouble with keeping to-do lists is that crossing things off is too much fun. At the end of the day, we take delight in crossing off twelve of the fourteen tasks. Unfortunately, the ones we cross off are too often the routine and petty tasks; we transfer the unpleasant or difficult ones to tomorrow's list. However, these are often the most important items on our list. If you are going to keep a daily to-do list, it is essential to indicate in some form the priorities of the list items. One way is to put an asterisk in front of the most important two or three items. Try to do the top-priority items first.

- Whenever you find yourself with a few minutes of free time, look at your list to see whether you can chip away any items. Many of the jobs, such as returning a phone call or sending a note, may take as little time as a minute.

- Some find it more convenient to keep their to-do list on their calendar. This works well if you use a daily calendar that gives you one full page for each day. An alternative is to keep your list on sticky notes that you apply to the calendar each day. Rather than rewriting the list at the end of the day, scratch out those items accomplished, pull the list from today's page in your calendar, and stick it on tomorrow's page.

- Instead of keeping a daily to-do list, some people keep only a master list. The projects and tasks on this list do not have to be done today but do require attention within the next week or month. They need to be done but are not urgent—yet. Of course, if put off long enough, they could become urgent.

- Examine your list to see which ones someone else can do. Which are really not important to you? Ask yourself, "What is the worst thing that would happen if I didn't do that?" Scratch out items that really don't have to be done. Some wise persons believe success is derived not so much from what we choose to do but rather from what we choose not to do. Effective time management is largely the ability to eliminate those activities that distract from the truly important ones.

- Duplicate and use copies of the to-do form included at the end of this chapter. Printing them on brightly colored paper makes it harder to misplace them.

> *Everything I didn't do yesterday, added to everything I haven't done today, plus everything I won't do tomorrow completely exhausts me.*
>
> **—Anonymous**

ASSESSING STUDENT TIME-ON-TASK

For at least a century, educators have touted the importance of attention and time spent on learning activities, but the idea has gained renewed attention during the past decade. A growing body of evidence shows that student time-on-task is a modest predictor of learning. Research also emphasizes that increasing time-on-task is likely to have a greater effect for below-average students.

High engagement rates on ineffective or irrelevant instructional activities are of doubtful benefit. To result in learning gains, the instruction must be at the appropriate level for that individual student: too high and the student does not comprehend and is lost; too low and needless overlearning and perhaps boredom occur. Some educators have been guilty of focusing solely on time-on-task without attending to the other variables that contribute to instructional effectiveness. Time-on-task is best viewed as a necessary but insufficient condition for academic success.

Past research has generally found time-on-task rates to be around 70 to 75 percent. However, it is important to remember that this is an average. Researchers have reported rates as low as 30 percent for individual classrooms. If you experience engagement rates at the lower end of the range, it may be time to develop a plan of action. While striving for higher time-on-task, do not ignore the half of the teaching day that is lost to nonacademic activities. It accounts for a greater proportion of time lost than does student off-task behavior. A complete school time-management plan must focus on decreasing noninstructional activity, as well as increasing student engagement rates. If the teacher isn't on task, the students can't be.

How effectively do your students spend their in-class time? Are they engaged more or less than the 70 percent norm? What are they doing when they are off task? These questions can best be answered by direct, systematic observation.

Your gut-level assessment may be a valid clue as to your students' on-task rate, but it may be biased and inaccurate. It is difficult to observe the rest of the class when you are preoccupied with one student or with a small group.

Trade observations with a fellow teacher, giving each other feedback and support. Select someone who is reasonably objective and candid. A single observation may not be representative of your teaching. Try to have at least three separate observations on different days. Avoid special days, such as right before or after holidays, as the results are likely to differ from typical days. Devise an observation form that fits your classroom situation and provides the information you want.

At five-minute intervals the observer should scan the entire class in the same sequence. For each student a tally is placed on the chart. If the observer cannot tell, after a few seconds of watching a student, whether the behavior is on task or off task, record it as being on task. Students should be recorded as out of class if they leave for the restroom, go to the principal's office, arrive late to class, or are told to leave.

Once the observations are complete, divide the number of students scored as on task by the total number of students included in each observation segment to arrive at your engagement rate.

Here are some things the observer can look for:

- How long does it take to get a class started?
- How much time is spent in clerical tasks, such as taking attendance and reading announcements?
- Which part of the class period suffers the most off-task behavior?
- How smooth are the transitions from one task to the next?
- What proportion of class time is allocated to seatwork?
- How much class time is spent on discipline?
- How many interruptions are there? How much time do they consume?
- How much time do students spend waiting for help?

The answers to these questions may assist in setting goals for improvement. Later observations can help assess whether your class is making progress in increasing time-on-task.

CONQUER PROCRASTINATION NOW!

Are you eligible for membership in the Procrastinator's Club but haven't gotten around to sending your application? Some teachers have accepted the group's motto, "We're behind you all the way." Are you one? Test your eligibility right now! Don't put it off another minute.

Educators' Procrastination Society
Eligibility Form

Answer each of the following now.

	Yes	No
Do you have a set of papers that has been waiting to be graded for a week or more?	____	____
Do you frequently finish jobs just before the deadline?	____	____
Are you regularly late handing in grades, reports, and so on?	____	____
Do your students usually have to wait a week or more to receive their papers back?	____	____
Do weeks pass before you respond to your mail?	____	____
Does your principal regularly remind you that a deadline has passed?	____	____
Do you find it difficult to get started on the big projects?	____	____
Do you frequently tell people you work better under pressure?	____	____
Do you frequently feel guilty because you have not completed a task?	____	____
Do you have difficulty getting jobs completed because they may not be perfect?	____	____

Count the number of "yes" responses. Compare your score with the following scale:

0–3 *Early starter:* By doing things today you are free to do them again tomorrow if you choose.

4–7 *Amateur procrastinator:* Some potential problem areas may create stress for you and annoyance in those around you.

8–10 *Professional procrastinator:* Putting things off until the last minute is a way of life.

Procrastination Payoffs

Psychologists and motivational researchers have studied procrastination for decades in an attempt to uncover its causes and cures. People procrastinate because they expect to gain or avoid something.

Procrastination likely develops over a period of years, beginning in childhood. Research suggests that many procrastinators tend to be perfectionists, immobilized by deadlines until they feel a masterpiece is achieved. They may feel that their work is of value only if it is perfect, and their self-worth is a reflection of their performance.

By doing jobs at the last minute, procrastinators may protect their egos, since their true ability is not judged, only their skill in doing jobs at the last minute under pressure. "Of course, I could have done a much better job if I had had more time!" may even elicit sympathy from some listeners. Another secondary gain is that if a person puts off a job long enough, someone else may do the job. Many adolescents are aware of this game. Their parents become impatient waiting for the garbage to be taken out or for their children to clean their bedrooms, so they do the chores for them. What motivation do these children have to change? None—they have a good thing going. Unfortunately, that pattern may continue into adulthood.

Procrastination may also serve as a defense to avoid difficult or unpleasant tasks, although the habitual procrastinator may begin to delay even minor and enjoyable activities. Seldom is the procrastinated task totally avoided; it is only delayed.

Sometimes procrastination is the result of poor skills or insufficient knowledge. Being poorly organized, setting goals without deadlines, attempting to make decisions with insufficient information, and being unable to say no may all contribute to procrastination.

Which of the following are you most likely to procrastinate?

- Grading papers
- Completing report cards
- Meeting with parents
- Writing letters
- Returning phone calls
- Writing lesson plans
- Making important decisions
- Planning a speech
- Meeting with your principal
- Writing a grant request
- Applying for a new position
- Confronting a colleague
- Cleaning off your desk
- Buying presents

If you confess to occasionally experiencing stress, guilt, and anxiety from procrastination, you may be ready for a change. If procrastination is a way of life for you, the following suggestions may help; but be patient. You will not undo a lifetime of learning in a day, a week, or even a month. Not only new ways of behaving but possibly new ways of viewing yourself may be needed.

Identify the task you would like to quit procrastinating and answer the following questions:

1. What do you gain from procrastinating this activity?

_____

_____

_____

2. What do you fear might happen if you attempt this activity?

_____

_____

_____

3. What do you lose by putting off this task? What price do you pay?

_____

_____

_____

4. What are the positive consequences that would result from doing this particular activity?

_____

_____

_____

5. Wh.at do you tell yourself to justify your procrastination?

_____

_____

_____

Attacking Procrastination

The easiest thing to procrastinate is doing something about procrastination. You may be tempted to allow short-term avoidance to overpower the longer-term advantages. If you have become a slave to deadlines, immobilized by the big and small projects you face, it may be time to combat procrastination. In the previous activity, you had an opportunity to analyze the motivation and costs of one problem area. Using those insights, you can develop a plan of attack.

> *Procrastination is the art of keeping up with yesterday.*
>
> **—Don Marquis, Archy and Mehitabel**

It is best to pick one area in which you find procrastination most annoying (for example, grading exams, answering letters, filing papers). Begin small and progress as you experience success. Attempting to eliminate all procrastination from your life at once is much like dieting while trying to stop smoking. You are setting yourself up for failure. Adhere to the following guidelines to defeat procrastination:

- Establish your own deadlines, and announce them to others involved. Be realistic in setting a timetable.

- Break the project into smaller parts. Chip away at it in small bites. Don't wait for that big chunk of time.

- Set a definite beginning point. You must break the inertia of inactivity. If getting started is especially troublesome, set a timer for ten or fifteen minutes. Commit yourself to doing something on the project until the timer rings. Then you can decide whether to stop or continue. Chances are you will gain momentum and continue after the timer stops. If not, try another ten minutes later in the day.

- Do the most important things first. Avoid the distractions of the trivial and routine tasks when a higher-priority job needs to be done. Examining each task in light of your goals will help you set priorities.

- Reward yourself for completing parts of a major task. It may be something as simple as a ten-minute walk, a soft drink, or a social phone call. Contract with yourself for a big reward for completing important tasks. A night on the town, sleeping late on a weekend, or a purchase you have been wanting to make may help motivate you to complete the job. Be nice to yourself.

- Avoid perfectionism. Excellence is a sufficient level of performance for most things in life; and for many tasks (doing the dishes, pursuing a new sport or hobby, dusting the lampshades), adequacy is all that is necessary. Give yourself permission to be less than perfect. You might double the amount of time spent typing a test, attempting to get the spacing and typing perfectly. Could you spend that extra time in another activity that will better benefit your students or yourself? Probably so.

Procrastination is a learned habit and can be supplanted with a more constructive habit, giving you greater control over your life. If procrastination has limited your achievements, do something about it *now!*

TIPS ON GETTING ORGANIZED

Get as organized as you need to be to do your job well and no more. Some people become obsessed with the idea of organization to the point that it becomes an impediment to efficiency.

> Nothing is so fatiguing as the eternal hanging on of an uncompleted task.
>
> —**William, *Letters of William***

Know What You Want

People without goals in life are much like the airline pilot who radios, "We're making good time, but we're lost." You can be rushing through the pathway of life at ninety miles an hour; but if you don't know where you are headed, you might end up someplace you don't want to be.

Both in and out of the classroom, the very best teachers and the happiest people have a clear sense of purpose. On the grander scale, they have a dream, a vision, and a view of their world as they would like to see it become. But a goal requires three additional ingredients to become reality:

1. A plan for realizing that goal
2. A passion and commitment to devote one's personal time and energy to attaining the goal
3. A realistic deadline that holds one accountable

Plan for Success

Imagine trying to build a house without a blueprint. Just go with the flow. Do what you feel like doing on the spur of the moment. "Today let's do drywall. Tomorrow we will do the plumbing and electricity." What a mess we would make of the project.

Whether teaching a lesson or building a house, a good plan helps us get things done effectively, efficiently, and correctly. A good plan stimulates creativity. Plan the process of making decisions about what to do, when to do it, and how to do it.

Save a few minutes Friday afternoon for making general plans for the following week. You can fill in details later, but the perspective of what tasks need to be done the next week will likely be fresher on Friday. It will also highlight additional information or resources you'll need to get in order to complete the planning process.

Strive to plan at least a week in advance. Include in the lesson-planning process handouts to copy, supplies to gather, and audiovisuals to request. Anticipate the potential obstacles that could occur. For example, if you plan to take a class outside for a particular activity, have a backup strategy in case of inclement weather.

Discover Your Prime Time

Are you an early bird or a night owl? When are you most creative? Most energetic? Most adults' peak mental time is in the morning, though there certainly are exceptions.

Don't waste your most creative time doing menial tasks like photocopying, stapling, cleaning, filing, or grading objective tests. Safeguard those precious hours when you are at your intellectual peak to do the most cognitively challenging tasks: writing, planning, or creating.

Of course, you have to use common sense. You can't very well tell your principal that you're not a morning person, so you don't want classes before 11:00 A.M. We all have to adapt to reality. Just resolve not to waste your most valuable creative time doing the less intellectually challenging tasks.

Keep a Personal Calendar

The single most valuable time management tool is a daily calendar. It doesn't matter which kind you use, as long as it meets your needs.

Teachers may select from a broad range of calendars. Most teachers prefer to use academic year calendars that run from July 1 to June 30, minimizing the need to carry two calendars around during the first half of the school year. My preference has always been for calendars that provide one full five-by-seven-inch page for each day of the year. These provide ample room to jot notes to oneself, keep to-do lists, and record any special appointments.

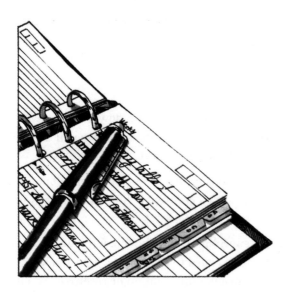

Many teachers now carry laptop computers or personal digital assistants (PDAs or handheld organizers) back and forth between home and work. A number of excellent calendar software programs provide the flexibility of interfacing with one's e-mail server, address book, to-do list, memo book, and other databases. These programs' reminder option is especially valuable in helping users keep abreast of important upcoming events. Many of these programs are available as freeware (see http://teachnology.com/downloads/time/ for a good selection).

At the end of each day, review your calendar to help plan your activities for the following day. Sticky notes can be used to make daily to-do lists to attach to paper calendars. Many of the software calendars provide a similar feature, often color-coded to help with setting priorities.

Many teachers use their calendars to record professional expenses (meals, mileage, lodging, and so on) that might be tax deductible.

Lead a Balanced Life

There was a time, early in my career, when I was teaching five preparations, coaching three sports, taking graduate classes in the evening, and trying to help raise two-year-old twins. Life seemed like a race between vacations. "Just wait until Thanksgiving, Christmas, spring break, ah, summer." Catching up seemed an impossible dream.

Then one day I had a tremendous emotional insight: "What if Easter doesn't come!" It was an early midlife crisis, for the first time confronting the limit of my own mortality. After a period of reflection, reading, and talking with some close friends, I came to a little different philosophy of life.

It may sound as corny as it comes, but it is the best I have been able to figure out. My life philosophy now contains two pieces.

First, lighten up a little! Grab a little gusto. Live each day as though it might be the last. There are no guarantees. Live a little more in the present and not so much on delayed gratification—working hard today for the pot of gold at the end of the rainbow.

But we can't hedonistically live only for today. For, like the squirrel, we must put away some nuts for the winter, just in case we are around. Hence, the second part of my guiding philosophy is a commitment to do at least one thing each day that will make for a better tomorrow—for my family, my community, and myself.

I once saw a television interview of famed ragtime musician Eubie Blake, on the occasion of his hundredth birthday. He said, "You know, if I had known I was going to live so long, I'd a taken better care of myself." At the age of one hundred! You never know, you might just make it. Do stop and smell the roses along the way.

A good place to begin is by resolving to save one hour a day to do something you really want to do. I know it won't always be possible or easy. It may mean getting up a half hour earlier or turning the television off for an hour.

Google Calendar

Check out Google calendar (www.google.com), a free online calendar service with many special features. Once you set up an account, you can create several calendars and invite others to access them. This enables a group (for example, your faculty, students, or family) to share schedules and collaborate in planning events.

Some teachers create Google Calendars for their classes, entering scheduled quizzes and tests, daily assignments, tests, holidays, and special events. Parents and students can easily access them from home. The calendar organizer can restrict who can access each calendar.

You can enter automatic event reminders, including cell phone notifications. Calendars are stored online, so you can access them from any browser anywhere in the world.

Other teachers use their Google Calendar for lesson planning. The calendars can also be printed in a variety of formats or uploaded onto your Web page.

A great time-management tool!

Finding Time for a Really Important Task

No matter how well organized we may be, unanticipated tasks occasionally demand our attention. It may be a report requested by an administrator, a favor for a friend, a school or personal crisis, or simply something important we just didn't have time to get done earlier.

The best advice is this: do not go to the faculty lounge! Social interruptions are inevitable. Here are a few tips teachers have found helpful in finding those few extra hours or minutes to accomplish a big chore that they must get done.

- Find a hideaway. During your planning period, find a place where you can work without interruption. This might be another teacher's empty classroom, the furnace room, or the bleachers on the football field. Let the secretary know where you can be found in case of an emergency.

- Close your classroom or office door. You will less likely be interrupted if you are not readily visible.

- If interrupted, be assertive. Let the person know you really have to get an important task done and agree to meet later if the other person desires.

- Arrive at school early. You can accomplish twice as much in the uninterrupted morning hours than you can once the building is full of people.

- Break a big task into several small chunks and chip away at it throughout the day or week. You may not be able to complete the whole job in five, ten, or fifteen minutes; but you can do something to move it along. Make a phone call, jot down one idea, write one paragraph, or grade two essays. Learn to think of big jobs as really just a bunch of little tasks that must be done one at a time. You will feel less overwhelmed and more in control of your time.

BEEN TO A GOOD MEETING LATELY?

In my workshops on effective use of school time, teachers continually list attending meetings as one of their greatest time robbers. Most teachers view meetings as a necessary evil

but usually don't expect them to be very productive. For better or worse, meetings are an essential part of every educator's job. This includes the myriad of committees, task forces, staff meetings, parent-teacher consultations, planning sessions, case conferences, and open discussions that consume a large portion of a teacher's calendar.

Not all meetings are a waste of time; some are productive, creative, energizing, informative, or morale boosting. Such outcomes do not occur by chance but because specific events happened that ensured success. With some basic training in effective communication skills, problem solving, and group dynamics, administrators and teachers can collaborate to make meetings productive.

Look for Alternatives to a Meeting

The easiest way to cut down on meeting time is to keep the number of meetings to a minimum. Too often educators attend or call meetings when the issues at hand could have been handled expeditiously in another fashion. If sharing information is the sole purpose of the meetings, consider using a memo, e-mail, or telephone call, saving both time and money.

A democratic value system and sensitivity to others' viewpoints can entice teachers into the paralysis of analysis, the inability to make even minor decisions without eliciting everyone's opinion. Decisions that affect the others' lives or are costly must be considered carefully, yet in many cases it would be just as effective to make a decision yourself or ask someone else to decide.

Standing committees that have a regular meeting date should cancel their meetings if the business at hand does not require a meeting. Many organizations have successfully adapted the Delphi technique, in which a committee functions largely by written communication and surveys.

Have an Agenda

Although spontaneity has its role in life, this generally is not the best way to run a meeting. An agenda will help focus the attention of a meeting's participants. Distribute the written agenda a day or two before the meeting if possible. Include not only an outline of topics but also questions to be considered or background information that participants should know before the meeting. Invite advance preparation.

The agenda should reflect clear-cut goals for the meeting. Is it to share information, solve a problem, seek advice, or sell an idea? Clear-cut tasks convey a businesslike atmosphere and a respect for other people's time.

Too often 80 percent of the meeting time is devoted to the items constituting only 20 percent importance. Schedule discussion of the most important items first, lest they be hastily decided at the end of the meeting. Limit discussion time on less important items.

Guard against an overly ambitious agenda. A crowded agenda decreases the group's effectiveness, leaves participants frustrated, and wastes time.

Begin on Time

Estimate how much time you have spent in the past year waiting for meetings to begin. Could that time have been better spent on other instructional-related tasks? If so, resolve to reduce your waiting time in the future. The world can be divided into two groups of people: those who are early for everything and those who are habitually late. Waiting for all of the latecomers to arrive punishes those who are punctual.

If people expect a meeting to begin late, the normally punctual people begin arriving after the scheduled starting time. The absurdity of this is that the habitually late people must now come even later to preserve their reputations. Convey the expectation that the meeting will begin on time and then make sure it does. If you are not in charge of the meeting, suggest to the chairperson that the meeting begin. Those who arrived promptly will applaud you, and after a few such instances, even the habitual latecomers are more likely to arrive on time.

Send out the notice and agenda for the meeting stating the beginning and ending times. Try scheduling meetings to begin at off-hour times, such as 2:40 or 11:10. This conveys a more specific time than 2:00, which often gets interpreted as "twoish."

Include Only Necessary People

Do you frequently sit through meetings wondering why you are there? Too often meetings are called with little attention to who really needs to be there. Large-group meetings become a series of small-group discussions, involving only a few participants, while the others sit idly observing them.

> Our age will be known as the age of committees.
>
> —**Ernest Benn**

Invite only those persons whose presence is directly related to the meeting's goals. If someone's input is needed for one item on the agenda, have that person attend only that part of the meeting. This is a sound practice for two reasons. It limits the size of the group, and people may spend their time on tasks of higher priority. Unless the purpose of the meeting is primarily to share information or persuade, efficiency greatly diminishes once more than ten or twelve people are included.

Attend only those meetings at which your presence is essential. If your input is needed for only a portion of the agenda, attend only that segment. If all else fails and you must attend a meeting in which you have little stake, take something to do. Work on your to-do list or outline your correspondence.

Select a Conducive Environment

Some forethought as to the meeting place can assure a more inviting atmosphere. The major criterion should be to have a place where interruptions can be kept to a minimum. Repeated interruptions may greatly impede a group's progress, whether it is a counseling group or a formal meeting. Not only does the group lose the time the distraction takes up, but it also loses momentum, requiring the group to refocus its attention.

Seek a location that avoids traffic flow. Close the door. This communicates that you value the meeting and plan to give it your full attention. If you are fortunate enough to have a secretary, inform him or her to interrupt only for emergencies. Group meetings should institute a policy of not allowing cell phones. The real estate office where my wife works instituted a $20 fine for any cell phone ringing during the weekly staff meeting.

Give consideration to the physical attributes of your meeting site. Is the temperature comfortable? Most people find a temperature of about sixty-eight degrees most conducive to mental activity. Rearrange the chairs to fit the meeting's purpose. Move empty chairs out of the way. If you seek interaction, form a circle. Follow the lead of fast-food restaurants and avoid overly comfortable chairs; this can lead to inertia—a body at rest tends to remain at rest.

Indeed, for some brief, informal meetings, you may choose not to have chairs at all. Stand. It will keep interaction brief and to the point. Why have a twenty-minute session if you have a five-minute task? What else could you be doing with that time that might have a greater payoff for you, your students, and the school?

Keep the Meeting on Task

If I were king or superintendent, whichever is higher, I would mandate that every meeting room throughout the land must have a clock, whose face shows not the traditional numerals reflecting the hours but the cumulative salary of every person sitting in that room. Thus, everyone would clearly recognize that a ten-minute digression on last week's football game cost this organization $380.

Time is money, at least when it comes to calling professional meetings. Whenever someone decides to call a meeting of five or ten paid staff members, he or she has made a decision to allocate that portion of the organization's resources. A teacher in a meeting cannot at the same time be teaching, tutoring, or planning a lesson. In some instances the organization and the students are better served by the meeting, but in others it is a misplaced priority. Time is finite; therefore, it is the educator's most precious resource. Choose well where to invest it.

Use your communication skills to keep meetings on task and follow a predetermined agenda. If someone begins to digress, inject gate-keeping questions such as "What do we need to decide today?" or "What are our options?" to refocus the group's attention. Summarize significant points, paraphrase crucial points, and confront discrepancies in the discussion. Educators have at their disposal a variety of effective communication techniques that they can use to play a valuable leadership role in any group, even when the educator is not the designated chairperson.

Observe the group process and intervene when necessary to invite full participation. Although consensus in every group decision is not essential, you can intervene to ensure that all viewpoints are aired. Solicit the contributions of silent members. Be especially sensitive to the nonverbal or nonparticipating people and tactfully but assertively quell the overly dominant member.

Remain sensitive to the hidden agendas that participants may bring to the meeting. Some observers believe that every meeting occurs at two levels. Hidden conflicts unrelated to the meeting agenda can greatly influence the group process. Remember that the spoken reasons are not always the real reasons for or against an issue.

Record Progress

Keeping a written account of the discussion is essential, especially in problem-solving groups. At the minimum, one person should take informal notes, to serve as the group memory. Decision making can proceed in a more orderly way if a visual display of the process is available. This may take the form of writing lists on newsprint or the chalkboard. Seeing one idea written may stimulate another.

Making a storyboard on note cards or using flowcharts or the diagrams from the Program and Evaluation Review Technique (PERT) have proven to be valuable techniques for recording and stimulating group problem solving. A planning process, PERT was adapted by a NASA project to help manage large projects, like putting a man on the moon. PERT charts (sometimes called network diagrams) are similar to flowcharts but read from left to right, with the final goal appearing in the node (or box) farthest to the right. (For more about PERT diagrams, see NASA's Web site at http://appel.nasa.gov/ask/issues/11/practices.) Such written stimuli are especially valuable if the group must continue the meeting at a later time.

Someone should be assigned to summarize the decisions made, either in formal minutes or in a brief memorandum to all the participants. It is also helpful to include a list of any responsibilities assigned to specific members for follow-up action. If the group is meeting again, include the meeting time and agenda.

End on Time

Remember Parkinson's Law: "Work expands to fill the time available." Avoid open-ended meetings except in genuine emergencies. Participants should agree on a specific ending time at the beginning. Everyone is more likely to stay on task if they know that the meeting will conclude at a specific time. One technique for forcing meetings to end on time is to schedule your meetings back-to-back. At the beginning indicate that you have another meeting scheduled and the time it must begin. As time approaches for the next meeting, announce that you have another appointment or meeting and must be excused.

If your group plans to meet again, try to set the time for your next meeting before this meeting adjourns. It will be a lot easier than trying to coordinate each member's schedule later.

Two heads can be better than one. When channeled constructively, the group process can be a source of valuable creativity and may even increase morale and the sense of community. The group process cannot be left to chance, however. The specific skills described here can ensure that your meetings are more likely to be productive and perhaps even fun.

STUDENT HELP

Allowing students to help with many classroom tasks not only saves valuable class time but also gives them an opportunity to assume responsibility and may help them feel needed and included. It may in some instances also give students a chance to learn new skills. The best time to introduce the idea of student assistance is the first week of school when you are establishing your classroom routines. Some tasks that teachers have delegated to students include the following:

Collecting papers, books, and materials

Distributing papers and materials

Tutoring other students

Constructing bulletin boards

Collecting lunch money

Taking attendance

Running errands

Filing papers

Tending classroom plants

Running audiovisual equipment

Taking inventory of books and supplies

Checking completed assignments

Picking up litter in the room

Constructing or arranging holiday decorations

Rearranging desks and furniture

Dusting erasers

Erasing or cleaning chalkboards

Recording brainstormed ideas on the board or newsprint

Videotaping class presentations

Keeping time for class activities

Putting away lab equipment

Setting up experiments, demonstrations

Greeting classroom visitors

Answering the telephone

Tending fish and other pets

Keeping the class calendar

Straightening the bookcase

Making in-school deliveries

Collating papers

Posting assignments and special events on the board

Some teachers ask for volunteers for each task as the need arises. Others allow students to sign up for a job for a week or month. Some draw names (or assigned numbers) whenever a role needs to be filled. Occasionally, teachers award particularly attractive jobs as rewards for outstanding performance. Some teachers assign teams of students to different responsibilities. In some classrooms every student is assigned a job on a rotating basis.

- Sometimes assigning groups of students to complete specific tasks can be successful. One elementary teacher assigned pairs to each task, trained each pair in the job, and then rotated the assignments on a staggered schedule every week, so that one person of each pair moved on to a new job. The experienced partner trained the new partner in the job.

- It is helpful to arrange a couple of brief after-school training sessions for some of the more demanding jobs, such as running audiovisual equipment. Demonstrate what needs to be done and then give the helpers a chance to practice. When delegating responsibilities be specific in communicating your expectations. Consider your students' capabilities and interests in assigning the more difficult jobs. Another possibility is to construct a job chart listing the various functions and the person responsible. You might color code it for easier reading.

- Some creative teachers draw up official-looking contracts with official-sounding names, like Director of Distribution or Multimedia Technician. The students sign the contracts, which detail their responsibilities and the duration of the agreement.

- Construct a board with the list of duties printed on the left side. On the right side, attach clips (or wooden slots) into which you insert cards with the names of the students assigned each task. To change duties each week, just rotate the name plates. (This works well in shop and art classes for cleanup assignments.)

- With some particularly hostile classes, you'll probably have a difficult time getting students to volunteer as teacher helpers. Their peers would put them down. It's probably best to privately ask individual students to do particular tasks as the need arises. The less official their role, the more likely they will comply with your request.

- Always remember to thank students for completing their tasks. For students who are particularly helpful, write them or their parents a note, award them a certificate, or allow them some small privilege as a thoughtful way to express your appreciation.

Note: Remember that many of the sample templates, letters, handouts for this chapter are available for download from the *Classroom Teacher's Survival Guide* Web site josseybass.com/go/classroom-teacher.

Teacher Time Survey

Directions: After reading each question, indicate whether it is generally true for you.

Do you frequently . . .   Yes   No

1. Have to rise early to prepare that day's classes? ____ ____
2. Set deadlines for yourself? ____ ____
3. Get up late? ____ ____
4. Stop in the lounge to socialize before classes begin? ____ ____
5. Fret and agonize when interruptions outside of your control occur? ____ ____
6. Begin classes on time? ____ ____
7. Visit the lounge between classes? ____ ____
8. Allow sufficient time at the end of the period (or day) for assignments, clean up, summary activities, and so on? ____ ____
9. Disrupt your own classroom momentum? ____ ____
10. Begin the day without interest in what you are teaching? ____ ____
11. Teach lessons without clear objectives? ____ ____
12. Schedule tests, movies, seatwork primarily to occupy students while you get caught up? ____ ____
13. Relate the amount of instructional time spent on a particular objective to its importance? ____ ____
14. Procrastinate grading papers and tests? ____ ____
15. Wait more than five minutes for staff meetings to begin? ____ ____
16. Write down ideas as they occur rather than relying upon memory? ____ ____
17. Anticipate problems and alternative solutions to them? ____ ____
18. Handle extracurricular activities during the academic hours? ____ ____
19. Make decisions systematically rather than "muddling through"? ____ ____
20. Spend time complaining to peers? ____ ____
21. Run out of prepared lesson material before the period or day is over? ____ ____
22. Find yourself going to the office to duplicate materials more than once per day? ____ ____
23. Bring up unscheduled business at faculty meetings? ____ ____
24. Set reasonable limits on parent conferences? ____ ____
25. Use student volunteers to help with routine tasks of which they are capable? ____ ____
26. Copy information from one form to another? ____ ____
27. Use parent volunteers whenever possible to assist in instructional activities? ____ ____
28. Spend instructional time dealing with disruptive behavior? ____ ____
29. Prevent duplicated effort by systematically filing and saving curricular materials, lesson plans, tests, and so on? ____ ____

(Continued)

Teacher Time Survey (*Continued*)

30. Arrive late for meetings? _____ _____
31. Participate in a regular schedule of physical fitness? _____ _____
32. Get a sufficient amount of rest each night to begin each day fresh? _____ _____
33. Think of a creative idea, only to forget it later? _____ _____
34. Do work for which others are paid? _____ _____
35. Have a balance of interests, including leisure activities, apart from your teaching? _____ _____
36. Choose to do menial tasks, such as stapling papers, as opposed to creative, productive tasks such as designing new instructional strategies? _____ _____
37. Strive to handle each piece of paper only once? _____ _____
38. Set priorities each day for the things you have to do? _____ _____
39. Have to repeat directions to students? _____ _____
40. Lose material because of a poorly organized, cluttered desk? _____ _____
41. Fail to make assignments clear and specific? _____ _____
42. Attend classes or workshops to develop new teaching ideas? _____ _____
43. Maintain contingency lesson plans in case of emergencies, sickness, and so on? _____ _____
44. Share ideas with colleagues? _____ _____
45. Review your long-term professional goals? _____ _____
46. Have difficulty saying "no" to requests for your time? _____ _____
47. Fall prey to perfectionism? _____ _____
48. Use vacation days and weekends to catch up? _____ _____
49. Begin class late? _____ _____
50. Make planning time a top priority? _____ _____

Scoring instructions: Give yourself one point for each of the following items to which you responded "yes": 2, 6, 8, 16, 17, 19, 24, 25, 27, 29, 31, 32, 35, 37, 38, 42, 43, 44, 45, 50. Give yourself one point for each of the following items to which you responded "no": 1, 3, 4, 5, 7, 9, 10, 11, 12, 13, 14, 15, 18, 20, 21, 22, 23, 26, 28, 30, 33, 34, 36, 39, 40, 41, 46, 47, 48, 49.

Total the number of points and find your score on the scale below.

40–50 *Peak Performer:* You are getting a high return on your investment of time and energy.

30–39 *Striver:* You are probably pretty effective, but still have a few inefficiencies.

20–29 *Plodder:* You're making your job tougher than it needs to be.

0–19 *Struggler:* How do you get anything done? Serious time-management problems impede your effectiveness.

School Interruption Survey

Directions: Using the scales under the subheadings, indicate when, how frequently, and how disruptive each of these interruptions is for you.

When	How Frequently	How Disruptive
BS = Before school	0 = Never	0 = Not at all
AS = After school	1 = Seldom	1 = A little
P = During planning period	2 = Occasionally	2 = Somewhat
C = During class time	3 = Quite frequently	3 = Quite
		4 = Constantly

Interruptions	When	How Frequently	How Disruptive
Messengers from:			
Principal's office	_____	_____	_____
Guidance office	_____	_____	_____
Other teachers	_____	_____	_____
The principal	_____	_____	_____
Former students	_____	_____	_____
Custodian	_____	_____	_____
Parents	_____	_____	_____
Other teachers	_____	_____	_____
Outside observers, visitors	_____	_____	_____
Aide or volunteer helper	_____	_____	_____
Classroom behavior disturbances:	_____	_____	_____
Student(s) leaving class	_____	_____	_____
Student(s) arriving late	_____	_____	_____
Assemblies	_____	_____	_____
P.A. announcements	_____	_____	_____
Audiovisual breakdowns	_____	_____	_____
Telephone calls	_____	_____	_____
Hallway traffic	_____	_____	_____
Noise from other classrooms	_____	_____	_____

(Continued)

School Interruption Survey (*Continued*)

Outdoor distractions:

Weather events	_____	_____	_____
Animals	_____	_____	_____
People	_____	_____	_____
Street traffic	_____	_____	_____
Airplanes	_____	_____	_____
Sirens	_____	_____	_____
Other noise	_____	_____	_____

Your actions:

Hunting lost items	_____	_____	_____
Changing topics	_____	_____	_____
Going back to previous topic	_____	_____	_____
Publicly reprimanding student	_____	_____	_____

Place asterisks (*) in front of the three interruptions you would most like to eliminate.

Things to Do

Date _____

Today's Schedule		Activity	Priority	Done
7:00				
7:30				
8:00				
8:30				
9:00				
9:30				
10:00				
10:30				
11:00				
11:30				
12:00				
12:30				
1:00				
1:30				
2:00				
2:30				
3:00				
3:30				
4:00				
4:30				
5:00				
Evening:				

Telephone Log

Date	Name	Phone	Comments

Weekly Schedule

Dates _____

Time	Monday	Tuesday	Wednesday	Thursday	Friday

Attendance Record

Date _____

Teacher _____ Period _____

Name	Absent	Excused	Comments

Book Sign-out Record

Teacher: _____

Name	Book Title	Date Out	Date In

End-of-Year Checklist

_____ Turn in grades.

_____ Collect any book damage fees.

_____ Select and turn in any books in need of repair.

_____ Take home plants and animals.

_____ Store textbooks.

_____ Make a list of needed supplies for next fall.

_____ Submit list of room repairs needed.

_____ Submit items to file in students' cumulative folders.

_____ Order textbooks for next year.

_____ Back up all critical computer files.

_____ Take home a backup disk of crucial files.

_____ Delete outdated e-mails.

_____ Run an antivirus program on the computers.

_____ Delete unneeded documents and programs from computer(s).

_____ Unplug all computers and peripherals.

_____ Inventory all hardware and peripherals.

_____ Cover computers and printers with cloths to shield from dust.

_____ Return all library books.

_____ Return all audiovisual equipment to media center.

_____ Take home any files, materials needed to plan for next year.

_____ Secure any confidential files.

_____ Organize and file any papers and folders to be saved.

_____ Send any thank-you notes to volunteers, support staff, and others.

_____ Throw out papers and materials no longer needed.

_____ Complete any required paperwork for the principal.

_____ Pack and label any items to be moved.

_____ Jot down successful teaching ideas to use next year.

_____ Turn in keys if required.

_____ Celebrate!

Things to Do

Date _____

Today's Schedule		Activity	Priority	Done
7:00				
7:30				
8:00				
8:30				
9:00				
9:30				
10:00				
10:30				
11:00				
11:30				
12:00				
12:30				
1:00				
1:30				
2:00				
2:30				
3:00				
3:30				
4:00				
4:30				
5:00				

Evening:

Memo

Please do not disturb!

Testing in progress

STOP

please do not disturb!

learning in progress!

Restroom Pass

Good for one five-minute visit to the restroom.

For emergency use only.

Restroom Pass

Good for one five-minute visit to the restroom.

For emergency use only.

Restroom Pass

Good for one five-minute visit to the restroom.

For emergency use only.

Hall Pass

Name _____ Date _____

From _____ To _____

Period _____

Reason for Pass:
_____ Get a drink   _____ Guidance office
_____ Main office   _____ Restroom
_____ To locker   _____ Telephone
_____ Run errand   _____ Do makeup work
_____ Tardy, please excuse _____ To nurse
_____ To see Mr/Ms _____

Teacher _____

Hall Pass

Name _____ Date _____

From _____ To _____

Period _____

Reason for Pass:
_____ Get a drink   _____ Guidance office
_____ Main office   _____ Restroom
_____ To locker   _____ Telephone
_____ Run errand   _____ Do makeup work
_____ Tardy, please excuse _____ To nurse
_____ To see Mr/Ms _____

Teacher _____

Hall Pass

Name _____ Date _____

From _____ To _____

Period _____

Reason for Pass:
_____ Get a drink   _____ Guidance office
_____ Main office   _____ Restroom
_____ To locker   _____ Telephone
_____ Run errand   _____ Do makeup work
_____ Tardy, please excuse _____ To nurse
_____ To see Mr/Ms _____

Teacher _____

Hall Pass

Name _____ Date _____

From _____ To _____

Period _____

Reason for Pass:
_____ Get a drink   _____ Guidance office
_____ Main office   _____ Restroom
_____ To locker   _____ Telephone
_____ Run errand   _____ Do makeup work
_____ Tardy, please excuse _____ To nurse
_____ To see Mr/Ms _____

Teacher _____

Teacher Time Log

Teacher _____ Date _____

Time	Activity	Importance	Comments

Creating Successful Lessons

4

PLANNING EFFECTIVE LESSONS

The aim of any lesson is change—purposeful transformation. Each day that you walk into a classroom, you should know exactly what you expect to accomplish and how you are going to do it. What will your students know how to do when they leave your classroom that they did not know when they entered?

Generally, too little time is spent on instructional planning. A list of assignments or textbook pages to cover is not a plan. A lesson plan is simply a sequential guide to how you will accomplish your instructional objectives or goals. Can you imagine a builder trying to construct a house without a blueprint? Lesson plans tell you what you will be doing and what your students will be doing. Lesson plans also help identify the resources, including time, needed to accomplish these activities.

Although you may not always be able to precisely follow your plan, you are more likely to intentionally affect your students' learning if you start with a plan. Some subjects will require more detailed planning than others. At least early in your teaching career, clearly written plans are essential for success. There is no one right format for these plans. Develop a format that works for you. It should be simple yet complete. Here are some practical planning tips that veteran teachers have found useful:

- First, make a general plan for the year. It will necessarily be vague and deal with general concepts, topics, and skills. These are usually drawn from any written program of study the school is obligated to follow. Monthly plans begin to add more detail. Weekly plans should be quite specific in both objectives and instructional strategies.

- Try to plan at least a week in advance. The first time you must unexpectedly be absent, you and your substitute will appreciate it.

- Make a master lesson-plan form, filling in all the details and activities that will remain the same each week. Place these in a large loose-leaf notebook. In each class's notebook, also keep any additional information needed for that class, such as rosters, form letters, phone numbers, and so on.

- The first step in every lesson is to focus on the goal(s) you hope to accomplish. State these in terms of how the students should be different after encountering your instruction. You are planning to intentionally change the students' knowledge, skills, or attitudes. Be specific. Also be reasonable in what you can realistically accomplish in a week or a day. It is better to teach less but do it well than to give superficial coverage to more content that students quickly forget.

- Don't overrely on knowledge-level objectives. Within one year students forget 80 percent of what they learn, most of that being facts they were required to memorize. Skills and attitude changes tend to have a much more permanent effect.

- Keep a notebook for each class to organize the lesson plans, handout masters, tests, quizzes, and lists of audiovisual requirements for each subject. It will save you much time next year.

- Some teachers prefer to develop and store their lesson plans on their computers. This makes revision much simpler. Of course, a paper copy will be needed for classroom use in most instances.

- First, schedule the blocks of time your students have to be out of the room. Then schedule the topics and content that you are responsible for teaching. Effective teachers cover the curriculum but teach more than the written course of study. Embellish and enrich the established curriculum with your interests, talents, and creativity.

- In planning any lesson, develop the body of the instruction first, including specifics on what you will do and what the students will do. Then give special attention to developing a powerful and interesting opening and ending. These are often overlooked in planning, yet they are the parts students are most likely to remember. Be sure to list any equipment, supplies, and preparations that you will need to arrange before the class.

- Where possible, schedule challenging and new content early in the day. Generally, student attention and concentration wane in the afternoon. Ideally, save the less mentally challenging, more energizing activities for afternoon. Of course, that is not always possible, particularly in secondary schools.

- Likewise, schedule the most demanding content on Monday, Tuesday, and Wednesday. Student productivity and enthusiasm diminish after Wednesday. Friday shouldn't be discarded, but save it for more active learning experiences and fun review opportunities. Simulations, field trips, films, guest speakers, and other special activities can keep students motivated at the end of the week.

- Always have several sponge activities available for students to work on if they complete an assignment or test early. These should have an educational purpose yet be interesting, lest students perceive them as punishments.

- After you teach each lesson, note on your lesson plan which parts of the lesson went well and which need to be improved. Don't rely on your memory to make those changes next year.

- Use colored folders to arrange each day's lesson plan and student papers. Use a different color for each class. Use the same color to identify any materials for that class.

- Some teachers choose to put their lesson plans on note cards, a single idea or activity on each card. That makes it easier to reshuffle the order or add and delete items in the future. (*Tip:* Punch holes in all your cards and put them on a large ring. If you drop them, they stay together.)

- Use checklists to help organize your lessons. For example, if you use a simulation game, develop a checklist to record any items you'll need or tasks to include.

- Some tasks, such as ordering films or arranging speakers, must be done well in advance. Ideally, you'll save time by ordering all films for the semester at one time. Though doing such long-term planning may be difficult the first year or two, it will become easier.

- Try to have materials for the next day's lesson ready before you leave school. Even if you have to stay after school to copy handouts or prepare other materials, it will prove less stressful than racing in the next morning to complete your preparation. Even early morning preparation periods can't always be counted on to be free to handle those last-minute tasks. A hallmark of any professional is being prepared.

- Develop a card file or loose-leaf notebook to collect teaching ideas. These might include copies of ideas you find in professional magazines. At least once a month, scan your file to see if you can incorporate any of the activities into your upcoming lessons.

- If you see another teacher or presenter use a successful technique or strategy, brainstorm ways you might adapt the idea for one of your lessons.

- Visit teachers who teach the grade above or below yours to discover how your lessons fit into the larger picture.

- As you develop each lesson plan, include a brief note indicating the state or national content standards that the lesson addresses. These will prove valuable in assessing the degree of alignment of course content with these standards.

- Save a few moments at the end of each day to reflect on your day's lessons. What went well? What clearly needs to be improved? Any ideas on how to make your lesson more effective the next time? Jot these down on your lesson plan and file them in your notebook.

BEGINNING A CLASS

Students are most likely to remember the first and last things you do in a lesson. Indeed, many people believe the first three minutes of a class are the most important. An effective opening can serve several valuable purposes. It can focus students' attention on what they are about to learn. It can also arouse students' curiosity and interest in the lesson. It helps motivate them to become involved in the lesson.

The beginning sets the tone for the rest of the lesson. It creates psychological readiness to engage in learning. The opening of the lesson stimulates your students' emotions, such as puzzlement, curiosity, tension, empathy, wonderment, excitement, amusement, pride, skepticism, or fascination.

Remember that students of all ages approach any lesson with the question "What's in it for me?" If your opening addresses that question, you will have a motivated learner.

It is essential to get your students actively involved within the first two minutes of the lesson. You can accomplish this in many ways, and it need not take a big chunk of time; a three- or four-second response actively draws their attention to the lesson. Here are several strategies that effective teachers successfully use to engage their students in the lesson:

- Learning begins before the bell rings. Use posters, door signs, music, transparencies, and other techniques to engage the students' minds, capture their attention, and arouse anticipation before the class officially begins. Many teachers have music playing as students enter to set the appropriate mood. Attention-grabbing cards containing trivia or interesting facts related to the day's topic might be suspended from the ceiling, hung upside down, or otherwise interestingly displayed.

- Be sure you have everyone's attention before you begin. Don't try to talk over the group noise. Convey enthusiasm for the lesson. It can be contagious. If you don't sound very interested in what you are teaching, it is improbable that your students will be. Be especially cognizant of maintaining eye contact with your students during the opening. Scan the entire class to include everyone.

- The opening must be connected to the main lesson. Your students must be able to see that the opening is relevant to the rest of the lesson.

- Avoid beginning the class with routine, procedural tasks (taking attendance, collecting homework, general announcements, and so on). Remember, your students most remember the first and last things that happen in class. Later, while students are working individually or in small groups, you can unobtrusively take attendance. Get your lessons off to a good start; give them punch.

- Begin with a personal anecdote. A personal illustration that ties to the topic makes it more interesting. Remember, it must be relevant to the lesson you are teaching.

- Pose a challenging question. Give careful thought to your opening questions. You may have students respond by jotting down their answer, volunteering to share it aloud, or simply answering silently to themselves. It is often helpful to ask a question to which all students are likely to raise their hands (for example, "How many are ready for a vacation?").

- Present a startling statistic or fact about some aspect of the lesson. Collect interesting statistics related to your course content. As an option, make these into an overhead transparency. Have the statistic on the screen as students enter the classroom. Examples:

The Earth's population increases by eighty-six hundred people every hour.

Two percent of American homes had electricity in 1900; 99 percent do today.

U.S. corporations spend $9 billion each year combating spam.

In 1910, 13 percent of the adults in the United States were high school graduates; 83 percent are today.

Some bristlecone pine trees in California are over four thousand years old, making them the oldest living things on Earth.

Life expectancy of people born in the United States in 1900 was 48.2 years. Today it is 77.8.

- Open the class with an unusual, surprising behavior or event.

- Present an interesting, relevant problem.

- Start with a funny story. It can be a true incident or a fictional tale. Even better is something that really happened to you. Don't try for jokes. Most important, the story must pertain to the day's topic.

- Use a true-or-false quiz reflecting major issues or research related to the topic. Before you give students the right answers, devise ways for them to share their answers. You might tabulate their responses on the board or move their bodies to different spots on a "live" continuum to indicate how sure they are of each answer.

- Display interesting visuals: a cartoon, poster, or quotation. In groups or as a whole class, you might have them discuss their reaction to the visual.

- Use a prop—an unusual piece of equipment, artifact, collection, toy, or creature.

- Use a gimmick to grab your students' attention. Walk into class with a portable telephone. Carry on a conversation over the phone in which you introduce the day's topic. Add humor or a personal anecdote. Use your imagination.

- Use drama to let students introduce the issue or problem that will be the focus of the day's lesson.

- Experiment with using costumes or hats related to the topic being introduced. Pull off a shirt to reveal a T-shirt depicting a quotation or graphic related to the lesson.

- Make a promise ("By the end of this lesson you will be able to . . . ").

- Draw analogies between what students have learned previously and the new skills or content they are learning in the current lesson.

- On a large sheet of newsprint ask groups to draw three large circles at least a foot in diameter. Label them "What I know about [the topic being studied]." Give the groups five to ten minutes to brainstorm and record anything they know about the topic under consideration. They should then label the second circle "What I hope to learn about [the topic]." Give them five minutes to list in that circle any questions they hope to have answered about the topic. The students then post all their sheets on the wall. At the end of the lesson, direct the groups to retrieve their sheets and to label the third circle "What I learned about [the topic]." Give the groups ten minutes to list everything new they learned about the subject. (*Source:* Reprinted with permission from the *Heart of Teaching* newsletter, Performance Learning Systems, Inc.®)

- Initiate a memory-dump activity. Pair students and give them the following directions: "Tell your partner everything you know about [the new topic]." Allow ninety seconds. Have students switch and repeat the process. Allow another ninety seconds. Switch and continue for sixty seconds. Switch and repeat for sixty seconds. Switch and continue for thirty seconds more. Switch a last time for thirty seconds. (*Source:* This idea was adapted from Cerylle Moffett, a consultant for the Association for Supervision and Curriculum Development.)

- Use a magic trick. Many good books can suggest simple tricks you can easily master. Or visit a magic shop to look for gimmicks or tricks that might fit into one of your lessons. Your banter during the trick is what ties it into your lesson. Don't let it just hang by itself.

- It is a sound practice to frequently build in some form of review of the previous lesson at the beginning of a lesson. However, to be effective, strive to make the review segment interesting and active. Mind maps, analogies, brainstorming, role playing, or a cooperative learning activity will generally be more effective than just telling the students what they studied previously.

- To maximize their impact, vary your openings. Strive to be creative and occasionally use the element of surprise. If your openings become the best part of the lesson, you'll have much less problem with tardiness!

ACTION VERBS FOR WRITING INSTRUCTIONAL OBJECTIVES

Effective teachers know what they are trying to accomplish in each lesson. Their instruction has a purpose or clearly focused objective. That goal may be for students to master a new skill; to change a behavior, attitude, or value; or to memorize a fact. Some research suggests that students forget within one year as much as 80 percent of what they learn in school. Most of what is lost are facts—those pieces of data learned solely through rote memory. Most likely to be retained are the skills, attitudes, and values learned in the classroom.

Objectives that remain at the knowledge level include verbs such as *memorize*, *list*, *name*, or *know*. Although a degree of factual information must be retained to allow higher-level thinking, most educators recognize the value of teaching higher-level critical thinking. You are seeking to answer the question "What will my students be able to do as a result of my instruction?" Action verbs assure that you are focusing on doing, not merely knowing. Here are some verbs that will help you construct objectives at a higher level:

Advise	Devise	Participate
Analyze	Direct	Perform
Appraise	Discuss	Place
Arrange	Draw	Plan
Assemble	Establish	Prepare
Assign	Estimate	Process
Assist	Evaluate	Propose
Build	Execute	Provide
Calculate	Exercise	Rate
Collaborate	Explain	Recommend
Collect	Formulate	Report
Compare	Furnish	Represent
Compile	Implement	Research
Compute	Improve	Resolve
Conduct	Initiate	Review
Consolidate	Inspect	Revise
Construct	Instruct	Schedule
Contrast	Interpret	Secure
Coordinate	Investigate	Select
Criticize	Locate	Show
Debate	Maintain	Solve
Decide	Manage	Submit
Deliver	Measure	Teach
Demonstrate	Negotiate	Train
Design	Obtain	Transcribe
Determine	Operate	Verify
Develop	Organize	

LEARNER-CENTERED LESSONS

For much of the previous century, traditional schools were predominantly teacher centered, focusing primarily on the needs, abilities, and goals of teachers (and other adults). Students were rarely involved in decisions about what or how things happened in their classrooms. Schools tended to follow the factory model of the Industrial Era, with a largely one-size-fits-all curriculum. The teacher-centered (or curriculum-centered) paradigm emphasizes covering content and meeting standards. Success tends to be determined largely by how well students do compared with their peers.

In the past decade, many teachers and education leaders have passionately advocated moving from curriculum-driven schools toward more learner-centered schools. Students are seen as cocreators on knowledge. Learner-centered lessons frequently stress critical thinking and problem-solving skills over rote memorization.

The learner-centered paradigm stresses student growth through experiences incorporating each student's unique needs and interests. They are involved in some decisions, with options in how things are learned and how their progress is assessed. Students are more likely to experiment, explore, and create. The curriculum becomes much more personalized, focused on meeting the needs of the students.

Many excellent teachers incorporate an amalgamation of the two styles into their classrooms. External standards and assessments are a reality that cannot be ignored.

- Emphasize connecting new material with students' prior knowledge. For example, briefly review previously learned skills and concepts immediately before presenting new ones.

- Create a classroom that is inviting.

- Design lessons where students set their own goals.

- Encourage students to think about the learning process and how, with their teachers, they can improve their learning.

- Provide "open-ended" experiences, without prescribed right or wrong answers.

- Provide choices in learning activities, assessment, and schedules, whenever feasible. Often there are several ways in which students might prove they have mastered content. Flexibility is a valuable asset in a learner-centered classroom.

- Focus on helping students transfer new knowledge and skills to other situations in their lives. How does it apply to outside challenges, such as the world of work or dealing with practical problems in the home?

- When feasible, allow students to learn at their own pace.

- Incorporate problem-based learning, cooperative learning, simulations, inquiry methods, and hands-on learning experiences into your lessons.

- Use performance-based assessment techniques that use student-made products as the outcome. Examples: a multimedia presentation, a bulletin board, a concept map, a flowchart, a model, a digital video, or a Web site.

- Employ rubrics in assessing students' achievements and products.

- Use praise and critical feedback wisely, without overdoing either.

- Encourage reflection about what they have learned. Learning logs or brainstorming are useful tools in promoting this insightful thinking.

- Model your thinking process aloud.

- Use student-led conferences with their parents and teachers.

- Communicate with parents to convey what learner-centered classes are.

- Attend workshops or conferences that focus on developing learner-centered classrooms. Even better, attend with one or more of your fellow teachers.

For More Information

Lipton, L., & Hubble, D. (2009). *More than 100 ways to learner-centered literacy* (2nd ed.). Thousand Oaks, CA: Corwin.

McCombs, B. L., & Miller, L. (2009). *The school leader's guide to learner-centered education: From complexity to simplicity.* Thousand Oaks, CA: Corwin.

Tollefson, M. K., & Osborn, K. (2008). *Cultivating the learner-centered classroom: From theory to practice.* Thousand Oaks, CA: Corwin.

PLANNING UNITS OF INSTRUCTION

Hurwitz and Day (2007) defined a unit of instruction as "a series of lessons organized around a single theme, topic, or mode. The unit plan should provide the teacher with a concise overview of the unit, including information about art works, art materials, and special preparations that need to be considered. The unit should be organized to emphasize sequences of learning activities" (p. 358).

Units of instruction usually focus on a major theme (for example, developing cultural awareness, inventions that changed the world, supply and demand, developing hand-eye coordination). Often they are interdisciplinary, drawing on two or more subject areas.

Here are some questions that will help in planning units of instruction:

- What subthemes are suggested by the topic or theme?

- What are the outcomes expected of students? Skills? Affective or cognitive objectives?

- How is the unit supportive or aligned with the state and other standards?

- What is the time line? How much time should be allotted to each subtheme or activity?

- How should the units be sequenced (chronologically or conceptually)?

- What special resources or materials are needed (for example, supplies, software, handouts, PowerPoint presentations, rubrics)?

- What instructional activities or methods would support the unit (for example, guest speakers, simulations, computer software, Internet activities, cooperative learning)?

- What opening activity will arouse students' interest, curiosity, and enthusiasm?

- How will progress and success be measured (for example, through portfolios, journals, models, video presentations, reports)?

For More Information

Brigham, D., Fell, J., Simons, C., & Strunk, K. (2006). *Units of instruction for gifted learners.* Waco, TX: Prufrock.

Erickson, H. L. (2007). *Concept-based curriculum and instruction for the thinking classroom.* Thousand Oaks, CA: Corwin.

Hurwitz, A. & Day, M. (2007). *Children and their art: Methods for the elementary school* (8th ed.). Belmont, CA: Thomson Wadsworth.

THIRTY-EIGHT HOT TIPS FOR MAINTAINING INTEREST

It is absurd to expect all students to be constantly on the edge of their seats, mesmerized by masterful instruction. Students do bring outside distractions into the classroom. Divorces, deaths, infatuations, conflicts, and the normal growing pains can divert the attention of even the most conscientious students. Although you cannot control these outside events, you do have a significant effect on most students' learning. Some teachers have greater skill at teaching lessons that hold students' attention and that result in higher achievement than other teachers.

All teachers have a few lessons that always excite and interest students. Those successful attention-holding lessons likely adhere to most of the following principles. Here are some ideas that may help gain and maintain learners' interest:

1. Learning begins before class starts. Challenge yourself to devise creative ways to capture students' attention and engage their minds the moment they enter the room. Every day plan to have something available related to the day's topic to arouse curiosity and stimulate thinking before the bell rings. Examples: a quotation on the board or overhead, a word puzzle for individuals or groups to complete, a couple of thought questions, a startling statistic, a related cartoon.

2. Get the class actively involved in the lesson's first three minutes. This might be through raising their hands in response to a question related to the day's lesson (for example, "How many have ever visited a dairy farm?"), participating in a small-group brainstorm, or writing a response. Strive to create an atmosphere of active involvement, not passive listening, early in the class period.

3. Plan carefully and fully. Lessons that are run smoothly keep students' attention and minimize interruptions. This has little to do with charisma. Lessons run smoothly because they are carefully planned and organized. Time is invested up front to ensure that materials are ready, the teacher knows what to do next, and the unexpected is anticipated. This helps create a businesslike, task-oriented atmosphere.

4. Clarify the specific objective(s) for each lesson. The single most important question you can ask yourself each day is "What do I want my students to learn from this class?" Unfortunately, some teachers have no clearer notion of where they are headed than "to make it through the textbook" or "to make it to the Civil War by Christmas."

5. Share your objectives with your students. Let them know what they should get out of this lesson. Of course, you cannot tell them if you don't know yourself. With purposes clear and instruction systematic, students will more readily master that lesson.

6. Divide learning tasks into smaller subskills. Present those subskills in logical and manageable lessons. Sequence your lessons so that you aren't trying to teach skills for which students have not yet mastered necessary prerequisites. Otherwise, both you and your students will be frustrated.

7. Design lessons that encourage students to contribute their views and knowledge. Many have special talents or experiences they might enjoy sharing and from which other students can learn.

8. Make a conscious effort to connect your lesson to students' lives beyond school. Incorporate their interests as illustrations. Provide opportunities for them to apply what they are learning to daily life and the problems they face.

9. Employ visual aids—transparencies, pictures, slides, props, demonstrations, and posters. Overall, the visual is the most powerful learning modality. Maximum learning is likely to occur when the instruction is both auditory and visual and, where possible, also kinesthetic (involving doing things and motor movement).

10. Keep moving while you talk. An easy way to lose any group's interest is to become the stationary talking head in front of the room. Talking while seated is also more likely to lead to speaking in a monotone. An additional benefit of moving while teaching is that you are better able to monitor the class, nipping in the bud any potentially disruptive misbehavior.

11. Generally, it is best not to start each class with housekeeping chores. The reason is that students most remember the first and last thing you do in a class period. Don't waste this valuable learning time on mundane distracting content.

12. Build a breath of fresh air or energizing activity into your lesson about every eight to ten minutes. It doesn't have to be long, but inject something that changes the pace and refocuses the students' attention. Examples include a humorous cartoon, a prop, personal illustration, sharing a response in pairs or small groups, a role play, demonstration, visualization. Anything that actively engages their brains is likely to be helpful in refocusing attention. Provide opportunities for active involvement through exercises and activities that break up long formal presentations. When asked, most students prefer lessons in which they act out parts, build things, interview people, or carry out projects. Least favored are those classes in which they are allowed only to listen.

13. Variety is the spice of life and the secret to successful lessons! Effective teachers don't use the same teaching techniques day after day. They employ an assortment of instructional strategies. Most ineffective teachers tend to use the same few techniques for every lesson—usually lecture and worksheets.

14. Strive to develop the broadest range of teaching approaches and employ that variety. Experiment with simulations, role playing, videotaping, and cooperative learning. Students generally are more excited about working in groups.

15. Involve students in real-life activities that have a practical usable product. For example, in the remarkably successful Foxfire project, students interviewed their Appalachian neighbors and relatives and produced and sold books they wrote and published. Other classes have developed handbooks for teenage consumers, constructed solar walls, or set up community carpools. Hands-on activities are most successful by far in arousing student interest.

16. The element of surprise works wonders in building student enthusiasm and motivation. Some teachers dress up in costumes, have surprise guest speakers, or use drama to capture students' attention. (For example, students are much more excited about reading Shakespeare when they act it out using an exaggerated Southern drawl—or Bostonian accent if they are from the South!). Occasionally, do the unexpected. Allow suspense to build in anticipation as the class unfolds. Questions, storytelling, and props are especially effective in creating intrigue.

> It is by surprises that experience teaches all she designed to teach us.
>
> —**Charles Sanders Pierce,**
> ***Collected Papers***

17. Use anecdotes. Personal illustrations of events from your and your students' life experiences make academic content come alive. It is essential that such stories pertain to the topic being studied. Irrelevant war stories add nothing to the lesson.

18. Try to relate new content to things the students already know. As much as possible, encourage the students to make those connections themselves. Personalize as much of your content as possible.

19. Minimize criticism and offer praise when appropriate. If students are too frequently criticized, they quickly learn to avoid volunteering their answers or opinions. There is no quicker way to squelch creativity or participation than to criticize the first couple of contributors. Use praise judiciously. Praise specific behaviors, not general characteristics. Be aware that public praise can backfire for many adolescents, whose peers may taunt them for being the teacher's pet.

20. Become aware of your voice level and speaking patterns. Tape a couple of classes and listen for your tonality, verbal tics (for example, *um, er, so*). Solicit feedback from a speech-and-hearing specialist as to the pitch of your voice.

21. Vary your speech pattern. Use pauses or stage whispers for emphasis. Always remember to talk to the students at the farthest corner of the room. If students must strain to hear you, you will have trouble holding their attention.

22. Make your presentations clear. Use vocabulary appropriate to your students' developmental level. Speak at a pace they can understand. If your voice tends toward the monotone, work on developing more animated speech. Periodically record or videotape your lessons. Seeing or hearing yourself as your students do may reveal areas that need improvement.

23. Remain flexible in your teaching. Read your audience and adjust accordingly. Furrowed brows and frowns will tell you that some students did not grasp a point. Squirming, fidgeting, or daydreaming may cue you to pick up the pace or change your approach. Good planning must remain flexible. There is little sense in plowing ahead with a lesson plan that isn't working.

24. Use your sense of humor. Do not try to become a stand-up comic, but don't be afraid to laugh or add humorous remarks to your presentation. The guiding principle for using humor in the classroom is that it should be relevant to the topic under discussion. Resist the temptation to entertain with jokes that don't have an educational point. Interesting lessons make learning fun, and a natural response to fun activities is the occasional laugh. You need not strive for a belly laugh, but when a humorous incident or anecdote presents itself, use it to your advantage.

25. Incorporate students' names in your presentations. For most people, their name really is their favorite sound.

26. Use appropriate analogies, especially humorous ones.

27. Use props whenever possible. Student interest is piqued when they enter the room and see a jar of beans, a model airplane, guitar, telephone, or parrot sitting on the teacher's desk. Almost any lesson can benefit from the inclusion of one or more props. If what you need is not immediately available, try using "invisible props." Describe the needed item in detail, using gestures as though you were actually holding it in your hand.

28. A special form of prop is the collection. Campaign buttons, artifacts, insects, leaves, rocks, tools, costumes, or postcards are among items that interest students and enrich their knowledge of the academic subject. You can develop your own collections or invite parents and other community members to share theirs. It is best if they can bring their collection and talk briefly about it. Ask students questions about the items in a collection to encourage them to think about its value, purpose, and meaning.

29. Use music. Many effective teachers successfully incorporate music into their classes. Having music playing as students enter the classroom begins to set the mood for the day's class. You can let students take turns bringing their favorite tapes or CDs to play before class or during breaks or recess. Soft music playing quietly in the background during individual seatwork can be pleasant and inviting. The beat of baroque compositions seems to work best for this.

> Give me a lever long enough and a prop strong enough, I can single-handed move the world.
>
> **—Archimedes**

30. Music related to the topic (for example, the Civil War, Ireland, China, the Roaring Twenties) can bring the topic to life and enrich students' understanding of the subject. Use recordings of sound effects for emphasis of important points. Some teachers even write new lyrics for familiar tunes. The new song conveys a message related to the day's lesson or an upcoming school event. It is fairly easy to devise your own composition using a rap beat. Either you can sing it or get a group of students or even the whole class to perform. Try reading the day's assignments to a rap beat!

31. Take timely breaks. Continually monitor your students' nonverbal expression. When nodding heads and drooping eyelids suggest you are losing their attention, insert a thirty-second stretch break. It can be something as subtle as standing up as soon as they have figured out an answer or turning their chairs to face a different direction. Of course, you don't want to create chaos or disrupt the flow of your lesson. A mini-break works best if it ties into your lesson.

32. Avoid becoming too involved with one student during class discussions. The rest of the class may assume they are not a part of the discussion and turn their attention elsewhere. While being sensitive to individuals, teach to the whole class. Maintain control of the discussion. If one student is monopolizing the interaction, ask questions of others to get them involved.

33. Assume the role of a character (an old woman, Superman, George Washington, a Civil War soldier). Embellish your character with props or a costume. (Garage sales and thrift shops are good sources for inexpensive costumes.) You might teach part of the lesson as your "character" for a few minutes or the whole period. Or alternate between two characters, debating with yourself. Consider acting out a real historical role in the actual setting as part of your vacation. Dress in authentic costumes and have someone videotape or take slides as you reenact some historical event or journey. These can be edited and used in class (or at all-school assemblies).

34. Use quotations to make an emphatic point. Sometimes the impact of this technique can be enhanced if a brief quotation is read aloud to the class directly from the original source rather than merely from your notes.

35. Build in brief, one- to three-minute pauses for reflection or writing. Give students a question to consider. For variety you may have all students stand and share their responses with someone else.

36. End each lesson answering the *so what* question. Encourage your students to consider why this content is important. Help them connect their new content with previous knowledge and with their personal lives wherever possible.

37. If a lesson falls flat, refine it or discard it. Why intentionally bore your students? Learning isn't happening. Spend your time on something that is working.

38. Most important, remember that you are unlikely to get students enthusiastic about a topic or activity if you are not enthusiastic about it yourself. Conversely, if you believe that what you are teaching is interesting, fun, or useful, that view might become contagious.

Mock Cell Phone Call: Attention-Grabbing Technique

Generate student interest with a mock cell phone conversation. Put a cell phone in your pocket and pretend that it is vibrating. Apologize to the class for taking the call during class. Then proceed to have a mock phone call with a well-informed caller. Select a famous person (for example, a scientist, politician, or writer) who is associated with the content you are teaching.

Carry on a conversation with the celebrity, in which you repeat his or her part of the conversation, allowing students to hear both ends of the discussion. You'll need to give some thought to the questions you would ask and the expert caller's responses. This strategy might be successfully used as an introduction to a new topic, as an energizer, or as a review of a lesson.

Source: Originally published in the *Heart of Teaching* newsletters, © 2001–2005 Performance Learning Systems, Inc.®, an educational services company located in Allentown, PA, and on the World Wide Web at www.plsweb.com. Used with permission.

SEVEN CARDINAL RULES FOR EFFECTIVE VISUALS

Good visuals have the potential to enhance attention and retention. Most learners perform better when they receive information through more than one learning modality. Slides, transparencies, multimedia projector visuals, flip charts, and posters all can be used to effectively embellish any presentation.

Any material you write on the chalkboard or whiteboard each time you teach a lesson is a good candidate for a permanent visual, such as an overhead transparency or slide. Visuals prepared in advance can also be much easier to read, more eye-catching, and faster than hand printing on the board or newsprint.

Have you ever heard a teacher or presenter say, "I know you can't read this, but . . ." as he placed a transparency on the overhead projector? Some feel that should be grounds for instant dismissal or worse. Visuals that can't be read are as useless as a parachute that doesn't open! Some simple rules will make your visuals more effective. These same principles generally apply to overhead transparencies, slides, or multimedia projectors.

1. To construct visuals that will be readable, remember the number six: no more than six lines on a visual and no more than six words on a line.

2. With the near universal availability of computers and printers, there really is no excuse for poorly constructed visuals. However, resist the temptation to clutter up your visuals with too many cute graphics and all the fonts at your disposal. No more than two font styles should be used on any one visual, and sans serif fonts (such as Geneva, Arial, or Helvetica) tend to be more readable. Use type that is at least twenty-four points and preferably thirty-six points. If you still doubt whether your slides can be read, put one on the projector and view it from the last row of your classroom.

3. It is better to put long lists on several slides than to cram too much on one. It is more effective to use progressive exposure, where each successive visual reveals one more line of information.

4. Whenever possible, use graphs and charts instead of tables for your visuals. Tables are more difficult to read and understand.

5. In preparing projected visuals, use a horizontal format rather than vertical. Since most screens are horizontal rectangles, your visual will fit more neatly on the screen. When you project onto the screen, try to use the upper three-quarters of the screen. The bottom quarter tends to be difficult for some participants in the back to see.

6. Don't read your visuals aloud. It's insulting to your audience.

7. Square the projector in front of the screen to minimize the keystone image: because the distance from the projector image is farther from the top of the screen than the bottom,

the image will always appear wider at the top than at the bottom. Using a screen that tilts forward about seven degrees can cure this. Many projectors have a built-in keystone correction feature. Learn to take advantage of it.

Additional Tips for Using Overhead Transparencies

- Use colored, erasable, water-soluble pens to highlight transparencies during presentations.

- Arrange your transparencies in the order you will display them, and place them near the projector.

- After placing a transparency on the projector, step away so that you do not block any student's view.

- Use frames on your transparencies. This looks more professional and makes them last longer. You can make your own out of scrap cardboard. Many presenters use the transparency frames as cue cards, writing key words in large print. A quick glance as you place the transparency on the projector reminds you of points to emphasize.

- When you are done talking about a transparency, turn off the projector. Don't just remove the transparency, leaving a blinding and distracting white screen. Instead, hinge a five-by-eight-inch card with tape on top of the projector lens. Simply flip the card down to block the light when you are done with a transparency.

- Try something other than just black-and-white overhead transparencies. Use variety; experiment with color. Photocopiers that run black-and-white transparencies can also produce transparencies with color backgrounds. Or use overhead transparency markers to add some color. White on dark colored backgrounds produces very readable transparencies.

- When using flip charts or newsprint, experiment with using a variety of dark colors. Print large and legibly. Notes to yourself can be penciled lightly on the newsprint beforehand. Tape sheets to the wall when they are completed.

- Tape four pennies along one long edge of a sheet of paper to make a mask to place over transparencies and pull down, gradually revealing one line at a time. The pennies keep the paper from slipping off as you get to the bottom of the transparency.

STORYBOARDING

The storyboard, originally a creative tool for moviemakers, has been adapted by many businesses to stimulate creative thinking and organize projects. In designing multimedia programs (movies, videos, or Web sites), storyboards are used to describe everything that the viewer will see, hear, or experience.

Storyboards help capture and stimulate imagination and visualization. They are especially valuable in facilitating collaborative creative designs. Writers sometimes use storyboards to help them organize their novels' plots.

Although storyboards were originally done on paper, storyboarders now have the option of using computers to generate storyboards.

A four-by-four-foot sheet of corkboard (or regular blank bulletin board), pushpins, felt-tip markers, and four-by-six-inch index cards are all the materials required. Some teachers use three-by-five-inch sticky notes instead of cards. This works fine if you don't intend to keep the storyboard for more than a day.

As the group brainstorms ideas, they are pinned into clusters or under specific headings on the board. Storyboards can be adapted to a variety of uses in the classroom.

Teach your students how to storyboard as a way of stimulating their creativity. To begin, present small groups of three or four students with a question to consider. As they take turns individually brainstorming ideas, they should jot down their ideas on index cards or sticky notes.

Ideas are hung in sequence on the corkboard, much like the frames of a comic strip. An alternative is to draw a large window with up to nine cells on a sheet of newsprint. Beginning at the top left block, ideas are depicted in words or drawings.

Storyboarding is also an effective device for organizing a lesson plan or other interactive presentation. It would prove especially valuable in designing an online course.

Interestingly, many high schools now teach storyboarding skills as part of their visual communications or digital arts courses. As part of its project-based curriculum, students in Utah's Granite School District learn storyboarding as early as the fifth grade.

For More Information

Simon, M. (2007). *Storyboards: Motion in art* (3rd ed.). Boston: Focal Press.

Internet Resources

Digital Storytelling Resources for Educators

www.techteachers.com/digitalstorytelling.htm

Storyboard Template

www2.hawaii.edu/~ricky/etec/sboardtemplate.html

Storyboarding: Using Pictures to Teach Words

www.education.com/activity/article/Storyboarding_Use_pictures_help/

Success Is in the Planning: Storyboarding Video Projects

www.create.cett.msstate.edu/create/howto/Storyboard_Handout.pdf

Storyboard Pro is a freeware software package available at http://movies.atomiclearning.com/k12/storyboardpro/ in Macintosh or Windows versions. Use this helpful software to lay out video production sequences. Digital storyboards are easy to save, revise, duplicate, and share with others.

REVIEW TECHNIQUES

Successful teachers allow ample time for reviewing new concepts and skills and integrating them into students' prior knowledge. The purpose of review is to clarify, reinforce, and set the stage for new content. The challenge is to make review interesting. It is probably a good idea to include a brief review each day of some content covered in the previous lesson. Here are some options that may help.

- Have each student draw three large balloons (or box cars, apples, or diamonds) on a sheet of paper. Ask them to write the three most important (or interesting) things they learned about the day's topic in the balloons. After a couple of minutes, invite them to share their ideas in pairs. Finally, you can solicit ideas from the whole class, providing three separate opportunities to review some aspect of the day's content.

- In the middle of a lesson, you can stop and ask each student to jot down one idea from the lesson he or she most wants to remember. Allow a minute for reflection, and then solicit ideas from various class members.

- Post on the walls several sheets of newsprint, each listing a major idea or concept studied during the previous lesson. At a signal, students are to move from one sheet to another, adding one fact or idea they know about each topic.

- Another fun way to stimulate review is for one student to draw on the board or newsprint a picture representing an idea related to the previous lesson. The rest of the students attempt to guess the word or topic in a Pictionary or Win, Lose, or Draw format.

- One of the most powerful techniques for organizing ideas and concepts is the mind map. The mind map (see below) is also a most useful note-taking device. Every student should have this tool in his or her repertoire. It can also be used in a variety of ways to stimulate reflection and review.

- Use computer software to create crossword puzzles or word games that include content being reviewed. (See Chapter Nine for sources of several useful software programs).

- Games are high-interest review techniques. Create your own versions of *Jeopardy*! or *Cash Cab* TV game shows. Have students write the questions and break the class into several teams.

MIND MAPS

The mind map is started by writing the key word or general topic (for example, PRESIDENTS) in a circle in the middle of a sheet of blank paper. The subtopics (for example, the WHITE HOUSE, ELECTIONS, FIRST LADIES, POLITICAL PARTIES, ASSASSINATIONS) are written on spokes drawn out from the circle. A good way to generate the subtopics is to ask students to brainstorm the main chapters they would include if they were going to write a book on the topic. Ideas and facts associated with the subtopics are drawn on shorter lines branching from the spokes containing the subtopics. Encourage students to use symbols or small pictures whenever possible. Using different colored markers or pens for the subtopics also helps stimulate creative thought.

After individual students have developed their mind maps of the topic, a useful option is to ask them to join another person and combine their two separate mind maps into one. After several minutes, redirect each pair to join another pair and again combine their mind maps into one. An option is to finally have all the students then gather around one large sheet of newsprint (or tape four regular sheets of newsprint together to form a gigantic one). Write the topic in a circle in the middle of the paper and give them the task of compiling a final mind map that includes all the ideas that their individual mind maps generated.

Some teachers have employed the mind map as an assessment device. Students complete mind maps to reflect their understandings of complex concepts. All students should be taught the mind-mapping process as an aid to note taking.

For More Information

Buzan, T. (1983). *Use both sides of your brain.* New York: E. P. Dutton.

Buzan, T., & Buzan, B. (1994). *The mind map book: How to use radiant thinking to maximize your brain's untapped potential.* New York: E. P. Dutton.

Margulies, N. (1991). *Mapping inner space: Learning and teaching mind mapping.* Tucson, AZ: Zephyr Press.

Shmaefsky, B. R. (2007). E-concept mapping. *Journal of College Science Teaching, 36*(4), 14–15.

Mind Mapping Software

Several excellent software packages facilitate the mind-mapping process. The features and prices vary. Check out the following:

iMindMap ($99). For Windows, Macintosh, and Linux.

    www.imindmap.com/

PersonalBrain. ($150, $250; free edition available). For Windows and Macintosh.

    www.thebrain.com/#-42

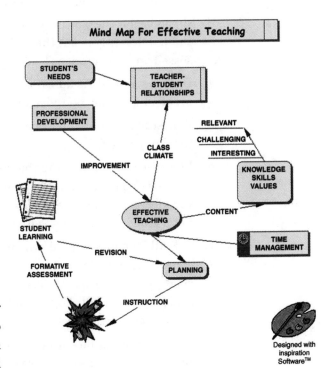

NINETEEN TIPS FOR CLOSING A LESSON

An outstanding lesson can be spoiled with a poor ending. Remember that students are most likely to remember the first and last things that happen in class. For this reason it is essential to give careful thought to each lesson's ending. A good ending allows students to connect what they learned in a lesson with their previous knowledge.

An effective closure provides students with a sense of accomplishment. It helps them reflect on what they have learned in a lesson and integrate new skills and concepts with their previous knowledge. The ending also provides an opportunity to plant seeds of curiosity for the next lesson. Each activity should be followed by some processing experience to allow students to reflect on what they have learned. The challenge is to present interesting, creative closure activities that keep students actively involved rather than serve as a cue to pack up their books. Here are nineteen suggestions for providing effective closure to your lessons:

1. Make a commitment to allow time in each lesson for a proper closure. Shouting the next day's assignment to your class as students rush out the door is ineffective. Allotting five to ten minutes of each class period for closure and debriefing is a valuable investment. Think of your lesson as a gift to your students; the ending is the bow on the package. It ties the whole experience together. It adds the finishing touch to your masterpiece.

2. Have students draw three balloons on a blank sheet of paper. In each balloon they are to write one important thing they learned in today's class. Have the students then pair with another and share what they wrote. It is a subtle way of encouraging them to review and reflect on what has happened during that lesson. (Of course, don't tell them it is review or they may disengage their brains from the activity!)

3. If you began the class with a question, you might now solicit their answers. Do they think differently about the topic now than they did at the beginning? Have they reassessed any assumptions?

4. Design a guided visualization. Leave parts open-ended, such as the best solution to a problem. Process their visualizations as a small-group or whole-class activity.

5. Pair students and allow one to interview the other about what he or she learned in the day's lesson.

6. Place a cartoon related to the lesson on the overhead projector. Always read the cartoon section of the newspaper with an eye for cartoons that might pertain to any of your lessons. Enlarge them on the photocopier and make them into transparencies. Let a student color them with colored markers.

7. Ask all students to jot down one idea from the lesson they most want to remember. Allow a minute for reflection, and then solicit ideas from various members of the class. As an alternative, you can have them share in pairs or small groups. Or you could give students topics and have them generate answers and use a *Jeopardy!* format for teams to generate appropriate questions.

8. Connect this lesson with previously learned content. This might be achieved through reflective questions or as a cooperative learning activity.

9. Provide an opportunity for application. Structure an activity that encourages reality testing a new skill or concept. Ideally, students should receive immediate feedback on their success.

10. If you have been teaching a controversial topic, have pairs of students do a force field analysis of the topic. They draw a line down the middle of the page. On one side they list all the arguments for and on the other side all the arguments against the proposition. You might summarize their grids as one large chart on the board.

11. Use a crossword puzzle that incorporates key concepts, names, or vocabulary included in the day's lesson. You can easily create crossword puzzles with inexpensive computer software such as Crossword Construction Kit (Insight Software Solutions) or Crossword Compiler (Anthony Lewis Software). You may let students work in pairs or alone for three minutes, and then they are free to help one another.

12. Let students write themselves a letter to encourage goal setting and self-monitoring of progress. Have students complete three sentence stems on a sheet of paper:

    • One thing I am doing well and will continue to do is . . .

    • One thing I will start doing in the next month is . . .

    • One thing I will stop doing in the next month is . . .

    You may substitute other questions or statements related to your lesson's objectives. Students place their completed sentences in envelopes, seal them, and write their names on the outside. Collect the envelopes and return them unopened one month (or a longer time period) later.

13. Have each student write one quiz question about the topic being studied. Collect them and then ask teams of students to respond to the questions in quiz-bowl style. Teams of students compete, accumulating points by giving answers.

14. Provide one or more sentence stems on a transparency or write them on the board, for example:

    I learned . . .

    I was surprised that . . .

    I discovered . . .

    I realized . . .

    I am puzzled about . . .

    I noticed . . .

    I recognize . . .

    I now appreciate . . .

Give your class two to three minutes to complete any one or two of the stems. Solicit several from volunteers. Be sure to thank contributors for offering their ideas.

15. Let students draw mind maps summarizing the content from the previous lesson. After individual students have developed their mind maps of the topic, ask them to join another person and combine their two separate mind maps into one. After several minutes redirect each pair to join another pair and again combine their mind maps into one. An option is to finally have all the students gather around one large sheet of newsprint (or tape four regular sheets of newsprint together to form a gigantic one). Write the topic in a circle in the middle of the paper and give them the task of compiling a final mind map that includes all the ideas generated on their individual mind maps.

16. Remind students of what they already know that ties into the new content they have just learned.

17. End with a teaser or promo for the next day's lesson. The "coming attractions" hook leaves students in suspense and enhances their motivation to show up next time. Be creative; borrow from television and theater promos. You might pose a couple of startling questions that the class will address next time. Post an intriguing problem or challenge. Make a promise. Exaggeration is permitted. Whatever you do, do it with enthusiasm.

18. Ask each student to write down on a blank sheet of paper one thing he or she learned about the topic today. After everyone has finished writing, instruct the students to wad up the paper and throw it across the room. Each person picks up one and reads it aloud. Assign a volunteer to collect all the papers with the wastebasket or recycling bin.

19. Of course, remind them if there is a test or assignment due or they need to bring special materials to the next class. It is also important to add a word of encouragement if the day's lesson has been particularly difficult for many students. Acknowledge their efforts and successes. Thank them for working so hard. You might even invite them to give themselves a standing ovation.

DIFFERENTIATING INSTRUCTION

One of the earliest lessons most teachers learn is that one size does not fit all. Most classes include a broad range of students with a broad range of maturity, ability, motivation, temperament, home environment, and interests.

Multiple Intelligences

Since 1905, when psychologists Alfred Binet and Theodore Simon first developed an intelligence scale for identifying those students who would most benefit from special education, schools have placed much emphasis on measuring and reporting students' levels of intelligence. It is worth noting that Binet explicitly did not intend his measure to be used to rank students by intellectual ability or even to identify their innate potential. He also did not believe intelligence to be a single quality, measurable by a number. The struggle to define and assess intelligence is probably articulated most clearly by Harvard psychologist Edward Boring's quip that intelligence is defined as what intelligence tests measure.

In the mid-1980s Howard Gardner, professor at the Harvard Graduate School of Education, popularized the concept of multiple intelligences. Gardner offered an alternative view of intelligence, defining it as "the ability to solve problems or fashion products that are valued in at least one culture" (1999, p. 33). He views intelligence as biopsychological potential.

Gardner and his followers have identified specific sections of the brain that control each of the eight intelligences he proposed:

- *Logical-mathematical:* verbal skills and sensitivity to the sounds, meanings, and rhythms of words
- *Linguistic:* possessing a mastery of language and ability to express oneself rhetorically or poetically
- *Spatial:* ability to think in images and pictures, to visualize accurately and abstractly
- *Musical:* ability to recognize and compose musical pitches, tones, and rhythms
- *Bodily-kinesthetic:* ability to control one's body movements and to handle objects skillfully
- *Intrapersonal:* possessing a high degree of self-knowledge, including awareness of one's own strengths, weaknesses, and inner feelings
- *Interpersonal:* competent in leadership skills, communication, understanding of others' feelings
- *Naturalist:* capacity to detect significant patterns in nature and distinguish and categorize items of various classes (plants, animals, chemicals)

Schools have traditionally stressed and rewarded linguistic and logical-mathematical intelligence. Many contend this narrow conception of intelligence has shortchanged those students whose talents lie in other forms of intelligence. Recognizing and nurturing the students' individual patterns of multiple intelligences allows teachers to help all students maximize their success, both in and out of school. Not all students have strong logical or linguistic intelligences. However, capitalizing on their strengths allows these students to excel in other arenas.

Tom Armstrong, author of *Multiple Intelligences in the Classroom,* suggests that knowledge of multiple intelligences provides teachers with eight unique pathways to learning, enabling them to more effectively personalize instruction. Skills can be learned and applied in a variety of modes. Attending to multiple intelligences will invariably change the teacher's role in the classroom. It must become less focused on textbooks and lectures, encouraging teachers to be more creative in designing lessons.

Gardner frowned on tests that were designed to measure students' intelligence. However, through observation, teachers can usually identify students' natural inclinations. Armstrong suggests that noting how students misbehave provides valuable clues to students' preferred intelligences. For example, students with high spatial intelligence may spend a lot of time doodling in class. Interviewing students, their parents, and previous teachers will provide insights into individuals' dominant intelligences. Finding out how students prefer to spend their free time out of school usually reveals their talents.

Gardner suggested that memory is intelligence specific. There is no such thing as a good memory or bad memory. He argues that memory will accompany one's predominant intelligences. For example, an individual with strong musical intelligence may be able to hear a composition once and play it back on a musical instrument, but that person may have a very difficult time remembering names or memorizing multiplication tables.

Armstrong suggested that by using multiple ways of teaching content, teachers encourage students to tap their strengths in accomplishing more challenging tasks. For example, a teacher might encourage the musically inclined student to sing the multiplication tables at home as a memory aid.

Gardner and his colleagues have promoted nontraditional forms of assessment to evaluate student achievement. Such authentic assessments may incorporate student portfolios or demonstrations. Ongoing teacher observation and student self-evaluation are significant aspects of instruction oriented toward multiple intelligences. Gardner (1993, p. 178) concludes that "it is extremely desirable to have assessment occur in the context of students working on problems, projects, or products that genuinely engage them, that hold their interest and motivate them to do well. Such exercises may not be as easy to design as the standard multiple-choice entry, but they are far more likely to elicit a student's full repertoire of skills and to yield information that is useful for subsequent advice and placement."

Teachers determined to implement multiple-intelligence strategies in their classroom face real-world obstacles. The time and energy needed to redesign instruction can be significant. Not all administrators encourage deviating from the focus on upping standardized test performance. Parents may not readily see the advantages of emphasizing talent development beyond the traditional three R's.

Research suggests that instruction organized around multiple intelligences can stimulate increased responsibility in students, enhanced academic achievement, and more cooperative classroom behavior. To learn more about multiple intelligences, see Howard Gardner's Web site (www.howardgardner.com/), check out the books listed in the resources below, or take a course or workshop.

HELPFUL RESOURCES

Arnold, E. (2007). *The MI strategy bank: 800+ multiple intelligence ideas for the elementary classroom* (2nd ed.). Chicago: Zephyr.

Bellanca, J. (2009). *200+ active learning strategies and projects for engaging students' multiple intelligences.* Thousand Oaks, CA: Corwin.

Fogarty, R., & Stoehr, J. (2008). *Integrating curricula with multiple intelligences: Teams, themes, and threads* (2nd ed.). Thousand Oaks, CA: Corwin Press.

Gardner, H. (2006). *The development and education of the mind: The selected works of Howard Gardner.* New York: Routledge.

Shearer, B. (2008). *Creating extra-ordinary teachers: Multiple intelligences in the classroom and beyond.* New York: Continuum.

Multiple Intelligences in Teaching

Logical-mathematical	Calculating, analyzing, questioning	Calculation, experiments, problem solving, computer games, library research
Linguistic	Writing, reading, telling stories	Books, discussion, reports, compositions, debates
Spatial	Drawing, visualizing	Art, puzzles, maps, visual images, mind mapping
Musical	Singing, playing instruments	Sing-alongs, musical instruments, background music, song writing
Bodily-kinesthetic	Dancing, running, touching	Gymnastics, hands-on activities, constructing things, physical games, drama, handicrafts, model building, skits, manipulatives
Intrapersonal	Reflecting, meditating	Independent study, introspection, self-paced learning, journaling
Interpersonal	Listening, helping, talking, leading, socializing	Peer tutoring, games, cooperative learning
Naturalist	Sorting, categorizing, collecting specimens	Animals, ecology, plants, experimenting

Emotional Intelligence

Daniel Goleman, author of the best-seller *Emotional Intelligence,* popularized the concept of emotional intelligence, which roughly corresponds to Gardner's interpersonal and intrapersonal intelligences. Goleman's five dimensions of emotional intelligence include self-awareness, self-regulation, empathy, motivation, and social skills.

Research indicates that conventional intelligence tests can account for only about 5 to 10 percent of the variability in real-life success and life adjustment. In one investigation, Dulewicz and Higgs (2000) found that emotional intelligence accounted for 36 percent of the variance in predicting successful managers, whereas traditional IQ accounted for only 27 percent.

THIRTY-EIGHT STRATEGIES FOR NURTURING EMOTIONAL INTELLIGENCE

1. Encourage students to strive for excellence, not perfection.

2. Teach reframing to help students see events from a more positive perspective.

3. Incorporate goal-setting activities in your lessons.

Traits of People with High Levels of Emotional Intelligence

Emotional self-awareness	• Distinguishes and labels one's emotions • Comprehends the causes of emotions • Discerns the difference between emotions and behaviors
Managing emotions	• Exhibits frustration tolerance and anger control • Avoids verbal put-downs, fights, and classroom misbehavior • Expresses anger appropriately, without fighting • Exhibits less self-destructive or aggressive behavior • Has positive feelings about self, school, and family • Handles stress well • Experiences less loneliness and social anxiety
Motivation: harnessing emotions productively	• Focuses on the task at hand; pays attention • Is seldom impulsive; shows self-control • Behaves responsibly
Empathy: reading emotions	• Takes another person's perspective • Displays sensitivity and empathy to others' feelings • Listens well • Conveys warmth and understanding to others
Handling relationships	• Comprehends relationships • Resolves conflicts and negotiates disagreements • Works at solving problems in relationships • Behaves assertively • Tends to be popular and outgoing • Is friendly and invests in relationships with peers • Shows kindness • Cooperates in groups • Is helpful

SOURCE: Goleman, D. (1995). Emotional intelligence. New York: Bantam.

4. Let students construct collages called Goal Posters, representing personal goals they hope to achieve.

5. Have students draw a picture of the hurdles they must clear to accomplish one of their goals.

6. Have students pick cards listing various feelings to mime, or have them charade emotions for their classmates to identify.

7. Have students rate their feelings on a scale of one to ten as a way to encourage them to think about the intensity of their emotions. They can draw a feeling thermometer to indicate the intensity of their feelings.

8. Frequently use reflection-of-feeling statements to develop empathy with your students. (For example: "You feel disappointed because you didn't make the quiz-bowl team.") Encourage students to develop a rich vocabulary for feelings, beyond *mad, glad,* and *sad.*

9. Teach students to confront their own "stinkin' thinkin'"—to identify their own negative self-talk.

10. Invite students to suggest what different characters in a story might be feeling at different points in the story.

11. Obtain pictures of people expressing a variety of emotions. Devise learning activities or displays in which students try to detect what emotion the person in the picture is expressing.

12. Help students differentiate wants from needs.

13. Encourage them to think in terms of preference rather than musts. (For example, "I would prefer to be chosen first" rather than "I must be picked first!")

14. Use puppets, stuffed animals, or other props to gain insights into students' thought patterns. These can prove especially valuable for encouraging introverted children to express themselves.

15. Encourage students to get involved in community service projects or help individuals in need.

16. Teach students to use I-statements to express emotions more responsibly and without aggressiveness.

17. Help students see that people can have different opinions on how to accomplish the same goal, without either necessarily being wrong. Debates can be a constructive way to help students analyze contrasting viewpoints.

18. Have students draw a line down the middle of a page and list the pros and cons or advantages and disadvantages of a specific issue (for example, year-round school or a requirement that students wear school uniforms).

19. Infuse the development of listening skills into your class content. For example, have students paraphrase others' comments before adding their own.

20. Structure cooperative learning activities, which provide opportunities to develop a variety of social competencies.

21. Expose students to other cultures as a part of your regular lessons. Field trips, guest speakers, films, stories, projects, and ethnic celebrations present opportunities to experience diversity.

22. Teach basic conversation skills. Teach students interviewing skills such as clarifying questions or paraphrases. Encourage students to interview adults as a part of class assignments.

23. Use brainstorming activities to encourage students to generate alternative ways of handling daily problems.

24. Have students brainstorm a variety of ways to express a particular emotion.

25. Continually remind students that "to have a failure is not to be a failure." Emphasize the value of failures and mistakes as part of the learning process. The key is to learn from our mistakes. Selectively share your own mistakes and failures with students to let them know that these are part of being human.

26. Get a peer mediation program started if your school does not already have one.

27. Encourage students to come up with several different solutions to problems discussed in class. Anticipate the consequences.

28. Teach problem-solving skills as a part of your regular content.

29. Encourage students to develop self-contracts for small goals.

30. Help students see the difference between having a feeling and acting on the feeling. Help them see that they have choices and can exercise control over their actions.

31. Teach some basic stress management techniques, such as deep breathing or progressive relaxation.

32. Help students think of large projects or goals as a series of little tasks. This makes the project seem less overwhelming.

33. Include anger-management strategies in your lesson. Devise an option for students who become too upset to cool off.

34. Strive to develop flow in your lessons.

35. Invest in a psychological bank account with your students. Build up goodwill by treating them with compassion and respect. It will pay dividends.

36. Never emphasize that there is one right emotion for any specific situation.

37. Work closely with your school counselor to develop classroom guidance activities reinforcing the components of emotional intelligence.

38. Most important, model high emotional intelligence. Actions speak louder than words.

FOR MORE INFORMATION

Bar-On, R., Maree, J. G., & Elias, M. J. (Eds.). (2007). *Educating people to be emotionally intelligent.* Westport, CT: Praeger.

Emmerling, R. J., Shanwal, V. K., & Mandal, M. K. (Eds.). (2008). *Emotional intelligence: Theoretical and cultural perspectives.* New York: Nova Science Publishers.

Lantieri, L., & Goleman, D. (2008). *Building emotional intelligence: Techniques to cultivate inner strength in children.* Boulder, CO: Sounds True.

Matthews, G., Zeidner, M., & Roberts, R. D. (Eds.). (2007). *The science of emotional intelligence: Knowns and unknowns.* New York: Oxford University Press.

Trout, J. D, (2009). *The empathy gap: Building bridges to the good life and the good society.* Princeton, NJ: Princeton University Press.

> *Helping people better manage their upsetting feelings—anger, anxiety, depression, pessimism, and loneliness—is a form of disease prevention.*
>
> —**Daniel Goleman,**
> ***Emotional Intelligence***

Preferred Learning Modalities

Research suggests that people learn through their senses and perceptions. Not only does perception supply much of what we remember, but it also anchors events in our memory to a particular place and time. Though virtually everyone applies all the senses in learning, most individuals learn best through a particular sensory or perceptual channel—kinesthetic, tactile, auditory, or visual. That is, most people prefer to learn through their sense of touch and feeling, their sense of hearing, or their sense of sight. Their learning style, or modality, is the channel through which they best receive and retain information.

Every classroom likely contains a mixture of preferences—students who are kinesthetic or tactile learners, auditory learners, and visual learners. Research indicates that visual learners make up 65 percent of the population. Approximately 30 percent are auditory learners, leaving about 5 percent as kinesthetic or tactile learners. Research suggests that most teachers rely almost totally on print and aural modes of presentation.

Sensory preferences are developmental, with younger children being more kinesthetic and tactile. Typically, during the sixth grade, girls become more perceptually mature in the auditory channel, with boys following shortly. At about the eighth grade, girls usually develop greater visual-perceptual acuity, with boys catching up a year or two later.

Visual learners tend to process information through what they see, to think in pictures, and to have fertile imaginations. Auditory learners deal with information through what they hear. They tend to enjoy listening and like to talk things through. Kinesthetic learners manage information by doing, touching, and experiencing. Hyperactive students, 95 percent of whom are male, may have an extremely high kinesthetic preference.

Research suggests that matching teaching style with students' learning styles may increase student motivation and improve performance. The research also indicates that teachers almost always teach in their own preferred learning style. Visual teachers generally rely on visual techniques; auditory teachers depend on oral and listening techniques; and kinesthetic or tactile teachers tend to prefer Montessori methods.

Learning-style researcher Rita Dunn suggested that not every student need be assessed for learning style, only those who are having difficulty learning. Teachers accommodate different sensory modality needs by designing multisensory instruction. Because most children are able to learn through all sensory channels, teaching them through all modalities will help them attain optimal learning; what they don't learn from their preferred modality, they may attain from another. Teaching with varied multisensory techniques helps increase achievement of slow learners who had not progressed with conventional strategies.

TEACHING TO STUDENTS' STRENGTHS: HOMEWORK THAT HELPS

Homework, like any other instructional technique, is only a means to an end. Its value is determined by how effectively it enhances learning. If it does not, it is busywork and serves little constructive purpose. Many critics argue that too little homework is assigned and that learning time can be increased cheaply by requiring more homework. A recent national study emphasized that more than two-thirds of seventeen-year-olds reported spending less than one hour a night on homework. It is not surprising that the same study revealed that higher-achieving students spent more time per week on homework than their classmates and that hours of television viewing and time spent on homework were inversely related.

How much homework you should assign is a complex question. The answer depends on your students' age, abilities, and habits, as well as your instructional objectives. It is probably reasonable to expect students to spend an hour per day on homework by the end of elementary school. High school students who have study halls should be able to complete two or three hours of work per day out of class.

Attributes Signifying Modality Preferences

Auditory	Visual	Kinesthetic or Tactile
Likes music	Doodles	Likes handling objects
Enjoys talking	Notices details	Gestures while talking
Long, repetitive descriptions	Verbal directions often difficult	Often in motion
Distracted by noise	Enjoys drawing	Tapping feet or hands
Sings	Vivid imagination	May be fidgety
Talks to self	Solves problems deliberately	Likes to try things out
	Tends to be quiet	Jumping, pushing
	Distracted by movement	Often seems impulsive
	Remembers faces but forgets names	May be a poor speller

Helpful Instructional Strategies for Learning Modalities

Auditory	Visual	Kinesthetic or Tactile
Discussions	Drawing	Manipulatives
Debates	Note taking	Building models
Oral presentations	Watching videos	Hands-on activities
Listening to lectures	Guided imagery	Field trips
Listening to music	Demonstrations	Drama, role playing
Reciting content aloud	Computer instruction	Allowing to stretch or stand
Studying with peers	Color coding	Making flash cards
Reading aloud	Mind maps	Labs
Talking problems through	Time lines, flowcharts	Walk-and-talk activities
Verbal mnemonics	Visual mnemonics	Stories with lots of action
Verbal analogies, metaphors	Use written directions	Interviewing
Reading dialogue and plays	Use pictures, diagrams, maps, and charts	Puppetry
Musical concerts	Flash cards	Writing at the board
Brainstorming	Highlight text with colors	Action games
Verbal directions	Independent learning	Sculpture
	Visual displays	Workbooks
	Transparencies	

When students have several teachers, some coordination is needed among the faculty on the homework schedule. Otherwise, some students may end up with five or six hours of homework in an evening, an unreasonable amount. Students, like teachers, need some rest and recreation.

Merely assigning more homework will not guarantee learning gains. Assignments that are not completed or are done incorrectly are of little benefit. Like seatwork, homework assignments that are too difficult or misunderstood will prove counterproductive.

Activities such as reading the text usually can be done out of class, preserving class time for activities that students cannot do independently. Homework provides a valuable opportunity to practice and reinforce new skills. It also provides an opportunity to connect new knowledge and skills with the outside world. Homework also serves an assessment function, providing the teacher with information on the success of his or her teaching.

Homework can be assigned to provide remedial instruction to students who lag in skill development. When the purpose of homework is to provide remediation, giving a blanket assignment to all students is hardly justified, as students progress at different rates. Assigning homework provides the golden opportunity for individualization, although it does require advance planning.

Although reading assignments, short essay answers, and drill problems make up the bulk of homework assignments, long-range projects seem to be of greater benefit. Such projects encourage students to use higher-level cognitive skills in gathering information, analyzing data, planning sequences, and synthesizing a variety of skills. Another valuable function of homework is to allow parents an active role in their child's education.

Do not use homework as a punishment. That practice only communicates to students that homework is an unpleasant activity, something to avoid. Such negative attitudes will not benefit either the teacher or the students. The first week of school, teachers must establish a fair and consistent homework policy.

Interesting Homework

Used effectively, homework reinforces practice and synthesis of skills and concepts developed in class. When asked by his father whether he had any homework, a boy replied, "No, the teachers ran out of toner." This anecdote reveals that many teachers lack imagination in assigning homework.

Professional journals, in-service programs, and other teachers are sources for gathering ideas on worthwhile homework assignments. A bit of imagination and planning can yield high-interest assignments and help develop students' skills. Here are a few ideas that other teachers have tried successfully.

- Write a new myth.
- Conduct experiments.
- Do volunteer work.
- Use math skills to measure common objects around the home.
- Plan a trip; include itinerary and costs.
- Develop a budget.
- Write a computer program.
- Observe and record birds, traffic, or weather.
- Plan a week's balanced menu.
- Trace family trees to personalize history.
- Interview an older person about a historical event he or she experienced.
- Plan and produce a film or skit.
- Write new endings to old stories.
- Teach someone a skill.
- Keep a journal.
- Invent a game; teach it to the class.
- Write a handbook for consumers.
- Construct a Web page.
- Research a topic and create a bulletin board display.

- Interview people about their jobs.
- Develop a creative solution to a problem.
- Develop an advertising campaign to promote a product, solution, or idea.
- Attend a public meeting.
- Design an ideal house, car, school, or government.
- Take sides on an issue; prepare a debate.
- Design a costume.
- Draw a map of the neighborhood or yard.
- Develop a case study.
- Prepare a photo essay on a community problem.
- Collect specimens of rocks, leaves, and wood.
- Draw a political cartoon.
- Participate in a political campaign.

Such "fun with a purpose" assignments can greatly increase students' motivation to learn. The relevance of the skills you are teaching becomes apparent. They must not only be fun but also have a legitimate educational purpose to justify their use.

Making Assignments

The first week of school, clarify your expectations regarding homework. Will work that students do not finish in class automatically become homework? If you do not make a specific assignment for the next class, will you expect students to read in their textbooks or review previous work? The procedures for assigning homework must be taught as part of the classroom routine. Here are some practical suggestions for effectively making homework assignments:

- Do not compete with student noise when giving oral directions. Stop talking and wait for their attention. Otherwise, you will end up repeating the directions.

- Save time and stress by putting directions for assignments on the board. If you prefer, cover them with a map until you are ready to discuss them. Some teachers instruct students to immediately take their seats and copy the assignments into their notebooks, without waiting for the bell to ring. Many teachers choose to put all assignments on handouts for distribution. This minimizes later student remarks such as "I didn't hear you" or "I didn't know you wanted it done that way." Be sure to write clearly. Save the master copy for use next year. If any problems of understanding arise in completing the assignment, make a note on the master to refine the directions next year. Avoid shouting the next day's assignment over students gathering books as they scramble for the door.

- Students are more likely to complete homework assignments that are highly structured and have very specific directions. In assigning major projects, displaying completed sample projects will clarify your expectations and save time answering questions. Some teachers take pictures or slides of completed products for next year's demonstration.

- Set up a homework center on your class Web page. Parents and students can access this site. Add supplemental materials to assist students who need additional practice.

- It may be helpful to reserve specific days for regular assignments. For example, on Tuesdays students are to read the next chapter in the text; Thursdays they review the drill questions at the end of the chapter. You will have fewer assignments to plan every week, and students will be less likely to forget what their assignment is.

- Try to be creative in designing some homework tasks that will be fun as well as educationally sound. Experiments, interviews, math games, and active assignments tend to have a higher completion rate. One technique for creating suspense in the next day's lesson is to give students an unusual assignment but not explain its purpose. For example, ask them to count the number of light bulbs in their house or to bring in the next day an empty egg carton or a baby picture. Of course, that activity must be incorporated into the next day's lesson.

- Early in the year, communicate with your students' parents what role you wish them to play in helping with their child's homework. This can be done in a newsletter and again at any open houses scheduled. Some teachers send a special sheet home to parents, titled "How to Help Your Child with Homework." Add the same information to your online homework center, if available.

The Internet and Homework

Many teachers now post their homework assignments on their school or class Web sites. Parents can pull up the site to check whether their children have homework that day. This technology also provides a valuable communication tool for improving teacher-parent relationships, encouraging parents to take an active role in the learning process. It is a good idea to post your homework policy on the Web site as well. Seeing the assignment on a Web page, forgetful students can download directions and worksheets from home.

A few schools have begun to experiment with using personal digital assistants (PDAs) and wireless technology as learning tools. Teachers can download homework assignments and accompanying worksheets onto every student's PDA.

Collecting and Grading Homework

Students must receive feedback on their homework for it to enhance learning. Not every homework assignment must be collected and graded. Use a variety of techniques to help students check their own or each other's assignments.

Create homework teams with one student in each team responsible for collecting everyone's work and reporting to the teacher who did not complete their assignments. On some days simply circulating the room with a clipboard and checking off that students have completed the day's assignment may be sufficient.

Some teachers give each student a "no homework" pass at the beginning of each term. A student may redeem it once when he or she does not complete a homework assignment. One option would be to allow students to turn in any unused passes at the end of the term for bonus credit.

The Homework Lottery

One strategy that teachers at all grade levels use successfully for motivating students to complete homework assignments is the lottery. The idea is relatively simple and easy to implement, yet it can encourage otherwise apathetic students to complete their work. All students who successfully complete their homework for the day put their names on small cards that they drop in a jar or box. On Friday the class holds a drawing, selecting one or more winners.

What the winners receive is quite secondary. Just the recognition of having their names drawn is rewarding for most students. Most will value a privilege, such as being first in line all week or using the DVD player or computer. Some teachers become proficient at scrounging for freebies such as tickets, posters, coupons, and prizes. Students soon learn that the more times their names are in the jar, the greater are their chances of winning. Of course, you must ensure that the only way to get their names in the jar is to complete their homework. It may be wise to specify a criterion of correctness for work submitted if students begin handing in hurriedly completed assignments.

One prize that students value is a pass good for one night of no homework. Instead of handing in homework, the holder may redeem the coupon. If the student did the assignments necessary to win the coupon, one night of missed work will not likely be irreparable.

Handling Makeup Work

Whenever possible, put directions for assignments, projects, or homework in writing, being as explicit in your directions as possible. You might also notify parents that this is the practice. This avoids possible misunderstandings as well as saving you time in giving directions to absent students. Be sure to save a copy for next year.

Every teacher faces the challenge of getting students who were absent to make up missed assignments.

Over the course of the year, this task can consume huge amounts of time that might better be allocated to other duties. The first week of school, clarify the procedures you expect students to follow for making up missed assignments after an absence. There is no one right routine for accomplishing this. The most successful approach will depend on your students' ages and maturity levels. Here are some ideas that veteran teachers have found helpful in dealing with this problem:

- For each subject or class you teach, attach a clipboard to the wall. Each day hang copies of the next day's assignments on the clipboard. Absent students (or students who lose their copy) can pick up the assignment as needed.

- For projects in which students are to create a product (for example, drawing, model, report), first demonstrate what is to be done, then post directions along with a sample. Save some of the best projects to use next year as models. This helps clarify your expectations and gives students an idea of what level of work you expect.

- At the beginning of the year, assign each student a partner. Have them exchange phone numbers. If one partner is absent, the other is responsible for gathering assignments, handouts, or materials and helping the partner catch up when he or she returns. Ninety percent of your students will successfully handle this. You may still have to help the other 10 percent get caught up, but this saves you a huge amount of time dealing with the others.

- Make a large calendar with numbers one to thirty-one for the days of the month. Laminate it so it can be reused. Each day write the day's assignments. Absent students can check missed assignments quickly.

- Audiotape your directions as you give them to the class. Pencil the day's date and class on the tape and file it in a box. Students who are absent that day listen to the taped directions when they return. Have a tape recorder available in a set location.

- If makeup work involves handouts, put the date and the student's name on them. Then, on a designated spot on the bulletin board, tack the handouts and any assignment for each student absent that day.

- Develop a homework form to record the exact assignments for absent students. The student's partner or another responsible student should fill out the form with the missing assignments.

- Keep a homework notebook. Have a separate section for each class. Each day record what work was done in class and any homework assignment with any special directions. Also include copies of any handouts needed. When students return after being absent, they are responsible for checking the homework notebook.

- Tape five small cardboard boxes together to make a large mailbox with five compartments. Label the dividers with the days of the school week. As you give out each day's assignment, place any leftover photocopies into that day's slot. When students return from being absent, they are responsible for gathering the necessary materials from the mailbox.

Degree of Effort and Challenge

Percentage responding "yes" in a representative sample of American teenagers:

It is important to me that I do my best in all my classes.	72 percent
The amount of work I do in school now is important to my success later in life.	66 percent
I try to take the most difficult and challenging courses I can.	51 percent
Doing homework is a priority for me. I complete it before participating in other activities.	43 percent

Source: Horatio Alger Association. *The State of Our Nation's Youth 2001–2002.* Alexandria, VA: Horatio Alger Association of Distinguished Americans, 2001.

PUTTING MORE PIZZAZZ IN YOUR PRESENTATIONS

Making presentations is an inescapable part of the teaching profession: class lectures, in-service workshops, parent open houses, faculty reports, board of education updates, and community service organization speeches. The person who can give a lively, interesting, stand-up presentation is in demand.

Although lecturing is only one tool in your instructional kit, teacher talk is a vital part of any classroom. Even those who employ a workshop approach must clarify, give directions, help process experiences, and share information. Great speakers are not born but made—through practice, reflection, feedback, and effort. Remember that the great Greek orator Demosthenes began with a speech impediment yet strove to become a competent public speaker. Many actors and politicians overcame shyness to confidently address hundreds. With determination, you can become a better public speaker. Here are a few suggestions to help.

Voice

- Record yourself teaching a variety of different kinds of lessons. Try to listen to yourself as objectively as possible. Is your voice soft, drowned out by background noises? Is the pitch reasonably pleasing? Note the speed at which you speak. Is the pace so fast that words jumble together? Do you occasionally mumble? Do you fill gaps with *OK* or *you know*? Do you clip the end of some words (for example, *goin'* for *going*)? Is there a nasal quality to your voice?

- Vary the pace and pitch of your presentation voice to avoid slipping into a monotone. A current mannerism of many young people is to continually raise the pitch at the end of each sentence, making them all sound like questions. This can be most distracting and makes the speaker sound very unsure of what he or she is saying. Equally distracting is dropping the volume at the end of each sentence.

- Be aware of the messages you send simply with your voice, independent of the content you are uttering. Your speaking style may communicate confidence, passion, excitement, enthusiasm, and joy; or it may convey boredom, self-doubt, or fatigue. Always remember that your students will echo your emotional tone.

- Is your throat sore at the end of the day? This is not uncommon among teachers the first couple of weeks of school, but if it persists it may be a sign that you are using your voice mechanism improperly. Consult with a speech therapist for training in more effective and less harmful use of your voice.

- When talking in front of the class, always project your voice as though you were talking to the person in the remotest corner of the room. However, speaking too loudly is also unpleasant for your listeners. Some variation in your voice level is most effective.

- Use pauses for impact. Slight pauses refocus students' attention. Do avoid fillers, such as *um, uh,* and *er.*

Nonverbal Communication

All teachers should be students of effective nonverbal communication. A rich understanding of the nonverbal level of expression will allow you to more accurately read students' messages, to remain congruent and accurate in the messages you send, and to avoid negative or incongruent messages you might inadvertently send to others. You are continually expressing nonverbal messages to everyone around you. Indeed, research suggests that the overwhelming portion of what you communicate is expressed nonverbally, not verbally. Here are a few tips on using nonverbal communication more effectively in teaching.

- Avoid leaning against the lectern or grasping it with a death grip. As much as possible, move away from the lectern. It is generally best to keep moving while providing whole-class instruction, such as lecturing. Not only does that allow you to monitor student behavior better, but you are also more likely to be animated while moving than when remaining stationary.

- Teaching the whole class while seated at your desk encourages you to speak in a monotone with subdued gestures, two traits that convey a lack of enthusiasm. Move about the room, but don't zip around like a gazelle. You'll wear your students out trying to follow you.

- Be aware of using the same gestures repeatedly. Students may begin to mimic such nonverbal tics.

- Strive to achieve a relaxed, natural posture while talking. Too many as well as too few gestures tend to inhibit your message.

- Talk facing your class; avoid talking to the chalkboard or the screen. Not only is it an ineffective speaking style, but you will also be less able to monitor your students' behavior with your back to them.

- Although there are cultural differences among different ethnic groups, generally it is best to offer eye contact with your audience. Eye contact conveys that you are interested in the listener. Keep your eyes moving around the classroom, holding your gaze on clusters of four or five students at a time for three to five seconds before moving to the next group. From ten feet away, this provides the illusion of individual eye contact, even though you aren't maintaining direct eye contact with any one of the students in the cluster. This is not a natural practice; doing it in a natural way takes concerted effort.

- When calling on a student, avoid pointing. Rather, gesture with your palm up, a more inviting message.

- As much as possible, try to talk with individual students at their eye level. Stoop when helping them, rather than looking down on them. This is especially helpful with small children.

- Many see a smile as a visual hug; it conveys warmth and acceptance. The smile is likely your most powerful social reinforcer. Remember, a genuine smile is conveyed as much with the eyes as with the mouth. Practice in front of the mirror to achieve the twinkle in the eyes.

- Occasionally videotape a class. Turn the volume down and just observe your nonverbal behavior. Do you like what you see? Are you directing eye contact equally around the room or only teaching to the students in the front center? Do you look animated or bored? Do you project confidence and enthusiasm through your nonverbal expressions? Do you look relaxed or stiff? Do you exhibit nervous gestures, such as rattling coins in your pocket, biting your lip, rubbing your nose, twirling your hair, stroking your beard, popping the top on your Magic Marker, or playing with your watch or jewelry? These can be very distracting mannerisms. Chances are you have one or more such habits of which you are unaware. That is why videotaping is essential. The camera does not lie. Although you may be unaware of your idiosyncratic gestures, your students aren't. And likely they will begin to joke about them among themselves. One of students' favorite pastimes is mimicking their teachers' quirks. Don't make it too easy for them!

Improving Your Speaking Effectiveness

- Teach to a variety of sensory modalities. Employ interesting visuals to augment your lecture. Props add interest and give a visual anchor to your oral presentation.

- Use vocabulary that all students can understand. Though you may want to introduce new vocabulary as part of your lessons, be sure you define unfamiliar terms. Your goal is to help them understand, not impress them with your expansive vocabulary. Simple, direct language usually will be easier to follow.

- Consider joining Toastmasters International, which teaches public speaking in almost every community. It is an excellent way to improve your speaking style. Toastmasters provides outstanding training programs and valuable practice with a supportive audience.

- If you are not sure of the pronunciation of a new word you are introducing in your lesson, look it up in the dictionary before class. Remember, you are serving as a model; and your students may copy your mistakes.

- Don't let your dress upstage your message. Though wild, flashy costumes may express who you are, your students may be paying more attention to your fashion statement than the content you are trying to teach.

HUMOR IN THE CLASSROOM

Mary Pettibone Poole's observation that "He who laughs, lasts" is probably nowhere more true than in teaching. A moderate touch of humor can nurture an inviting class climate. Bob Hope suggested that humor serves as a welcome mat between speakers and their audiences. It is a powerful tool that can break the ice and get the listener on your side. Humor recaptures students' attention and anchors their memory, improving achievement. One classic study found students to be more creative after listening to a humorous recording. Humor can defuse tense situations, combat resistance, and reduce stress in the classroom. It provides comic relief from the serious, sometimes tedious, business of learning. Humor tends to make any experience more fun and brings a group closer together.

Laughter has been called internal jogging. It's good for the soul, the mind, and the body. As John Kennedy and Abraham Lincoln so capably demonstrated, we can be quite serious about our subject yet still infuse it with humor.

The cardinal rule for using humor in the classroom is that it must never be used to harm, humiliate, ridicule, or otherwise make fun of students. Cruel, sarcastic humor is totally inappropriate and must not be tolerated. Likewise, humor that is sexual or involves ethnic or gender slurs is taboo. If you have a doubt as to whether an anecdote, quip, or joke is appropriate, don't use it in school. The safest target of humor is you. Make a self-disparaging remark about your handwriting or stick figures drawn on the board.

Humor can be spontaneous or planned. Some people have a natural gift for finding humor in the everyday ironies and foibles in their world. Just in the normal course of daily classroom interactions, amusing predicaments will emerge on their own. A smile or chuckle on our part communicates that we are also human and can enjoy a good laugh, granting permission to our students to do the same. Good-natured kidding and puns can be forms of spontaneous humor. If you are not spontaneously witty, plan your humor by looking for cartoons, anecdotes, and quotations that you find amusing and can share with your students.

Your humorous quips or observations need not evoke knee-slapping, rip-snorting belly laughs. Lighthearted humor that brings a twinkle to the eye, a smile to the face, or a groan or chuckle serves its purpose. You're not running a comedy shop. You don't have to be hilarious to weave humor into your class presentations.

Tips on Using Humor in Your Classroom

> There is little success where there is little laughter.
>
> **—Andrew Carnegie**

- Props, such as costumes, hats, masks, or unusual objects, can inject some levity into otherwise very serious subjects. Many teachers collect unusual pencils and pens. Accumulate inexpensive toys and puzzles with which students can spend a few minutes playing before class or during breaks.

- Use odd or funny noisemakers to signal the class to be quiet and give you their attention.

- Some teachers convey their sense of humor through their dress and accessories. Colorful, funny ties, scarves, sweaters, socks, and watches are widely available.

- Successful teachers develop a repertoire of stories and anecdotes illustrating various aspects of the subjects they teach. Some of the tales may be naturally amusing or can be made so with a bit of exaggeration, animated gestures, or surprising twists. Begin by drawing on funny things that have happened to you.

- Most people who believe they are not funny argue, "I can't tell a joke. I never remember the punch line." If so, then don't try to tell jokes in class (or if you do, overrehearse it until it flows naturally). Jokes are probably overrated as a source of humor; they are the most difficult form to use successfully. Even a teacher who is a good joke teller should not overuse the technique. If you do tell a joke, make sure it is pertinent to the topic you are teaching. If it bombs, you've at least made an academic point.

- If a joke bombs, don't try to explain the punch line. Better to use a self-disparaging comment: "That's why I keep the day job," or "I told my writers that wouldn't work."

- In most classes you'll have at least one student who will be spontaneously, genuinely witty. Sometimes all you have to do is play straight man to the amateur comedian. Such a person often enjoys the attention, so take care not to let it become disruptive or excessive.

- An easy source of humor is the comic section of the newspaper. Read it every day with an eye toward cartoons that illustrate some point related to your curriculum. Comic strips that frequently feature school- and child-related topics include *Peanuts, Sally Forth, For Better or for Worse, Dennis the Menace,* and *Family Circus.* Gary Larson's *Far Side* cartoons are rich with off-the-wall quips students love; his past cartoons are still available in books. Educational journals such as *Phi Delta Kappan* and the *Chronicle of Higher Education* include cartoons related to various aspects of education. Clip these and make them into transparencies. It helps to enlarge them and add color with markers. Post some cartoons on the door, use others on tests or handouts, or post some on the bulletin board. If you are going to reproduce a cartoon for instructional use, most cartoonists will freely grant you permission. Call the local newspaper for their addresses.

- Quotations and proverbs are another planned source of humor. You don't have to be funny, just recognize what people find amusing. Chances are that if a quotation makes you laugh, it will also make your students laugh. Periodicals such as *Reader's Digest* are good sources for quotations. Invite students to be on the lookout for ones they find funny and relevant to your subject. You might even designate a section of a bulletin board where they might post humorous clippings. Specify that they must make some point relevant to your course.

> *Laughter is the shortest distance between two people.*
>
> **—Victor Borge**

- Construct your own variation of David Letterman's top-ten lists or allow your students to brainstorm their own lists. Do remind them to stay within the bounds of good taste.

- When a lesson isn't going well, carry on a monologue with yourself in a stage whisper. Some teachers pick up a puppet, stuffed animal, or other object and begin talking to it. Pull out a picture of the person you are studying and have a chat. Or talk to the class goldfish or hamster. You can ask it questions and then answer them yourself. Personification, treating objects as though they were people, can be funny. Give your chalkboard eraser a name and talk to it. Students will chuckle. They may lock you up, but they will chuckle.

- When several unexpected events disrupt your class, react with humor rather than stress. "Well, it went better in rehearsal."

- Suddenly shifting to an accent for emphasis gets attention. Or have students try doing a routine task in a different accent than normally expected (such as reading Shakespeare or Poe in an exaggerated Southern drawl or Bronx accent).

- Intentionally slaughtering a foreign phrase (*mercy bow-cup* for *merci beaucoup*) can be amusing. Of course, the students need to be familiar with the phrase to recognize what you have done. It isn't essential that everyone catches it, and don't pause to wait for a laugh.

- Insert a touch of humor into your tests, perhaps by using the name of your principal (in a tasteful way), a local celebrity, a rival school, or alluding to a current school event.

- Find a humorous poem or song to celebrate a special occasion or holiday. Teach it to the class.

- Check bookstores and educational supply catalogues for humorous posters. Draw your own if you are artistic.

- A humorous song related to the topic being studied can grab students' attention and inject a touch of levity. This can be a good way to open a challenging or controversial subject.

- Cultivate inside jokes within your class. Some funny things just happen, without planning. They can become part of the class lore, which can be referred to from time to time throughout the year.

- Create a comedy file. Save in a folder or a notebook items that you might use later in your class. Include news items, cartoons, anecdotes, jokes, and quotations. As your file expands, you might categorize your items by topic.

- Discover your own humor style. Rather than forcing some brand of humor that is unnatural, experiment and rely on the kinds of humor that you already enjoy and use.

- Observe your students to see what works. Listen to them talking among themselves to discover what they think is funny.

- Become a student of humor. Read the daily comics, watch funny movies, read humorous books, go to comedy clubs, watch the good (though rare) situation comedies on television.

- One last piece of advice: don't try too hard. With experience, you'll discover what kind of humor works and how much helps but does not hinder.

For More Information
BOOKS AND ARTICLES

Hellman, S. V. (2007). Humor in the classroom: Stu's seven simple steps to success. *College Teaching, 55*(1), 37–39.

Minchew, S. S., & Hopper, F. (2008). Techniques for using humor and fun in the language arts classroom. *Clearing House: A Journal of Educational Strategies, Issues and Ideas, 81*(5), 232–236.

Reeves, A. (2007). *Cartoon corner: Humor-based mathematics activities: A collection adapted from "Cartoon Corner" in mathematics teaching in the middle school.* Reston, VA: National Council of Teachers of Mathematics.

Rightmyer, J. (2008). *A funny thing about teaching: Connecting with kids through laughter . . . and other pointers for new teachers.* Fort Collins, CO: Cottonwood Press.

INTERNET RESOURCES

The Lighter Side of Teaching

teachers.net/gazette/APR08/humor/

Reach Every Child—fun stuff for teaching

www.reacheverychild.com/feature/humor.html

The Humor Project—array of humor-related materials

www.humorproject.com

HUMOR RESOURCES & SUPPLIES

Archie McPhee—fun and funny novelties

www.mcphee.com/

Clown Supplies, Inc.—magic and clown supplies

www.clownsupplies.com/

Humor Mall—jokes, humor tips, comedy tips

www.HumorMall.com/

> My way of joking is telling the truth. That is the funniest joke in the world.
>
> —**George Bernard Shaw**

SEEKING STUDENT FEEDBACK

Listening to your students' views will help develop an inviting classroom. The following open-ended statements can be used to stimulate feedback on how your students see the classroom's day-to-day operation. Students can occasionally anonymously write their responses to one or more of these sentence stems. They are also useful to stimulate discussion during class meetings.

- I like this class because . . .
- I would like this class better if . . .
- In this class I wish we spent more time . . .
- I like it when the teacher . . .
- The most interesting part of this class is . . .
- I feel special when the teacher . . .
- One thing I feel proud about in our school is . . .
- I would like our class to improve . . .
- When I enter our classroom I usually feel . . .
- When I leave our classroom I usually feel . . .
- I am most bored when . . .

- My favorite part of school is . . .
- I feel left out when . . .
- My favorite activity in class is . . .
- This class is most fun when . . .
- I feel challenged when . . .
- I don't like it when other students . . .
- I think I could learn better if . . .
- One thing I would like to achieve in this class is . . .
- I would like to have more choice in . . .
- I believe our teacher wants us to . . .
- I think the teacher most values me when . . .
- Every day I look forward to . . .
- I become discouraged when . . .
- One thing in our class I would like to see changed is . . .
- I wish we spent less time . . .
- The best teachers seem to . . .
- When I must be corrected by the teacher, I would prefer . . .

GUIDELINES FOR FAIR USE OF COPYRIGHTED EDUCATIONAL MATERIALS

Federal statute guarantees copyright protections of one's creative products. A fair use policy was established to specify conditions under which teachers and others can legally use copyrighted materials without first seeking permission of the copyright holder.

The guidelines are somewhat complex and have evolved from both law and judicial rulings. The law providing for fair use is guided by four basic assumptions:

1. The purpose and character of the use: nonprofit, educational uses are given more leeway than commercial uses. The principle of fair use permits more protection when the purpose is for criticism, research, comment, teaching, or news reporting.

2. The nature of the copyrighted work: for example, the courts have been more accepting of fair use of nonfiction than fiction.

3. The amount and substantiality of the portion used in relation to the copyrighted work as a whole: this is a murky area, for it is not an absolute guarantee of protection. Copying only a small portion of a work may still be seen as a violation if that tiny portion captures the heart of the creative work.

4. The effect of the use on the potential market for or value of the copyrighted work: How much harm is the copying likely to do to the copyright holder?

The guidelines for fair use are not always clear and absolute. From copyright laws and court interpretations, the following guidelines are generally accepted as defining the boundaries of fair use of copyrighted material:

- Teachers may copy one chapter from a book, provided the material copied does not exceed one thousand words or 10 percent of the total book.

- A single copy of a story or article, not to exceed twenty-five hundred words, from an encyclopedia or anthology may be copied.

- A poem no longer than 250 words may be copied.

- A single article from a periodical may be copied.

- One cartoon, photograph, or chart may be copied from a book.

- Copying a copyrighted computer program without permission is illegal.

- Video recordings of television programs may be recorded and shown to students. Programs from noneducational television channels may be shown to students twice within ten days of the original broadcast. Teachers are permitted to keep such recordings for up to forty-five days for evaluation purposes. Video recordings from educational channels may be used for seven days only.

- Such copying must be done on the spur of the moment at the teacher's initiative. The intent of the fair use policy is to permit limited use of instructional items for which there is not time to request permission from the copyright holder.

- The same item may not be repeatedly copied year after year.

- Students may not be charged for the costs of copying the item(s).

- Only one item by the same author may be legitimately copied.

- Only nine individual items may be copied per semester or term.

- Consumable items, such as workbooks or standardized tests, may not be copied.

Public Domain

Items not protected by copyright are considered to be in the public domain. Anyone is free to use such items without permission. Works that were never copyrighted or for which the copyright has expired will generally fall under public domain. Facts, ideas, slogans, and titles cannot be copyrighted. Government documents generally are not copyrighted, unless an independent contractor authored the item and may still hold the copyright.

Generally, items published before 1922 are in the public domain. For a list of songs now in the public domain, check the Public Domain Info Web site at www.pdinfo.com/.

Seeking Permission to Use Copyrighted Material

In soliciting permission to copy items, it is essential to contact the actual copyright holder, which may not necessarily be the author. Most periodicals include information on how to request such permission. For book publishers or other sources, start with their Web site to identify the appropriate contact information. A reference librarian can be very helpful for locating names and addresses.

The safest practice is to get permission from the copyright owner before using copyrighted materials.

Protecting Your Creative Works

Add the following copyright notice on all items you create and want to protect:

> Copyright © 2009 (your name)
>
> All Rights Reserved

It is probably wise to insert this copyright notice on any Web pages you design, as well as your original worksheets, study guides, stories, poems, or other creative works. Technically, copyright protection is provided immediately and automatically when you add the copyright notice to your creative work. However, by registering your work with the U.S. Copyright Office, you gain the right to sue in case of copyright infringement. The current fee for registering a copyright is $35 for a single document. You can download the necessary forms from the U.S. Copyright Office at www.copyright.gov/.

Note: Remember that many of the sample templates, letters, handouts for this chapter are available for download from the *Classroom Teacher's Survival Guide* Web site josseybass.com/go/classroomteacher.

Sample Letter Requesting Permission to Copy

Rebecca Cabaniss
Chenoa High School
1330 Hazel Avenue
Bowling Green, OH 43402

October 22, 2009

Permissions Department
Popular Culture Magazine
60 Beaumont Drive
San Francisco, CA 94103

Greetings,

    I teach U.S. History at Chenoa High School. I am requesting permission to photocopy and distribute to my classes the article titled "Fads and Fancies of the 1920s" by Charley Rogers. The article appeared on pages 40–43 in the April 2004 issue of your magazine. I have approximately sixty students in my classes each year. This article would provide valuable supplemental information for my class and would likely prove valuable in capturing my students' interest.

    If permission is granted, please sign below and return this letter to me in the enclosed self-addressed stamped envelope. Thank you.

Sincerely,

Rebecca Cabaniss

....

Permission is granted to Rebecca Cabaniss to copy and distribute the above article for use in her U.S. history class.

_____   _____
Date   Signature

Storyboarding Form

Project _____ Sheet no. _____

Assignment Log

Assignment	Date Due	Grade	Comments

Homework Pass

Good for one
homework assignment.

_____
Student's signature

Homework Pass

Good for one
homework assignment.

_____
Student's signature

Homework Pass

Good for one
homework assignment.

_____
Student's signature

Interactive Teaching and Learning Strategies

5

Because most teachers were taught primarily by lecture, their natural choice for a favored mode of instruction is to be the proverbial talking head in front of the class. Despite a growing body of research demonstrating lecture's limitations as the primary instructional strategy, many persist in the practice. Drooping heads and whiplash are pervasive in these classrooms as students struggle to stay awake. Although lecture can be useful in certain situations, many other more valuable teaching tools are available. The most outstanding teachers have a variety of instructional techniques in their repertoire.

QUESTION AND ANSWER

Questions are a most valuable instructional skill when used skillfully. The question-and-answer method can be a powerful instructional tool. Most commonly, teachers ask questions and students answer. The Socratic method of stimulating creative or critical thinking in students through skillful questioning can be especially valuable. On a lower level, it may take the form of rote drill, with the teacher firing a barrage of questions around the room and soliciting answers. This form of question and answer is most effective when the content is fairly concrete. See the following section on questions for tips on the effective use of teacher questions.

The question-and-answer method may also consist of students asking the teacher questions. The least effective method of doing this is to simply ask, "Are there any questions?" especially at the very end of the class period. Most students are hesitant to openly ask questions in front of the whole class, even if they have some in mind. One useful technique is to have each student jot down one question about the topic on a sheet of paper. Then you might collect them and respond to a few. Another possibility is to have small groups generate a list of two to five questions to submit. Rather than answering these questions, direct some of them back to the class, to consider either in a whole-group discussion or in small groups.

In facilitating question-and-answer sessions, try to stand across the room from the student speaking. This forces the student to speak in a louder voice, allowing everyone else to hear him or her. This will require you to keep moving during the discussion but will pay off in better interaction. As you call on students, you might nonchalantly pace toward the opposite side of the room. A secondary benefit of maximizing your distance from the student speaking is that it broadens your range of vision, allowing you to better monitor the rest of the class.

TWENTY-TWO HOT TIPS FOR ASKING EFFECTIVE QUESTIONS

A substantial body of research affirms that questions are still the most frequently used teaching tool. However, not all questions are created equally. Some are highly effective; others can be useless or even harmful. There is an art and a science to effective questioning. Here are twenty-two tips gleaned from outstanding teachers and research for improving teachers' use of questions:

> The important thing is not to stop questioning.
>
> —**Albert Einstein**

1. As part of lesson planning, list the process questions to ask. Effectively worded questions can make a good lesson superb. Develop a logical sequence and strive for clarity in your questions.

2. Challenge the whole class to mentally respond. When you ask a question, pause and then select the person to respond. Choosing the answerer randomly provides the opportunity for even the shiest child to become involved in the class discussion. The teacher's encouragement and support can reduce anxiety and make the lesson a successful learning experience. It is best for the teacher to build on small successes by asking open-ended questions rather than factual-recall questions. Unfortunately, researchers have observed that teachers ask low-ability students fewer questions and praise them less often when they respond correctly.

3. Wait at least five seconds after directing a question before saying anything else. Most teachers allow their students less than two seconds on the average to answer a question. Permitting the student a reasonable amount of thinking time is essential, especially if you are asking for more than recall of a single fact. The length and quality of students' responses increase when teachers allow more wait time.

4. Use closed-ended questions when you are seeking information, facts, or a commitment. In attempting to assess student mastery of specific facts, the closed-ended question is most effective. Generally, avoid asking yes-or-no questions in your lessons.

5. Open-ended questions (beginning with how, why, or what) usually allow greater latitude in the student's response with a variety of possible answers (How can air pollution be decreased? Why do people change careers?). A single correct answer does not exist. Such open-ended questions are most crucial in stimulating students' creative abilities and developing higher-level cognitive processes such as evaluation, hypothesis generation, analysis, and synthesis.

6. What the teacher does after a student responds to a question significantly influences the group discussion process. Students who are ridiculed or intimidated will become increasingly reluctant to participate in discussions. No constructive end can come from put-downs, whether the teacher or students initiate them. People, including students, have a right to make mistakes and a responsibility to learn from those mistakes. A positive class climate is attained when students feel accepted and sufficiently open to take risks—even at the price of sometimes being incorrect.

7. Encourage students to respond in some fashion, even if they aren't completely sure of the answer. Rephrase the question or provide cues, but don't just accept "I don't know."

8. Probe students' responses for clarification and to stimulate further reflection. "Why?" is an effective probing question to force the student to a deeper level of thought.

9. Avoid multiple questions. Barraging students with a series of questions often only confuses them and obscures the lesson's purpose. One question at a time posed clearly and concisely will more likely yield a clear and concise response.

10. Effective teachers keep a balance between calling on volunteers and nonvolunteers. Particularly when it is likely many nonvolunteers know the answer, calling on a non-volunteer is better.

11. Occasionally have all students jot down an answer to your question before calling on one person to share the answer.

12. For variety have all students share their answer to your question in pairs or small groups. Call on a few groups to report their best answers to the whole class.

13. Difficult and challenging questions seem most effective for classes of high-ability students. A mixture of higher-order and lower-level cognitive questions seems to work best with mixed-ability classes. Low-level cognitive questions seem to work best when teaching basic skills. Effective teachers ask a combination of both low- and high-level cognitive questions.

14. Strive to ask questions that yield a high level of correct responses; research suggests around 70 percent is the optimal success level. Some evidence suggests that the most successful strategy is to begin a lesson with lower-level questions and to use higher-level questions as the lesson progresses.

15. Learn to allow students to talk more. Typically, teacher-talk consumes 70 percent of class discussion time.

16. Acknowledge correct responses, but be specific in your praise. What exactly was appropriate or creative about the student's response? Avoid the cliché "Very good" in response to every question. Save genuine praise for the response that is truly exceptional.

17. Occasionally ask the student to repeat the question before replying. This assures students are listening and understand the question.

18. Give students an equal opportunity to respond to your questions. Research shows that students down the middle and across the front of the classroom get called on more frequently. Also, higher-ability students tend to get called on more than lower-ability students when they raise their hands.

19. Research supports permitting call-out answers with students of a lower socioeconomic level, particularly at the elementary level. With classes at a higher socioeconomic level, students should be acknowledged before giving their answers. In the latter case, students are typically more assertive and eager to respond, creating more chaos. Without having to seek permission to speak, lower-ability students are more likely to contribute. A risk of permitting call-out responses is that a few students may dominate class discussions.

20. Don't accept an obviously incorrect answer. Gently yet clearly help identify a more appropriate response. Acknowledge if an answer is partially correct, but solicit a more complete response from the class before continuing. Have the student reflect a bit more on the question or your rephrasing of it. Don't immediately call on someone else.

21. Encourage students to ask questions, but don't just do it by saying, "Any questions?" Have each student write down one question, or have them pair up to make a list of questions related to the topic. Real learning is most likely when students are genuinely curious and enthusiastically generate their own questions. Encourage them to ask questions of each other as well as of you.

22. Be wary of asking *why* questions to confront misbehavior. When we ask *why* questions in reference to a person's behavior ("Why did you do that?"), we are generally seeking an argument, not an explanation. *Why* questions often put the student on the defensive, yielding a wisecracking defensive answer. A question such as "What are you doing?" is more effective in focusing the student's attention on his or her misbehavior.

> The key to wisdom is knowing all the right questions.
>
> —John A. Simone Sr.

INQUIRY LEARNING

Students tend to be naturally curious. The four-year-old eagerly absorbs everything she sees in her environment. Along the way, that natural inquisitiveness wanes in too many children.

Rekindling that curiosity is a major side effect of inquiry learning. It is based on getting the students actively engaged in the subject being studied.

Though inquiry learning has long been practiced in the science classroom, it can be used in a wide spectrum of subjects. Its core focus is empowering students to competently frame questions and seek answers. It is more than merely asking questions; it helps generate knowledge that students can transfer to other aspects of their lives. It seeks to develop students' critical thinking abilities, problem-solving skills, and inquisitive attitudes.

When done well, inquiry learning converts information into useful knowledge and makes students into lifelong learners. In an inquiry-focused classroom, teachers take on the role of the facilitators rather than that of all-knowing experts. It becomes an invitation to learn and explore the unknown. Inquiry learning most commonly occurs in groups,

What Works in Education

Check out Edutopia, the George Lucas Foundation's superb Web site (www.edutopia.org/video), to view video clips of outstanding teachers in action.

The videos highlight what works in education—best practices supported by research. Includes many examples of project-based learning. Interviews of top educators are also featured.

A sampling of superb videos available for viewing:

- *Quieting the Classroom*
- *Using a Fishbowl for Discussions*
- *Student Body: Classroom Exercise Makes Learning Lively*
- *Cooperative Arithmetic: How to Teach Math as a Social Activity*
- *Developing Minds: Learning How to Rebuild a Town*
- *High Expectations: Students Learn to Rise to the Occasion*
- *The Forum: Students Learn the Skill of Conflict Resolution*

providing opportunities to develop their collaborative abilities. It can be combined with co-operative learning or problem-based strategies.

For More Information

Callison, D., & Preddy, L. (2006). *The blue book on information age inquiry, instruction, and literacy*. Westport, CT: Libraries Unlimited.

Henning, J. E. (2008). *The art of discussion-based teaching: Opening up conversation in the classroom*. New York: Routledge.

Wilhelm, J. D. (2007). *Engaging readers & writers with inquiry: Promoting deep understandings in language arts and the content areas with guiding questions*. New York: Scholastic.

BRAINSTORMING

Brainstorming, first introduced by Alex Osborne in the advertising industry, can be an effective technique for stimulating creative thinking in groups. It can be incorporated into almost any lesson. Brainstorms lasting one to four minutes are a quick and effective means of energizing a group when interest wanes. Some advance training on the principles of effective brainstorming is essential. Consider displaying the four basic rules of brainstorming as a poster or transparency. When you first explain brainstorming, discuss the following rules:

- **Generate as many ideas as possible.** The more ideas a group has, the greater the probability of discovering a good one. The emphasis for now is on quantity, not quality.

- **Delay evaluation.** Later the group will evaluate its ideas, but to nurture free and open brainstorming, students must not be worried about whether others are going to criticize their ideas. Innovation only occurs when individuals are able to see with fresh eyes, stripping away the tunnel vision that usually limits creativity. Positive evaluation is also prohibited, as those not receiving positive comments from the group will assume their ideas are inferior. Record each idea without evaluation. Introduce the idea of creativity crunchers that we commonly use to squelch each other's creativity.

- **Encourage wild, zany, half-baked ideas.** Even if it doesn't quite make sense now, a suggestion might be the stimulus for a great idea. Record it; later it may blossom into something worthwhile.

- **Build on others' ideas.** Listen to their ideas and use them to stimulate additional ideas.

Each group should have a scribe record on paper—ideally on a large sheet of newsprint for all to see—all ideas as the group generates them. After the initial brainstorming exercise, you might assign the group the task of discussing their ideas and selecting (and possibly ranking) their top five or ten solutions.

When you first introduce brainstorming, give your students an opportunity to practice applying it to unusual, interesting, and novel problems, for example, generating lists of unique uses for common items. You might even hold up an object when assigning the brainstorming task. Here are some suggestions:

- Chalkboard eraser
- Cafeteria tray
- Box of unmatched socks
- Wallpaper sample book
- Softball
- Carpet scrap
- Used auto tire
- Empty paper towel tube
- Soda straw
- Used CD
- Pie pan
- Plastic milk jug

Another fun activity for practicing brainstorming is to encourage students to project what would likely happen if some major change occurred. How would the world be different? Just suppose any of the following were true:

- All people looked the same.
- Everyone had the same voice.
- We no longer had trees.
- Televisions were banned.
- Men could not vote.
- Everyone was given a million dollars.
- There were no telephones.
- We had no thumbs.
- There were no traffic laws.

Curriculum expert and teacher trainer Cerylle Moffett suggests an interesting adaptation of the brainstorming technique that she calls carousel brainstorming. Several topics are listed on newsprint and posted on the wall around the room. The class is divided into an equal number of groups. Each group gathers at a different post. Give the groups three to five minutes to brainstorm and record their ideas on the topic written on the sheet in front of them. When you call time, everyone rotates clockwise around the room to the next post. Give them a set time limit to read the previous group's ideas and continue the brainstorming process, recording their ideas on the sheet. Repeat the cycle until each group has considered each of the ideas posted.

Another technique, sometimes called rapid brainstorming, involves posting a variety of topics on separate sheets of newsprint displayed around the room. A group is assigned to each topic and gathers in front of its sheet of newsprint. All groups brainstorm as many responses as they can in two to three minutes. Each group then shares its ideas with the whole class. Another variation is to have each group rotate to the next topic and spend two minutes trying to add ideas to those already posted. Continue rotating until each group has brainstormed on each topic. Another variation is to have the groups remain seated in their groups and to pass the sheets of paper around the groups.

Another idea from Cerylle Moffett is the mail call. This technique works well when considering several related problems. Break the class into groups of four or five. Identify several problems for brainstorming. Each group needs a set of envelopes with each problem written on a different envelope. Place all the envelopes in the center of a table. Each person in the small group writes one idea on a note card and puts it in each envelope. Use newsprint or the chalkboard to record the various brainstormed solutions generated in each group.

One more option: instruct students to silently brainstorm their ideas for a minute. Each student then jots down his or her ideas on a sheet of paper. Then, in the small brainstorming groups, each shares two ideas. Afterward the group follows normal brainstorming procedures.

CREATIVITY CRUNCHERS

Have you ever heard other teachers—or possibly even yourself—say any of the following? If you have, then creativity and brainstorming have been crushed. Avoid saying these at all cost!

No way!	We don't have the money.
You're dreaming.	Let's form a committee.
Don't be silly.	You've got to be kidding!
It's a nice theory, but . . .	It will never work.
It's too risky.	Yes, but . . .
You don't understand.	They'll never let us.
We tried that before.	It'll never sell.
We're too big for that to work here.	That's not our problem.
It would take too long. Why?	The time isn't right.
The administration will never go along.	The main office won't let us.
Maybe someday.	It's too new.

Put it in writing.

We'll discuss it later.

Why do it now?

It will never be approved.

What for?

Nobody needs it.

It's against our rules.

The union won't go along.

It's too faddish.

What will the community think?

Let's table it for now.

Don't rush into things.

It's politically unwise.

Too radical.

We're too small.

It's too much work.

Let's wait and see.

Let me think about it.

What good will it do?

We already have enough problems.

It'll never happen.

It'll never fly.

They'll laugh at us.

We have too many obstacles.

It's reactionary.

We don't have proof it will work.

It will offend someone.

It's too late.

It's not our policy.

Are you serious?

We need more data.

It didn't work the last time.

Costs too much.

Baloney!

Someone else should do it.

They aren't ready for it yet.

There's no use trying.

It's not our job.

Dud!

Nobody cares anyway.

We don't have enough details.

Don't you think there is a better way?

Too corny.

It's too soon.

That's not new.

It's illogical.

Get practical.

Here we go again.

That's fine, but . . .

Whose idea is that?

It's too simple.

It's too complicated.

That's just plain dumb.

BRAINWRITING

Brainwriting is a variation on the brainstorming technique. It ensures that everyone has an opportunity to participate and minimizes the effects of premature evaluation of each other's ideas. A topic or problem is assigned to a small group (four to seven members), and each student is given three note cards (or small sheets of paper). Each student writes a different idea about the problem on each card, then places the cards facedown on a table or desk. When all cards are facedown, the students take turns drawing one card and reading it aloud. It is then placed face up on the table for all to see. As similar ideas are read, they are grouped into clusters. After all the groups have read and grouped their ideas, they can be shared with the whole class and recorded on the board or newsprint. This is a useful technique for generating class rules at the beginning of the school year.

The card swap is an extension of brainwriting: students pass one of their cards to the person on their right. Recipients read the card they received. Next they can be instructed to do one of several things with the card:

- Allow the card to stimulate a new idea.
- Modify in some fashion the idea on the received card.
- Simply pass the card on around the circle.

LIST MAKING

List making can be combined with several other techniques, such as brainstorming or brainwriting. It may be done individually, in small groups, or as a whole class. Here are some ideas for possible lists:

- Causes (economic depressions, the Civil War, fights, fires, success, trust, decay of organic matter, substance abuse, the civil rights movement)
- Effects, real or projected (of chemical fertilizers, unemployment, alcohol abuse, global warming, soil erosion, television, decline of communism)
- Characteristics or traits (properties of organic matter, components of a healthy diet, parts of an airplane, forms of mental illness)
- Criteria for judgments (selecting a college; choosing a friend, a good novel, a successful employee)

- Members of sets (countries of Africa, religions of the world, elements of the periodic table, nineteenth-century American authors, species of birds, proverbs)
- Solutions (for decreasing crime, lengthening our life spans)

Lists are easily incorporated into consensus-building activities. Students are assigned the task of first individually ranking the list in priority. Afterward small groups discuss their lists and attempt to arrive at a final group ranking. It is important to prohibit simple voting; students must present and negotiate the issues.

For examples of how lists can be used in various classes, see the following: Ron Partin's *Social Studies Teacher's Book of Lists* (Jossey-Bass, 2003); or Marian D. Milliken, *The Physical Education Teacher's Book of Lists* (Jossey-Bass, 2005).

CLASS DISCUSSIONS

Class discussion is a useful strategy for stimulating critical thinking and encouraging students to reexamine their attitudes. For a discussion to be effective, students must possess some general information about the topic under consideration, unless you are using the discussion as an advance organizer to introduce a new topic.

The teacher's role in a class discussion is as a moderator. The teacher poses the initial question, facilitates thinking with follow-up questions, and ensures that everyone has an opportunity to participate. He or she also introduces bits of information, but generally it is best if the teacher refrains from offering an opinion. If you do choose to take a position, it is probably wise to wait until the end. It is essential that you merely facilitate, not dominate, the discussion.

- Whole-class discussion is best facilitated with the group seated in a large circle or a horseshoe. If they can see each other, students are more likely to respond to each other rather than engage in a series of successive dialogues with the teacher.

- Do give some forethought to the stimulating questions you will ask to promote the discussion. It is best to write them down. Overall, the less you have to participate to keep the discussion going, the better. It is also essential to establish the procedures for taking turns speaking. Does the student need to be acknowledged by the teacher before speaking?

- Begin the discussion by introducing the topic. Students need to be aware of the discussion's general theme and have a sense of its purpose. A couple of sentences and an opening question may suffice.

- Discussions can serve a variety of purposes. They may focus on examining a problem, analyzing its causes, effects, and potential solutions. A discussion may be used to debrief an activity such as a simulation, role play, or experiment. Discussion may focus on predicting some future event or explaining some past phenomenon. To meet any of these aims, the discussion must progress beyond the knowledge level. Higher-level cognitive questions must be asked.

- The class may be broken into small groups to stimulate discussion. Each group might discuss the same topic or have separate topics to consider. It is helpful to provide the groups a written list of questions, either as a handout or displayed on the overhead projector or chalkboard. Without a clear purpose and a task for which students will be accountable, the discussion will quickly degenerate into a conversation. It is usually a good idea to appoint a group leader who is responsible for keeping everyone on task, recording the group's ideas, and reporting back to the whole class. (See the handout Strategies for Selecting Group Leaders at the end of this chapter.)

- To facilitate only one person talking at a time, bring a sponge ball or other soft object to class. In order to speak, a student must be in possession of the ball. When a student wants to contribute to the discussion, he or she must raise a hand. The individual may speak only after he or she receives the ball from the previous student.

- Avoid overrelying on high-ability students in an effort to keep the discussion going.

- A tactic that teachers commonly use to prevent several persons from dominating the discussion is to allocate each student three or four poker chips or other tokens. Each time a student makes a comment, he or she must turn in one token to the teacher. Once their chips are gone, they may add no more comments to the discussion. Another way to control the monopolizer is to first break students into small groups and designate a reporter from each group to share the group's conclusions. Another option is to appoint the monopolizer to a role that inhibits his or her participation, for example, as a silent observer or recorder.

- Don't allow the discussion to deteriorate into a shouting match. Emphasize the value of having a free and open discussion and supporting positions with facts. Emphasize that reasonable people may sometimes interpret those facts differently.

- End the discussion before it begins to stagnate. Do something different: have each student take one minute to write an answer to a question, introducing some relevant facts.

- Provide some structure to the discussion so that it is not too divergent. It must have focus to encourage serious reflection. An exchange of unexamined opinions is of minimal educational value.

- Provide closure to the discussion. One way is for the teacher or volunteers to summarize the main points emphasized. Another is to have students reflect or write about how the discussion may have changed their views of the topic.

- Thank students for their contributions. It generally works best to reinforce but not grade participation in discussions. Provide a transition to the lesson's next phase. Point out how the discussion fits into the overall lesson objectives.

- Occasionally, it is helpful to lead a post-discussion review of the discussion's process and techniques. Encourage the class to analyze what went well and which areas might need improvement. Encourage reflection on the level of thinking that occurred during the discussion. Sometimes appointed observers can provide feedback on the group dynamics.

FISHBOWLS

A fishbowl consists of a small group that discusses an issue while seated in the center of the classroom, with the rest of the class seated in a larger circle around the fishbowl. This technique is most effective for topics in which students have a lot of interest and some disagreement exists. Often an empty chair is included in the fishbowl. Anyone in the outer circle who wishes to inject a comment may temporarily join the fishbowl. The student contributes a comment, then returns to his or her seat on the outside, leaving the chair vacant for the next volunteer.

It works best to prepare a list of questions in advance to structure the discussion and keep it on task. It is essential that those in the outer circle remain quiet during the discussion. They may talk only if they join the fishbowl in the empty chair. Observers should take notes during the discussion (for example, recording the topic's pros and cons). One option is to have the fishbowl participants and observers reverse roles and continue the discussion. Allow time for debriefing at the end of the discussion. The fishbowl technique can also be used as a lesson in effective group processes.

Another option is to break the class into several smaller discussion groups to examine a controversial topic. Each group then selects a representative to participate in the fishbowl and express his or her group's concerns on the issue. After fifteen or twenty minutes of discussion, the representatives might return to their groups for feedback and new "ammunition" to share once they rejoin the fishbowl.

ARTWORK

Most students love to draw, especially if they are not being evaluated. For variety, experiment with art media in your regular classes. Crayons, colored markers, colored pencils, and chalk seem to immediately grab students' attention. Students who otherwise find self-expression difficult may be able to communicate deeper ideas and feelings through artistic media. Art has been used successfully to build students' self-esteem and self-confidence. It can tap all students' creativity and imagination.

- Experiment with inserting a five-minute art activity into a lesson. Rather than having students write out their responses to a discussion question, have them draw a depiction of their answer. It provides a reenergizing break from the left-brain focus of most lessons.

- Added motivation comes with the use of scented markers (Mr. Sketch is one brand) available at most office supply stores.

- Play music in the background while students are doing their artwork to further stimulate creativity.

- Encourage students to draw in their journals to represent some of their ideas. Have them take a sketch pad along on field trips to record their observations. Drawing helps students focus their attention and process their perceptions.

- Drawing murals cooperatively can enrich students' reflection about the academic content while developing social skills.

- Discourage competition among students in their artwork. Be cautious of effusive public praise for obviously talented students. It may discourage less artistically inclined students. Private praise is probably much more effective.

- Have students draw a vertical and a horizontal line to create four equal boxes. In each box the students draw a different item in response to four different questions about the topic being studied in class. (For example, it could be four causes of the Civil War, four kinds of clouds, four effects of inflation, or four career possibilities.) Or each box might be used to address a different question. (For example, the first box might show a cause of some problem being studied. An effect and two possible solutions might be drawn in the other three boxes.)

- Keep the directions to any art assignments general. Let the students use their creativity and imaginations to construct their vision of reality. Give them as much freedom

as possible to choose the form and media they believe best expresses their ideas.

- Encourage the use of color by having assorted markers, pens, crayons, or pencils available for students to use if they do not provide their own.

- Incorporate the construction of advertisements into your lessons. Ads may take the form of posters or magazine layouts. Their ads should express some relevant concept related to the topic being studied.

- Collages can be adapted to a great many purposes in classes other than art. Though most art collages consist of pictures and captions clipped from magazines, most any item that can be pasted to a piece of poster board can be included in a collage (for example, photographs, fabrics, drawings, leaves, buttons, ribbon).

- Individuals or groups can compose collages. Ask students to bring in a variety of old magazines as sources of pictures to cut out. Have students attach titles to their collages.

- Check out George Szekely's book, *How Children Make Art: Lessons in Creativity from Home to School* (Teachers College Press, 2006), for many practical ideas for incorporating drawing into your lesson plans.

MUSIC

Music has many uses in the classroom. It can be used in the background to set the mood for a lesson; to energize, relax, inspire, cue transitions, focus attention, reinforce a theme; or for fun. Music affects our physiological systems, our emotions, and our spirit. Music can influence your students' moods and behaviors.

It is generally best to select instrumental music, although vocals might be used during breaks or if the lyrics pertain specifically to the lesson. Pay special attention to the musical selection's beat. A march is hardly going to soothe and calm a group of hyperactive, rowdy students. Baroque and soft New Age instrumentals work well as background music during individual seatwork.

When words leave off, music begins.

—Heinrich Heine

- Special effects or emphasis can be achieved by using themes from famous movies or television programs. (The theme from *Jeopardy!* during a spelling bee or oral quiz lightens the atmosphere.) Be aware of the purpose you want to achieve with each musical selection.

- Incorporate humorous novelty songs into your lessons. This is especially effective if the song's theme relates to the topic under study.

- Put a part of your lesson to music. If you are bold, try singing an announcement or assignment to a rap beat.

- Allow students to bring a favorite tape to play before class begins or during lab or project work. The privilege of selecting the tape for the day can be used as a reward for outstanding performance.

- If you play a musical instrument, bring it to class and feature a brief selection as part of the lesson or use it as a novelty reward. It reinforces the value of music.

- Some teachers play music before class. Stopping the music is a cue that it is time to begin class. Be sure to cue your recordings at the appropriate spot and adjust the volume before class begins. You'll lose momentum and effect if you have to waste class time searching for the segment you want to use. Have them out of their boxes and clearly labeled and ready to use.

GUIDED IMAGERY

Guided imagery can be used effectively to stimulate students' problem solving, goal setting, and hypothesis building in studying complex issues. In affective education, guided imagery is used to help students explore their feelings and attitudes. The guided imagery lesson aims to immerse the students in the subject. Guided imagery is the next best thing to being there. It is an active, not passive, instructional strategy.

Careful thought must be given to the topic chosen as the focus of a guided imagery. Some teachers employ guided imagery to help students focus on a reading assignment. For example, in teaching about the drafting of the Constitution, a teacher might lead the students through a visualization of the scene in Philadelphia, with vivid descriptions of the people present, the debates, the weather, and other details, setting the stage for the drama to unfold. The students' prior experience and knowledge about the topic must be considered in designing the lesson. It may be necessary to present some background information before introducing the imagery. The questions to be included must be given careful consideration.

Here are some ideas to help you use guided imagery:

- It is best to allow students the option of not participating in fantasy trips or visualizations. Though this is rare, some students might not wish to participate for religious or emotional reasons. Don't make a big fuss, but avoid forcing student participation. Provide an alternate assignment, perhaps a written theme on the same topic.

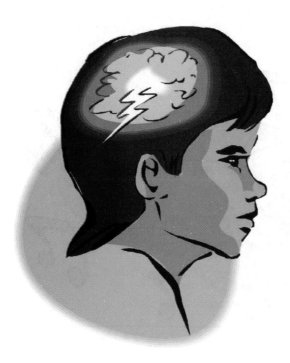

- When you introduce the visualization, make clear that no one will be forced to share their thoughts or feelings afterward. In debriefing, call only on volunteers for responses.

- Introduce the visualization by encouraging students to make themselves comfortable, to take several deep breaths, and to relax. You may choose to turn the lights off. Some may prefer to close their eyes to eliminate distractions, but do not insist that they do so.

- Carefully script the visualization the first time. Pause after each line to allow time for students to create their fantasy response.

- Design visualizations that encourage students to use all their senses as they progress through the visualization. For example, "What sounds are outstanding?" Or "What do you see from the top of the hill?"

- In debriefing the visualization, invite students to share whatever observations they choose. This might be perceived as safer if done in pairs or small groups. A large-group discussion might then elicit any generalizations or conclusions.

> To imagine is everything.
>
> —Anatole France, *The Crime of Sylvester Bonnard*, 1881

JOURNAL KEEPING

A valuable instructional device for encouraging reflection, review, application, and creativity is the student journal. As most commonly used, each student periodically makes entries into a spiral-bound notebook, which is occasionally handed in to the teacher. The teacher scans the journals, making relevant comments in the margin or a separate column. Student journals can serve a variety of purposes: to improve writing skills, to remind the student of important things to remember, or to strengthen self-reflection skills. The following will help you get started:

- Learning logs or journals function as course diaries. Students enter summaries of the major content they have been studying. These might be major points from class lectures, formulas and other important pieces of information they need to memorize, or procedures and directions. It might be kept in the form of a mind map.

- Reflective journals serve as a medium to stimulate and record thinking about what students experience in the class. This form of response journal may be turned in to the teacher and returned with the teacher's comments, creating a teacher-student dialogue. Each can ask the other questions.

- Journals can also serve as logs, helping the students and the teacher track the books read, experiments completed, Web quests finished, or learning activities done or objectives attained. Journals can also help students monitor their progress. Experiment with assigning specialized journals, such as a conflict journal. Students record instances in which they encounter conflict in their daily lives, their response to the conflict, the outcome of their reactions, and other options they might have taken. Other topics for specialized journals might include stress, use of time, successes, anger, joys, positive and negative consequences, nutrition, or exercise. Of course, the journal assignments should be relevant to the subject you are teaching.

- Journals can also function as field notebooks for recording observations of processes or phenomena you want students to examine over time. Students can keep journals on weather patterns, wildlife observed, progress of experiments, social or psychological observations (for example, violence on television, smiles), child development, political developments, books read, or field trips.

- Provide instructions as to the format of students' journals. What medium (spiral notebook, notebook paper, computer disk) may be used? How frequently will they be writing in it? What is the minimum amount they should write? When will the teacher read it?

- When you give a journal-keeping assignment, be sure to explicitly describe its purpose. Journals are frequently used as a learning log to record new knowledge gained each day. This is especially valuable with experiential learning.

- When emotions become aroused during heated discussions, it is often helpful to call a time-out for students to reflect on the issue at hand and enter their thoughts and feelings into their journals. This encourages them to summarize the main points on both sides of an issue.

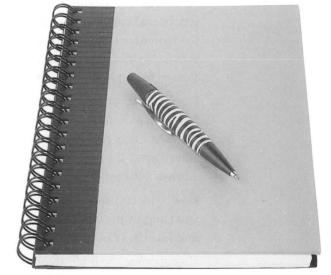

- Another strategy for using journals is to have students list three important points or ideas from the day's class that they think will be most helpful to them. You might then encourage them to share these thoughts in pairs or seek volunteers from the class at large. This facilitates review of the day's lesson and encourages application.

- To stimulate students' journal writing, ask them to answer specific, open-ended questions in their journals.

- As part of introducing a new topic, particularly those of natural interest to students, ask each student to enter in their journals two or three questions they hope the upcoming lesson will answer. Near the end of the lesson, you might ask students to check their list of questions for any that remain unanswered.

- Have students assume a role related to the topic being studied (for example, antebellum plantation owner, colonial merchant, entrepreneur, union organizer, Underground Railroad conductor, or explorer). Students write their journal entries as though they were the person in the role they are assuming. Or the student might be assigned to study a real person, such as George Washington, Clara Barton, Eleanor Roosevelt, Madame Curie, or Albert Schweitzer. Instruct students to make their journal observations as they believe their assigned persons would have responded.

- Some teachers have successfully employed the use of team journals. Teams of five students are each given a journal. Periodically the teacher assigns a topic for the class to consider and enter their reactions in their team journal. The team leader, a rotating position, writes the first entry in the journal. Other members are then responsible for adding their comments. Each student, except for the team leader, is supposed to comment on at least one previous entry. The teacher then reads each journal and adds an entry. It encourages students to write regularly and to assume a position and defend it.

- Consider having students keep their journals on computer files that they can exchange and forward to the teacher.

FIELD TRIPS

The entire world can be a learning resource if a knowledgeable guide shows the way. Well-planned, organized field trips can be one of the most valuable ways of helping students apply their textbook and classroom learning to the greater world. Here are twenty-three practical tips for making field trips into profitable learning experiences.

1. Any class trip should have a meaningful purpose that is directly related to the subject being taught and is explicitly communicated to the students. It is also essential to communicate that purpose to any off-site presenters and any parents or others serving as chaperones. A class trip cannot be justified if its sole purpose is to entertain or fill time. It should enrich and expand your regular curriculum.

2. Clarify your school's procedures and requirements before you begin planning a field trip. Will parental permission be required? If so, is there a special form you must use? (See the Field Trip Permission Form handouts at the end of this chapter.) When and where must the permission forms be filed? Will chaperones be required? How many? Always notify your principal in writing.

3. How will transportation be provided? Going in buses is generally preferable to traveling in private automobiles. It is simpler, easier to control students' behavior, and less likely to create liability issues.

4. If chaperones will be accompanying you on the trip, be sure to communicate your expectations of the role they should take. It is best to send a note to each chaperone detailing when they should be at school and exactly what you expect of them. Are they only to monitor student behaviors? Which behaviors are unacceptable? How should they handle rowdy students? Will the chaperones have a role in the learning associated with the trip?

5. Send information to the parents about your field trip, describing its purpose and specifics of the travel arrangements. If you are seeking parents to accompany the class, be sure to give ample notice (ideally, at least two weeks). Are any costs involved? If so, how are they to be handled? Will lunch be provided?

6. Be sure the proposed visit is age-appropriate for your students. Is this site used to having visits from students? Will a guided tour be provided? If so, are the hosts used to talking to students of this age group? Will cameras be allowed? Is any special attire required?

7. Strive to make the field trip an active learning experience. The more hands-on the experience, the better. If it is a guided tour (for example, a factory or battlefield), provide students (either individually or in cooperative groups) specific tasks to accomplish during the visit. The class should in some way be accountable for learning that occurs during the trip. This can be in the form of word puzzles, word scavenger hunts, or a study guide to help direct their attention and reflection. It is often useful to break the class into learning teams, each with a different task to accomplish. The next school day, they can exchange their insights and completed tasks.

8. As much as possible, the field trip should be integrated into a sequence of planned class activities. Before the trip, prepare the students with background information about the field trip's topic. The day after the visit, allow class time for reflection and discussion of the experience. Plan a lesson that allows them to apply this new knowledge.

9. Be reasonable about what you can get done on a field trip. Often teachers try to accomplish too much, especially if it is a daylong trip. Once students become bored or tired, less learning and more misbehavior are likely.

10. Be sure to confirm the field trip a couple days ahead of time. Contact the site, chaperones, transportation providers, and your principal.

11. Try to arrange for parents to meet with you fifteen minutes before the group is to leave so that you can share any last-minute details and coordinate efforts. It's generally a good idea to have one more chaperone than you think you'll need. If parents will be driving, be sure to give each one a map of the route to take.

12. Adequately prepare your students before the day of the trip. Clarify your expectations for appropriate behavior and for any learning assignments associated with the trip. Are there special dress requirements? Will seats be assigned on the bus? What should students do if they get separated from the group?

13. If possible, give your planned trip a dry run. How long will it take to get there? Try to meet any guides or presenters who will be leading your group. Will eating arrangements need to be made en route or on-site? Make note of details, such as locations of bathrooms, parking, and so on. Is the site fully accessible for any students with disabilities? Determine precisely where and when you are to arrive with your group. How will any admission fees be handled?

14. Count noses before you leave the school and again when you meet to return home.

15. With older students, identify a landmark where all should meet at a set time if they become separated.

16. Carry a notepad or cards with you on the field trip. During the excursion jot down ideas for processing questions or points to emphasize back in the classroom.

17. It is probably wise to take along a first-aid kit, tape, safety pins, needle and thread, tissues, and coins or a cell phone for emergency phone calls. On a long bus ride, carry a couple of bags for students who experience motion sickness—and hope you don't need them.

18. Be sure to make a provision for a restroom stop during the field trip.

19. Take along a digital camera to take shots that can be made into a PowerPoint presentation, included on your class Web site, or used in bulletin board displays.

20. During a tour carry an easily identifiable object, such as a colorful umbrella, that you can hold up to help students find their group. With small children some teachers use a rope, instructing the children to cling to it in a single file throughout the walking tour.

21. After the field trip, send a thank-you note to the organization or person that facilitated the visit. If appropriate, you might encourage your students to draft a letter to send.

22. Evaluate the field trip. Did it fulfill your educational purposes? Solicit feedback from the students. What would have improved the experience?

23. If you plan to use that field trip site in the future, jot down any reminders of changes that would make the trip more profitable next time. You might file these along with copies of your form letters and permission slips, student activities, and any promotional brochures.

Ideas for Potential Field Trips

Airport	College or university
Amusement park	Concert
Aquarium	Conservation area
Arboretum	Conservatory
Art exhibit	Courthouse
Artist's studio	Cultural fair or festival
Assisted living facility	Factory
Bank	Farm
Battlefield	Fire department
Book publishing company	Forest
Botanical garden	Geological site
Brokerage firm	Historical museum
Cemetery	Historical site or building
City council meeting	Hospital

Laboratory

Law enforcement agency

Legislative session

Library

Military base

Museum

Neighborhood

Newspaper office

Observatory

Park (local, state, national)

Planetarium

Political rally

Power plant

Presidential library or home

Printing plant

Science museum

Seashore, river, or lake

Sewage treatment plant

Ship

Special exhibition

State capitol building

Television or radio station

Theatrical performance

Train ride

Weather station

Zoo

Field Trip Supply List

- Binoculars
- Camcorder
- Cell phone
- Clipboards
- Digital camera
- Drinking water
- Driving directions and map
- First-aid kit
- Flashlight
- Food
- Garbage bag
- Important phone numbers
- Insect repellent
- Money
- Name tags
- Parental consent forms
- Pencils
- Resealable plastic bags for collections
- Spare pencils
- Student medications
- Sunscreen
- Trip schedule

- Two copies of the participant roster
- Water bottles
- Whistle

Field Trip Follow-up Activities

- Allow teams of students to create a CD or DVD of the trip using digital photos or video clips taken during the outing. Share the product at a parent-teacher open house.

- Encourage the class to send thank-you notes to the on-site field trip guides.

- Create a display depicting the material learned and featuring any specimens collected. Invite other classes to view the display.

- Solicit volunteer students to help create a bulletin board depicting the content of the trip.

- Invite students to evaluate the field trip experience. What was their favorite part of the field trip? What would they suggest to make the trip more worthwhile? Did it meet the preannounced goals?

- Select a student to write a story about the field trip for use in the class newsletter to be sent to parents.

- Assign teams to make reports on various aspects of the trip. These might be presented in a variety of modes (PowerPoint presentation; a video; oral presentation; learning center).

Virtual Field Trips

The Internet offers easy access to a broad array of virtual field trips relating to almost every subject area. Many historical, art, and science museums now host splendid online educational tours.

Virtual field trips allow students to visit remote places that would normally be impossible to visit. Online tours avoid the hassle of arranging chaperones and transportation, and they can be completed during normal class hours.

Several excellent catalogues of online museums and field trips can be found on the Web:

Best Virtual Field Trips Online

surfaquarium.com/virtual.htm

The "OOPS" Virtual Field Trip Page!

http://oops.bizland.com/vtours.htm

Virtual Schoolhouse

www.ibiblio.org/cisco/trips.html

- As with off-campus field trips, virtual trips require planning. Be sure to meticulously preview any virtual field trip before introducing it to your students. You want no surprises.

- Some teachers send home a permission form for virtual field trips, just as they would for off-campus field trips. Be sure to include the site's URL so that parents can check it out. It is always wise to forestall problems by keeping parents informed.

- Prepare goals and instructional activities for students to complete as they explore the site's offerings. For example, design a scavenger hunt with information that small groups of students work on together. Design a follow-up activity for students to complete to extend and crystallize the knowledge they gained.

- Teachers must monitor students to ensure they are on task and not abusing Internet privileges.

- Questions to guide evaluation of potential virtual tours include the following:
  - Who is sponsoring the site?
  - Are there any costs?
  - Is the content nonpartisan and factual?
  - Is the site easy to navigate?
  - Is the site sufficiently interactive?
  - How current is the information?
  - Where do any external links lead?

GUEST SPEAKERS AND PANELS

The use of guest speakers, either individually or as a panel, can provide a valuable educational opportunity. Outside presenters can enrich a lesson, provide special expertise, stimulate interest, and help students connect classroom learning to real-world applications. Guest speakers provide variety: a different voice and a new face. A bonus benefit is the public relations value of inviting parents and community members to share their wisdom, skills, and views with young people.

However, as with any instructional approach, planning and preparation are crucial for success. A poor speaker is worse than none at all. Not only

Sample Virtual Field Trips

American Museum of Natural History

www.amnh.org/ology/

At the Tomb of Tutankhamen

www.nationalgeographic.com/egypt/ index. html

Boston Museum of Science

www.mos.org/

Fisheye View Online Camera

www.fisheyeview.com/

Library of Congress

www.loc.gov/exhibits/

Metropolitan Museum of Art

www.metmuseum.org/

National Aeronautics and Space Administration (NASA)

http://www.nasa.gov/

Ontario Science Centre Online

www.ontariosciencecentre.ca/

Smithsonian American Art Museum

www.nmaa.si.edu/

will precious educational time be lost, but also the speaker may leave with a lower opinion of schools and your students.

Here are some ideas for potential speakers:

- Anyone who has traveled to a foreign country
- People representing different careers
- Persons with unusual hobbies or interests
- College and university professors
- Elected officials
- Local citizens of other nationalities
- Area business owners or executives
- International students attending local schools or colleges
- Governmental agency employees
- Someone with an interesting collection
- Physicians, lawyers, and other professionals
- School alumni
- Representatives of trade associations, unions, service organizations
- Local radio, television, or newspaper celebrities
- Federal government employees
- Local newsmakers
- Better Business Bureau, consumer agencies, advocates

Guest speakers should be arranged well in advance. Here are some ideas for guiding your planning process:

- Determine why you are using the speaker (or panel). What benefit do you expect students to gain from being exposed to this speaker or panel? Without using jargon, communicate your objective to the speakers when you invite them.
- Give careful thought to whom you invite to participate in your class. What are their credentials? Parents, senior citizens, local celebrities, civic leaders, skilled artisans, artists, professors, and local businesspersons can potentially contribute much to your students.
- When you extend an invitation, be specific as to the date, topic, and time limits. What format are you suggesting: lecture, demonstration, question and answer, a panel discussion? Have they spoken before in front of groups this age? How will they relate to students? Some persons are more comfortable participating as a member of an informal panel discussion than as the sole presenter.
- Confirm the visit two or three days ahead of the scheduled presentation.
- Give your speakers as much support as possible. Tell them about the kinds of students you have. Alert them to potential behavioral problems they might encounter and your plans to deal with such disruptive students. See if the speakers need any special equipment or supplies. Encourage them to use props and to involve students as much as possible.

- Encourage the speaker to solicit questions from students. This makes the experience more interactive and responsive to students' interests.

- Short presentations are generally preferable, at least the first time you have a speaker present on a specific topic. If it is well received, more time can be allotted the next time.

- Prepare your students for the speaker(s). Before the speaker arrives, clarify who is coming and why. Clarify what behaviors you expect from your students. You might suggest they formulate some questions ahead of the presentation. Make it an active learning experience.

- Ask permission to videotape the speaker's presentation for use in the future or with students who were absent.

- Be sure to send thank-you notes to your panelists or presenters. If students express high interest in the subject, invite them to write thank-you notes, either individually or as a group.

- Invite persons who have some expertise in the subject under discussion to share their knowledge in a panel discussion. These might be parents, community members, or representatives of a particular organization, occupation, or interest group. Most people feel more comfortable participating as a panel member than giving a stand-up solo presentation. Generally, a panel consists of three to five participants. The panelists might discuss the topic among themselves as well as respond to questions from your students. Another option is to select a group of students who study a particular topic and present it to the rest of the class as a panel discussion.

- Before the panel takes place, it is often a good idea to give students a few minutes in class (or as homework) to write one or two questions they could submit to the panel. This might also be done as a small-group exercise. You serve as a moderator, posing questions when the discussion lags. However, avoid dominating the discussion.

- Arrange chairs at the front of the room so that the panelists can see each other and be seen by all the class. Keep track of the time and try to allow for some closing thoughts by each panelist.

- Another useful variation is to allow fifteen to twenty minutes at the end for the panelists to meet with small clusters of students and permit individual questioning and discussion.

DEBATES

The debate can be a powerful motivational and instructional device. Though formal debate has perhaps become a lost art, seldom practiced outside of law schools, the debating process can successfully be adapted to any educational level. Informal debates can be used in almost any subject. Debates are an effective tool for honing students' thinking skills. The debate also reinforces data gathering, persuasion, public speaking, and listening skills. The ability to analyze a position and persuasively present a case for or against that position will benefit students throughout their lives. One of the most valuable gains from debates is the appreciation for more than one way of viewing issues.

Informal classroom debates need not follow all the procedures of a formal debate, though you will need to teach some basic rules to structure the debate. Each side should have the same amount of time to present its case. Students take turns presenting their arguments with time to rebut the opponent's points.

Any topic on which people might disagree can be selected for a debate assignment. This might include local or school-related issues, national or international events. Most any proposal for change meets resistance, with advocates for both sides. Though some students may initially be reluctant, most really do find classroom debates exciting; and even the academically less-talented students can become involved. Debates frequently are quite lively and elicit postdebate discussion on the issue.

- The first time you use the debate in class, keep it fairly simple. With experience, your students can successfully take on more complicated issues. The more complex the issue, the more time needed for preparation. Adjust your expectations to your students' intellectual level.

- Present some of the basic principles of effective argumentation, such as distinguishing opinions and emotions from facts. If you aren't familiar with these skills, find a book from the library (see the suggestions that follow). Invite a lawyer or a debate coach to speak to your class about effective debating.

- Debates generally work best as a cooperative learning activity. Students will feel much more comfortable as a member of a panel than as a sole debater. Emphasize the collaboration within each team more than the competition against other teams.

- Another adaptation of the debate is to assign a variety of debatable topics to pairs of students. Each pair works collaboratively to identify the best arguments for and against their assigned proposition. The teacher then randomly assigns one student to present the pro and another student to present the con position in a five-minute presentation. Allow them two minutes to review their notes before presenting to the whole class. Everyone in the class gets to speak, but the time is brief enough not to arouse undue anxiety in most students.

- For variety debate with yourself in front of the class. Choose a stimulating issue and argue one point of view, perhaps in a relevant hat or shirt. Then quickly don the other costume and argue the other position. Switch back and forth for rebuttal. With a bit of practice, you can present a most entertaining as well as enlightening debate. The hat serves as a cue that the roles are shifting back and forth.

- Provide the option for your students to demonstrate their debating skills by presenting their argument to an outside audience, perhaps the board of education, city council, the school administration, or viewers of the local cable television channel. This would require students to carefully research the issue, analyze the supporting data, and rehearse their presentations.

- For inspiration, show the film *The Great Debaters,* which depicts the story of Melvin B. Tolson, a professor at Wiley College in Texas. Tolson motivated students to create the school's first debate team and successfully compete at the national level against the top university debate teams.

- Check out Debate Central at www.debate-central.org/ for valuable information on organizing high school debates. Sponsored by the National Center for Policy Analysis, the site provides access to information on key current issues.

For More Information

Azzam, A. M. (2008). Clash! The world of debate. *Educational Leadership, 65*(5), 68–72.

Daley, P., & Dahlie, M. S. (2001). *Fifty debate prompts for kids.* New York: Scholastic Professional Books.

Driscoll, W., & Zompetti, J. P. (2003). *Discovering the world through debate: A practical guide to educational debate for debaters, coaches, and judges.* New York: International Debate Education Association.

Ericson, J. M., Murphy, J. J., & Zeuschner, R. B. (2003). *The debater's guide* (3rd ed.). Carbondale: Southern Illinois University Press.

Fine, G. A. (2001). *Gifted tongues: High school debate and adolescent culture.* Princeton, NJ: Princeton University Press.

Freeley, D. L., & Steinberg, A. J. (2009). *Argumentation and debate: Critical thinking for reasoned decision making.* Boston: Wadsworth/Cengage Learning.

VIDEOS AND DVDs

Video media (primarily DVDs or online videos) can be tremendous instructional assets. The challenge facing teachers using video presentations in class is that their students have been overexposed to the medium at home. Many students spend more time in front of a television or movie screen each year than they do in class. And much of what they have seen is action-packed, lusty, and very professional. Educational films or videos that are usually low budget and often of low technical quality can be weak competition for students' attention.

Yet when used effectively, films and videos can be powerful learning aids. The visual media can take students places they could never visit, help them see things they might never experience, and make the things they have read about come alive. Good films and videos can be very effective in arousing interest and motivating students. Many excellent documentary videos are available via commercial or educational broadcasting stations. *The Civil War* series produced by Ken Burns demonstrated the power and appeal of well-done video broadcasting. (See Chapter Four for information on fair educational use of video-taped programs.)

Selecting the right video is crucial. It must clearly fit into the lesson, not simply be an add-on or time killer. It is only a tool for helping you attain your instructional objective. A good film or videotape does not replace good teaching; it complements it.

- Check with your local library or television station about the availability of these programs. Many commercial organizations lend free films and videos. Colleges and governmental organizations are also sources of free or inexpensive films or videos.

- Whatever the source, the cardinal rule in using any audiovisual material is to preview it first to determine its appropriateness. You don't want any surprises in class! Evaluate the film or video for accuracy, age-appropriateness, cultural or gender bias, relevance to your class, and production quality. A bad program is worse than none at all.

- As you preview a film or videotape, jot down potential processing questions and main points you want to stress in the debriefing. If only portions of the film or video are worth showing, observe the timer to determine when the desired segment begins and ends.

- The biggest risk of audiovisual media is that it can become a passive learning experience for students, little more than a recorded lecture. Successful learning from films and video hinges on the teacher's ability to actively engage students in the experience. One way is to assign students a task to accomplish while viewing the presentation. This may take the form of two or three questions to answer, behaviors to count, words to define, or examples to observe.

Free Educational Videos

A broad spectrum of free instructional videos are accessible via the Internet. They can be used in a variety of ways to enrich and support your classroom instruction. Here are some of the better sites:

- National Geographic Video
  video.nationalgeographic.com/video/player/
  kids.nationalgeographic.com/Videos/VideoGallery
  Broad array of video clips on science, geography, current events, nature. Most clips contain short intro ads.
- Best Online Documentaries
  best.online.docus.googlepages.com/
  Hundreds of free online videos.
- Edutopia
  www.edutopia.org/video
  From the George Lucas Foundation. Great videos on What Works in Education—clips to outstanding teachers in action.
- Nova Online Videos
  www.pbs.org/wgbh/nova/programs/index.html
  Video clips from the popular PBS *Nova* series can be viewed online. Most cannot be downloaded due to copyright restrictions.

It is important to abide by fair use practices in using copyrighted material, including videos, in your classes. A helpful guide, *Code of Best Practices in Fair Use for Online Video*, is available free (http://centerforsocialmedia.org/).

- Another way to keep students actively involved in visual media is to stop the film or video occasionally and ask them questions about what they've seen or ask them to predict what they think will happen next. To affect learning, the subsequent processing of the film or video is as important as what students see and hear. Ask questions that stimulate reflection about the experience. Help students connect what they have learned in this presentation with prior knowledge and skills.

- Do not put on a film or video and then leave the room while students watch it, even if you have seen it fifty times. Apart from the liability issues of leaving a classroom unmonitored, your absence suggests to students the film is just being used to fill time and really isn't very important.

- Don't feel compelled to rewind the film immediately. Proceed directly to your debriefing activity and rewind the film later.

- Experiment with just using small clips from films and videos to augment lectures. A brief two- or three-minute segment illustrating an important point adds variety to any lesson and can enhance attention and retention. It is crucial that you cue up the desired segment and set focus and volume levels before the lesson begins. It is also imperative to adjust the lighting for optimal viewing of the screen.

- After the film or video, solicit candid feedback from your students as to how helpful it really was. If it gets low marks, don't use it again. You might even have them complete a brief rating form. Don't just ask if they liked the film; ask what they learned from it.

- If you have not learned how to operate the DVD player or LCD projector, find someone in the school to teach you. It is much better to know how to do this than to always depend on finding someone else to do it.

- Be sure you know where to quickly locate a projector replacement bulb and how to change it if help is not immediately available.

Digital video equipment and editing software are now available in most schools. All video-editing software comes with self-paced tutorials. However, it is best to learn under the tutelage of an experienced user. This may be a techie student!

With user-friendly software, teachers and students can add high-end special effects and export their project to the Web, DVD, or videotape. Macintosh users may find Apple's iMovie and Final Cut Express reasonably easy to learn. Adobe Premiere Elements or Avid Xpress are two of the more popular software packages for video editing on PCs.

PODCASTS

Cutting-edge teachers are increasingly realizing the instructional potential of students' ubiquitous iPods. In addition to music, many iPods can carry audiobooks and video. Innovative teachers are beginning to adapt lessons for new technology. Some teachers audiotape or videotape their lectures and post them online, allowing students to download them onto their personal computers or iPods.

Podcasting can work with both Mac and PC systems. Audio files recorded in MP3 format have the advantage of being accessible by students owning other brands of MP3 players or iPods. Sophisticated podcasts can include video, images, and text, as well as audio.

Instructional uses of iPods might include having students create radio programs, recording and presenting oral histories and interviews, or to aid in learning a new language. Union City (New Jersey) Schools pass out iPods to bilingual students as an aid in helping them learn English.

As part of their classroom lessons, some teachers play music from their iPods connected to a good speaker. Teachers can access hundreds of education-related podcasts online at sites such as the Education Podcast Network (http://epnweb.org/). For an excellent example of a student-made podcast, check out Cary Academy's 7th grade's "Plug It In" project at https://web1.caryacademy.org/facultywebs/joselyn_todd/podcasts/default.htm. Check out the superb podcast *12 Byzantine Rulers: The History of The Byzantine Empire,* created by high school teacher Lars Brownworth (www.anders.com/lectures/lars_brownworth/12_byzantine_rulers/).

Next trend to watch: Vodcasts (or Video-on-Demand-casts), which allow movies to be downloaded and shown.

For More Information

Brown, A., & Green, D. (2008). Video podcasting in perspective: The history, technology, aesthetics, and instructional uses of a new medium. *Journal of Educational Technology Systems, 36*(1), 3–17.

Internet Resources

iPod in the Classroom: Lesson Plans

> www.apple.com/au/education/ipod/lessons/

iPods: Poetry and Writing Across the Curriculum Prompts

> www.writingfix.com/ipod_prompts.htm

Start your own Podcast, *MacWorld*

> www.macworld.com/article/44428/2005/04/junecreate.html

A Dozen Helpful Podcasts for Teachers

- ADHD Podcaster
  www.theadhdspecialist.com/adhdblog/podcast.html
  Recent developments related to ADHD.
- Bit by Bit
  www.bobsprankle.com/bitbybit/blog/B88463452
  Using technology in instruction.
- Broward County Public Schools Professional Development for Teachers
  www.broward.k12.fl.us/hrd
  An array of practical educational topics.
- Connect Learning, with David Warlick
  http://davidwarlick.com/connectlearning
  Topics of interest to today's teachers.
- EdTechTalk—21st Century Learning
  www.edtechtalk.com/taxonomy/term/9/9
  Help in planning and implementing instructional technology in the classroom.

BLOGS

One of the newest large-scale communication tools to arise on the Internet is the blog. Blogs (short for Web logs) are online personal journals that are updated regularly, often daily. They typically offer information on a specific topic. The range of topics is vast, with someone writing a blog on virtually any conceivable subject.

Most blogs offer the opportunity for readers to comment online about what the blogger has posted.

Thousands of teachers have incorporated blogs into their instruction. Some are intended only for their students. Some teachers offer their writings to the cyberworld for all to see. Teachers must be very careful about what they put onto blog. Whatever enters cyberspace can be seen by anybody. Assume that colleagues, administrators, and students may read what you post. Insensitive or slanderous content must be avoided.

See the sources below for examples of blogs related to educational issues.

- Bridging Differences (*Education Week*)

  blogs.edweek.org/ edweek/Bridging-Differences/

  Deborah Meier and Diane Ravitch focus on issues related to improving education.

- Digital Education (*Education Week*)

  blogs.edweek.org/ edweek/Digital-Education/

- Education Podcast Network
  http://epnweb.org/
  Access hundreds of teacher-related podcasts.
- Educational Podcasts
  http://homepage.mac.com/deyestone
  How to do your own educational podcasts.
- New Teachers' Hotline
  www.newteacherhotline.com/
  Practical tips for beginning teachers.
- Teach with Tech
  http://teachwtech.blogspot.com/
  Valuable information on integrating instructional technology.
- Teachers' Podcast
  http://teacherspodcast.org
  News, views, research, and resources for teachers.
- Today's Middle Level Educator
  www.nmsa.org/Publications/TodaysMiddleLevelEducator/tabid/1409/ Default.aspx
  News from middle school educators, leaders, and experts.
- UW-Madison: e-Pedagogy Sessions
  http://academictech.doit.wisc.edu/workshops/epedagogy/
  Presentations on pedagogical practices and strategies.

Web 2.0

The introduction of Web 2.0 is an exciting evolution in the Internet, making it vastly more powerful with many creative options. The Internet-based software programs referred to as "Web 2.0" are rapidly making an impact in education. Web 2.0 is a two-way medium, based on collaboration, and information sharing. It not only provides access to content but also invites users to help create that information. *Wikipedia*, blogs, wikis, and podcasting, photo-sharing sites like Flickr and Ringo are outstanding examples.

Collaboration and creativity are the hallmarks of Web 2.0. Popular sites like You Tube and Facebook have connected broad audiences. Creative teachers are finding a myriad of strategies for incorporating the powers of the new Web into their lessons.

For more information on the educational applications of Web 2.0 technologies, check out these sites:

- Classroom 2.0
  www.classroom20.com
- Web 2.0 Is the future of Education
  www.stevehargadon.com/2008/03/web-20-is-future-of-education.html
- 100+ Web 2.0 Ideas for Educators
  www.teachinghacks.com/?p=269

Regular discussions of Tech Topics and Trends in K–12.

- Schools Matter

schoolsmatter.blogspot.com/

Jim Horn, Monmouth University professor, offers incisive commentary on current education policies.

- Teachers Teaching Teachers

teachersteachingteachers.org/

INTERACTIVE TECHNOLOGY IN THE CLASSROOM

Increasingly, teachers from elementary to graduate schools are incorporating clickers (marketed as student response systems) into their instruction. These electronic gadgets look like remote controls and allow students to simultaneously submit answers to the teacher's multiple-choice or true-false questions. Only the teacher knows which student submitted each answer.

This technology provides teachers with instant feedback on the success of their lessons, indicating which students are learning and which students need immediate help. The immediate feedback allows teachers to adjust instruction to reinforce knowledge and concepts not being mastered by students.

Teachers report that clickers keep students more actively involved in lessons, turning them from passive observers to active participants. Clickers are also environmentally friendly—saving reams of paper traditionally allotted to quizzes!

For More Information

Bell, A. (2006). *Handheld computers in schools and media centers.* Worthington, OH: Linworth.

Martyn, M. (2007). Clickers in the classroom: An active learning approach. *EDUCAUSE Quarterly, 30*(2), 71–74.

VIDEO RECORDING

Digital video recorders are widely available in schools and homes. Used wisely, video recording can be a versatile, powerful instructional tool. It can also motivate reluctant students. Current models of camcorders are simple to use, requiring little experience to operate. As with any other instructional technique, the key to success is careful preparation and planning.

- Before you attempt to use a video recorder in class, be sure you have practiced using it. Double-check that the battery is fully charged.

- If you use the same videotape repeatedly, mark on the label the length of time the tape consumes. That will make allotting the correct amount of class time easier in the future. Also file processing questions and any related student activities with the tape for easy access.

- One teacher can videotape parts of the opening day discussion of rules, routines, expectations, and grade policies. If the principal has an opening presentation, that might also be included on the tape. Students joining the class after the first day sign out the video to view it in the library or at home in the evening. This can also be a useful option for assisting hearing-impaired students or others for whom English is not the primary language. Any student who wants to review the first day might choose to check out the tape overnight. Some parents might even be interested in viewing it to learn more about your class.

- Take the camcorder along to tape field trips, special speakers (with their permission), or other interesting lessons.

- Videotape class activities to send to students who are absent with extended illnesses.

- Record various interesting class experiences throughout the year to show at the parents' open house or when making a presentation at a parent-teacher association meeting.

- Use a camcorder to record various activities and events throughout the school year. On the last day of the year, show the videotape in your class. Students will love seeing themselves and recalling some of the highlights of their year.

- As more schools turn to portfolio assessments, videotaping will be incorporated as part of the student evaluation process. Each student might have his or her own videotape to periodically update.

- Some high-quality class-produced videotapes might be shown on the local cable channel. While providing a valuable educational service, you are also creating good public relations for your school.

Internet Scavenger Hunts

Students love Internet scavenger hunts. Lessons in any subject area can incorporate scavenger hunts that require students to gather information from the Internet. The hunts usually include a series of questions and sometimes suggest reliable Web links where answers may be found. Older students can be taught to use search engines and instructed to locate and evaluate their online sources.

High-quality scavenger hunts incorporate questions that encourage in-depth research, higher-level thinking, and problem solving. Treasure hunts may be completed by individuals, pairs, or teams. Many ready-made scavenger hunts can be found online. See these sources for a sampling:

- Adventures of Cyberbee: Treasure Hunts
  www.cyberbee.com/hunts.html
- Internet Hunt Activities created by Cindy O'Hora
  http://homepage.mac.com/cohora/ext/internethunts.html
- Scavenger Hunts: Searching for Treasure on the Internet!
  www.education-world.com/a_curr/curr113.shtml

- Videotape students involved in successful lessons. Send these clips home with students to show their parents or play them when parents come to an open house. Most parents will love the opportunity to see their kids involved in schoolwork.

- Don't overlook the value of reviewing videotapes of your own teaching as a means of self-improvement and professional development. The videotape creates a truthful memory of the lesson. Use the videotape to stimulate reflection on your teaching. Retain videotapes of successful teaching experiences to include in your professional portfolio.

For More Information

PRINT PUBLICATIONS

Branzburg, J. (2007). You can take it with you: How to integrate video segments in curriculum—Without worry. *Technology & Learning, 28*(3), 40–42.

Moore, P. (2007). Camera operator and videographer. *Tech Directions, 67*(2), 36–37.

Stinson, J. (2008). *Video: Digital communication & production* (2nd ed.). Tinley Park, IL: Goodheart-Willcox.

ONLINE RESOURCES

Digital Video in the Classroom

    http://techintegration.cciu.org/Digital%20Video/index.html

Discovery Channel online Video Editor and Mixer

    http://dsc.discovery.com/convergence/sharkweek/video-mixer/video-mixer.html

Dr. Alice Christie's Digital Media Resources for Teachers

    www.alicechristie.org/edtech/dmedia/

Video for the Classroom

    www.mackzone.com/video/tips/default.htm

Videomaker Magazine

    www.videomaker.com/article/3249/

FREE ONLINE TUTORIALS

Creative COW Video Tutorials

    http://library.creativecow.net/video_tutorials.php

Kids' Vid

    http://kidsvid.altec.org/

Videography for Educators

    http://edcommunity.apple.com/ali/story.php?itemID=365

DESIGNING EFFECTIVE POWERPOINT PRESENTATIONS

Well-done PowerPoint® presentations can greatly enrich interest and the effectiveness of any subject. With practice, teachers can create powerful, professional-looking lessons with PowerPoint software. Many teachers encourage students to develop PowerPoint or other slide presentations as a part of their learning experience. A few tips for developing effective presentations are presented below.

- Apply a design template.
- Keep slides simple; avoid clutter.
- Avoid wordiness: use key words and phrases only.
- Remain consistent in fonts, backgrounds, and colors.
- Use clip art to create interest.
- Don't overdo the clip art, fancy transitions, and sound effects.
- Less is more. Avoid information overload.
- Use animation sparingly.
- Use at least an 18-point font.
- Rely mostly on common font types (Arial, Times New Roman).
- Fonts should contrast sharply with the background.
- No more than seven lines of text or seven words per line.
- Proof your slides for spelling and other errors.
- Use one or two slides per minute of your presentation.
- Practice your presentation.
- Stand off to the side so that you do not block anyone's view.

Free PowerPoint Lessons

Free PowerPoint Templates and Music Loops

www.pp.heyda.net/

Free PowerPoint Tutorials

http://office.microsoft.com/en-us/training/

Powerbacks: Free PowerPoint Templates

http://powerbacks.com/

Sources for Free Images and Sounds

FSX: Free Sound Effects

www.freesoundeffect

Gif.com

www.gif.com

Hassle Free Clip Art.com

www.hasslefreeclipart.com/

Microsoft Office Online

http://office.microsoft.com/en-us/clipart

Morgue File: Free photos

http://www.morguefile.com/

Royalty Free Music and Sound Effects

www.partnersinrhyme.com/

DYADIC ENCOUNTERS

A dyadic encounter is a structured dialogue between two (or occasionally three) students. It works best to prepare a sheet or a small booklet of directions and questions. A booklet of ten to twenty pages works better than a single sheet, as the students are more likely to fully focus on one question at a time and not race ahead. (Hint: make booklets by cutting an 8½-by-11-inch sheet of paper into four smaller sheets.) On the first page, include a brief paragraph giving directions on how to proceed through the stimulus questions.

A dyadic encounter can work with any topic in which you want students to reflect on their experiences, opinions, or attitudes. The booklet may contain questions (for example, "What qualities do you most value in a friend?" or "What do you think are the most pressing problems facing our country today?") or sentence stems (for example, "One thing I would like to be better at is . . . "; "The character in *Moby Dick* most like me is . . . "; or "If I could have dinner alone with one historical character it would be . . ."). Both students respond to each question or stem and take turns going first. Encourage students to ask each other's questions and to help clarify each other's responses. The intent of the dyadic encounter is to stimulate thought about a specific topic.

A variation on the dyadic encounter is the talk-walk exercise. Students conduct their dyadic encounter while walking around. This can work well on a nice day when you can take the class outside. Establish restrictions on where they may roam. As they walk together, they discuss the assigned topic. At a whistle or other cue, they all return to the classroom.

DEMONSTRATIONS

Demonstration is an essential step when you are teaching a skill, providing an opportunity for students to see the task modeled. Adequate preparation is the key to effective demonstrations. Have any needed equipment or materials readily available. Pay attention to the details in your preparation. Assure that all students can clearly see the demonstration. If necessary, allow those in the back to stand to gain an unobstructed view. One option is to have someone who has mastered the skill demonstrate it while you narrate the process.

As you introduce the demonstration, be sure to explain its purpose. Focus students' attention on each step as you proceed. You might choose to demonstrate a task or skill at regular speed and then repeat the demonstration in slow speed, stopping to discuss each step in more detail. Explain why you are doing each step as you proceed. You might occasionally ask students questions at crucial points in the demonstration. In most instances it is best to keep your demonstration short, probably no longer than five minutes. Attention will begin to wane if it drags on much longer.

Ideally, your demonstration should be followed by an opportunity for the students to practice the skill you have just demonstrated. Supervise their practice and permit opportunities to receive feedback from the teacher or from peers.

BOARD WORK AND WHITEBOARDS

Math teachers have traditionally had students work through problems at the chalkboard (and now the whiteboard). While this can be an effective means of giving students practice at problem solving and assessing progress, with some creativity it can be even more instructive and fun in most subject areas.

Some teachers have problems already written on the board before the class begins. As students enter the room, they might be assigned to work on these problems at the board in pairs. The teacher can offer hints to pairs who are having difficulty. Students who are not working at the board are called on to analyze the completed problems. Following are a few tips for effectively using chalkboards or whiteboards.

TIPS FOR USING CHALKBOARDS

- Use legible handwriting. Make sure it is large enough to be read from the back of the room.

- Erase items from the board (or ask a student volunteer to help) at the end of the lesson so that a clean board will be available when needed.

- Put a cloth towel into a plastic sandwich or freezer bag along with a few drops of lemon oil. The oil will soak into the towel, creating a superb blackboard cleaner. Add oil as needed to keep the cloth damp.

- Use an eraser covered with a lanolin-soaked tissue as a nifty board cleaner.

TIPS FOR USING WHITEBOARDS

Here are a few useful tips from experienced teachers:

- Use a variety of colored markers on whiteboards for emphasis and increased interest.
- Old white socks work well for cleaning whiteboards.
- Check the view of the whiteboard at various times of the day to detect reflection from sunlight.
- Clean the whiteboard periodically; markings left for a long time leave a faint stain.
- Avoid using light-colored pens on the whiteboard. Red often doesn't show well from the back of the room.
- Use a digital camera to capture whiteboard graphics or writing that you want to save. Download images to a computer for manipulation.
- Use the full capability of the interactive whiteboard. Add video and audio where appropriate.

Interactive whiteboards (aka SmartBoards), which connect to a computer, offer tremendous instructional potential. Software can capture images and video from any electronic source—multimedia CDs or DVDs, the Internet, or any software program—and project it onto the whiteboard.

The whiteboard technology offers a multitude of creative instructional applications. Anything written on the interactive whiteboard (such as a mind map) can be saved to a computer for later retrieval. Teachers can write notes and drawings with a stylus on an electronic tablet and project their writings onto the whiteboard.

Originally developed for use in business meetings, this new technology has begun to find its way into a few classrooms. Unfortunately, the price sets this technology beyond the reach of most K–12 classrooms. As with most technology, declining prices will likely spread its use in the next decade. The technology will be particularly valuable to teachers involved in distance education courses.

ACTION RESEARCH

Action research is an effective learning device for teaching the process of scientific investigation and systematic problem solving. Involving students in gathering data and systematically studying real-world problems enhances the relevance and authenticity of classroom instruction. This may take the form of a case study, an experiment, a survey, or interviews.

Students learn how to ask the right questions, gather data, tabulate results, draw conclusions, and present findings. Action research can be conducted in cooperative teams or as a whole-class project with various delegated tasks. Guest speakers may be invited to provide the class with some background information on the problem under investigation.

The final report might be presented orally or in written form to a group or organization, such as the city council or board of education.

INTERVIEWS

Many lessons can be enriched with the use of interviews, which are best used as a homework assignment. Potential targets of interviews might include parents, grandparents, local government leaders, peers, civic leaders, neighbors, or businesspersons. Besides enriching students' knowledge and motivation through active learning, interviews are also a good public relations tool. People in the community, especially parents, generally enjoy being asked about their experiences and opinions. Interviewing allows adults and young people to have discussions that might never otherwise occur.

It is best to have students develop in class a set of questions that they will use to structure their interviews. Give them sufficient time and specific instructions on whom to interview and a deadline for reporting their results. The interview results can be submitted as a written assignment or discussed in class as a large group or in small groups.

One variation of the interview is a mock press conference, in which one or more class members assume the role of a person or group being studied in the class (astronaut, president, explorer, author, scientist, and so on). They should be given time to research their roles and instructed to answer all questions from the assigned character's point of view.

The rest of the class assumes the role of television or newspaper reporters who then interview the celebrity. A moderator or panel can also be appointed, and a *Meet the Press* format can be used.

In another interview variation, students research the lives of historical characters, notable scientists, or people from another culture. Their peers then interview the students who assume the role of the character whom they researched.

Hands-on Learning

Students from Martin Luther King Middle School in Berkeley, California, learn firsthand about food production from seed to table. They grow, prepare, and eat their own lunches in a project labeled the Edible Schoolyard.

Alice Waters, celebrated chef and food activist, initiated the Edible Schoolyard program at the school in 1994. Students, working with community volunteers, plant and tend a one-acre garden in a lot adjacent to the school, engage in hands-on learning about food production, ecology, and nutrition.

Students not only help grow the food but also prepare seasonal recipes emphasizing fresh and natural food in a kitchen located in a small house on the school property. They also serve and eat the food.

Lunch tables are adorned with flowers grown in the school's garden. Everyone pitches in to help with clean up. Vegetable scraps are composted after each meal, completing the seed-to-table cycle.

All sixth-seventh- and eighth-grade students are involved in the kitchen and garden. A carefully planned interdisciplinary curriculum guides instruction.

Sources: Originally published in the *Heart of Teaching* newsletters, © 2001–2005 Performance Learning Systems, Inc. Used with permission. For more information, see The Edible Schoolyard at www.edibleschoolyard.org.

CONSTRUCTION

Building or making things is an integral part of many courses. Examples include baking cakes, building models, sewing a tie, constructing a house, making a stained-glass window, reconditioning a piece of furniture, taking and developing photographs, reproducing a chair, making a clay pot, composing a song, making a quilt, or constructing a poster.

Such hands-on projects are among the most valuable learning experiences. They closely approximate reality or rehearse activities actually used in the world outside schools. Students tend to become highly motivated when involved in real-life tasks. It is important to clarify the assignment's boundaries, including any evaluation criteria. Deadlines must be specified. For very large projects, it is often desirable to have several checkpoint deadlines prior to the final due date.

Tell students what help they may receive from others. There are many advantages to using group projects where feasible.

See that particularly outstanding products are publicized, with the student's permission. Some might be exhibited in government buildings, malls, fairs, festivals; on local cable television; or at school open houses. Consider inviting the local newspaper or television to do a feature story on your students' noteworthy accomplishments.

Almost daily, local and national newspapers, television, and professional journals highlight outstanding learning activities. Keep an idea notebook of ones you might adapt to your class.

CARD SORTS

Card sorts are useful devices for helping students narrow a range of options, clarify criteria, or set priorities. Potential topics for a card sort might include career options, life goals, interests, criteria for selecting a career or college, or school funding priorities. Any choice in which more than a dozen alternatives are available can be adapted to a card sort.

The first step is to generate a list of alternatives. This can be done as a large-group brainstorm, listing the alternatives on the chalkboard or newsprint. After the list is constructed, each student prints each option on a separate card or slip of paper. (It works well to precut or have students cut 8½-by-11-inch sheets of paper into eight equal slips, each 4¼-by-2¾ inches.) After each student has a complete deck of cards, give directions for the card sort. Instruct the students to sort their cards into three piles: Yes, Maybe, and No. After the initial sort, have them count the number of cards in the Yes pile. If they have more than ten or twelve, ask them to sort through one more time, sorting that stack into two more piles: those they feel red hot about and those they feel lukewarm about. The goal is to get the options down to fewer than ten.

Once the cards in the Yes pile are down to ten, instruct the students to spread out all the cards in their Yes piles so that they can see them all at once. Direct the class to study their cards carefully. After a pause instruct them that they may have only one card. "Which one will it be? Pick it up and hold it in your hand." After everyone has made their selection, tell them they may have one more card, which they are to pick up and place behind their first choice. After everyone has made their second choice, instruct them to continue picking up their cards one at a time until the entire stack of Yes cards is in their hand. They should then record the list in order on paper.

After the card sort is completed, you may process the activity in a large-group discussion or in small groups. Another option is to construct a large grid on the board revealing the group's top priorities. Experiment with variations on the card sort. It can be used successfully in almost any subject.

SURVEYS AND QUESTIONNAIRES

Instruments such as surveys and questionnaires can serve a number of valuable purposes: to enhance interest and motivation in a topic; to introduce a new lesson; or to assess prior knowledge, attitudes, and experiences. Tell students whether they will keep their answers private or be asked to share them. Experiment with using soft music in the background while students are completing the instrument.

Teachers can construct their own surveys or questionnaires, or they can easily adapt them from newspaper and magazine articles, especially those reporting survey results pertaining to topics the class is studying. Many teacher guides also include brief surveys or questionnaires.

A variety of follow-up activities can be used with the survey or questionnaire. A large-group discussion might be held to process the students' answers. Students can talk about and compare their answers in pairs or small groups. Tabulate the answers on a chart or graph to synthesize the group data. A small fishbowl discussion in the middle of the class can be used to facilitate examination of the content. If comparison data are available from other groups, you might share them with the class.

As an introduction to a new topic, construct your own questionnaire to include significant facts related to the subject. Be clear that it is not a quiz and will not be graded. As each question is scored, you are reinforcing the information included in the questionnaire.

ORAL PRESENTATIONS

Oral presentations have long been used as an instructional strategy in American schools. At their worst, they are frightening to give, boring to watch, and a waste of time. Used effectively, oral presentations can be stimulating and motivating learning aids. For an oral presentation to be of maximum benefit, the teacher must appropriately structure it. Most students do not know how to give a brief, focused presentation. When making the assignment, it is important to provide adequate coaching on the project's why, what, and how. The following suggestions might be adapted to improve your students' presentations.

- To reduce the anxiety of talking in front of the group, begin with safe topics the students know well. Themes such as "my dream vacation" or "my favorite game" tap a student's experiences. Permit students to teach a skill they know or talk about a favorite possession; these are topics students can present with little extra study.

- Letting two students do a presentation together provokes less anxiety for the speakers.

- Have students read magazine articles related to an assigned subject area. The students should take notes summarizing the key points of the article and prepare a four- to five-minute talk. Specify the main parts of their presentation. The talk could be split between two students, dividing the content between them.

- In most instances, individual oral presentations should be limited to ten minutes. Few students possess the skills and enthusiasm to hold their listeners' attention longer.

Little is gained and much precious time is lost if your class must endure a succession of long, boring reports. They probably won't be too exciting for you either.

- It is helpful to demonstrate the oral presentation you are assigning. Model the parts of the demonstration and process the presentation afterward, providing a written outline of its parts. Another option is to videotape your five-minute presentation and replay it, pointing out the different parts of the talk. Encourage the class to critique the presentation. It is best if it is not perfect. If you can point out your own errors or deficiencies, students will realize they don't have to be perfect.

- If students have some experience in giving oral presentations, allow two to three minutes at the end of the talk for the rest of the class to ask questions of the presenter. This develops the ability to think on their feet and to speak extemporaneously.

- Sometimes teachers provide an opportunity for the class to offer feedback to the presenter, perhaps in writing: "List one thing the speaker did well," or "Describe one part of the presentation that needs improvement."

- Another tactic for developing oral presentation skills is to develop a persuasive speech. This assignment requires students to take a stand on an issue, research it, and develop a brief persuasive presentation.

- It is best to set a time limit for student presentations. The time should be appropriate to your students' age and developmental level. Seldom should a solo presentation exceed ten minutes, even for high school students. For elementary students three to four minutes are generally sufficient, especially if everyone in the class is assigned to do one.

- The debate format is also a most useful alternative for developing the skills of oral persuasion.

- Require students to speak from note cards. Don't let them write out a verbatim script, and discourage them from trying to memorize the whole speech. Encourage them to use a visual aid or prop. This serves as a cue, creates added interest, and gives them something to do with their hands.

- Oral presentations can also be incorporated into cooperative learning activities, with each team member presenting a different part of the program. It is easier to stand in front of the class as a member of a supportive group than alone.

- Having students interview another student can be a valuable learning experience. Establish the focus of the interview ahead of time. Again, it is easier if the topic is one the student already knows. Another option is to assign students to various historical or fictional roles. The students then study the lives and times of the characters they are playing. The class interviews them as reporters with the role player answering in character.

- It is sometimes helpful to videotape the presentations and allow students to review them later either alone, in teams, or with the teacher. Students might be allowed to check the videos out overnight to show their parents. Some of the better ones might be saved for use at the parent open house.

ROLE PLAYING

Role playing is a valuable technique for simulating real-life situations. Role plays provide a safe environment for students to experiment with new behaviors and skills. The role play can arouse interest in a topic, as well as encourage students to empathize with differing viewpoints. Because students become totally involved in their roles, the learning is holistic, involving their emotional and psychomotor domains as well as the cognitive. The role play is one activity in which students don't have to be anxious about coming up with the single right answer. Giving them permission to make mistakes encourages even more risk taking and experimentation. Even low-ability students can experience success. The creativity of all students can be unleashed through role-playing activities.

Role plays are typically very short, seldom more than fifteen minutes. In a role play two or more students improvise a specific, assigned scenario. These roles may be familiar (for example, introducing a new student to a friend) or beyond their realm of experience (for example, a World War II resistance fighter, a nuclear scientist, or a U.S. president). The actors receive only a sketchy outline of the scenario. Role plays may be set in the past, present, or future. The directive may be no more than a sentence or two. For example, two students in a French class may role play a job interview or order a meal from a menu.

Here are some suggestions for using role plays effectively:

- Plan role plays to support your instructional objectives. Depending on their function, role plays can be used in the beginning of a lesson to introduce a new topic, in the middle to help teach a skill or concept, or at the conclusion to tie together and reinforce the whole lesson. Whenever used, role plays should have a sound educational purpose.

- Generally, you should clearly explain the purpose of the role play ahead of time. In some role plays, where the purpose is to sensitize students to their attitudes, it would be detrimental to fully explain the intent beforehand. In such instances seek their cooperation by explaining that you'd like their help in an experiment. It is important to avoid forcing students into roles that may prove embarrassing.

- To overcome some of the initial resistance to role playing, it may be best not to use the word *role play* the first time you do the activity. Many students have preconceived notions about role plays. Describe it as an experiment or simply say, "Assume for a moment you are . . . " or "Respond as though you really were . . . " It's usually best to seek volunteers for the role play unless everyone is going to be participating. You will likely encounter less resistance to role plays if everyone participates in small groups. (Groups of three seem to work well.) When people assume roles, they must talk: there is no place to hide as in group discussions.

- You must provide a safe climate for students, or they will not get into the roles. After students have gained some experience in small-group role plays, some (but not all) will feel more comfortable role playing in front of the class. Do invite and encourage participation by the introverts as well, but it's probably best not to force very shy children to role play in front of the whole class.

- Explain the roles or give brief written descriptions to each role player. Keep the scenarios and role descriptions brief. A sentence or two is usually sufficient. Assign nonparticipants to make structured observations of the role play. An observer's worksheet is helpful in focusing their attention. Rearrange the room to enable everyone to see. If several simultaneous role plays are occurring, spread out the groups so that they do not interfere with each other.

- Students are more receptive to role plays if they have some freedom in choosing how to play them.

- Keep the introduction to the role play simple. The more you build up the role play, the more anxiety you are likely to create. Succinctly convey the essentials. One tactic that some teachers use is to wave a wand and say, "You're a [role to be played]!"

- Giving the role players props, a costume, or a hat sometimes adds a touch of realism and increases their motivation to assume the role. Having something in their hands seems also to reduce anxiety.

- At least the first time you use role plays, assign roles they can easily play. You may have to provide some prompts for initial dialogue.

- Have students use fictitious names rather than their own. It makes getting into the role a bit easier. It adds a touch of humor to make up funny nicknames for them to use.

- One tactic often used is to interrupt the role play and have two people reverse roles. Or have another student step into a role and continue the role play.

- Immediately after one group completes a role play, have a second group repeat the same role play with a different twist.

- Another option is to have the audience participate by giving the role players directions. For example, in a foreign language class, the audience might suggest a scenario or responses to help structure the role play.

- Adapt the empty chair technique that Gestalt therapists use in exploring conflicting situations. It is a good way to look at two sides of an issue. Only use this technique with content that is safe and doesn't evoke strong feelings in the student. A student volunteer sits in a chair facing an empty chair. The student begins by arguing for a particular issue or course of action (for example, compulsory education, banning cigarettes, curfews). After fifteen to twenty seconds, say "Switch." The student then moves to the other chair and argues the opposite point of view. After another fifteen to twenty seconds, again call "Switch." Repeat three to four times or until the student runs out of things to say. A safe way to introduce this is to have everyone in class do it simultaneously, or break the class into groups of three with one volunteer in each group who engages in the empty chair.

- The press conference is a commonly used role play. One or more students assume roles, such as famous historical characters, scientists, explorers, or authors. The rest of the class act as reporters and interview the celebrity. As a variation, use a *Meet the Press* format, with a panel of two to four journalists who conduct the interview with a moderator.

- Videotape the role play. As it plays back, occasionally stop it to process significant points. This is especially valuable in

Debriefing Role Plays

Morry van Ments, author of *The Effective Use of Role-Play* (Nichols, 1989), suggests the following steps for debriefing a role play:

- Bring players out of the role.
- Clarify what happened (get the facts).
- Correct any mistakes or misunderstandings.
- Dissipate any anxiety or tension.
- Discuss the assumptions, feelings, and changes that occurred during the role play.
- Give the players an opportunity to develop self-observations.
- Develop observation skills.
- Relate the outcome of the role play to the original objectives.
- Analyze why things turned out as they did.
- Draw conclusions about the behaviors observed.
- Reinforce or correct concepts learned.
- Draw out new points for consideration.
- If appropriate, deduce ways of improving behaviors.
- Generalize to other situations.
- Link with prior learning.
- Provide a plan for future learning.

introducing new skills. Students might even take the video home to study their own progress.

- Don't allow the role play to run on too long. Try to cut it off at a high point. If the scenario has run its course, cut off the role play and debrief. If it isn't working, cut it off but don't belittle the actors for their efforts.

- Thank students for participating in the role play. If they have been asked to take a special risk, such as performing in front of the class, praise or a small reward is sometimes appropriate.

- Don't criticize students' role-playing performances (unless it's a theater class). The threat of evaluation will surely stifle students' willingness to engage in role plays. Keep the focus on the actions, not the acting.

- Be sure to always allow time afterward for processing the role play. This is the most important part of the role play; don't rush it. Debriefing is absolutely essential if the role play has evoked conflict or negative emotions. Ideally, it should immediately follow the role play. Solicit feedback from the observers as well as the role-play participants. Ask questions that explore content as well as feelings. It is important to help students make connections between the role-play situation and real-world events.

- Be patient. Role playing may be a new experience for some students. As a more trusting class climate emerges, students will feel more comfortable taking risks and less inhibited.

- If the role play went well and you would like to use it again with future classes, make notes on any refinements you might want to make the next time.

DRAMATIZATION

In dramatization students act out a skill or situation before the class, with or without scripts. A dramatization is a miniplay. The roles are much more defined than in a simple role play. Students receive instructions as to the role they are to demonstrate and suggestions as to the behaviors and techniques to include. Students will usually rehearse the dramatization before presenting it to the whole class.

Strive to minimize participants' potential embarrassment by matching the roles to the students' personality as much as possible. Creating a safe atmosphere for the dramatization is important so that all participants feel at ease. Generally, it is best to explain what you will be asking the students to do before soliciting volunteers. Don't force anyone to participate.

Some dramatizations will require advance preparation. Rather than using verbatim scripts, assign roles and provide guidelines for the students' roles. Occasionally, you may employ improvisation to encourage students to develop their creativity.

Experiment with using puppets to create your dramatization. Most students find it much easier to become involved in a role by using a puppet. Costumes, props, hats, or masks can also arouse students' enthusiasm for the skit.

Group processing of the dramatization is an integral part of the learning experience. Give careful thought to developing good open-ended process questions. Help the class clearly understand the purpose and different aspects of the dramatization.

Here are some examples of dramatization that teachers have used in various subject areas.

- Some foreign language teachers have students enact soap operas in their new language.

- Conduct a mock constitutional convention.

- Present past or current U.S. presidential debates.

- Conduct a press conference of famous scientists, artists, explorers, or inventors about their accomplishments.

- Present a public hearing of an agency on some social or environmental issue. Each side has to prepare testimony and present it to the panel, which must ask the witnesses questions.

- Conduct a mock trial of either a character from literature or a historical figure.

- Allow the class to write their own drama and then present it to the rest of the school. Be sure to videotape it for parents.

GAMES AND SIMULATIONS

Games and simulations can be powerful learning strategies. However, only use them when they have sound educational purposes related to the topics you are teaching. Academic games should require some use of intellectual skills, rather than chance, to succeed. The skills students use in this game should have application to the real world. Academic games may be very brief, requiring only a few minutes of class time; or they may continue over a number of days, perhaps stretched out over several weeks or longer.

- Besides using games to build skills, use them as rewards for good performance.

- It is best to avoid games that end with only one winner. Though the winner feels good, the negative emotions that the losers experience make it an unpleasant experience for most students. They will have plenty of opportunities outside the classroom to confront defeat and know how losing feels. Team competition is preferable to individual competition.

- As with all learning activities, explain the purpose of the game or simulation. There may be some emotional insights you expect to explore and may not want to describe overtly ahead of time.

- Some form of scoring system should be included in the game's structure. To score well one must be required to use the academic skills rather than luck.

- Ask the following questions in considering a game for use in your class:

  - Is it fun?
  - Is it challenging for your students?
  - What is the purpose of the game?
  - How will this game further my learning objectives?
  - What skills does this game develop?
  - Is this game age appropriate?
  - Are skills, rather than luck, required to win?
  - Are the rules relatively simple? Do they need modification?
  - Does the game require team rather than individual competition?
  - Will the game reward inappropriate behavior?
  - How are scores determined and recorded?

- Consider redesigning an existing game to fit your classroom needs.

- Educator Robert Slavin promotes the use of teams-games-tournament as a cooperative learning activity. Students are broken into heterogeneous teams allowing students within each team to collaborate in mastering new content. The teams then compete against each other in academic contests. For the tournament phase, students compete against students of similar ability, and their success contributes to their teams' score.

- To keep track of small game pieces, store them in plastic sandwich or freezer bags.

- Laminate any paper game items that will be used repeatedly.

- One kind of game students love is the television quiz show. Adapt the format of *Jeopardy!, Who Wants to Be a Millionaire, Hollywood Squares,* or other popular television programs to entice students into review, reinforcement, and assessment of your classroom content. Such activities add variety, energy, and enthusiasm to your curriculum. Although some element of competition is involved, try to structure the game so that everyone wins; downplay the competitive aspect.

- Read the group energy level. When the enthusiasm for the game begins to wane, end the game and proceed to the debriefing phase.

In simulations students assume roles and make choices as though they were the person in that role. A simulation is more complex and evolving than a role play that focuses on a single incident. As a structured activity, the simulation provides consequences for the choices the players make. For a simulation to succeed, students must be convinced to realistically act out their roles. They must try to think and act like a real-world person in that role.

Margaret Gredler, author of *Designing and Evaluating Games and Simulations* (Gulf Publishing, 1994), categorized simulations according to the types of tasks and nature of interactions between participants. Tactical-decision simulations require students to interact in resolving a complex problem or crisis and to arrive at a logical, safe resolution. The participants must interpret data, develop options, and implement strategies. Simulations that require management of economic resources fall under this category. In contrast, social-process simulations encourage students to interact to address social challenges or to attain a political or social goal. Participants must interact and react to each other in a social milieu. Such simulations often involve interviewing, negotiating, cooperating, questioning, or persuading. Communication or empathy-building simulations are of this variety.

The most important learning occurs after the simulation, when the participants reflect on what happened during the game. This debriefing should encourage them to examine the thoughts, feelings, and actions that the simulation elicited. Generalizations of these insights for future real-world application should also be examined. Teachers must facilitate this reflection, not leaving it to chance.

Processing done in small groups may ensure that more people actively participate. A good way to facilitate small-group thinking about the game is to provide several written questions for each group to discuss. Each group should have a recorder. Later the whole class discusses the groups' answers.

The latest development in the world of academic games and simulations is the wide availability of the computer and thousands of computer games and simulations. Much of it is commercial, although many good free or shareware programs are also available and easily accessible through the Internet or computer user clubs. There are indeed some pearls in this sea of computer simulations and games, but there is also a lot of garbage.

Although the potential of computer applications with multiple graphics, sounds, and instantaneous feedback is attractive and possesses a great deal of potential, the teacher must use valid criteria in selecting those games and simulations to use in class. A risk is that the eye-catching graphics can distract the player from the game's real purpose. Don't just use a game because you have it. Use as rigorous criteria in selecting a computer game as you would a board game. Is it worth class time?

For suggestions on how to effectively use games and simulations, consult the helpful resources below.

Helpful Resources
PRINT RESOURCES

Biech, E. (Ed.). (2008). *The trainer's warehouse book of games: Fun and energizing ways to enhance learning.* San Francisco: Jossey-Bass.

Buckingham, D., & Burn, A. (2007). Game literacy in theory and practice. *Journal of Educational Multimedia and Hypermedia, 16,* 323–349.

Cohen, S., Portney, K., et al. (Eds.). (2006). *Virtual decisions: Digital simulations for teaching reasoning in the social sciences and humanities.* Mahwah, NJ: Erlbaum.

Ferdig, R. (Ed.), (2008). *Handbook of research on effective electronic gaming in education.* Hershey, PA: IGI Global.

Olson, J. C. (2007). Developing students' mathematical reasoning through games. *Teaching Children Mathematics, 13,* 464–471.

Shelton, B. F., & Wiley, D. A. (Eds.). (2007). *The design and use of simulation computer games in education.* Rotterdam: Sense.

Squire, K., & Klopfer, E. (2007). Augmented reality simulations on handheld computers. *Journal of the Learning Sciences, 16,* 371–413.

ONLINE RESOURCES

Historical Simulations in the Classroom

   www.historicalsimulations.net/index.htm

North American Simulation and Gaming Association

   www.nasaga.org/webx/resources/

Quest Atlantis

   http://atlantis.crlt.indiana.edu/#%20

Simulation Nation—The Promise of Virtual Learning Activities

   www.edutopia.org/simulation-nation

Simulations & Learning e-Games

   http://agelesslearner.com/intros/simulations.html

Virtual Learning: 25 Best Sims and Games for the Classroom

   www.collegeathome.com/blog/2008/06/03/

COOPERATIVE LEARNING

The traditional argument for adhering to the bell-shaped normal curve in distributing class grades was that students needed to be prepared for the competitive, dog-eat-dog world of work. However, the dramatic changes in the global economy have forced a revolution in the workplace. The emphasis is on teaching employees to work cooperatively. Quality circles and work teams are now in use almost universally. Employers realize that to be competitive in the world economy, their employees must be skilled in working collaboratively.

Cooperative learning consists of a variety of techniques that require students to collaborate in mixed-ability groups, helping each other learn the material. Students are taught to take greater responsibility for their own learning. The ultimate goal of cooperative learning is to enable each student to become more successful in school.

The essential focus of cooperative learning is that students are not competing with other students for success. They are seeking to top their own level of achievement. By helping each other, all students can improve. How many people a student defeats in the race for grades would no longer define success. Cooperative learning succeeds when students become convinced that their success is determined by how well they help each other. They must become interdependent in their use of the available learning resources.

Numerous research studies have found cooperative learning does work. Indeed, it may be the most validated instructional strategy in practice today. It results in achievement gains in every grade level, for both high- and low-ability students. Research has found cooperative learning to enhance student self-esteem, mutual helping, and more positive attitudes toward teachers and learning. Contrary to what some people fear, high-ability students do not suffer when they work cooperatively with middle- and lower-ability students. Direct teaching of the interpersonal skills necessary to collaborate is an essential component of cooperative learning.

Cooperative learning is widely used across all grade levels and subjects; probably every school in the United States has some teachers using cooperative learning. The major spokespersons for it have been Roger and David Johnson and Robert Slavin. These educators are among those offering outstanding training programs on using cooperative learning. A thorough presentation of cooperative learning is beyond the scope of this book, but do consider taking a course or workshop to learn more about implementing the various cooperative learning strategies available. See Performance Learning Systems (www.plsweb.com) for an example of one such course, or contact a college of education near you.

The following tips may prove helpful in implementing cooperative learning activities in your classes:

- Merely participating in a group activity will not assure success. Several conditions must exist. The students must be working toward a common goal, and their success in attaining that goal must depend on their interdependence. Ideally, students must also have to depend on each other to share resources. There is evidence that the use of group rewards enhances students' cooperative learning efforts but only if the rewards are contingent on all group members' individual learning.

- Cooperative learning activities can succeed only if a supportive class climate is established. Students must feel free to take risks and make mistakes.

- Be creative in how you form groups. For most temporary groups, randomly dividing the class into the desired number of groups will assure a sufficient degree of mixed abilities in each group. Simply counting off and grouping the ones, twos, threes, and so on is the most common tactic. Inject some humor and interest by using unconventional ways of forming equal-sized groups. For example, have students line up against the wall in order of their birthdays, without talking. Then break them into the desired number of groups.

- Group size can vary with the activity's objective. Generally, a maximum of five seems to be advisable. Heterogeneity in gender, ability, and ethnicity is desirable. The research shows that students involved in cooperative learning become much more accepting of other students, including those different from themselves.

- Clear directions are essential for the success of cooperative learning groups. Provide written instructions in assigning any complicated tasks. Give careful thought to your directions' completeness and clarity. Encourage students to ask questions if they do not understand what to do.

- Each person in a group has a job. The number of jobs required to complete the assignment determines the size of the cooperative learning group. Sometimes the teacher may assign each member specific jobs; other times the group may decide how to break up the functions.

- Cooperative learning develops the social skills necessary to work with others: seeking and giving help, listening to others' points of view, and resolving conflicts. Provide students special training to develop the skills they need for collaborative work. Assessment of each student's social skills is an essential component of successful cooperative learning. Training in the constructive management of conflict is vital for success. For many students cooperation may be a new mode of classroom learning. Patience and guidance will be necessary.

- Cooperative groups can be especially valuable in editing group members' written compositions. Students should be provided with a checklist of criteria to use to evaluate each other's compositions. The peer editor places his or her signature on the criteria checklist. At each step of the writing process—from conceptualization through polished product—the cooperative team members aid each other. Ideally, everyone submits a high-quality written product and the teacher saves much time reading and rereading rough drafts.

- Some teachers have their students explain and grade their homework assignments in cooperative learning groups. An efficient routine must be established for the procedures to follow, with several roles assigned (accuracy checker, grade recorder, coach, explainer). An advantage of this group approach is that students have the opportunity to help each other understand why they made the errors they did and to obtain corrective feedback.

- Cooperative learning groups are sometimes permitted to take examinations or tests together. The day prior to the test, groups may help each other review. It is essential that the groups be heterogeneous in ability. On the test day, students may take individual examinations. After turning in the answer sheet, students meet with their cooperative learning group and collaborate on the examination. They turn in the second answer sheet, with the teacher recording each student's performance on both exams.

> Cooperative learning methods are creating a classroom revolution. No longer is a quiet class thought to be a learning class; we know now that learning is often best achieved in conversation among students. Teachers all over the world are breaking up the rows in which students have sat for so long, and are creating classroom environments in which students routinely help each other master academic material.
>
> —**Robert Slavin, *A Practical Guide to Cooperative Learning***

For More Information

BOOKS AND JOURNALS

Gillies, R. M. (2007). *Cooperative learning: Integrating theory and practice.* Thousand Oaks, CA: Sage.

Gillies, R. M., Ashman, A. F., & Terwel, J. (Eds.). (2007). *The teacher's role in implementing cooperative learning in the classroom.* New York: Springer.

Johnson, D. W., & Johnson, F. P. (2009). *Joining together: Group theory and group skills* (10th ed.). Upper Saddle River, NJ: Pearson.

Jolliffe, W. (2007). *Cooperative learning in the classroom: Putting it into practice.* Thousand Oaks, CA: Sage.

Orvis, K. L., & Lassiter. A.L.R. (Eds.). (2007). *Computer-supported collaborative learning: Best practices and principles for instructors.* Hershey, PA: Information Science.

Williams, R. B. (2007). *Cooperative learning: A standard for high achievement.* Thousand Oaks, CA: Corwin.

Willis, J. (2007). Cooperative learning is a brain turn-on. *Middle School Journal, 38*(4), 4–13.

ONLINE RESOURCES

Cooperative Learning Center (David and Roger Johnson)

   www.co-operation.org/

International Association for the Study of Cooperation in Education

   www.iasce.net/

Jigsaw Classroom

   www.jigsaw.org/

Kagan Publishing and Professional Development

   www.KaganOnline.com/

The Tickle Guide: Technology & Cooperative Learning

   www-acad.sheridanc.on.ca/scls/coop/TCL.htm

Note: Remember that many of the sample templates, letters, handouts for this chapter are available for download from the *Classroom Teacher's Survival Guide* Web site josseybass.com/go/classroomteacher.

Software Evaluation Guide

Title _____

Company _____ Cost _____

Multiple user and site licenses available? ___ No ___ Yes

Platforms supported: ___ Macintosh ___ Windows ___ Linux

System requirements _____

_____

Age or skill level _____

Objectives of software _____

_____

Target audience: ___ Individual ___ Collaborative Groups

Assess each criterion with a score from 1 (poor) to 5 (excellent).

Criteria					
	Poor			Excellent	
	1	2	3	4	5
Ease of installation					
Alignment with standards and curriculum					
Accuracy of content					
Technical quality					
Interest and motivation					
Degree of interaction					
Multicultural and gender sensitivity					
Effectiveness					
Clarity of directions					
Documentation					
Ease of use					
Internal record management					
Total Points					

Recommend software? _____ No _____ Yes _____ Undecided

Strategies for Selecting Group Leaders

First person to stand up

Whoever got up earliest this morning

Last leader tap the person on your right and congratulate him or her

Drives the oldest car

Lowest last two digits in their phone number

Draw cards

Youngest or oldest person in the group

Born farthest or closest from school

Stayed up the latest last night

Most or fewest brothers and sisters

Traveled the farthest to get here

Has the most animals

Been to the movies most recently

Nearest birthday

Shortest pinky

Last name comes first in alphabet

Moved most recently

Most recent vacation

Born earliest in the year or month

Went swimming most recently

Person to left of the last group leader

Came into the room last

Has the most eyelets in their shoes

Ate peanut butter most recently

Wearing the largest (smallest) shoe

Has moved the most times

Mowed the grass most recently

Rented a video most recently

Most years in their current home

Appointed by the last leader

Shortest or tallest

The most letters in name

Bought a _____ most recently

Lives closest to where they were born

Most recent airplane ride

Longest or shortest hair

Sitting closest to the door

Sitting nearest the instructor

Everyone points to the next leader on the count of three

Ask for a volunteer who then appoints the next leader

Field Trip Checklist

Site: _____ Date of Trip: _____

Contact person: _____ Phone: _____

Departure Time: _____ Return Time: _____

Chaperones: _____

Done Before the Visit

_____ Identify the purpose of the trip.

_____ Contact site to arrange date and time.

_____ Obtain administrative approval if necessary.

_____ Distribute permission forms.

_____ Send letter to parents describing details of the visit.

_____ Solicit chaperones.

_____ Arrange transportation.

_____ Make any necessary lunch arrangements.

_____ Develop active learning worksheets.

_____ Collect and turn in permission forms.

_____ Construct map/directions to the site.

_____ Discuss behavioral and academic expectations with students.

_____ Remind chaperones and students the day before the trip.

Day of the Visit

_____ Meet chaperones a few minutes early.

_____ Give drivers maps if necessary.

_____ Distribute any worksheets.

_____ Remind students of when and where to meet.

After the Visit

_____ Debrief students and help students connect the visit with prior learning.

_____ Write thank-you note(s) to chaperones and site coordinator.

_____ Note any changes to be made in next field trip.

_____ File forms, brochures, lesson plans to use next time.

Field Trip Permission Form

We are planning a class field trip to _____

on _____. We are seeking your approval for your child to participate.
We will be leaving at approximately _____ and will return to the school at
_____. We will be traveling by _____. The trip will be appro-
priately supervised. I believe this visit is of sound educational value. Please call me if you
have any questions. I need this form returned to the school by _____.

The above student has my permission to participate in the above field trip.

_____

(Parent or guardian)

Field Trip Permission Form

We are planning a class field trip to _____

on _____. We are seeking your approval for your child to participate.
We will be leaving at approximately _____ and will return to the school at
_____. We will be traveling by _____. The trip will be appro-
priately supervised. I believe this visit is of sound educational value. Please call me if you
have any questions. I need this form returned to the school by _____.

The above student has my permission to participate in the above field trip.

_____

(Parent or guardian)

Audiovisual Request Form

To: _____ Today's Date _____

From: _____ Room No. _____

Equipment	Date Needed	Time	
		From	**Until**

Team Record

Team Name _____ Class _____

Team Members	1	2	3	4	5	6	7	Totals
Team Score								
Average Score								

Tasks:

1) _____

2) _____

3) _____

4) _____

5) _____

6) _____

7) _____

Assessment and Testing Tools

6

ASSESSING STUDENT PERFORMANCE

Assessing and grading students' achievement and progress are inescapable parts of every teacher's job. *Assessment* means gathering information about individual students' level of performance or achievement. *Evaluation* is the process of making judgments about that information. Evaluation involves comparing a student's achievement with a peer group (norm referencing) or with a set standard (criterion referencing). (*Norm-referenced grades* are calculated by comparing an individual student's performance relative to the rest of the class. *Criterion-referenced grades* are determined by assessing how well a student has met a specific set of standards, independent of how well anyone else did.) *Grading* is the subsequent assigning and reporting of a symbol (letter, number, or category) to the evaluation.

FORMATIVE VERSUS SUMMATIVE ASSESSMENT

Two forms of assessment exist. *Formative assessment* is diagnostic in that it provides relatively immediate feedback to aid teachers and students during the learning process. Using this feedback, teachers can alter instruction to help students learn more effectively. Indeed, research has suggested that good formative assessment is one of the most powerful instructional devices in a teacher's toolbox.

Summative assessment is designed to determine what students know at a specific point in time, usually at the end of a term or year. Examples would be high school exit exams and final semester exams. Most standardized tests are summative. Summative evaluation is inescapable. Parents, students, administrators, and colleges expect end-of-course grades. States mandate exit and proficiency exams.

Done well, formative assessment is an extremely valuable means for improving student learning. It helps identify areas in which students are struggling in time for teachers to take corrective action. It assists teachers in making instructional decisions.

Ideally, student assessments provide teachers feedback on how well they are succeeding and diagnose areas needing additional attention. Assessment of students' progress is essential in determining whether instruction successfully met the lesson's objectives.

Good formative assessment deemphasizes marking and grading and depends less on rote memorization than most standardized tests do. Feedback on specific errors and gaps in learning are more valuable than are overall grades in enhancing learning. Receiving a B– on an essay is not of great value in helping students comprehend what they need to do to improve. Specific comments and grading rubrics provide useful data, particularly when paired with remediation and practice.

Formative assessments tend to be embedded within the learning process. Helpful formative assessment options include the following:

- Some tests
- Homework
- Quizzes
- Research reports
- Oral questions with adequate time for students to answer
- Feedback on seatwork
- Thoughtful, reflective class dialogues
- Grading rubrics
- Comments
- Checklists
- Self-evaluations
- Teacher conferences
- In-class writing assignments
- Lab worksheets
- Student journals

Self-assessment is an essential ingredient in the formative assessment process. In a 1998 *Phi Delta Kappan* article, Paul Black and Dylan Wiliam wrote, "Self assessment by pupils, far from being a luxury, is in fact an essential component of formative assessment. When anyone is trying to learn, feedback about the effort has three elements: recognition of the desired goal, evidence about present position, and some understanding of a way to close the gap between the two. All three must be understood to some degree by anyone before he or she can take action to improve learning" (p. 143). Ideally, formative assessment encourages students to assume responsibility for their own learning.

Feedback on performance is crucial for improvement. Hence, good formative assessment is a prerequisite to effective teaching.

MONITORING STUDENT PROGRESS

Special education programs have long emphasized the importance of tracking students' progress on a variety of essential academic, social, and behavioral criteria. Many schools require their staffs to monitor students' progress toward mandated grade-level benchmarks, which are usually aligned to state or national standards.

Progress monitoring applies a scientific approach to data collection and instructional fine-tuning to allow students to get the most out of their educational experiences. This helps teachers make better-informed instructional decisions based on concrete data about what is or is not working.

Professional educators stress the importance of frequent monitoring of each student's progress. This formative assessment allows teachers to make adjustments in their lessons. Increased accuracy in formative classroom assessments are likely to yield increases in student achievement. Self-assessment by students is often an important part of that formative assessment process.

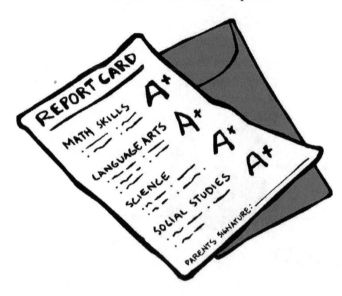

Student grades are not very accurate or reliable measures of their progress. The variety of data sources used to effectively monitor progress include structured interviews, teacher-made tests, rubrics, student portfolios, curriculum-based assessments, checklists, rating scales, and observations.

Progress monitoring is aided by addressing the following questions:

- What outcomes are you monitoring?
- Which data will provide the information needed?
- What evidence will verify whether individual students are making gains?
- To whom should the data be presented? Principals? Parents?
- How will progress data be reported?
- What changes do the data suggest are needed?

Research shows that about 60 percent of the nation's teachers have access to electronic student data systems. Unfortunately, only about half of those actually use that data to help them improve their instruction.

VARIABILITY IN ASSESSMENT

Remember that different teachers grading the same materials show a variability of grades, especially for essays and other subjectively rated products. Different teachers employ different criteria in assigning grades. Even when using the same criteria, teachers may judge differently how well students have met those criteria.

Teachers' grades reflect many factors besides students' academic achievement: students' efforts, persistence, classroom deportment, and a host of subtle biases that can creep into subjective assessments. Research studies have found that each of the following biases can influence teachers' judgments of essays:

- Students with neat handwriting get higher marks on essay tests, especially from teachers with neat handwriting.
- A halo effect exists in the assignment of grades: students who performed well on previous essays tend to receive higher ratings on subsequent ones, even if the quality diminishes.

- Longer essays get rated higher than shorter essays, even when the shorter ones are better in argument, organization, and grammar.

- Students with common names (Sally, Mike, Jane) get rated higher than students with unusual names (Elmo, Zeke, Evangeline).

- Students deemed attractive tend to be rated higher than students rated as homely or unattractive, even when the essays are identical.

An objective view of the research reveals that grades do somewhat predict one thing: future grades. However, the higher up the educational ladder, the less accurately do previous grades predict grades at the next level. However, grades have proven of little value in predicting individuals' success in any field after they finish school.

GRADING STUDENT PERFORMANCE

Grading students' work is intended to meet a variety of educational and social purposes. For some students (mostly those already doing well), grades motivate and control behavior. Grades make categorization of students easier—for promotion, selection, and grouping. Parents also expect feedback from the school on how well their children are performing in school. Traditional grading schemes (A, B, C, D, and F; satisfactory or unsatisfactory) still prevail. But teachers, subjects, and schools vary so much that deciphering the meaning of one student's B provides little information about that student's level of achievement.

There are risks in assigning grades to student performance. Traditional norm-referenced grades, approximating the normal curve, probably work very well for the top one-third. They can develop positive academic self-esteem and generally reap the bulk of rewards that schools dole out. The lowest one-third, however, suffer from overtly competitive grading systems. They enter an environment each day that communicates "You are a loser. You are valued less than others." Howard Gardner suggested that these students may possess important intelligences (musical, spatial, interpersonal, intrapersonal, or bodily-kinesthetic). Unfortunately, our schools tend to value and reward only the logical-mathematical and linguistic intelligences. We should not be surprised that research reveals that students who drop out of school experience an immediate increase in self-esteem.

Student evaluations must be based on a variety of measures: assignments, projects, exhibits, tests, quizzes, observations, journals, presentations, products, performances, self-evaluations, and peer evaluations.

Though assessment and evaluation play important roles in the learning process, research provides little evidence that grades themselves have much educational value. Yet the practice persists, and most every teacher is mandated to submit a grade (usually a letter) for each student at the end of periodic grading terms. The next section offers concrete suggestions that experienced teachers have used to make that process as painless and as fair as possible.

TWENTY TIPS FOR MAKING GRADING AS PAINLESS AS POSSIBLE

1. Involve students in the grading process to minimize disagreements over grades. Make sure they fully understand how grades are assigned.

2. Have students grade some in-class assignments for immediate feedback. Sometimes it is valuable to allow them time to improve their effort after the self-assessment.

3. An elementary school teacher may use recess time for grading the previous period's papers. The teacher goes around to each pupil's desk and grades all the papers at once. On returning from recess, the students receive immediate reinforcement of their work. This saves time at night and also saves the time needed for passing out and collecting papers.

4. It is not essential for the teacher to correct every student assignment. As much as possible, allow students to swap and grade papers. Spot-check to prevent cheating.

5. For seatwork or some homework, provide rubrics that the students use to score their own work and add up their point totals for the week. Spot-check a few papers.

6. For checking students' homework, assign a set number of points to an assignment if it is complete and on time. Let the students check their own answers in class as a whole group. This allows homework to be a learning experience and saves time grading papers.

7. Require students to keep a page in their notebook on which they record each test or quiz grade when they receive it. That way they always have a tally of their scores and need not continually check with you.

8. Some teachers find it more efficient to keep the cumulative total of each student's test and quiz points. When entering a score, add it to the previous total. You might mark this new sum on the student's test paper. You'll save time at the end of the semester by not having to refigure each student's grade. This is an especially easy task if you use a computer grade-keeping system.

9. Stagger the due dates for major projects, papers, and examinations. Receiving a barrage of papers can be overwhelming. You'll manage your time more efficiently if you space out the assignments. Students who have you for more than one class will also appreciate it and probably do better work.

10. It is also a good idea to insist that students keep all graded papers until the end of the term. If there is a discrepancy in what you have recorded in your grade book and what they believe they have earned, they have the final proof.

11. Some teachers have each student turn in a cassette tape with their name on it along with their writing activities. The teacher records comments about the written work as they read it. Students may take the tape home to listen to it or do so on a recorder in class during free time.

12. Some teachers assign each student a number, which may correspond to the one appearing beside their name in the grade book. Each assignment or test must include that number. It is much quicker to find that number when entering scores than to hunt for the student's name.

13. One advantage of seating students alphabetically is that papers you collect are already in alphabetical order, making grades easier to record in your grade book.

14. To keep clear records in the small spaces in most teachers' grade books, code many events that influence the grade. For example:

    Writing A in a corner of the box means "absent."

    Outlining the box means the work was handed in late.

    D means the assignment was done over.

    S indicates a parent signature on the paper.

    (*Source:* Contributed by Betsy Redd)

15. Generally, it is better to record test and quiz grades as numbers, not letters. Numbers are easier and quicker to convert into grades at the end of the term.

16. When grading multiple-choice examinations, use a computer scoring system if one is available. If not, develop answer sheets and a master key that you hold over the answer sheet to facilitate scoring.

17. Require students to double-space all essays or other written assignments. That provides more room for comments than just using the margin.

18. Develop rubrics for evaluating essays and other products. List the specific criteria you are assessing and provide a separate rating for each criterion. Some criteria might be weighted higher than others. If you are only concerned with whether the feature is included in the assignment, a simple checkmark beside that item will suffice. Structure the form to minimize the amount of writing required of you.

19. Teach students to edit and revise their papers before turning them in to save you the time of repeatedly reading rough drafts. Let them work in cooperative groups to help edit each other's papers.

20. Some elementary teachers send home a weekly work folder with each student. The parents read the week's projects and then sign and return the folder with the student. This is a valuable way to maintain effective home-school communication.

TESTS AND QUIZZES

The most effective teachers assess student learning often. This discourages student procrastination and cramming and provides a more accurate assessment of student learning. Here are some tips for making evaluation of student work easier and more effective:

- Strive for higher-order levels of thinking in your questions. The biggest disadvantage of multiple-choice questions is the overreliance on rote memorization. One research study found that students forget 80 percent of what they learn within one year. Most of what students forget are facts they memorized for one quiz or test.

- Develop a file for your old tests and worksheets. A large three-ring binder or manila file folder will work. After using a test, jot notes on the top as to which questions need replacing because they are too hard or too easy.

- If you give diagnostic tests at the beginning of the year, code the test items related to each skill area. Students then receive a checklist indicating their deficiencies. The checklist can also reference pages in the textbook. On the final exam, students only have to complete those areas in which they did not show mastery on the pretest. (*Source:* Contributed by Barb Wagner)

- To build students' confidence, some teachers choose to make the first test relatively easy.

- Run two-page tests on both sides of a sheet of paper and grade one side at a time. When done with the whole stack, just turn it over and begin grading the other side. This way you don't waste time turning all the pages over before you can start grading the second page. Also, you don't have to flip the pages back to page one to begin scoring. Just turn the stack over again. Tests run double-sided do not require collating and stapling, and they also save paper. Answer sheets help with multiple-page objective tests. You may only have to grade one sheet instead of flipping through several pages. You can then save the test copies for future use without having to run them off again. (*Source:* Contributed by Barb Steinhauser)

- Use publishers' textbook tests when possible, but feel free to adapt them to your objectives.

- Use as few items as necessary to assess a skill or knowledge. Why use a fifty-item test if twenty items will give you the same information?

- Some teachers give makeup exams only for extended absences. By allowing each student to throw out his or her lowest grade, the teacher makes sure a single missed test does not penalize the student.

- Develop a computer test file. A variety of software is available to develop a test bank. Tests and quizzes are easily and quickly generated. Some software lets you save performance data, allowing you to eliminate ineffective questions.

- Provide adequate notice and help in preparing your students for examinations.

- Let students review in study teams before an exam.

- Set up a self-checking station for students to grade their own multiple-choice quizzes and homework assignments. Have a laminated answer key and colored marking pens available. Students are not allowed to bring their own pens or pencils to the checking station, and only one student at a time is allowed at the station. When done, the corrected work is left in a tray at the station. As you record grades, spot-check the work for accuracy and honesty. Research shows that students are generally quite accurate in their self-scoring.

- Fill out evaluation sheets on a computer or PDA as you assess the student's essay or product. Print or e-mail a copy to the student, keeping the data on file.

- Experiment with giving collaborative tests. Groups of three students get to work together on the test. You might randomly assign groups each time or carefully select a stratified sample to include one high- and one low-ability student in each group. Success requires that a cooperative climate be already established in your room.

- Give some attention to reducing test anxiety among your students. One tactic for reducing test anxiety and helping students prepare for an examination is to permit them to ask any questions about the test that you can answer with "yes" or "no." (*Source:* Contributed by Barb Wagner)

- Immediately before an examination, lead the class in some relaxation exercises: focused breathing, positive affirmations, stretching, perhaps even shoulder rubs.

- Provide adequate feedback on students' test performance. Help them to understand where they erred and to correct mistakes and misunderstandings. Any assessment should help a student learn.

- Some teachers use cooperative learning groups to take weekly quizzes together and then individual final examinations. The cooperative group members may then meet after the examinations are scored to help each other understand questions missed.

- If any students are very upset about their exam scores, offer to meet with them the next day. Give them some time to cool off first. Make it a policy never to argue with a student about a grade in front of the class. Nobody wins, and the results usually will be unpleasant.

- If a large number of students do poorly on an exam, reconsider its worth. Though it is tempting to blame large numbers of failures on incompetent, apathetic students, sometimes it is the instruction or assessment that is defective. Try to remain objective.

GRADE CONTRACTS

The grade contract is an option that many teachers use, especially in middle and high school. A contract is an agreement between two parties stipulating that when a specified event has occurred, a particular positive consequence will follow. Because completion of the grade contract is dependent on attaining a preset standard of performance rather than relative position within a group, it is a criterion-referenced form of evaluation rather than a norm-referenced one.

In the most common form of a grade contract, the teacher specifies a relatively small number of assignments that are required of all students, with each higher-level grade requiring one or more additional tasks. Generally, the student signs a contract at the start of the course for an A, B, or C. Students who contract for an A but fulfill only the required tasks for a lower grade present a dilemma for the teacher. Should these students be penalized for failing to reach the contracted goal or rewarded for the performance level that they successfully attained? Another option is to specify the tasks required for each grade category but not to require students to identify their target grade ahead of time. At the end of the grading period, students receive the grade corresponding with the contract tasks they completed.

The contracted tasks reflect the course's expressed or hidden objectives. The teacher may wish to attain other goals, but students will tend to emphasize the ones being evaluated.

THE MULTIPLE-OPTION GRADE CONTRACT

An extension of the grade contract system, the multiple-option grade contract maximizes the advantages of a criterion-referenced contract system while eliminating some of the deficiencies of standard grade contracts. The model presented here is a flexible grade contract that teachers have used successfully with a variety of grade levels and subjects. The multiple-option grade contract may incorporate the teacher's teaching style, needs, and objectives while also considering differences in students' learning styles and individual talents.

At the first class session, students receive a handout describing the contract's terms and specifying the minimum number of points needed to qualify for each letter grade. A sample contract might list the following cutoff points: one hundred points equal an A; eighty points equal a B; sixty points equal a C.

Don't specify a target grade of D. Suggest instead that those shooting for a D should come see you later and you'll negotiate a number; this often gets a laugh. Rarely will anyone ever take you up on such an offer. Identify a grade of C as the minimum competency level for your class objectives.

Each week students receive a set of two to ten activities and projects. These assignments are keyed to the course objectives. Successful completion of each task is accepted as mastery of a particular objective or skill. Some activities, reflecting vital skills or concepts, may be required of everyone. There may be alternate means available for demonstrating attainment of the same skill. Many learning tasks are optional; students choose those that best reflect their individual needs, interests, and learning styles. The fact that students may choose among several options, even among a limited set of alternatives, enhances motivation.

The total number of points available should exceed the sum required for an A, usually by at least 50 percent. The contract is cumulative and positive. The student receives points for achievement and effort. Points are not subtracted for poor performance; rather, nothing is added to the student's total.

Students are encouraged to propose assignment options that will demonstrate their learning. Class presentations, reports, book reviews, and interviews are all valid learning experiences that should be encouraged. The student and teacher can negotiate a mutually acceptable point value for such assignments. It is essential that at least an approximate point value be negotiated as part of the contract.

Individual assignments may be evaluated as pass or fail, indicating that the student achieved minimal criteria or that a student's assignment may be prorated and thus receive partial credit. If a pass-fail assessment is used, you may give students the option of redoing assignments until they fulfill the minimum criteria for success. (These criteria can be set quite high, as students have the option of taking more time to attain the prescribed level of success.)

It is possible to grade tests and quizzes on a point basis. Give each a specified point value, such as five, ten, or twenty points. Reward students for high performance. Poor performance is not rewarded, but one bad test score does not doom students for the duration of the term. Because the points are cumulative, not based on an average, test anxiety is decreased.

The contract must clearly specify assignments for it to be successful. Students should not have to guess what you expect. What are the minimal criteria for success? It helps to have high-quality sample products or assignments received from previous classes. Students will not perceive the contract as fair if they have to constantly rewrite because they guessed wrong about what you wanted. This is where rubrics prove invaluable. To discourage procrastination, set specific deadlines for all the assignments.

The multiple-option grade contract places the responsibility for grades on the students. The relationship between performance and grades is apparent. Students always know how many points they have accumulated and how many they need to attain the grade they seek.

The multiple-option grade contract provides an opportunity to individualize instruction and assignments. A menu is presented to the students. Essential skills or experiences may be required of all students, but in many instances alternative routes to a goal often exist. Students may be able to demonstrate mastery of a skill or concept in a variety of ways.

This method of grading forces the teacher to carefully reflect on the desired course goals. In what way will students be different when they leave from when they entered this class? How will the teacher know whether students have achieved skills or mastered concepts in the course objectives?

Students are competing with themselves, not against their peers. No one's grade is dependent on how well others in the class perform. The student is striving toward a preset standard of performance. The emphasis is on mastery.

It is a fair grading system. Students know where they stand and are in control of their destiny. The contract minimizes the subjective elements of psyching out the teacher, leaving the teacher in the role of a resource person. There are no last-minute surprises. This also minimizes disputes over grades earned.

The primary purpose of grades is to communicate a level of performance. The flexible contract represents a fair and consistent method of evaluating academic accomplishment without damaging students' self-esteem.

AUTHENTIC ASSESSMENTS

In 1949, the distinguished educator Ralph Tyler proposed an enlarged concept of student evaluation, encompassing other approaches besides tests and quizzes. He urged teachers to sample learning by collecting products of their efforts throughout the year. That practice has evolved into what we now call authentic assessment, which encompasses a range of approaches including portfolio assessment, journals and logs, products, videotapes of performances, and projects.

Authentic assessments have many potential benefits. Diane Hart, in her excellent introduction to authentic assessment (1994), suggested the following advantages:

- Students assume an active role in the assessment process. This shift in emphasis may result in reduced test anxiety and enhanced self-esteem.

- Authentic assessment can be successfully used with students of varying cultural backgrounds, learning styles, and academic ability.

- Tasks used in authentic assessment are more interesting and reflective of students' daily lives.

- Ultimately, a more positive attitude toward school and learning may evolve.

- Authentic assessment promotes a more student-centered approach to teaching.

- Teachers assume a larger role in the assessment process than in traditional testing programs. This involvement is more likely to ensure that the evaluation process reflects course goals and objectives.

- Authentic assessment provides valuable information to the teacher on student progress as well as the success of instruction.

- Parents will more readily understand authentic assessments than the abstract percentiles, grade equivalents, and other measures of standardized tests.

Authentic assessments are new to most students. They may be suspicious at first; years of conditioning with paper-and-pencil tests, searching for the single right answer, are not easily undone. Authentic assessments require a new way of perceiving learning and evaluation. The role of the teacher also changes. Specific assignments or tasks to be evaluated, as well as the assessment criteria, need to be clearly identified at the start.

It may be best to begin on a small scale. Introduce authentic assessments in one area (for example, on homework assignments) and progress in small steps as students adapt.

Develop a record-keeping system that works for you. Try to keep it simple, allowing students to do as much of the work as feasible.

PORTFOLIO ASSESSMENTS

Portfolio assessment is a valuable form of authentic assessment being widely adapted in schools today. Hart (1994, p. 23) defined a portfolio as "a container that holds evidence of an individual's skills, ideas, interests, and accomplishments." The ultimate aim in using portfolios is to develop independent, self-directed learners. Long-term portfolios provide a more accurate picture of students' specific achievements and progress and the areas that need attention.

Portfolios make it easier to develop grading schemes that emphasize assessing individual student growth rather than competition with other students. Because self-evaluation is an integral part of portfolio assessment, a highly competitive climate will prove counterproductive.

Students will be reluctant to focus on their deficiencies if they believe this will put them at a disadvantage in the competition for the top grades. Often portfolios are used to supplement, not replace, traditional assessment procedures.

Here are some useful tips from veteran teachers on how to effectively incorporate portfolio assessment into student assessment:

- Students should develop their own portfolios, not the teacher. Students should have freedom in selecting items to include in their portfolios. Making the whole portfolio process a collaborative teacher-student effort allows the teacher to become more of a consultant to the student; the teacher functions more as a coach than a director.

- Any item that provides evidence of a student's achievement and growth can be included in a portfolio. Commonly used items include the following:
  - Examples of written work
  - Journals and logs
  - Standardized inventories
  - Videotapes of student performances
  - Audiotapes of presentations
  - Mind maps and notes
  - Web pages
  - Group reports
  - Tests and quizzes

- Charts and graphs
- Lists of books read
- Questionnaire results
- Peer reviews
- Self-evaluations

- Each item in the portfolio should be dated to facilitate the evaluation of progress through the year.

- Typically, teachers hold periodic individual conferences with students to review their portfolios. During this interview it is important to listen to the student's assessments of the portfolio items. The focus of the discussion should be on the products included in the portfolio. The teacher and student work together to set a limited number of objectives for future work. Strive to achieve a dialogue, not a lecture.

- Much of the portfolios' value derives from the students' reflection on which items are worth including in their portfolios.

- The portfolios may be kept in folders, file boxes, assigned drawers, or other appropriate containers. Whatever the storage container, it must be readily accessible to the student.

- Portfolios are especially useful at parent conferences. Help the parent examine the portfolio, pointing out evidence of progress and areas that need improvement.

- Be patient. Portfolios are a new concept to most students and parents. There is a learning curve involved in adapting to the process. Experiment to determine what works, and feel free to modify as needed.

- In some schools, students' portfolios are made available to their teachers the following year to aid in diagnosis. A few schools are experimenting with developing a permanent portfolio that follows the students throughout their total school experience. (This would be separate from their cumulative record folder.) On graduation the students would keep their portfolios.

- Prepare your own teaching portfolio as a means of facilitating your professional development. It also can prove invaluable in tenure assessments and future job searches. Your professional portfolio might include videotapes of successful classes, curriculum materials you have developed, course syllabi, sample lesson plans, professional development goals and objectives, workshop classes attended, published writings, student evaluations, awards, certificates, professional affiliations, principal's and supervisor's evaluations, and your teaching philosophy.

- A large three-ring binder is a practical way to organize your portfolio. Use tabs to indicate the various categories. You might occasionally share your portfolio with students to model the processes you are urging them to follow.

- With the wide availability of computer technology, many teachers encourage students to develop electronic portfolios. These multimedia presentations may incorporate student-designed Web pages, pictures, sounds, video, and text. Electronic portfolios are stored digitally on computer hard drives or on removable media such as CDs or DVDs. Helen Barrett in *Learning & Leading with Technology* (2000) developed a guide to help students create electronic portfolios. The rubric, which helps both teachers and students in developing and evaluating the portfolios, can be found online at http://electronicportfolios.org/portfolios/iste2k.html.

PERFORMANCE ASSESSMENTS

Performance assessments require students to demonstrate mastery of a skill or procedure by demonstrating it. Performance assessment has long been a part of the curriculum in some courses, such as shop, home economics, physical education, or the arts. Directly evaluating a student's sewing, welding, dancing, typing, piano playing, or woodworking is not a new idea.

Direct assessments have the advantage of greater validity because the objective being assessed is observed directly. Indirect measures, such as a paper-and-pencil test on cooking a soufflé, may not accurately predict how well a person would perform baking a real soufflé. Performance assessments are more useful in assessing complex skills and higher-level understanding.

Though not new, the trend toward including live performances and products in educational assessment schemes has grown in recent years. The expanding interest in performance or authentic assessments is largely a reaction to the limitations and disparities of paper-and-pencil tests. Here are some useful ideas from successful teachers:

- The events or activities to be assessed are content specific and emerge from the course objectives. The tasks may be very brief or long and complex. The performance tasks may be completed individually or sometimes in groups.

- Problem-solving tasks related to real-world problems are often used in performance assessments. They may be embedded in a simulated or case-study scenario.

- Some schools have adapted a rite-of-passage experience, often required for graduation. These might consist of mastery exhibits, oral presentations, a résumé, essays, products, artwork, and role plays.

- Classmates may be able to evaluate performance tasks. It is essential to provide a rubric with the evaluative criteria listed with some form of rating scale for each criterion.

- Sometimes students have a choice in the types of products they will develop to prove mastery of the skill or knowledge.

SELF-ASSESSMENT

The ultimate aim of education is to produce lifelong, independent learners. An essential component of autonomous learning is the ability to assess one's own progress and deficiencies. Student self-assessment can be incorporated into every evaluation process. Its specific form may vary with the student's developmental level, but the very youngest students can begin to examine and evaluate their own behavior and accomplishments.

- Instead of grading all assignments, allow students to correct some themselves. You may choose to spot-check these for accuracy.

- Share the specific evaluation criteria (or rubric) that students should employ in assessing various tasks or assignments. Provide them with rubrics (or have the class generate them) that specify exactly what constitutes a good product.

- Provide models of successful products, answers, or performances. These might be tacked to the bulletin board, set in a display case, or played on videotape. Share the model before students begin the project. For creative activities, avoid encouraging students to simply copy someone else's product. Lead students through an evaluation of the outstanding model, using the evaluation criteria to demonstrate why the model is an exemplar. To minimize peer pressure or harassment, use a previous student's work for the model rather than a current student's.

- Schedule individual sessions to discuss students' progress. Have each student evaluate his or her own performance, applying specific criteria.

DESIGNING RUBRICS

Rubrics are grids that help students understand what is expected and valued in any assignment. They specify *performance criteria*—the standards by which students' products or performances will be assessed. Rubrics communicate to students what is being considered in rating their work. They will perceive assessments as fair when they don't have to guess at what their teachers want. Performance criteria also force teachers to clarify their expectations and to focus on conveying what is important to them in assessing any student performance.

Rubrics are valuable authentic assessment tools for evaluating students' performances on tasks that reflect real-life challenges. Traditional assessment devices—tests and quizzes— are of little value in evaluating a student project, such as designing a Web page, drawing a landscape, making a PowerPoint presentation, or participating in a debate. Rubrics are extremely valuable in project-based learning, cooperative learning, or performance classes such as art, music, or physical education.

A rubric helps teachers organize and interpret information gathered while observing students' performance and products. Rubrics convey detailed explanations on students' levels of achievement using clearly specified criteria.

The main purposes in using rubrics are to provide teachers with information on how successful their lessons are in helping students learn and to provide students with clear feedback on how well they are performing. Rubrics also help students become more competent at self-assessment.

After examining several good examples of rubrics (see suggestions below), begin by specifying the criteria you will be using to evaluate a project or performance. Many teachers design a generic rubric that can be adapted to a variety of tasks. See the sample below.

Sample Generic Rubric

TASKS	LOW QUALITY	MEDIUM QUALITY	HIGH QUALITY
1. Task or objective			
2. Task or objective			
3. Task or objective			
4. Task or objective			
5. Task or objective			

The next step in creating a rubric is to generate benchmarks for each of the levels of achievement (low, medium, high in the above example). Each of the empty boxes would include the respective performance characteristics reflecting each level of performance on that particular task or objective.

Try out one of the online sites where you can custom-make your own rubrics. A fine example is TeAchnology at www.teach-nology.com/web_tools/rubrics/. Another top-notch site worth exploring is Rcampus (www.rcampus.com/index.cfm), an open-source online resource that permits teachers to create free custom-designed rubrics.

An excellent resource to aid in designing rubrics is the Educational Testing Service's publication *Creating and Recognizing Quality Rubrics* (2007).

Check out the following rubric archives for many excellent examples covering an array of subjects:

Rubrics for Assessment from the University of Wisconsin–Stout

www.uwstout.edu/soe/profdev/rubrics.shtml

Rubrics for Teachers

www.rubrics4teachers.com/

The Rubric Bank from the Chicago Public Schools

http://intranet.cps.k12.il.us/Assessments/Ideas_and_Rubrics/Rubric_Bank/rubric_bank.html

THIRTY ALTERNATIVE ASSESSMENTS

The two main purposes of student assessments are to determine what students have learned and to reveal their strengths and weaknesses. Besides tests and quizzes, teachers can tap an array of alternative assessment devices. Here are thirty alternative assessment techniques that other teachers have found helpful:

Develop a portfolio	Design a game
Teach a class	Draw a map
Maintain a journal	Present an oral report
Design a Web page	Conduct a debate
Demonstrate a skill	Make a storyboard
Conduct an experiment	Compile a notebook
Write a report	Write a poem
Implement a group project	Draw a picture
Create a chart or diagram	Take photographs
Make a mind map	Make a slide show
Present a drama	Draw up behavioral checklists
Build a model	Create a poster or bulletin board
Produce a musical interpretation	Record an interview
Solve a real-world problem	Prepare a self-evaluation
Produce a video	Create an exhibition

For More Information

DiMartino, J., & Castaneda, A. (2007). Assessing applied skills. *Educational Leadership, 64*(7), 38–42.

Frey, B. B., & Schmitt, L. (2007). Coming to terms with classroom assessment. *Journal of Advanced Academics, 18*(3), 402–423.

Janesick, V. J. (2006). *Authentic assessment primer.* New York: Peter Lang.

Kingore, B. (2008). *Developing portfolios for authentic assessment, PreK–3: Guiding potential in young learners.* Thousand Oaks, CA: Corwin.

Sternberg, R. J. (2008). Assessing what matters. *Educational Leadership, 65*(4), 20–26.

INTERPRETING STANDARDIZED TEST SCORES

School counselors usually have responsibility for interpreting standardized test scores, but it would be helpful for teachers to have at least a general understanding of what different standardized tests scores mean. Too often, standardized test scores have been misused or misunderstood. It is essential to have a basic understanding of terms commonly used in reporting and interpreting standardized test scores.

Standardized tests: Such tests are administered under consistent and equitable conditions (same instructions, same time limits) to assure fairness and enhance validity.

Norms: The test is given to a large sample and data is gathered creating norms or records of how well students generally perform. The data are reported in statistical terms, such as percentiles, grade equivalents, T-scores, or stanines.

Raw scores: The number of test items answered correctly is called the raw score. Without additional statistical information, like that reported in the norms, it would be difficult to interpret the raw scores.

Percentiles: Results of standardized achievement tests are often reported in percentiles, which describe where a particular student stands relative to all in the norming group. The highest score would be the 99th percentile, indicating that that student scored as well as or better than 99 percent of those who completed the norming group. A student scoring at the 55th percentile scored as well as or better than 55 percent of those in the norming group.

Grade equivalent scores: These scores indicate the grade and month of the school year for which a score is average. The average score for a fourth grader being tested in the third month of the school year would be 4.3. A student with a grade equivalent score higher than his or her grade in school (for example, a sixth grader with a grade equivalent score of 8.1 on a math test) doesn't indicate that the child can do eighth-grade work, but that he or she scored equal to an average beginning eighth grader if that student had taken the fifth-grade test.

Mean: This is the statistical average of a group of numbers. It is calculated by adding all numbers in a set of numbers and then dividing by the number of observations in the set. Examples would include grade point average, the Dow Jones, or average daily temperature. The mean is the most commonly used measure of central tendency.

Normal distribution: A bell-shaped graph of data. It is highest in the middle and lowest on the sides, and the right and left halves are symmetrical.

Standard deviation: A statistic that describes how tightly all the data are clustered around the mean in an array of data. When the instances are closely bunched together and the bell-shaped curve is steep, the standard deviation is small. When the data are wider apart and the bell curve is flatter, the standard deviation will be large.

Standard scores: Frequently standardized test results are reported as standardized scores. The Standardized Achievement Test (SAT) and Graduate Record Examination (GRE) provide standard scores.

Remember that important decisions affecting a student's future should never be based on only one standardized test score.

HIGH-STAKES TESTING

With increasing pressure from the federal government, by 2003 nineteen states had mandated standards-based exit examinations, often called proficiency tests or competency tests. Research from the Center on Education Policy indicated that by 2012, 74 percent of the nation's public school students will be required to pass an exit exam before they can graduate. This national trend is often labeled high-stakes testing.

California's High School Exit Exam is fairly representative. Students take the exam, consisting of English language arts and mathematics sections, in the tenth grade and may retake each section of the pass-fail exam up to five times. Also fairly typical is the mandate that schools must offer assistance to students who do not demonstrate progress toward passing the exam. However, the state does not provide districts with additional funds for this purpose.

Arguing for making tests a cornerstone of educational improvement practices, the Educational Testing Service, which produces many of the standardized tests used in the effort, states: "Tests provide answers. They help teachers make better instructional choices for their students. They help students—and their parents—understand how well they are learning what they are supposed to know and how they compare to other students. Good tests identify strengths as well as weaknesses" (ETS Web site at www.ets.org/letstalk/formula.html).

On the other hand, respected education researchers Sharon Nichols and David Berliner (*Phi Delta Kappan,* May 2008), strongly asserted, "The high-stakes testing provision of NCLB has wreaked havoc with our education system, causing irreversible harm to many of our nation's youths and educators."

Harvard's Dan Koretz claimed that one of the major flaws of the high-stakes testing phenomenon is that students with disabilities and nonnative speakers of English are frequently included in the same testing programs used with the general education students. Their failure rate often exceeds 50 percent, distorting the overall picture and discouraging those challenged students. Koretz concluded, "If used sensibly, test scores provide unique and valuable information about student achievement. The trick is using them sensibly, which requires recognizing the limitations of testing as well as its strengths."

The American Psychological Association (APA) cautioned that public officials and educational administrators using tests to make high-stakes decisions must be alert to "the instances when tests have unintended and potentially negative consequences for individual students, groups of students, or the educational system more broadly." Its Code of Fair Testing Practices in Education policy (APA, 2004) further stated, "It is only fair to use test results in high-stakes decisions when students have had a real opportunity to master the materials upon which the test is based."

Educators and public critics have become increasingly vocal in urging schools to use multiple indicators (including grades, performance assessments, attendance, and advanced placement coursework) in making decisions about promotion, graduation, retention, or rewards.

Most states have initiated incentives (and sometimes punishments) for schools and teachers when their students' test performance falls short of set standards. When California implemented incentive bonuses for teachers whose students showed gains in their SAT-9 scores, over one thousand teachers earned bonuses of $25,000 when their students attained 10 percent gains in their test scores.

Arguments for High-Stakes Testing

- They help schools focus instructional programs.

- They can provide teachers with valuable information about instructional programs' quality and individual students' achievement.

> Tests in and of themselves do not improve the quality of education; teachers do. Unless testing programs are coupled with comprehensive strategies for disaggregating and interpreting data and implementing curricular and instructional approaches to school improvement, it is unlikely anything will change.
>
> —Harold C. Doran of
> New American Schools

> School officials using such tests must ensure that students are tested on a curriculum they have had a fair opportunity to learn, so that certain subgroups of students, such as racial and ethnic minority students or students with a disability or limited English proficiency, are not systematically excluded or disadvantaged by the test or the test-taking conditions. Furthermore, high-stakes decisions should not be made on the basis of a single test score, because a single test can only provide a "snapshot" of students' achievement and may not accurately reflect an entire year's worth of student progress and achievement.
>
> —American Psychological Association,
> *Appropriate Use of High-Stakes Testing*
> *in Our Nation's Schools*

> *Decisions that affect individual students' life chances or educational opportunities should not be made on the basis of test scores alone.*
>
> —**American Educational Research Association, *Position Statement Concerning High-Stakes Testing in PreK–12 Education***

- The same high expectations and the same evaluation criteria hold for all students.
- Tests help identify children's strengths and weaknesses.
- They allow policymakers to reward high-performing schools and teachers.
- The exams force schools to better align curricula with state standards.
- It is easier to make school-to-school comparisons.

Arguments Against High-Stakes Testing

- Teachers feel they must use instructional strategies that they don't believe are good educational practices.
- State tests seldom take into account errors in measurement.
- School graduation rates decline.
- Teachers only teach to the test.
- Rote memorization tends to be rewarded more than critical-thinking skills.
- Standardized test scores correlate highly with parents' income and level of education.
- Too much time is spent preparing students to take tests.
- Content not tested tends to become neglected.
- As the curriculum narrows, students will become less well rounded.
- Less time is spent on noncore areas, such as the fine arts and foreign languages.
- They encourage teachers to work in ways that are lockstep and uncreative.
- Making such important decisions based on performance on one test is unfair.
- The tests have little correlation with success outside of school.
- Testing programs are extremely expensive.

For More Information

BOOKS AND ARTICLES

American Psychological Association. (2004). *Code of fair testing practices in education.* www.apa.org/science/fairtestcode.html.

Au, W. (2009). *Unequal by design: High-stakes testing and the standardization of inequality.* New York: Routledge.

Fisanick, C. (Ed.). (2008). *Has No Child Left Behind been good for education?* Detroit, MI: Greenhaven.

Hursh, D. (2008). *High-stakes testing and the decline of teaching and learning: The real crisis in education.* Lanham, MD: Rowman & Littlefield.

Nichols, S. L., & Berliner, C. (2008). Testing the joy out of learning. *Educational Leadership, 65*(6), 14–18.

ONLINE RESOURCES

Academic Benchmarks

   www.academicbenchmarks.com/search/

   K–12 standards for all states.

National Center for Fair & Open Testing

   www.fairtest.org/

   Extensive library of materials related to high-stakes testing.

National Center for Research on Evaluation, Standards, and Student Testing (CRESST) at UCLA Graduate School of Education

   www.cse.ucla.edu/

   Scientific approaches to improving the quality of education and learning.

Note: Remember that many of the sample templates, letters, handouts for this chapter are available for download from the *Classroom Teacher's Survival Guide* Web site josseybass .com/go/classroomteacher.

Skill Assessment Form

Name _____ Date _____

Subject _____

Teacher_____

Skill	Yes	No	No Evidence	Comments

Assignment Record

Name _____

Week _____

Subject	Monday	Tuesday	Wednesday	Thursday	Friday

Don't Forget!

Test Tomorrow

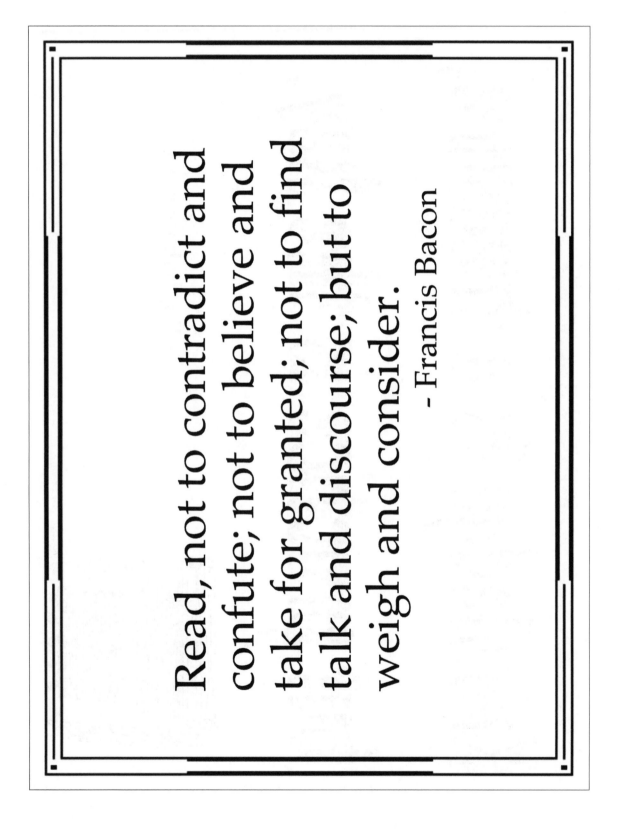

Read, not to contradict and confute; not to believe and take for granted; not to find talk and discourse; but to weigh and consider.

– Francis Bacon

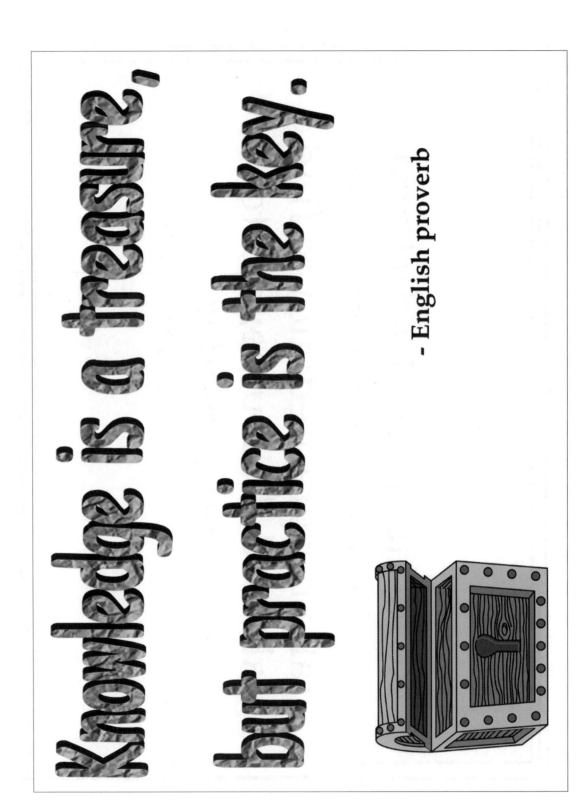

Knowledge is a treasure,
but practice is the key.

- English proverb

Performance Record

Class _____   Term/Year _____   Teacher _____

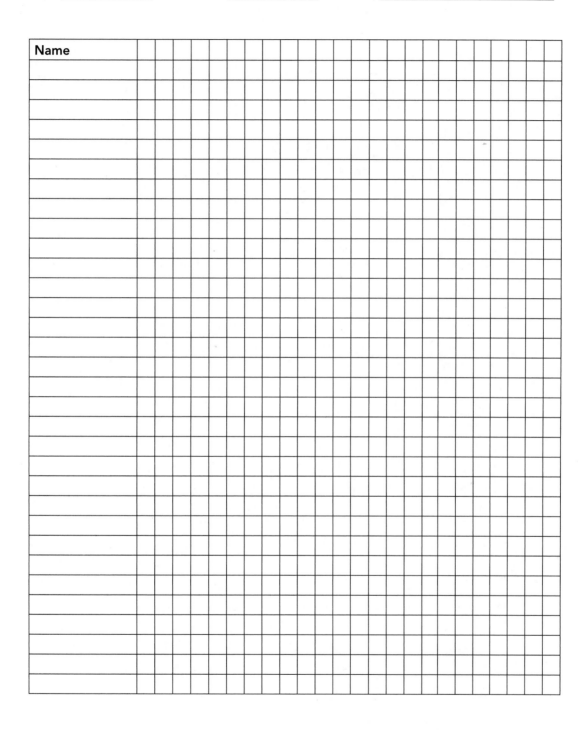

Building a Learning Community

7

TWENTY-FOUR HOT TIPS FOR WORKING WITH OTHER TEACHERS

Most experienced teachers have learned to avoid the potential isolation of the classroom. In many schools a teacher can go through an entire day with little more than superficial contact with other adults. What happens behind the closed classroom door is still seen as private in some schools. Beginning teachers used to enter the profession with full responsibility from the first day, learning to teach largely on their own by trial and error or the sink-or-swim method.

Fortunately, there are signs that the school culture is opening up. Increasingly, teachers are collaborating, working in teams, and engaging in peer coaching. Attention to developing collegial relationships and nurturing positive school climates is growing.

1. Talk with your colleagues about teaching. This should involve more than complaining about insufficient supplies or bemoaning how terrible kids are these days. Nor should conversations be limited to trading war stories. Encourage a positive focus on sharing strategies for improving classroom teaching, solving school problems, or seeking innovative ways of doing old tasks.

2. Experiment with peer coaching. Invite teachers whom you respect to observe your teaching and provide suggestions for improvement. Let the observers know which areas you are seeking to improve. Of course, if you solicit their feedback, listen to it objectively. Don't discount their views and become defensive. Ask for help from colleagues. Share your concerns about what you would like to do better. In every building there are successful teachers. Seek them out and learn from their experiences.

3. Acknowledge your fellow teachers' successes. Relay positive comments you hear from students about other teachers.

4. Send special notes and cards to your colleagues, recognizing their successes or offering words of comfort during difficult times. Eschew jealousy over other teachers' successes. Your value as a teacher or person is not diminished by others' accomplishments. To be appreciated is one of the most fundamental human needs.

5. Share curriculum resources or creative ideas that you bring back from professional workshops or read in journals.

6. After attending school in-service programs, discuss the content with other teachers. Try to remain open-minded in examining new ideas, always seeking new ways to improve your teaching. Convey to your colleagues that you value improvement and appreciate their ideas.

7. Avoid joining the staff saboteurs whose main function is to prevent any efforts at improvement. Their primary activities are complaining, gossiping, nit-picking, whining, and ridiculing. Rarely do they offer positive solutions or acknowledge their

own deficiencies. They blame all their problems on others. Often they will be found sitting in the back at faculty meetings or clustered in faculty lounges before and during school. Treat them cordially, but resist their venomous game. They are an emotional and economic drain on their schools, taking far more than they contribute. It is unlikely that they find much joy in teaching.

8. Avoid gossiping about other teachers, students, or the administration. Gossip serves no constructive purpose and poisons the school climate. It is unprofessional as well as destructive. If you hear gossip, don't spread it. Be especially careful in what you say about students or faculty outside of school.

9. Organize or join a study group or peer support group. Peer coaching is gaining acceptance in many schools. Do whatever you can to nurture mutual support and the development of collegial, professional relationships.

10. Participate in professional improvement activities with your colleagues. Attend workshops, classes, or conferences together. Watch videotapes or discuss education-related books. Nurture each other's professional development.

11. Strive to develop connections with teachers beyond your area or grade level. Much can be learned from all good teachers, regardless of the subject or grade they teach.

12. Observe outstanding teachers in their classrooms. The truly effective ones will welcome your presence. They are not threatened by having visitors in their classrooms.

13. Never criticize fellow teachers in front of students. Such unprofessional conduct serves no constructive purpose. Always assume that whatever you say about a colleague will eventually get back to that person.

14. Communicate directly with the other teacher if you believe his or her behavior creates a problem for you or your students. If the grievance is serious, pursue it through your principal. Remember, you will probably be working with that teacher for some time.

15. Be willing to do your share of the work. Volunteer for some committee assignments: chaperoning dances, organizing events, or supervising students. However, avoid overcommitting yourself to extracurricular activities.

16. A friendly "hello" or "good morning" plants the seeds of an inviting relationship with your colleagues, even those you don't know very well or who treat you coolly.

17. Help create goodwill. Celebrate special occasions by bringing cookies, fruit, or other treats to a faculty meeting or to the lounge in the morning.

18. Avoid associating only with a favorite clique. Try to develop cordial relationships with all teachers, even those with whom you disagree. Try to get to know them as people. Discover their interests, family news, and achievements.

19. Respect your colleagues' rights. Avoid causing students to be late to their classes. Don't undermine colleagues' authority and credibility with their students. Remain considerate of your fellow professionals' needs.

20. Don't borrow materials, books, supplies, or equipment without asking. If you do use someone else's things, be sure to return them promptly.

21. Be extremely cautious of reprimanding other teachers' students, especially while the students are under their teachers' supervision.

22. Try to resolve conflicts in a mature, assertive fashion. Any school will have occasional disagreements over policies, perceptions, solutions, or actions. Feelings can get hurt, intentions misperceived. Seldom is one person right and the other absolutely wrong. Colleagues are rarely evil, though occasionally they may be thoughtless or inconsiderate. Don't overreact. The first step is to let the person know in an assertive, not hostile, way that you perceive a problem to exist. Seek collaborative problem solving. Really listen to their point of view. Avoid petty squabbling.

23. Be patient with your colleagues. Like you, your fellow teachers are humans. They will have bad days and will make mistakes. Don't expect them to hold the same values and perspectives as you.

24. Treat all colleagues as professionals, even if you don't believe they are treating you with full respect. Work at being tolerant of those who have views different from yours. Treat all others decently. Your initial perceptions of people can be wrong; you don't know all that is happening in their lives beyond school.

WORKING WITH A MENTOR

Teaching is challenging work, even for the most experienced teachers. The most enthusiastic beginning teachers can find entering their very first class to be a frightening experience. Approximately a third of all new teachers leave the profession within three years. Clearly, new teachers need support.

You can learn much from the veterans in your school; ask for their advice. You don't have to reinvent the wheel. Others have faced the same challenges and taught the same content. Learn what works for them. It makes them feel valued if you are genuinely interested.

Many schools have established formal mentoring programs to make the transition smoother for beginning or struggling teachers. Indeed, some states have mandated such programs. An abundance of research supports the wisdom of well-implemented mentoring programs.

Seek out the best teachers in the school and ask their permission to observe their classes. It doesn't matter what subject they are teaching. There is no substitute for seeing outstanding teachers in action.

A number of excellent publications outline the procedures for setting up effective mentoring programs. Hopefully, your school has followed those guidelines. A well-matched mentoring relationship benefits both the mentor and the protégé. And in the end, students greatly benefit as well.

Having an effective role model to provide a friendly ear, objective feedback, support, and encouragement has tremendous potential for enriching one's professional development. Effective coaches and mentors help novice teachers gain confidence, improve their skills, and achieve their full potential. Mentored teachers are more likely to stay in the profession and enjoy teaching more.

A Hampton, Virginia, program matches beginning teachers with retired teachers. The program is a collaboration among the Virginia Education Association, the NEA-Retired Association, the local school district, and area universities.

Although the tendency is to focus largely on classroom management issues earlier in the mentoring process, it should move on to include lesson planning, curriculum goals, collegiality, and instructional improvement.

Here are some concrete tips on how to reap the most from a mentoring relationship:

- If your school doesn't have a formal mentoring program, ask your principal about creating one. Suggest one or two teachers you admire as potential mentors.

- If you are a beginning teacher or having difficulty, find a mentor. Identify a teacher whom you respect and whose style and personality is simpatico with yours. Seek someone who is genuinely enthusiastic about teaching and is an exemplary instructor. Share your difficult problems with them and listen openly to their advice.

- Get to know your mentor. If possible, meet him or her before the school year begins.

- Enter the mentoring relationship with an open mind. Your mentor is not there to judge or evaluate you. Even if you don't agree with something your mentor says, treat him or her with respect.

- Take responsibility for initiating contacts with your mentor when you need help. Your mentor cannot anticipate all your needs and concerns. Try to set up regular meetings.

- Being an effective mentor takes a serious commitment of time and effort. Be respectful and don't monopolize your mentor's time or become overly dependent.

- Accept suggestions and constructive criticism. Avoid taking criticism personally, and try to avoid becoming defensive. You are not perfect and you will make mistakes.

- If possible, visit your mentor's classroom to observe him or her in action. Take notes about what you see and initiate a discussion later about what you observed. Focus your observations on specific aspects, such as the way this teacher asks questions, the teacher's nonverbal behavior, the use of praise and encouragement, the teacher's way of handling transitions, or the pace of the lesson.

- Clarify what you think the mentor is communicating. Ask follow-up questions or paraphrase what you think you have heard. Clarify your assumptions.

- Periodically express your appreciation for your mentor's help. If your mentor is especially helpful, be sure to convey that message to the principal or superintendent. Doing so multiplies the effect of your gratitude.

- Share your successes with your mentor. Give your mentor credit for helping you improve.

- Develop a file of warm-and-fuzzy compliments, positive notes from parents or students, and mementos of any other successes you cherish. Paste these in a scrapbook and reread them anytime you begin to feel a bit discouraged.

- Keep a daily journal, noting concerns, challenges, questions, successes, and insights. Reflect on insights you gain. These notes may serve to structure meetings with your mentor. This writing is not a formal paper, so write whatever comes to mind in whatever style flows naturally. Reread your journal later in the year. Save it. Who knows? It might become a book someday!

- Give the mentoring relationship a fair chance to succeed. If after a couple of months, you find that your mentor is not very helpful, develop an informal mentor relationship with a teacher you admire. If you have a trusting relationship with your principal, candidly discuss your concern.

- At the end of the year, do something nice for your mentor. A letter of appreciation, an invitation to lunch, or a small gift would likely be most appreciated. For many, the mentoring relationship blossoms into a lifelong friendship.

TELEMENTORING

In a creative application of developing computer technology, many teachers have linked up in telementoring projects (also known as e-mentoring or telecoaching). Some telementoring projects are formally set up by schools or universities, some by for-profit organizations, and others by informal arrangements between two teachers. The University of California at Santa Cruz's New Teacher Center sponsors the eMentoring for Student Success (eMSS) program, which helps new science and math teachers use cyberspace to work with experienced teachers in their subject areas.

Most of the communication occurs through e-mail exchanges. The mentor can be thousands of miles away yet still develop a helpful relationship with the protégé. Some teachers videotape lessons and send them electronically to their mentors, making it possible for their mentor to see them in action. Some trendsetters are experimenting with viewing live-stream video from their protégés.

For More Information

e-Mentoring for Student Success (eMSS)

www.newteachercenter.org/eMSS/

Electronic Emissary

http://emissary.wm.edu/

Guiding Principles: Tips on Building Trust Online

www.edutopia.org/online-mentoring

Teachers.net

http://teachers.net/mentors/

GUIDELINES FOR COLLABORATIVE TEAMS

The ability to engage in group problem solving has become a vital skill for today's teachers, as schools increasingly incorporate site-based management (directly involving local staff in decision making), collaborative teams, and shared decision making. The opportunity to participate more broadly in the school decision-making process has several potential benefits. Giving teachers a greater voice in the school decision-making process, like the quality circles that businesses are adapting, ensures that those having the best available information will make decisions and be responsible for implementing them. Participatory decision making also gives the participants a greater sense of control and is more likely to yield a commitment to the resulting decisions.

The ability to effectively arrive at good group decisions requires a set of learned skills that teacher education courses of study rarely include. It is risky to assume that all members of a team are competent at group problem solving. Unfortunately, most people assume that everyone knows how to arrive at group decisions. A substantial body of research suggests this is a most erroneous supposition. To be effective, specific training in collaborative decision making should be available to any staff moving toward greater use of teams. The preponderance of evidence also shows training in group problem-solving skills leads to more creative ideas, both in quantity and quality.

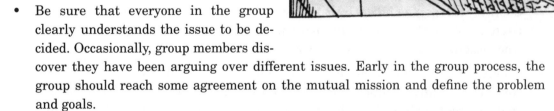

Whenever two or more persons must jointly arrive at decisions, expect two things: (1) the process will take more time, and (2) the process will bring friction. Although any group can arrive at a decision, the barometer of success is whether the group considered the best available information in making its choice. When groups effectively tap all their members' resources, they are capable of achieving synergy, meaning that the group product is superior to anything any one individual could have achieved alone.

- Be sure that everyone in the group clearly understands the issue to be decided. Occasionally, group members discover they have been arguing over different issues. Early in the group process, the group should reach some agreement on the mutual mission and define the problem and goals.

- Ask open-ended questions to elicit all points of view. Some participants are going to be more reluctant to share their views openly without encouragement. Paraphrasing for understanding and clarity is another valuable communication tool for group decision makers.

- Occasionally ask others to clarify with examples and specifics. Don't necessarily assume that you know what another person means.

- In the early stages of searching for possible solutions, employ the strategy of group brainstorming. To succeed, brainstorming must adhere to four rules:

- Elicit as many ideas as possible. The focus in this stage is on quantity, not quality. The more ideas you have, the greater the possibility of discovering a good one.

- Delay evaluation. Later you will apply judgment criteria to your ideas, but premature criticism nips creativity in the bud.

- Encourage wild, far-out, half-baked ideas. One may be the diamond in the rough.

- Listen to others' ideas and use them as springboards. Let their ideas stimulate your search. For this reason, it helps to record the group ideas on newsprint for all to see.

Elicit different points of view. View such disagreements as a healthy part of the group search for the optimal decision. Avoiding conflict is not productive in arriving at good group decisions. Research shows that the most effective decision-making groups encourage minority opinions to be aired. It is important to discuss sources of resistance openly rather than to let them fester and later sabotage the implementation of the decision.

- The goal should be to arrive at a win-win consensus rather than a compromise that elicits little enthusiasm. For that reason avoid such conflict-reducing techniques as voting or averaging. These may save time, but they often yield inferior decisions that lack all members' commitment.

- It is also important for groups to arrive at their own definition of consensus. It could mean that everyone must enthusiastically endorse any group decision, that everyone agrees the solution might work and should be tried and later reevaluated, or simply that everyone can live with the recommendation.

- Consensus building is most likely when all group members seek to identify areas of disagreement and the common ground. The group should fairly analyze the advantages and disadvantages of all possible solutions.

- Don't change your mind merely to avoid conflict. Disagreement among persons with different needs and assumptions is a legitimate part of the group process. Conversely, it is important to challenge others' ideas, especially when they offer little support for their position.

- When conflicting views emerge, strive to identify the needs and interests rather than merely the positions of the opposing group members.

- Show your respect for others by listening to their ideas. When you share your opinions, try to be nonconfrontational. Present your point of view without putting down those who disagree. Focus on issues, not personalities.

- If necessary, leave the decision for a later time. This permits some incubation time. New, more creative solutions may emerge from this reflection. Such a delay is especially warranted if the discussion has become excessively volatile or if the group lacks information necessary to make a sound decision.

- Groups have very limited attention spans and tend to digress from the issue at hand. Gently refocus the group's attention with such open-ended questions as "What additional information do we need?" or "Are there any other options we have not considered?"

- Be sure to have a team member keep a written record of your team's decisions and create the group memory. This helps the team keep focused on its task and assures a future record of what the group has decided.

- Create opportunities to celebrate your team's successes: a gag gift, a funny ritual, a special meal, or a party.

- A team must assume responsibility for decisions that don't succeed. Part of the price of the freedom to make decisions is accepting their consequences.

- Capitalize on each team member's strengths and talents. Match the tasks required with your team members' skills.

- Training should be available on group roles, group problem solving, planning, and stages of group development. The group might read and discuss some of the resources that follow.

- The members should be conscious of and occasionally examine their group process to see if it is working effectively. By enhancing their process, the team can arrive at better choices. Some teams find it helpful to take five minutes at the end of each meeting to complete a team process assessment form such as the one at the end of this chapter.

SUGGESTIONS FOR EFFECTIVE ACTION PLANNING TEAMS

- Select a group leader. Things seem to go more smoothly if one person serves as the facilitator.

- Do not prematurely seek the ultimate solution. Spend time clarifying the issues related to the problem, as well as its causes and effects.

- Discuss what additional information is needed to make an intelligent decision. Where can you get that information? Divide up the information-gathering tasks. Ask for help if you need it.

- After gathering relevant information, spend adequate time fully brainstorming options without prematurely evaluating. Remember the four rules of effective brainstorming:

  ○ Strive for as many ideas as possible.

  ○ Delay evaluation.

  ○ Encourage novel, creative ideas.

  ○ Build on others' ideas.

- Elicit ideas from other members without dominating the discussion. Remember to differentiate facts from opinions.

- Components of an effective action plan should include the following:

  ○ Specific steps to be taken

  ○ Who will be responsible for each component of the plan

Teacher Leadership

Teachers have increasingly taken on roles as active leaders in their schools. Much of their effort focuses upon studying effective practices and working toward their implementation within their schools. A primary objective is to use data from sound research to inform and reform educational practices. These exemplary practices are often shared with colleagues through action-planning teams.

Active teacher leadership has played a significant role in helping turn around many underperforming schools. Nurturing a cohesive learning community is a crucial component of these successes. Research shows that such efforts require teachers to assume active roles in their schools' decision making and that a school culture emerges valuing continuous improvement.

Teachers and administrators collaborate with parents at all stages of the improvement process: planning (including setting goals and priorities), implementing (putting the plan to work), supporting (soliciting necessary resources, time, and personnel), monitoring (measuring progress and effectiveness), and communicating (sharing the story with colleagues and the community).

- ◦ A reasonable time line for implementing each component
- ◦ Estimates of any costs for implementation and suggestions as to the source of these funds
- ◦ A target deadline for reevaluating progress toward implementation of your plan
- Set a time and place to meet again if needed.

Helpful Resources

Holcomb, E. L. (2009). *Asking the right questions: Tools for collaboration and school change* (3rd ed.). Thousand Oaks, CA: Corwin.

Jennings, M. (2008). *Dynamic educational leadership teams: From mine to ours.* Lanham, MD: Rowman & Littlefield.

Pellicer, L. O. (2008). *Caring enough to lead: How reflective practice leads to moral leadership* (3rd ed.). Thousand Oaks, CA: Corwin.

Wilson, L. W. (2008). *Improving your elementary school: Ten aligned steps for administrators, teams, teachers, families, & students.* Larchmont, NY: Eye On Education.

> Personal relationships are the fertile soil from which all advancement, all success, all achievement in real life grows.
>
> —Ben Stein

WORKING WITH YOUR PRINCIPAL

A principal who truly serves as an instructional leader is of immense value to any school. The role of the principal and the nature of school leadership are being redefined as increasing numbers of schools turn to site-based management, total quality schools, teaming, restructuring, peer coaching, and decentralization.

Whatever the exact configuration of leadership functions in a specific school, teachers and their principals are locked in an interdependent relationship; they need each other to succeed. The less friction and stress between principal and teacher, the more enjoyable both will find their jobs. Evidence also suggests that the quality of the teacher-principal relationship greatly influences the overall school climate, which in turn affects the students' success in the classroom.

Investing in a positive, professional teacher-principal relationship should be a top priority for any beginning teacher. Though some principals are more talented leaders than others, students are ultimately the winners when principals and teachers can work in harmony. No one gains—and students lose—when a poisonous, adversarial relationship exists between principal and teachers. Successful teachers strive to develop partnerships with their principals.

- Keep your principal informed of both budding problems and your triumphs. Don't wait to surprise the principal with major problems. It is best for the principal to have ample information directly from you before he or she hears about a problem from others. No decision can be better than the information on which it is based. Take time to communicate your interests and needs.

- Avoid visiting your principal only when you have problems. Share some good news or ask his or her advice. Invest time in nurturing a positive relationship. If you are experimenting with a new instructional technique or a novel assignment, alert your principal and seek his or her support. Only through frequent interactions does mutual trust evolve.

- When your principal has done something considerate or particularly helpful, drop him or her a note. Let the principal know that you appreciate his or her efforts. Like department store managers, principals often hear only the complaints.

- For special achievements, send an unsolicited letter of recognition or support for your principal to the superintendent. Anytime you want to give people major recognition, don't just tell them; tell their superior.

- Avoid dumping your problems on your principal. Especially avoid sending kids to the office for misbehavior unless it involves persistent or serious infractions, such as fighting. Relying on the principal to solve your student behavior problems on a daily basis creates the impression that you cannot control your own classroom.

- Avoid backbiting or ridiculing your principal, even if he or she falls short of your expectations. It simply isn't professional, and it really doesn't accomplish anything positive. Don't join in the game even if others are playing.

- If you have a complaint or disagreement with the principal on an issue, communicate your case clearly and rationally. This never calls for yelling, name-calling, or sarcasm. Stick to the facts. If you have difficulty controlling your emotions in direct conversation, articulate your position in a letter. Remember, you still have to work with him or her tomorrow. Your aim is to influence the principal's decision, not to alienate him or her. In all contacts act maturely and professionally.

- Choose your battles carefully. In any relationship you have only a limited amount of credit available in the other's emotional bank account. Don't squander your assets on minor skirmishes; save them for the truly important issues. If you rarely complain, you are more likely to be heard when you do.

- When you take a problem to your principal, prepare at least one or two possible solutions. Anticipate the consequences of each, the risks, and the resources needed. Be succinct in your presentation. Be rational in what you expect the principal to do to solve your problems. Avoid using the principal's time for petty problems.

- Find opportunities to make your principal look good. One way is to publicize in the community the students' outstanding achievements. Any noteworthy school accomplishment reflects positively on the principal.

- Don't make the principal's job more difficult than it needs to be. Submit grades, attendance records, and reports on time. Some amount of paperwork has to be done to make a school work smoothly. It may sometimes be inconvenient, but it must be done.

- Try to see things from the principal's point of view. Being principal is not an easy job. Principals have many interests to please: teachers, noncertified staff, boards of education, central office, students, parents, and taxpayers. Most every decision they make irritates someone, especially with the limited resources available to most schools. They are also sometimes obliged to enforce school policies that they may not like. Be a bit empathetic. That doesn't mean you have to sacrifice your principles or that you shouldn't advocate for those issues to which you are passionately committed. However, recognize that you won't always get what you want when you want it.

- Take the initiative in inviting your principal to visit your classroom. If you have a particularly interesting or successful lesson coming up, try to schedule an observation. Strive to view the principal as an instructional ally, even if you do disagree on your teaching effectiveness.

- Avoid interpreting criticisms of your teaching effectiveness as personal attacks. No teacher is perfect. Avoid becoming defensive. Reality-test any criticisms by asking other administrators or teachers to observe your teaching. Invite the principal to observe you again to reassess your teaching. A goal you both should share is to provide the best instruction possible to all your students. Build on that common purpose.

- Avoid asking for special privileges. It unfairly puts the administrator on the spot. If you have a request for special resources or exemption to school policies, consider how your fellow teachers would accept that request if it were granted.

- Share articles that you read on school improvement practices with your principal. Occasionally, ask his or her opinion on an educational trend or innovation.

- A good time to get to know your principal better is during the summer. Most are on an extended schedule. Stop by to see the principal during the summer. She or he will have more time than during the school year, when daily crises consume the principal's time.

- Show your principal you are thinking of him or her. Small considerations such as a birthday card, a holiday card, homemade cookies, or a vacation postcard are fruitful investments in a positive relationship.

IMPROVING PARENT-TEACHER RELATIONS

You have much to gain from developing a constructive working relationship with your students' parents and guardians. If invited, parents can play a valuable role in your teaching success. They can offer support and reinforcement for your academic and behavioral goals. Parents or guardians can provide assistance in a variety of ways, both in your classroom and in their homes. Many possess talents, interests, and ideas that can augment what you offer. Many parents (and other community members) don't become more fully involved in their schools simply because they haven't been invited. Here are some useful suggestions:

- Before the school year begins, send notes home to your students' parents or guardians introducing yourself and inviting them to become a part of the school community. Some teachers include a checklist of hobbies, talents, and interests that the parents might be willing to share with the class at some time during the year. Emphasize that you believe they play an important role in their child's education.

- Send periodic notes to parents, recognizing their children's positive achievements or behavior in your class. Typically, parents hear from the school only when their children are in trouble. Set aside ten minutes each week to send two or three notes to different parents. Don't just acknowledge the students who are getting A's. Recognize the student who has been reluctant to participate but is now contributing in class, the student who did an outstanding job on one project, or the student who had been getting C's and is now getting B's. It will pay dividends!

- Occasionally call parents to communicate some good news about their child's accomplishments. It will catch them off guard, but they will likely be most appreciative.

- Develop home-school contracts with the parents of students who are having difficulty completing homework or behaving appropriately in class. If the student fulfills the contract, the parents offer a special privilege or reward. You might have a checksheet that both you and the parent must sign each day or week. This forestalls students from reporting "I didn't have any homework" and other similar "inaccurate" communications they sometimes relate to parents.

- Set up a Web site, where parents may access information about your classes (grading policies, expectations, assignments, and so on).

- Invite parents to become involved in your classroom. Tap their talents as special volunteers not only for field trip supervision and class parties but also as teacher's aides and speakers. You might send a survey home to obtain information about their skills, interests, and willingness to help.

- If feasible, make home visits to meet your students' parents. Not only will you learn much more about your students through these visits, but you will also be communicating to the student's family that you genuinely are interested in their child.

- Be sensitive in making assumptions about the constellation of your students' families. It is likely that some of your students reside with only one parent (not necessarily the mother) or with grandparents, older siblings, aunts, uncles, unrelated guardians, or foster parents. It is also possible that some of your students have parents who are deceased, incarcerated, or hospitalized. Tactfully determine the child's living arrangements before contacting the home. You can avoid potentially embarrassing situations.

- Let parents know early if their child is having difficulty in your class. Don't wait until grades are sent home.

- Consider sending parents a class newsletter several times a year to let them know what is happening in your class. You might even give your students responsibility for writing, editing, and printing it. News of field trips, special class projects, guest speakers, birthdays, and features recognizing individual students' achievements are all good content to include.

- Sponsor a family fun night in which parents and their children come to school to participate in some enjoyable, interesting activities together. These might be related to your subject area or simply a chance to interact and have fun together. Some schools very successfully offer workshops in topics of interest to parents, anything from flower arranging to parenting skills. If your faculty cannot teach the workshop, find someone in the community who can.

- Designate one evening a month as an informal open session to which all parents are invited to visit your room to discuss any concerns or ask more about what their children are learning. Provide coffee, tea, or cookies. If no one shows, you can get some extra work done.

- Some elementary schools sponsor a grandparents' day. Students are invited to bring their grandparents to school for a visit. You might even encourage grandparents to participate in the lesson of the day (for example, a discussion of the 1950s or how technology has changed). Grandparents are also a valuable though underused source of school volunteers.

- Send special cards or notes to parents for special family celebrations: birth of a new child, a new home, special award received, and so on. Clip newspaper articles featuring any family members and send them to the parents with a note of congratulations.

Do whatever it takes to get parents or guardians involved in school. This is no small challenge. Not all adults have pleasant memories of school. They avoid schools, even in adulthood. Not all parents are responsible, caring adults. Nonetheless, we must do all that we can to break down the barriers between the school and the home. We must make schools inviting and persuade the adults in our students' lives to get involved in their education.

There are many examples, even in the most depressed schools, of programs that have experienced success in involving parents. Parental involvement is no panacea, but the odds of success are greater when schools and families make a team effort to help children get the most they can out of their educational opportunity.

> In teaching you cannot see the fruit of a day's work. It is invisible and remains so, maybe for twenty years.
>
> **—Jacques Barzun**

Parental Involvement Pays

Research shows that students are more likely to earn higher grades when their fathers are highly involved in school. This connection holds for fathers in two-biological parent families, for stepfathers, and for fathers heading single-parent families. Mothers' involvement is similarly related to high grades. When mothers are involved in school, students in sixth through twelfth grades have a lower rate of suspension and expulsion.

High parental involvement was defined by participation in at least three of four school activities: attending a general school meeting, attending a regularly scheduled parent-teacher conference, attending a school or class event, and volunteering at school.

Source: National Center for Education Statistics. (2001). Fathers' and mothers' involvement in their children's schools by family type and resident status. Available online at nces.ed.gov/surveys/. Reprinted with permission from the *Heart of Teaching* newsletter, Performance Learning Systems.

PARENT OR GUARDIAN CONFERENCES

The prospect of a parent-teacher conference can arouse intense emotions in both the teacher and the parent. Beginning teachers can be especially anxious about meeting parents or guardians for the first time. For adults whose memories of school are less than pleasant, parent-teacher conferences can be intimidating and dreaded. However, the reality is that most parents really do want their children to have a positive school experience and prefer to develop a cooperative home-school relationship. Professionally conducted parent-teacher conferences can prove a most valuable strategy for improving students' classroom behavior as well as enhancing learning. Here are some ideas that successful teachers have used to reap the maximum benefit from parent-teacher conferences:

> *If you promise not to believe everything your child says happens at this school, I'll promise not to believe everything he says happens at home.*
>
> —**English schoolmaster, *Wall Street Journal*, January 4, 1985**

- Before the conference date, plan what you hope to accomplish. What information do you want to share with the parent or guardian? What problems need solving? Do not overwhelm the parent. Settle on no more than two or three concerns to address. A laundry list of complaints will only discourage or alienate them.

- If you are requesting the conference in response to a specific problem with the child, allow some time to cool off before meeting with the parent. You'll be less emotionally charged and more objective after a couple of days. Remember, you are a professional educator.

- When a student begins to misbehave in class, record specific disturbances on an index card. Include the name, date, description of the problem behavior, and the action taken. Make your notes as soon after an incident as possible. This will help you to identify patterns and give more credibility to your complaint when talking with the child's parent.

- If possible, clarify ahead of time who will be attending the conference and their relationship to the student. Is this person the child's mother, father, guardian? Also verify from the school records the person's name. Do not assume their surname will be the same as the student's. Don't make a big point of it in front of the parent, but a bit of advance checking can help avoid potentially embarrassing gaffes during the conference. Some teachers have mistakenly assumed that an older parent was the student's grandparent.

- Within reason, try to accommodate the parent's schedule. Many parents cannot readily take off work to attend school conferences. If parents have more than one child, attempt to coordinate their appointments so that they have to come to school only once. Such small considerations can reap significant cooperation.

- Consider sending a reminder of the time, date, and place to the parent a couple of days before the scheduled conference. If special directions are needed for parking or for finding your room, include those as well. If you are seeing several parents back-to-back, inform them how much time is allotted for their appointment.

- Put your name on the door to make it easier for parents to locate your room.

- Create an inviting room atmosphere. Displays of students' work, projects in progress, bulletin boards, posters, learning centers, and "Welcome Parents" signs can all help create a warm atmosphere.

- Arrange the room setting to minimize potential distractions or interruptions during the conference. Close the door if necessary.

- Assemble samples of the student's work and a list of his or her grades before the conference. It will save you the time of having to look them up during the appointment. Some teachers have their students assemble a work portfolio. This might include a greeting from their child. You might also include a page where the parent can return a positive note to their child about the schoolwork.

- Many teachers keep a note card for each student, recording points to discuss at the parent-teacher conference. Try to anticipate any questions a parent might ask and note your thoughts related to that issue.

- Greet parents cordially when they arrive, again being sure to verify their names immediately. Ideally, try to greet them at the door. Thank them for coming to see you.

- Be the gracious host. Some teachers set up coffee, juice, or snacks for parents, especially if they might have to wait in the hallway while you finish a prior conference. If they must wait in the hall, provide some chairs and perhaps copies of your textbooks or other materials to scan while waiting.

- Practice the very best of manners, treating each parent with full respect and dignity. Whatever their occupation or socioeconomic status, treat all parents as you would the president of a corporation or a physician. Strive to make them feel as welcome and comfortable as possible.

- Address all parents by their last names preceded by the appropriate Mr., Mrs., or Ms. until they invite you to use their first names.

- Don't hide behind your desk. It can be a barrier to developing a working relationship. If possible, sit beside the parent at a table. Also avoid seating parents in small children's chairs.

- Begin the conference on a positive note. Think of two or three positive descriptors for each student (for example, "Brooke is so eager to help" or "Braedon seems well liked by his classmates"). You might jot these down on each student's card or file to stimulate your memory. It is important to find something to praise with each student.

- Establish rapport with the parent. This need not take long, but try to establish a personal connection and create an inviting atmosphere. If you know about the parent's job, hobby, or special interest, make a brief inquiry (for example, "Matt tells me you've been working on your family genealogy"). Help put the parent at ease.

- Do question the parent about the student's special talents, interests, or accomplishments. Express a genuine interest to better understand their child's successes and strengths as well as challenges.

- Be specific when discussing difficulties the student is experiencing. It is generally better to be candid but not place blame. It is unwise to mislead the parent into thinking all is well if there is a problem with their child. Stick to the facts, giving concrete examples rather than broad generalities.

> The only reason I always try to meet and know the parents better is because it helps me to forgive their children.
>
> —Louis Johannot, headmaster, Institut Le Rosey, Switzerland, *Life* magazine, May 7, 1965

- Don't dwell on any student's attributes that are unlikely to change or over which the parents have little control.

- It is best to avoid getting emotional in discussing problems you may be having with the student. Remember, your goal is to enlist the parent's cooperation in resolving any difficulties the student may be experiencing in your class.

- Actively listen to the parent. Practice the reflection of feeling skills discussed in Chapter Two. Respond empathically to feelings that the parent expresses (for example, "You are disappointed Laurie isn't getting more individual attention in class"). This communicates that you really are trying to understand the parents' perspective; it does not imply that you necessarily agree with their view. Such active listening is an especially effective way to handle the angry parent.

- Encourage parents to ask questions, and respond fully yet tactfully. Avoid jargon, "educationese," or psychological labels. Allow parents time to talk.

- Inquire about home routines (responsibilities, homework habits, play, and so on). Seek information that might help you gain a better understanding of the student's talents, interests, and challenges.

- Try to offer two or three specific suggestions that the parents might implement at home to help their child. Offer them not as commands but as ideas that have worked with other students.

- Invite the parents to contact you with any future concerns about their child's classroom progress.

- Some traps to avoid: discussing family problems, discussing other teachers' classroom treatment of the student, comparing the student with siblings, arguing with the parent, attempting to psychoanalyze the student, or blaming the parent for the student's misbehavior.

- End the conference in a hopeful tone. Summarize the main points discussed and any steps to be taken to resolve identified problems. The Parent Conference Record from the end of this chapter emphasizes the importance of following through on any actions. Again, commend them for coming to the conference.

- If other parents are waiting, be sure to end the meeting at the scheduled time. Ideally, allow yourself a few minutes between sessions to allow time to note any major points discussed during the conference. If necessary, offer to schedule another conference with the parent.

- Do follow up with a note or a phone call, especially if the conference has identified a particular problem for attention.

THE SUCCESSFUL OPEN HOUSE

Many schools sponsor open houses for parents and guardians. The open house can be a valuable opportunity to get parents more involved in their children's education.

- Videotape several interesting learning activities in your class. Have these playing on the DVD as parents enter the room. You might show selected segments to give them a flavor of what your class is like. It is best to edit your tape first to avoid having to fast-forward. Five or ten minutes of video are sufficient.

Facilitative Conferences

Alliances for Success

Betty Jo Simmons, professor of education at Longwood College, urges teachers to engage in facilitative conferences to nurture productive parent-teacher relationships. Simmons proposes five keys to successful problem solving in facilitative conferences:

- Be honest. Provide parents with specific and accurate information in a calm, nonaccusatory manner.
- Assure parents that their child is liked. Convey that you care about their child and that he or she is important.
- Describe the responsibilities to be shared. Clarify the roles of parent, teacher, and student in achieving success.
- Involve the student. Include the child in discussion of academic progress or behavior concerns.
- Provide encouragement. Reassure parents that whatever difficulties the student faces can be resolved with collaboration.

Source: Simmons, B. J. (2002). Facilitative conferences: Parents and teachers working together. *The Clearing House, 76(2)*, 88–93.

- Avoid getting into prolonged discussions with individual parents about their child's progress. Do offer to arrange appointments with any parents who would like to discuss their children's work in more detail.

- Create an especially inviting atmosphere. Remember, some parents do not have fond memories of school and may be a bit anxious about being in a classroom.

- Greet parents at the door. If you do not already know them, introduce yourself to each as they enter.

- Some teachers have each student create a folder of exemplary work throughout the term. Have these available for parents to examine as they first enter.

- Create a "Welcome" sign with your name and subject clearly posted on the door so that parents are sure they are in the appropriate room.

- Attractive bulletin board displays featuring student work is a plus. If students create or build projects, have these on display.

- If parents are visiting several rooms, do not keep them past the time they should be moving to the next class.

TIPS FOR HELPING SUBSTITUTE TEACHERS

Substitute teaching can be a challenging experience, but you can help ensure that it will be constructive for the substitute and your students. It is essential that learning continue even in your absence. Advance preparation can make a substitute's visit run more smoothly and ensure that useful learning occurs.

- Early in the year, inform the students of your expectations of acceptable behavior when a substitute is present.

- Agree with a nearby teacher to help the other's substitute when one of you is absent. The teacher can help the substitute get settled and become familiar with your procedures.

- Develop a substitute's notebook that includes all information he or she will need to make the experience successful. Be sure your notebook is clear and precise, avoiding special codes or abbreviations the substitute may not understand. Here are items many teachers include:

- ○ Lesson plans.
- ○ Daily schedule of activities.
- ○ Class roster(s). The substitute can make notes on these (for example, checking off homework completed).
- ○ Attendance forms and procedures.
- ○ Hall passes and procedures for going to the restroom, library, guidance office, and so on.
- ○ The names of teachers, administrators, clerical staff, or students the sub can turn to for help with special problems or questions.
- ○ Seating charts for each class.
- ○ Classroom rules. It is helpful if the students already have a copy and they are posted for everyone to see.
- ○ List and details of any special classroom routines or behavior management programs.
- ○ Note any special nonteaching duties you must perform (for example, playground or lunchroom supervision).
- ○ Bus information. Note times and procedures for dismissal and getting students to and from their buses.
- ○ A map of the school building.
- ○ Student handbook.
- ○ Instructions on where all textbook manuals and supplies are kept.
- ○ Teacher handbook.
- Don't forget to inform the substitute of any special scheduled interruptions (assemblies, class pictures, field trips, homerooms, and so on).
- If you know ahead of time that you will be absent, leave a lesson plan to cover the material you want taught. It may not be the same lesson you would have taught, but it should be something of instructional value. It is a good idea to have a couple of special learning activities that can be plugged into the schedule at any point in the year. Keep these in a special place with all the necessary materials and directions. Try to help the substitute by including something you know your students will enjoy. Don't just use tests and seatwork on the days that substitutes are covering your class.
- If your absence is anticipated, make a videotape for the substitute to show at the beginning of class. In this presentation you can give the students instructions on what you expect them to do that day. You might also videotape and save demonstrations or some lectures from previous years for the substitute to use.
- Expect the day to be used constructively. Most substitutes are qualified professionals with the training and motivation to do a good job. Treat them as professionals and with due respect.
- If you plan to be absent several days, invite your substitute to visit your class beforehand to meet your class and to discuss your lesson plans and classroom procedures with you.
- Ask your substitute to leave a note describing how the day went. It helps to remind your students ahead of time that you will be soliciting feedback from the substitute.

You might express your appreciation to your students (through praise or special privileges) if the report is favorable.

- If you have a substitute who does perform particularly well, drop him or her a note to express your appreciation. Let your principal know as well. Specify that individual to take your place when you are absent. That will permit that substitute teacher to become more familiar with your routines and your students. If you will have frequent absences, it also alleviates the stress of getting the students accustomed to another person. Trust the substitute to provide a meaningful learning experience for your students (with your help).

WORKING WITH SUPPORT STAFF

Successful teaching is a team effort. Teachers will be much more successful with the support of other competent professionals: counselors, secretaries, nurses, custodians, aides, cafeteria workers, and librarians. Each has a valuable function to play in creating a smooth-running and effective school. Special efforts should be made to ensure that they feel included and valued as part of the school community.

- Learn the names of the support staff. Ask them how they would prefer to be addressed. Don't assume they want to be called by their first names.

- Attempt to discover what is important to them. Their jobs and needs are different from yours. Wherever possible, help them get their needs met.

- Acknowledge their contributions. An occasional thank-you note for any special assistance or a particularly outstanding contribution will be most appreciated. Offer verbal comments that convey you do value their efforts. Seek genuine opportunities to offer sincere compliments.

- Let others know what is happening. If you are planning a special activity that is going to affect someone else's job, check it out with them first. Try to minimize any disruption of their work. Seek their advice on how to proceed. Even if they don't have any suggestions, they will appreciate being asked.

- Always treat support staff (and all other persons) with courtesy. Accompanying requests with a *please* or *thank you* will plant the seeds of a cooperative, mutually respectful relationship. Always greet them with a smile and pleasant acknowledgment in the morning.

- Whenever someone puts forth an extra special effort to help you, acknowledge it with a note, small gift (cookies, bread, flowers from your garden), or even a note to his or her supervisor.

- If you see a positive news article about any staff members or their family, clip it out and send it to them with a note of congratulations.

- Treat all, including those with less education, as equals. Never assume that more education makes you a superior human being. Chances are that persons with less education than you have experiences, talents, or knowledge you do not.

- Sooner or later you are going to need a favor from a support staff member. You are much more likely to gain his or her compliance with your request if you have invested in a collegial relationship.

WORKING WITH VOLUNTEERS AND AIDES

Time is the teacher's most precious resource. There is always too much to do in too little time. Someone other than a teacher could complete many essential tasks, if such help were available. Using aides, either paid or volunteer, is one valuable way to get more help in the classroom, freeing you to spend more time on the most important teaching tasks. One estimate is that over five million persons volunteer to help in schools each year, and probably many more would help if they were invited. Many adults in your community have valuable talents that could be tapped to enrich your instructional program.

One benefit of using aides is that they share the challenges and achievements of your school with the greater community. They can become valuable public relations spokespersons simply by sharing their experiences with friends and neighbors. These paraprofessionals from the community are more likely to become advocates for their schools.

There is also evidence that student achievement improves in schools that use volunteers extensively. Teachers who are freed from many of their noninstructional tasks have more time and energy to focus on their teaching responsibilities. Additionally, individual students gain more of the teacher's attention, as well as the added contact and reinforcement from the paraprofessional helper.

The paraprofessionals working in their community schools also gain. Many feel a greater sense of social responsibility and personal enrichment from using their time to aid children's development. Many feel more positively about themselves, knowing that their talents and knowledge are valued and needed. For others, especially college students, working in the classroom provides an opportunity to develop skills and knowledge that may enhance their employment prospects. All classroom assistants gain a greater appreciation and insight into the inner workings of their local school.

Volunteers can help in a variety of ways, depending on the students' age group, the volunteer or aide's skills and knowledge, and the teacher's willingness to delegate tasks and train the paraprofessional to assume these duties.

If your school does not regularly provide aides, discuss the idea of using volunteers with your principal. You will need to consider concerns such as legal limits and liabilities and delegated responsibilities. You might want to start small at first to determine how best to use classroom assistants.

Send out a call for all potential volunteers, not just to your students' parents. An announcement in the local newspaper or through the parent-teacher association newsletter may encourage others to volunteer. Senior citizen groups and your students' grandparents are also potential sources of volunteer aides. College students, especially teacher trainees, may value the opportunity to work in a classroom. Elementary teachers sometimes use high school students.

You might also survey local businesspersons to determine if they might be willing to help occasionally. Some companies provide release time for their employees to help in schools. The regular school open house is an excellent recruiting opportunity. Create and prominently display a recruiting poster describing the specific ways parents can help. Follow up the open house with a letter inviting parents to volunteer. Make a special effort to recruit parents who speak languages other than English.

Parents and others are generally reluctant to volunteer because they are unsure they have anything to contribute. Be sure to list specific tasks parents are capable of handling. Where possible, provide options, allowing parents to choose those activities they find most attractive. Although some parents may be able to work every week, let parents know that you value their help even if only for a onetime visit to share some talent or their jobs with your class or help with one activity. Some parents might be able to help even if they cannot come to school. Many tasks can be done in their homes: designing a Web site, sewing, baking, or entering computer data.

Many volunteer aides or paraprofessionals lose interest because they feel underused or taken for granted. Here are a few tips for effectively using the aides' services:

- Interview each volunteer, preferably in person, and assess whether you think you can work comfortably together. You likely will need more than one volunteer to cover the week. Determine how much time each day you want an aide or volunteer in your room. You'll also need to decide whether to schedule volunteers for specific tasks as needed or for the same block of time each week. Some persons might wish to help weekly; others will be able to assist only occasionally. Be sure to call everyone who volunteers.

- Appropriate training is essential for effective use of paraprofessional help. Allow time for them to observe you interacting with students and doing the tasks you will expect them to fulfill. They will also note the routines you have established. If you are using several volunteers, you might schedule an orientation session where you can provide training for all at once. Also provide ample time for them to ask questions. It is helpful to let them just observe for a day before you have them work directly with students.

- Develop a handbook for your assistants. It should describe tasks to be done (with samples when possible), disciplinary procedures, rules, and responsibilities. It is also important to emphasize confidentiality so that volunteers don't gossip about the individual children's problems.

- Do try to get to know your classroom helpers. Ask about their families and interests. When appropriate, seek their suggestions on how to make improvements in the classroom.

- Develop a file, tray, or box in which you place work for your aide or volunteer to do when time is available. This prevents them from having to interrupt you to get instructions on what to do. A desk or table designated as their workstation would be helpful. Be sure to provide an adult chair if you teach young children. Also designate where they can store personal items and clothing.

- Construct and post a chart depicting the schedule for your assistants. Ask them to call when they are not able to come. It is helpful to send reminders to volunteers who are coming for a special project. If you are scheduling a parent to help with one class, remember it is easiest for most parents to come first thing in the morning or late afternoon. Be considerate of their schedules.

- Make sure you always have something useful for them to do. They will get bored or discouraged if they arrive to find they really aren't needed. Keep a running list of things for your helpers to do. Try to give them meaningful, interesting tasks at least part of the time.

- Design a system so that you need to spend only minimal class time supervising your assistant.

- In front of students, always address your aide or volunteer as you would any other professional in the building, usually by title (Mr., Mrs., Ms.). Insist that students also address them as they would a teacher and that they treat any paraprofessionals with courtesy and respect.

- In the beginning delegate tasks you are quite sure the paraprofessional can handle, assuring initial success. As they gain confidence and your trust, assign more challenging duties. Provide an opportunity for your assistants to learn and grow. Encourage them to ask questions if they are not sure how to complete a task.

- Remain tactful yet clear in providing suggestions and feedback to your assistants. Always treat them with respect. Show them that you have confidence in their ability to fulfill their duties. When appropriate, seek their opinion on items related to classroom success.

- Allow your classroom assistants an opportunity to work with all students, not just the ones having difficulties. Discourage parent volunteers from working only with their child.

- Give ample recognition and appreciation to your aides. Never take them for granted; strive to always make your assistants feel needed. Here are ideas some teachers have used to show their appreciation to their paraprofessional helpers:

  ○ Give them certificates.

  ○ Award them plaques.

  ○ Praise them.

  ○ Send them special thank-you notes.

Common Tasks for Volunteers and Aides

Administer routine first aid
Assist with club meetings
Collect and distribute materials
Complete certificates for students
Compute grades
Conduct storytelling
Converse with individual students
Coordinate volunteers
Demonstrate an experiment
Design class Web site
Direct a play
Do desktop publishing on the computer
Do housekeeping chores: water plants, arrange desks, clean
Escort students through the hall
Facilitate small-group activities
File papers
Find materials in the library
Grade objective tests and quizzes
Help organize games
Help returning students make up missed work
Help students get on the bus
Help with computer software
Help with seatwork
Inventory books, supplies
Laminate materials
Listen to students read
Make costumes

Make phone calls
Mediate student disputes
Monitor computer use
Monitor students
Operate instructional equipment
Order free materials
Paint murals
Photocopy
Praise students
Prepare instructional resources
Prepare visual aids
Proofread
Provide enrichment activities
Put up bulletin boards
Record grades
Record observations about students and classroom activities
Requisition supplies
Restock supplies
Score objective quizzes and tests
Set up displays
Share a hobby
Share career guidance information
Supervise field trips
Supervise learning centers
Supervise recess
Take attendance or lunch count
Take students to the nurse
Tutor individual students
Type

○ Write newspaper features on volunteers.
○ Invite them to lunch.
○ Honor them at recognition ceremonies.
○ Give them small gifts.
○ Invite them to a staff development program.
○ Buy them a soft drink, coffee, or tea.
○ Send them a birthday or holiday card.
○ Delegate additional responsibility.
○ Seek their opinion.
○ Take them to the faculty lounge.
○ Introduce them to other school personnel.
○ Offer to write them letters of recommendation.
○ Celebrate their achievements.
○ Nominate them for volunteer awards.
○ Smile.
○ Send a letter of appreciation to their boss.
○ Treat them as professionals.

○ Bring a cake for their birthday.
○ Praise them in front of your principal.
○ Greet them by name.
○ Take time to listen to their ideas.
○ Give them a space of their own.

While volunteers do save the teacher time and having parents in the classroom may enhance parent-teacher relationships, the bottom line is that extra help in the classroom benefits students.

> **Note:** Remember that many of the sample templates, letters, handouts for this chapter are available for download from the *Classroom Teacher's Survival Guide* Web site josseybass .com/go/classroomteacher.

Invitation to Open House:
Sample Letter to Parents

(Date)

Greetings,

    Kalida Elementary School will be holding its annual open house on Monday, October 15. We ask all parents and guardians to first meet in the school auditorium at 7:00. After a brief introductory program, you are invited to join me in Room 68.

    I will have several samples of your child's work available for you to examine. While we will not have time to discuss your child's performance in detail, I would be willing to schedule a private conference if you desire. I do hope to briefly explain some of the activities we will be doing this year and to respond to any questions you might have about our classes.

    I very much value the help and support my students receive at home. Together, we can assure that your child has a successful year. I hope to see you at our open house.

Sincerely,

Mrs. Ritter

Team Process Assessment

At the end of the team meeting each member should indicate his or her assessment of how that meeting went. Circle the number that represents your rating of each dimension. The group should then spend a few minutes discussing their responses.

Participation

1	2	3	4	5	6	7

Some did not participate at all.

There was significant participation by all.

Group Focus

1	2	3	4	5	6	7

The group tended to digress from the session agenda or objective.

The group stayed on task throughout the meeting.

Listening Process

1	2	3	4	5	6	7

It seemed participants were not fully listening to one another.

Outstanding efforts were made to fully hear each other.

Commitment Check

1	2	3	4	5	6	7

I am not supportive of the meeting outcome.

I am very supportive of the group decision.

Quality of the Group Effort

1	2	3	4	5	6	7

The session did not produce an effective outcome.

The final outcome was excellent.

Team Meeting Form

Team _____ Date _____

Agenda Topics

_____

_____

_____

_____

_____

_____

Decisions

_____

_____

_____

_____

_____

_____

Assignments and Deadlines

_____

_____

_____

_____

_____

_____

Parent Conference Record

Teacher _____ Date _____

Student _____ Parent(s)_____

Objective: _____
_____
_____
_____
_____
_____
_____
_____

Suggestions for improvement: _____
_____
_____
_____
_____
_____
_____
_____
_____
_____
_____
_____
_____
_____

Signed: _____
                    Teacher

_____   _____
        Parent(s)/Guardian(s)   Student

Staying on Top of Your Game

8

TWENTY-TWO TIPS FOR BECOMING AN EFFECTIVE TEACHER

Teaching is a complex and challenging profession, and some teachers are more successful than others. Their students perform better on achievement tests, are more likely to succeed in future grades, and remember their teachers more fondly.

> Great teachers rely not on charisma. Instead, they rely on the inner qualities of love, integrity, and commitment.
>
> —Eric Jensen, *Teaching with the Brain in Mind*

Many outstanding teachers are creative and successful in facilitating their students' academic as well as personal growth. We need not search only for those gaining national recognition, such as Jaime Escalante, featured in the real-life drama *Stand and Deliver*, or Kay Tolliver, the East Harlem teacher touted in the PBS production *Good Morning, Ms. Tolliver*. Exciting, creative, and effective teaching is happening in every school. A growing body of educational research has focused on what these exemplars are doing that makes them successful. Use every opportunity to observe outstanding teachers in action; you can learn much from them.

What follows is a compilation of research findings on the characteristics of these effective teachers:

1. The A+ teachers tend to have realistic yet high expectations for their students. They require students to use higher-level mental processes, such as critical thinking, deeper understanding, creativity, and problem solving. They present the appropriate level of challenge in their lessons.

2. They incorporate student questions and comments into their lessons. Their classes tend to involve significant amounts of class discussion and group exploration. This is especially important in teaching high school students.

3. The best teachers actively involve their students in the learning process. Their students spend less time doing seatwork, passively watching, or waiting. When these teachers do employ seatwork, it is more interesting and varied.

4. Much thought and planning go into their instruction, yet they remain flexible in their teaching to allow for spontaneous discovery as opportunities present themselves. They are especially sensitive to cues that their lessons are not working, and they adapt them on the spot.

5. The best teachers tend to conduct their lessons in a businesslike, task-oriented style. They maintain a strong academic focus in their classrooms. They are effective in designing lessons that enhance student mastery.

6. Effective teachers match their instructional activities to their students' developmental level and then gradually lead them to higher levels of mastery. This involves recognizing and correcting deficiencies in students' skill levels.

7. They employ structuring comments or advance organizers at the beginning of their lessons. They are also careful to use language appropriate to their students.

8. Teachers whom students rated highest tend to use more humor in their classrooms. This humor does not typically come from telling jokes but rather from the

good-natured banter they carry on with their students. This contributes to developing good rapport with their students.

9. They genuinely believe in the value of their subject matter. Almost without exception, they exude enthusiasm for what they are teaching; and they teach in a manner that exhibits that passion. You can sense the energy and animation in their teaching. The research suggests this is especially important at the junior high and high school levels.

10. The best teachers possess a can-do attitude, sometimes referred to as efficacy. Although they face the same problems as less effective teachers, they have confidence in their ability to cope with the challenges they face. They feel that their efforts can make a difference in their students' lives.

11. Memorable teachers exhibit empathy toward their students, striving to see the world from their point of view. Such caring and desire to genuinely understand their students is sometimes characterized as teacher warmth. This includes sensitivity to the students' cultural background as well. One opportunity to do that is by arriving at class early to chat with students as they enter. These teachers' classes are more student-centered than subject-centered.

12. Top-performing teachers seek help from others. They discuss teaching ideas with colleagues and seek input from parents, students, administrators, and educational specialists. They also read more educational magazines and books and are more likely to attend professional development programs.

13. They provide opportunities for students to seek extra help if they fall behind. They are approachable. They are also observant of cues that individual students are not learning or are uninvolved. They more frequently check students' progress and proceed only when students have shown mastery of the content being taught.

14. The A+ teachers avoid embarrassing students and do not resort to intimidation to gain their cooperation. They avoid showing favoritism toward students. Not surprisingly, the better teachers tend to have more positive opinions of students, as well as of fellow teachers and administrators. Research shows that ineffective teachers are more prone to use sarcasm, shame, ridicule, shouting, and scolding. High-achieving classrooms are cooperative, warm, and convivial.

15. The top teachers give clear instructions in assignments and demonstrate clarity in their presentations.

16. Excellent teachers are more likely to incorporate a variety of instructional strategies into their lessons. They tend not to do the same thing in the same way for too long. They possess a broad repertoire of teaching skills.

17. They encourage more than they criticize. Indeed, criticism is negatively related to student achievement. However, outstanding teachers do provide corrective feedback whenever necessary to help students rectify.

Characteristics of Successful New Teachers

- Able to motivate students
- Child-centered
- Consistent
- Empathetic
- Team-oriented
- Willing to serve
- Cooperative
- Flexible
- Good interpersonal skills

Source: Breeding, M., & Whitworth, J. (1999). *Increasing the success of first year teachers: A synthesis of three studies.* Paper presented at the annual meeting of the American Association of Colleges for Teacher Education (ERIC Document No. ED428056).

18. The most effective teachers are in control of their classrooms but are not obsessed with the idea of control. They invest time and effort into preventing discipline problems by developing positive student relationships and planning well-organized, interesting lessons. To the outside observer, these teachers seem to exert relatively little effort to maintain an orderly environment. They are more apt to intervene to nip problems in the bud before they escalate into major disruptions. They are also less likely to send students to the principal, punish their students, or call parents to complain about students' misbehavior.

19. Successful teachers continually monitor their classrooms; they are aware of what is happening at all times. They often do this by moving about the room and maintaining frequent eye contact with all students.

20. Good teachers teach their students classroom routines, such as what to do when they finish an assignment early or how to obtain extra help.

21. Not surprisingly, effective teachers actually spend more time teaching. They use class time to maximize student learning and try to minimize distractions, chaos, and interruptions. Indeed, teachers who are less able to manage their time well tend to leave the teaching profession.

22. The truly outstanding teachers are not necessarily charismatic and dynamic individuals; but they enjoy and believe in what they are teaching, work hard at it, and spend time planning well-organized lessons.

Successful teachers are vital and full of passion. They love to teach as a writer loves to write, as a singer loves to sing. They are people who have a motive, a passion for their subject, a spontaneity of character, and enormous fun doing what they do.

—Thomas Cronin, 1991

Suggested Reading on Effective Teaching

Moore, K. D. (2009). *Effective instructional strategies: From theory to practice* (2nd ed.). Thousand Oaks, CA: Sage.

Reifman, S. (2008). *Eight essentials for empowered teaching and learning, K–8: Bringing out the best in your students.* Thousand Oaks, CA: Corwin.

Stronge, J. H. (2007). *Qualities of effective teachers* (2nd ed.). Alexandria, VA: Association for Supervision and Curriculum Development.

Turnbull, J. (2007). *Nine habits of highly effective teachers: A practical guide to empowerment.* New York: Continuum.

Wiseman, D. G., & Hunt, G. H. (2007). *Best practice in motivation and management in the classroom* (2nd ed.). Springfield, IL: Charles C. Thomas.

TEACHER EXPECTATIONS REVISITED

Since Rosenthal and Jacobson first proposed the idea of the self-fulfilling prophecy in their much-publicized 1968 study, *Pygmalion in the Classroom,* research has verified that teacher expectations are a complex and not yet fully understood variable. Many researchers have found that under certain conditions, teacher expectations can affect student behavior and achievement. Scholars are still debating the magnitude and predictability of these effects. However, UC–Berkeley psychology professor Rhonda Weinstein found that teacher expectations appear to affect the amount of effort that students are willing to put into their schoolwork.

Weinstein's research has also revealed that children as young as age six can sense where they fit in the academic pecking order. This is especially so in schools that strongly emphasize differences in academic achievement. Though many teachers believe students cannot detect favoritism toward "pet" students, empirical research suggests that students are indeed accurate in reading such favoritism through teachers' nonverbal behaviors (Babad, 1992). Teachers express their expectations differentially through their nonverbal cues.

In her book *Reaching Higher,* Weinstein (2002) argued that the current focus on extensive standardized testing fails to incorporate the substantial body of research on developing positive prophecies for students. She argues that the school culture should stress developing students' talents. This is instead of testing and sorting. She concludes that current massive testing programs will inevitably yield large numbers of student failures, resulting in increased special education placements, tracking, retention, and mandatory summer school—all approaches that research has shown to be damaging to children's opinions of themselves, destructive to their self-expectations, and generally counterproductive.

The Whistling Dog

A man reported to his friends that he had taught his dog to whistle. His friends coaxed the dog to whistle. Despite their fervent pleas, nothing happened. In exasperation one finally retorted, "I thought you taught him to whistle." The man replied, "I did. But he just didn't learn."

For More Information

Adams, C. (2008). What are your expectations? *Instructor, 117*(4), 26–30.

Green, R. L. (2008). *Expectations: How teacher expectations can increase student achievement.* Columbus, OH: SRA/McGraw-Hill.

Mawhinney, T. S., & Sagan, L. (2007). The power of personal relationships. *Phi Delta Kappan, 88,* 460–464.

Pardini, P. (2007). Higher expectations challenge teachers and students to succeed. *Journal of Staff Development, 28*(4), 10–13.

Weinstein, R. S. (2002). *Reaching higher: The power of expectations in schooling.* Cambridge, MA: Harvard University.

ARE YOU AN EFFECTIVE TEACHER?

Let's take a moment to see what you think. Complete the following checklist. Be honest about yourself!

Why Teachers Fail

Unfortunately, teachers sometimes do not succeed in their chosen profession. In a survey that asked school administrators about reasons for teacher failure (dismissal, reprimand, reassignment), Professor Jack Riegle found teachers are more likely to get fired because of poor human relations skills than lack of knowledge about their subject matter. Respondents most frequently mentioned the following reasons:

- Inability to organize and control a classroom of students
- Lack of knowledge concerning how children grow and develop as pertaining to pupil-teacher interactions
- Inability to work effectively with other educators
- Inability to work effectively with parents
- Subject matter inadequacies
- Other: immorality, insubordination, absenteeism, child abuse, senility, or drugs and alcohol

Source: Riegle, J. D. (1985). What administrators say about why teachers fail. *The Teacher Educator, 21*(1), 15–18.

Effective Teacher Checklist

Do You . . .

_____ Listen to your students?

_____ Know your students' names by the end of the first two weeks of school?

_____ Try to see things from your students' point of view?

_____ Smile in class?

_____ Believe all your students are capable of learning your subject?

_____ Convey your enthusiasm for what you are teaching?

_____ Continue to improve your teaching effectiveness?

_____ Believe in the value of what you are teaching?

_____ Have clear objectives for each lesson?

_____ Clearly communicate your expectations to your students?

_____ Strive to create an inviting room environment?

_____ Establish routines the first week of school?

_____ Try to get to know all your students as individuals?

_____ Encourage cooperation more than competition in your classroom?

_____ Demonstrate a sense of humor in working with your students?

_____ Praise your students for specific accomplishments?

_____ Fairly and consistently enforce your rules?

_____ Use more positive than negative statements in your classes?

_____ Vary your seating arrangement according to your teaching needs?

_____ Communicate the positive achievements of students to their parents?

_____ Make positive comments on students' papers?

_____ Permit your students to make mistakes as they learn new content and skills?

_____ Avoid overreacting to minor misbehaviors?

_____ Create interesting lessons that actively involve students?

_____ Encourage students to ask questions when they don't understand some part of your lesson?

_____ Capitalize upon spontaneous learning opportunities when they occur?

_____ Attend workshops or classes to continue improving your teaching skills?

(Continued)

_____ Maintain at least an 80 percent on-task rate in your classes?

_____ Compliment students, individually and as a group?

_____ Create a sense of family among your students?

_____ Make effective use of class time?

_____ Strive to link current lessons to students' prior knowledge?

_____ Provide reflection time for all students?

_____ Give students guided practice?

_____ Provide appropriate pacing for your lessons (neither too slow nor too fast)?

_____ Employ a variety of instructional techniques besides lecture?

_____ Regularly communicate with the parents of students having difficulties?

_____ Consider the variety of learning styles of your students in planning your lessons?

_____ Incorporate students' questions and comments into your lessons?

_____ Adapt your lessons on the spot when they aren't working?

_____ Provide opportunities for students to seek extra help if they fall behind?

_____ Feel confident in your ability to handle the challenges you face in the classroom?

_____ Greet your students as they enter the classroom?

_____ Avoid the use of sarcasm or ridicule in interacting with students?

_____ Have everything ready for the day when you enter the building in the morning?

_____ Are you in control of your classroom, but not obsessed with the idea of control?

_____ Are you able to effectively nip behavior problems in the bud before they escalate?

Scoring Directions: Count the number of items you checked and find your score in the categories below.

41–50	_Outstanding_	A master teacher. Others can learn much from you.
31–40	_Good_	You're on the way to success. There are a few areas needing attention.
21–30	_Challenged_	It's not too late to seek help in improving your classroom effectiveness.
0–20	_Struggling_	Teaching is probably not very enjoyable. Considering a career change might be wise.

TWENTY-SEVEN MISTAKES TEACHERS COMMONLY MAKE

1. Consistently talking in a monotone
2. Using sarcasm
3. Embarrassing students in front of their peers
4. Talking down to students
5. Not knowing students' names
6. Being inconsistent or unfair in classroom discipline
7. Using sexist or culturally insensitive language
8. Not being adequately prepared
9. Overrelying on lecture
10. Being disorganized
11. Using inappropriate humor
12. Allowing too many interruptions
13. Expecting perfection rather than excellence
14. Ignoring the bottom half of the class
15. Not clarifying expectations, rules, and routines
16. Screaming at students
17. Not knowing the subject
18. Talking to the blackboard or whiteboard
19. Trying to impress the students
20. Not using variety in instruction
21. Trying to fake it
22. Not having clear objectives in designing lessons
23. Setting expectations too low
24. Poor grooming or personal hygiene
25. Rewarding inappropriate behavior
26. Isolating themselves from colleagues
27. Not learning from their mistakes

THIRTY-TWO STRATEGIES FOR NURTURING PEAK PERFORMANCE IN OTHERS

Charles Garfield has made a career of studying high performers in an array of professions. His research has revealed that some work environments are more likely to elicit high levels of performance. Teachers can help their colleagues (from custodians to principals) do their jobs better. Here are thirty-two suggestions for helping your colleagues become peak performers.

1. Minimize criticism. Most people need role models more than they need critics. Criticize sparingly and in private. Praise often and in public. Use questions to encourage reflection and creative thinking.

2. Help others get what they want. In the end it is the surest way to get what you want.

3. Communicate clearly and concisely. Provide consistent but constructive feedback.

4. Use I-language in conveying your complaints. For example, "I would prefer we begin our meetings on time." Learn to be responsibly assertive rather than aggressive or nonassertive.

5. Clarify expectations and goals. Don't just assume others know what you need or expect. Check it out.

6. Assure that colleagues have access to the information and resources they need in order to do their jobs effectively.

7. Clarify priorities. Don't expect others to read your mind.

8. Do not promise what you cannot deliver, and keep the promises you do make. This is the root of trust.

9. Don't let the urgent things crowd out the important. Avoid overwhelming colleagues and subordinates with so many urgent tasks that they don't have time to deal with the most important ones.

10. Be more concerned with effectiveness than efficiency. One can be very efficient without being very effective.

11. Invite feedback from others. Listen with an open mind.

12. Always strive to be empathetic. Try to see things from the other person's point of view.

13. Nurture relationships. Develop a psychological bank account with every colleague; try to make at least a small deposit each day.

14. Master the art of saying thank-you. Seek every opportunity to provide genuine appreciation and recognition for others' successes and achievements.

15. Strive for excellence, not perfection.

16. Demonstrate respect for colleagues' time. Avoid creating unnecessary interruptions.

17. Follow the cardinal rules for effective meetings: always publicize the agenda; begin and end on time; keep them on task; record and circulate decisions made. Don't dominate the meeting.

18. Describe the traits of the worst boss or colleague you've ever had. Would your colleagues find any of these characteristics in you?

19. Support others when they are down. Learn to be a compassionate listener.

20. Share credit with as many people as possible.

21. The details are important. Be prepared.

22. Strive to view the challenges you face at work as problems in need of solutions. Seldom are they great moral choices with only one correct answer. Open-mindedly examine the advantages and disadvantages of each option. Relinquish the need to convince others you are right.

23. Be skeptical of simplistic solutions for complex problems.

24. Nothing conveys respect more than learning your colleagues' names.

25. View mistakes as an opportunity to learn; in fact, they are essential to effective learning. Fear of failure hinders taking risks and tackling challenging tasks. Encourage calculated risk taking and experimentation.

26. Don't punish desired behaviors or reward undesired behaviors. Do not ignore people when they do the job right.

27. Avoid participating in gossip. You have nothing to gain and much to lose. Others will assume you are talking the same way about them behind their backs.

28. Assign reasonable workloads. Students are most productive when challenged with meaningful tasks and least productive when they are overwhelmed.

29. Strive to reduce the stress level in your building. Increased illness, job burnout, and higher turnover are all related to high levels of stress.

30. Don't dump your problems on other people. Always treat colleagues with dignity and respect.

31. Share journal articles of value with your colleagues.

32. Encourage all to participate in quality professional development activities.

EFFECTIVE SCHOOLS

In the past two decades, scholars have given substantial attention to studying effective schools (see the work of Larry Lezotte, Michael Fullan, and Elaine McEwan). No universal blueprint exists, but we can draw some generalizations from the myriad of research studies available. The most outstanding schools possess a number of specific traits, although it is difficult to determine exactly what causes them. Research has identified the following characteristics as exemplifying the most effective schools:

- The professional staff is committed to the belief that all students can learn. The time required to learn the same content may vary greatly, however.

- Teachers hold high expectations for their students. Teachers also believe their efforts make a difference in students' lives.

- Students believe their success in school is related to how hard they work rather than just innate ability.

- The principal functions as an instructional leader, setting high goals for the school and inspiring staff to move toward those goals.

- A safe and orderly school environment is provided.

- Continued professional development is encouraged and facilitated.

- Firm, consistent, and fair enforcement of appropriate student behavior is emphasized. Disruptive and dangerous behaviors are not tolerated. Rules and expectations are clearly communicated to all.

- A climate of cooperation exists among the staff. The faculty works as a team. Collaboration becomes part of the school culture. Mutually supportive relationships exist between the principal and the staff.

- Students exhibit a high level of school spirit. They identify with their school and feel good about attending their school.

- Academic learning time is safeguarded. Frivolous interruptions of class activities are minimized.

- Parents feel welcome in the school. The community is supportive of its schools.

- Student progress is systematically monitored.

- Staff input into instructional decisions is invited.

- Students' level of on-task behavior is relatively high.

- The emphasis is on developing students' basic academic skills.

- Continuity of instruction from one grade level to the next is emphasized.

For More Information

Blankstein, A. M., Houston, P. D., & Cole, R. W. (2008). *Sustaining professional learning communities.* Thousand Oaks, CA: Corwin.

Fariña, C., & Kotch, L. (2008). *A school leader's guide to excellence: Collaborating our way to better schools.* Portsmouth, NH: Heinemann.

Hawley, W. D. (2007). *The keys to effective schools: Educational reform as continuous improvement* (2nd ed.). Thousand Oaks, CA: Corwin.

Lubienski, C., Crane, C., & Lubienski, S. T. (2008). What do we know about school effectiveness? Academic gains in public and private schools. *Phi Delta Kappan, 89,* 689–695.

McEwan, E. K. (2009). *Ten traits of highly effective schools: Raising the achievement bar for all students.* Thousand Oaks, CA: Corwin.

Nichols, B. (2008). *Improving student achievement: Fifty research-based strategies.* Columbus, OH: Linworth.

> Faced with the choice between changing one's mind and proving there is no need to do so, almost everyone gets busy on the proof.
>
> —*John Kenneth Galbraith*

INDICATORS OF QUALITY

The following indicators of quality summarize the findings of numerous research studies examining the most successful schools:

1. *Enriched environment*

   The physical environment is uncluttered and inviting.

   Flexibility in the room arrangement is possible.

   Students are actively involved in hands-on experiences.

   A variety of multimedia resources are used.

   Learning resources augment peripheral learning.

2. *Safe, supportive learning environment*

   Appropriate humor is used.

   Rules are fairly and consistently enforced.

   Opportunities for extra help are provided.

   Teachers treat students courteously.

   Teachers use students' names.

   Teachers monitor their classrooms with eyes and movement through the classroom.

3. *Choice*

   Students are involved in classroom decisions.

   Options are provided in learning activities.

   A variety of instructional techniques are employed.

   Teachers are sensitive to learning-style differences.

   Opportunities are provided for learning through different sensory modalities.

4. *Meaningful content*

   Relevant, real-life learning experiences are provided.

   New content is anchored to prior knowledge.

   Subject matter is age appropriate.

   Teachers convey enthusiasm for the content.

   Learning situations appropriately challenge students.

   Lessons support interdisciplinary and real-world connections.

   Critical thinking is emphasized more than seeking the right answer.

   Curiosity, novelty, and interest are embedded in learning experiences.

5. *Collaboration*

   Instruction is student centered rather than teacher centered.

   Time is provided for interaction with other students.

   A sense of community is evident among the students.

   School-home collaboration is nurtured.

   Students are provided with opportunities to learn in groups.

6. *Time usage*

   Teachers employ efficient routines for handling daily tasks.

   Students are appropriately engaged.

   Interruptions and distractions are minimized.

Students are allotted adequate time to totally process learning tasks.

Teachers adapt lessons to students' energy levels.

7. *Ongoing feedback*

Mistakes are treated as learning opportunities.

Teachers listen to the students.

High Schools That Work

What would the top 1 percent of high schools look like? The *Oregonian*, Portland's daily newspaper, assigned two reporters to gather data on the crème de la crème of West Coast high schools.

The investigators sought out high schools that ensured success for virtually every student. Selection criteria included high student achievement, a low dropout rate, a high rate of college attendance, and subsequent success in college. These outstanding schools also received no more funding than comparable area schools and had a mix of students, including significant numbers of minority, special education, and low-income students.

The paper concluded: "High schools must invigorate ties between adults and students, so teens aren't left to find their own way. And they must demand more challenging and meaningful work from students."

The *Oregonian* reported ten qualities that highly successful high schools possess. The high-performing schools they studied demonstrated nearly every one of these ten practices:

1. Expect high performance from all students and discontinue dumbed-down tracks. For example, one school required every student to take algebra. It did not offer general math or pre-algebra classes.

2. Assure that no teacher has more than 150 students. By adapting with block schedules or a trimester format, teachers had the same class size but spent longer time with fewer students.

3. Nurture teachers talking with their colleagues. The top schools made in-depth conversations about school effectiveness a top priority.

4. Assign schoolwork "worthy of being showcased." Many of the best high schools use student portfolios featuring authentic, high-quality projects. For example, students from San Diego's High Tech High

Teachers use more positive than negative comments.

Constructive peer feedback is encouraged.

Students are encouraged to ask questions.

Emphasis is on moving from extrinsic to intrinsic motivation.

Teachers use student feedback to modify instruction.

8. *Assessment*

Teachers clearly communicate expectations to students.

Learning is assessed in a variety of ways.

Assessment of progress is provided.

Mastery is valued more than memorization.

Assessment emphasizes application of lesson content.

Students demonstrate how-to knowledge.

Students are encouraged to assess their own performance.

Students have some choice in the assessment techniques used.

NATIONAL TEACHING STANDARDS

Standards, testing, and *accountability* have been buzzwords in the educational arena for the past decade. A significant portion of the nation's educational resources (money, time, and energy) has been devoted to accountability. Along with the offshoot buzzwords *curriculum alignment* and *high-stakes testing,* these phenomena dominate contemporary educational journals and professional educational conferences.

Some suggest that the origin of the movement for national standards dates to the successful Soviet launch of the Sputnik spacecraft in 1957. This event sparked an enormous response, focusing on what was being taught in our schools. Attention to national standards regained momentum in 1983 when the U.S. Department of Education's National Commission on Excellence in Education published the report *A Nation at Risk*. This much ballyhooed document strongly recommended that graduation requirements be strengthened and that higher standards be implemented for teacher preparation and professional growth.

In 1989, the National Council of Teachers of Mathematics published Curriculum and Evaluation Standards for School Mathematics; and the American Association for the Advancement of Science published *Science for all Americans*. Other subject areas soon had their own sets of standards.

Passage of the federal No Child Left Behind (NCLB) Act in 2001 greatly influenced the development of state standards, timetables of state exit exams, and local school districts' priorities.

Proponents argued that standards would boost achievement by clearly defining what is to be taught and what kind of performance is expected. The underlying theory is that higher expectations produce better performance. The intent behind the national standards movement is to set clear standards for what students must learn, to evaluate student improvement, and to

School made documentaries on World War I, built a working submarine, and sponsored a public debate on evolution.

5. Form student advisories. Many of the top schools see that every student has a faculty adviser. The authors concluded, "Making every educator an adviser helps ensure that no teen drifts through high school unnoticed."

6. Make every minute matter. The best schools are obsessed with eliminating absences and tardiness. Interruptions are discouraged, and classes begin on time.

7. Assist students in selecting courses. Some schools require students to obtain the permission of their most recent teachers in a subject before students can enroll in an advanced class. Students are encouraged to talk with teachers they respect about the most appropriate courses to take.

8. Turn seniors into mentors. Older students are encouraged to provide positive guidance to younger ones, creating a more inviting and friendlier school environment.

9. Give parents, students, and teachers more say. Site-based management with heavy involvement from teachers and parents is a hallmark of the most successful schools. Students have an active role in the running of the school.

10. Challenge students with authentic lessons. Connecting the academic curriculum to real-world problems and job-related skills captures students' interest and boost enthusiasm.

Source: Hammond, B., & Graves, B. (2004, January 13). Road map to success. *The Oregonian*. Online at www.oregonlive.com.

> If the school sends out children with a desire for knowledge and some idea of how to acquire and use it, it will have done its work.
>
> —**Richard Livingstone**

See One Hundred Outstanding Teaching Ideas

Alisa Miller has catalogued online videos of a hundred creative teachers sharing their classroom lessons. Check out this valuable Internet resource to gain some tips or polish your skills. A few examples:

- *Cooperative Arithmetic: How to Teach Math as a Social Activity*
- *Teaching Children Philosophy*
- *Blogging in the Classroom*
- *Developing Minds: Learning How to Rebuild a Town*
- *Classroom Jeopardy*
- *SMART Board in Action*
- *PowerPoints that Rock*
- *Ma and Pa Kettle Division*
- *Erosion Science Lesson*

Source: Alisa Miller, *100 awesome classroom videos to learn new teaching techniques* at www.smartteaching.org/blog/2008/08/100-awesome-classroom-videos-to-learn-new-teaching-techniques/

hold students and teachers responsible for the results.

Curriculum alignment is the idea that test content should be congruent with subject area content specified in state or national academic standards. Teachers and schools are continually urged to align their curriculum and assessments with state standards.

The No Child Left Behind program has faced significant opposition from educators, parents, and politicians. Writing in the February 2008 issue of *Clearing House,* Theoni Smyth captured much of the expressed frustration about the NCLB legislation: "Educators have discovered that the plan is flawed, developmentally inappropriate, ill funded, and leaving more students, teachers, and schools behind than ever before."

The overwhelming number of standards is the biggest impediment to successfully implementing standards, according to Robert Marzano, senior fellow at the McREL Institute. He argued that the number of standards should be cut at least by two-thirds. Marzano suggested that schools would have to switch from K–12 to K–22 to have time to cover all the standards. The McREL Web site (www.mcrel.org/standards-benchmarks) lists over forty-one hundred benchmarks distributed among 256 standards. In the McREL database, mathematics contains nine standards and 223 benchmarks. For example, one standard, "Understands and applies basic and advanced concepts of probability" encompasses eighteen benchmarks, such as "Determines probability using simulations or experiments" (grades 6–8) and "Understands the concepts of independent and dependent events and how they are related to compound events and conditional probability" (grades 9–12).

Lauren Resnick, Mary Kay Stein, and Sarah Coon noted that the NCLB legislation included all sticks and no carrots. Its punitive nature stressed penalizing students, teachers, and schools for failure. Other researchers (Duncombe, Yinger, & Lukemeyer, 2008) concluded that the massive underfunding of the legislation's mandates doomed it to failure.

Insanity is doing the same thing over and over again, but expecting different results.

—Rita Mae Brown,
Sudden Death

PROFESSIONAL DEVELOPMENT

Teaching should be more than just a job. It is a profession and a career. It is a long-term commitment to doing your best to help young people blossom intellectually, emotionally, and behaviorally. It is a position of incredible importance; teachers with passion and compassion can profoundly influence their students' lives. At the worst, teachers also have the power to discourage, humiliate, and crush their students' spirit. Either way, the lives we teachers touch become part of our heritage, our immortality.

Outstanding teachers are not born; they develop. True, some personality types are probably more attracted to education, but the art and craft of teaching is gradually honed through years of study, experimentation, reality testing, and reflection. Development of the effective teacher does not end with the receipt of an undergraduate or even master's degree. A diploma is but a license to learn. The more true professionals learn, the more they realize there is to learn.

Any teacher can become a better teacher; with enough determination and hard work, probably any teacher could become a successful teacher. However, teaching is hard work. Knowing your content is a necessary, though wholly insufficient, prerequisite to becoming an outstanding teacher. Many in the teaching profession are brilliant, possessing great knowledge and understanding of their chosen field of study, yet they will never be successful teachers.

The skills of effective teaching are complex. It is not enough to be a scholar; a good teacher is also part salesperson, entertainer, psychologist, counselor, leader, mediator, conductor, guide, evaluator, advocate, and cheerleader. Different teachers develop different combinations of these talents, but all are helpful.

Believe it or not, many teachers rarely read anything related to their teaching area. Their teaching repertoire is limited to what they knew when they walked into the classroom the first day. Imagine going to a physician, auto mechanic, or any other professional who had not remained current with the latest techniques, research, and technology related to their profession. Indeed, an argument can be made that the person who fails to learn and use the most effective practices available to his or her profession is being both negligent and unethical.

Create a purposeful plan of professional development. It is too important to be left to chance. Here are some ideas that successful teachers have used to enhance their professional skills.

- Continued learning keeps you fresh. Experiment with new ways of doing old tasks. Include new content and skills in your courses or volunteer to develop new courses. It is impossible to maintain enthusiasm and peak performance while teaching the same things the same ways year after year. "Rust out" or burnout is inevitable if we do not incorporate professional rejuvenation.

- Allow time, ideally each day, for reflection. Examine what works and what doesn't and how you might improve each lesson. Write it down in a journal or in the margins of your lesson plans. Keep an idea notebook to incubate and brainstorm teaching ideas.

- Peer-coaching groups are now an integral part of many staff development programs. This is an effective, proven approach to improving instructional and classroom management skills. If your school does not yet have a peer-coaching group, suggest it to your colleagues. Many will be threatened by the thought of another teacher observing them. The truly professional teacher will welcome the opportunity.

- Develop or join a support group among fellow teachers. It may take the form of a study group where you read and discuss relevant educational materials, or it might be a more unstructured gathering to offer mutual support and problem solving.

- Draw up a professional development plan each year, even if your school does not require it. It should target two or three areas for improvement. It might be in classroom management skills, developing specific teaching strategies, or in expanding your knowledge of some content area. Share your plan with your principal and seek suggestions. You are also more likely to later receive support (in either release time or money) if it is obvious your request is a part of a professional development plan and not a whim.

- Create your own independent study. Each year identify a new topic you intend to study in depth. Attend workshops or classes, read books and journal articles, interview experts, or develop your own field trips. Within a year of concentrated effort, you can develop a reasonable degree of expertise in most any subject.

- Don't overlook the benefits of acquiring a mentor, even if you are a veteran teacher. It may be a more experienced teacher, a supervisor or administrator, a professor, or perhaps an individual working in your subject area outside of a school setting. Working with a mentor should be a mutually rewarding experience. Show your appreciation of your mentor through verbal acknowledgment, token gifts, and time spent helping him or her in special projects.

- Learn by observing good role models. Every building contains creative, successful teachers. Find them and study their style, techniques, and ideas. Seek their advice.

- If you have an opportunity to participate in a sabbatical, take it—even if it entails some financial sacrifice. The trade-off in mental health and renewed vigor are well worth the price.

- Each year try to attend at least one state or national conference related to your teaching field. Ask fellow teachers or local professors which ones are most worthwhile. These programs can provide refreshing and energizing experiences. Bring back samples and ideas to share with interested colleagues. If you are a regular at a conference, consider sharing your classroom experiences as a presenter. If you can't attend, most conferences provide tapes of many sessions. Borrow or buy these to listen to while commuting.

- Subscribe to at least one useful publication related to your teaching area. You need not feel obligated to read every issue cover to cover, but do scan it looking for new teaching ideas.

- Regularly visit a few of the best Web sites related to teaching your subject.

- Subscribe to one or two outstanding blogs offered by experts knowledgeable in your content area. If podcasts are available, download them to an iPod or MP3 player to listen to them as you drive or exercise.

- Recognize that teaching as a profession cannot be limited to forty hours per week for nine months out of the year. If education is really a passion, you will eagerly devote the time necessary to improve your lessons, develop new skills, and reflect on the daily challenges of the classroom.

- Attend in-service programs and workshops with an open mind. It is easy to develop a red-pencil mentality and stubbornly refuse to rationally listen to new ideas. Of course, they have to be reality tested back in your classroom the next day, but give them a chance. Like developing any new skill—riding a bike, mastering a computer, or learning a new hobby—innovative teaching techniques will require a start-up learning curve. It may seem unnatural or awkward at first. Experiment. After a fair trial, discard those things that clearly don't work for you; and adapt those things that do. That is how we improve in any endeavor—whether golf, knitting, or painting; we keep the behaviors and ideas that work and eliminate those that do not. It is embedded in the concept of continuous improvement, constantly fine-tuning our performance.

- Develop options. If you have only one way to teach a concept or handle misbehavior, what will you do when your tactic does not work? If you have a smorgasbord of alternatives available, you can pragmatically experiment until you find one that succeeds.

- Use a student evaluation form appropriate to your students' age level. Carefully and objectively read the results to see how your students rate your teaching effectiveness. There are some limitations of student evaluations, but they do provide a valuable source of information that should not be ignored.

- Examine your students' scores on standardized achievement tests related to your subject area. Are there any areas in which they seem to consistently score low? Is it important for your students to master these skills or concepts? How can you better teach these concepts in your class?

- Resist the temptation to rationalize poor student performance or behavior in your classes. Claims such as "I'd be a better teacher if I had better students" may be true, but they don't excuse poor teaching. Imagine a physician lamenting that only sick people come to her office. Yes, kids are not the same today as when you went to school, and they probably never will be. Yet the fact remains that school represents the best hope that many kids have. A true professional is committed to doing the very best possible with the skills, resources, and students available.

- Don't automatically discount critical feedback you receive from others about your teaching performance. Supervisors' or principals' observations are one, though not the only, valuable source of information. Listen objectively, not defensively. If you disagree with some aspect of an observer's conclusions, rationally present whatever documentation or evidence you might have to rebut the point. However, avoid arguing or quibbling to protect your ego.

- Develop relationships outside the field of education. One way of recharging your batteries is to cultivate interests beyond school. Interacting only with other teachers invites too much shop talk and commiserating. Though you will likely include some colleagues in your circle of friends, seek a balance with others from diverse careers and experiences.

- Become a risk taker. Don't repeat the same half-baked lessons year after year from habit. Experiment. Try new things. Don't be afraid to make mistakes. Free yourself from the shackles of perfectionism. Strive for excellence, not perfection.

Personal Independent Study

For twenty-five years, I have satisfied my thirst for learning by annually setting up a personal independent study project. Each year I select a topic that piques my curiosity and embark on a quest to learn all I can about it in roughly a year. My research involves reading relevant articles and books, attending workshops and seminars, and interviewing any available experts. The Internet has facilitated access to a treasury of hard-to-find resources.

In my independent study, I am accountable to no one but myself. No grades or reports are required. No one is going to evaluate my progress. There is nothing magical about the length of time a project takes. Some topics run their course in less than a year. I sense it is time to move on when what I am reading or hearing becomes redundant or when the topic becomes less interesting.

While I was teaching college, the content of my inquiries tended to be academic; for example, the use of time in schools, stress management, creative problem solving, perfectionism, and classroom management. More recent topics have included learning to design Web pages, building stained glass windows, and calligraphy.

You can develop a fair amount of expertise on any topic if you focus on it for a year. Interestingly, the next topic often emerges from the previous year's study, appearing almost subconsciously as an itch that needs scratching. I anticipate that my independent study practice will continue as a lifelong habit.

- Become an actor, not a reactor, on the stage of life. You possess a free will to choose how you will conduct your life, both in and out of the classroom. When we become reactors, we surrender control of our thoughts, actions, and feelings to those around us. When we worry about possible disapproval from our colleagues or about not living up to others' expectations, we yield control of our lives. When we defensively respond with revenge, gossiping, backbiting, sulking, and withdrawal, we have surrendered our autonomy. When we become creative problem solvers, we affirm our competence and efficacy. When we become tolerant of the foibles of others while admitting and occasionally laughing at our own, we reap dignity and the respect of our colleagues and students. True power arises from acceptance of ourselves and of those around us.

NATIONAL BOARD CERTIFICATION

The pinnacle of professional accreditation for educators today is attainment of National Board certification. This is a voluntary national credential that complements state licensure. Administered by the National Board for Professional Teaching Standards, the rigorous certification process guides teachers through self-reflection and examination of their teaching practices.

National Board Certification is available for teachers in twenty-four fields and development areas. Over 65,000 of the nation's 2.5 million teachers have been designated as National Board Certified Teachers (NBCTs).

As of November 2008, all but one state had enacted special incentives and recognition for teachers achieving National Board certification. Most states subsidize all or part of the $2,300 certification fee. The state of Washington provides an annual

$5,000 salary enhancement for NBCTs. Ohio certification earners gain an annual bonus of $2,500 for up to ten years. Oklahoma offers $5,000 annually to certificate recipients. Maine offers a stipend of $3,000 for the life of the certification. Many local school districts offer additional annual payments (typically, $500 to $2,500) for successful attainment of this certification.

Over twelve hundred colleges and universities will grant graduate credits for completing the board certification process. The American Council on Education may award three semester hours of graduate credit to teachers who complete the application process and an additional six credit hours to those receiving National Board certification.

The National Board's mission, according to its Web site (www.nbpts.org), is to maintain "high and rigorous standards for what accomplished teachers should know and be able to do." The National Board certification process is based on five basic assumptions underlying the practices of excellence in teaching:

- Teachers are committed to students and their learning.
- Teachers know the subjects they teach and how to teach those subjects to students.
- Teachers are responsible for managing and monitoring student learning.
- Teachers think systematically about their practice and learn from experience.
- Teachers are members of learning communities.

The National Board assessment involves two components, a professional portfolio and a series of assessment-center exercises. The portfolios include videotapes of the applicant's teaching, samples of students' learning products, and additional teaching artifacts, as well as a detailed analysis of the teacher's instructional practices. Trained assessors examine how teachers put knowledge and theory into practice. The assessment-center component requires teachers to write answers to questions pertinent to their specific content areas. The intent of these exercises is to verify that the knowledge and competencies demonstrated in the portfolio truly reflect the applicants' performances and to allow applicants a chance to exhibit proficiencies not included in their portfolios.

Candidates may complete the computer-administered assessments at any of more than three hundred testing centers, located in every state in the nation. Teachers spend an average of two hundred hours working on their certification process.

National Board certification is valid for ten years, at which time a teacher must undergo a renewal requirement. A growing body of research relates National Board certification with improved student achievement. To learn more about receiving this certification, check the National Board's Web site at www.nbpts.org.

EDUCATIONAL RESEARCH

Every professional educator must be a savvy consumer of educational research. The obligation to follow the best practices that have been supported by sound, empirical research is a hallmark of any profession.

It is every professional's duty to continuously improve his or her skills and knowledge. A doctor who is practicing outdated procedures that have been scientifically shown to be inferior is in violation of his or her profession's ethical code.

A vast body of sound educational research is available. Some of it is pure muck—poorly designed, inaccurate, and misleading. The fact that it is in print offers no assurance that a research study is valid. Being able to separate the wheat from the chaff is an essential skill for professional teachers. This is why virtually all master's degree programs in education include research and statistics courses. To remain ignorant of the principles of sound research and basic statistics is to put oneself at the mercy of charlatans and zealots plying political and personal agendas.

Though a full tutorial in educational research and statistics is beyond the scope of this book, a general set of guidelines for assessing the quality of good educational research follows.

The Scientific Method

The scientific method is the foundation of sound research, enabling investigators to objectively gather data to solve problems. It consists of four parts.

1. *State the problem.* Einstein suggested that a well-defined problem is half solved.
2. *Form a hypothesis.* A potential solution is tentatively created after gathering information about the problem. This step involves examining the current body of knowledge related to the problem at hand, including observations, theories, and prior research efforts.
3. *Test the hypothesis.* An experiment is planned and conducted to determine whether the hypothesis solves the problem or not.
4. *Draw conclusions.* A conclusion is reached as to whether the hypothesis was correct or not. The results are often stated in research articles in terms of the statistical probability that the observed results could have occurred by chance.

Types of Research

Different disciplines may rely on somewhat different modes of research, depending on the types of problems being studied and the feasibility of collecting necessary data. Research designs fall into two broad categories: qualitative or quantitative.

Qualitative research designs involve compiling narrative data to learn about variables of interest. Data analysis includes coding data and synthesizing the information to draw conclusions about the phenomena under study.

Quantitative research designs rely on collecting numerical data to understand, predict, and explain phenomena. The analysis is essentially deductive, involving primarily statistical analysis.

Research designs tend to fall under one of the following seven categories:

- *Ethnographic research* strives to describe group behavior and social interactions. It employs qualitative techniques, particularly structured interviews, careful observation, and meticulous documentation of actions and social interactions.

- *Descriptive research* tries to depict and explain present phenomena. It uses both qualitative and quantitative data assembled from interviews, observations, surveys, written documents, and test results.

- *Historical research* seeks to describe and explain past events. It usually depends on qualitative data, such as oral histories or written documents.

- *Correlational research* explores relationships among variables or tries to make predictions. It analyzes the statistical correlation between two or more measures, such as test scores and attitudinal instruments.

- *Action and evaluation research* assesses the value of a procedure, program, or product. It often takes place on-site (such as in the classroom or school building). Its goal is usually to improve the organization. Action or evaluation research does not attempt to generalize results to a broader population.

- *Causal comparative research* attempts to explore cause-and-effect relationships. It relies on both qualitative and quantitative data such as written documents, interviews, test scores, and so on. Pretest and posttest control group projects in which the subjects are randomly assigned to the control group or experimental group provide an ideal research structure for making valid claims of causality. The difficulty in controlling relevant variables (such as students' home environment) makes pure control group experiments difficult in some areas of educational and social research.

- *Experimental research* examines cause-and-effect relationships. Experiments are designed to manipulate specific variables to create different kinds of effects. It uses primarily quantitative data such as test results and performance measurements. The independent variables are the factors the experimenter controls.

Common Flaws in Research Articles

CAUSATION VERSUS CORRELATION

The fact that the rooster crows every morning does not mean that its crowing causes the sun to rise; the mere fact that two events occur together does not mean that one causes the other. It reveals a relationship (what researchers call a correlation) between the two events but does not imply causation.

A common error in the public press is to misinterpret correlation between two variables as causation. Statistically, a clear correlation can be shown between the price of cigarettes and the salaries of ministers in this country. Would anyone be so naive as to suggest that somehow ministers are profiting from the sale of tobacco? Of course not; they are obviously both caused by a third variable, economic inflation. But equally invalid assumptions commonly find their way into the popular media and are spread as gospel.

Sound research designs can provide evidence of a causal relationship between variables. Some are too complex to cover here, but most involve some form of control group, which does not receive the procedure under study. It serves as a comparison group for the variable under investigation. Data from the experimental group, which does receive the procedure under study, is then statistically compared to that of the control group.

SAMPLING ERRORS

Seldom is it feasible to include every individual or event in a research project. A legitimate research practice is to study a representative sample of a particular population. The safest way to ensure that the individuals included are truly representative of the total population is to randomly select a sufficiently large group. Random selection means that every individual in the total population had an equal chance of being selected.

A research investigation may lead to erroneous conclusions if a poor sample of the population under study is selected. Erroneous conclusions are likely if the sample is drawn in a biased manner or from a group not representative of the population being studied. It would be risky to use data from ten teachers to generalize that all teachers would possess the same characteristics.

MEASUREMENT ERROR

Ineffective or inappropriately used instruments will usually lead to erroneous conclusions. Tests, questionnaires, and other assessment devices must be designed using fair and unbiased procedures. Two essential qualities, reliability and validity, must be evident and should be reported in any legitimate research article.

Reliability is a statistical indicator of the instrument's ability to obtain consistent results. Imagine trying to measure the length of something using an elastic ruler.

A test (or other instrument) possesses validity if it measures what it says it is measuring. One form of validity is predictive validity. For example, the SAT claims to be a valid predictor of student success in college. Note that reliability is a necessary but not sufficient condition for validity.

Biased test instruments can put some students at a great disadvantage. Much of the debate on intelligence testing and today's high-stakes competency tests centers on potential cultural biases. Fairness of testing may be questioned if the test penalizes students with disabilities or those with limited English proficiency.

Poorly worded questions on a survey can distort the results, intentionally or unintentionally yielding inaccurate interpretations. Unclear or incomplete directions can adversely affect test or questionnaire results.

LACK OF STANDARDIZATION

The instruments and procedures used in any research endeavor must be standardized, such that all subjects or cases in a comparison group receive the same treatment under precisely the same conditions. Studies comparing schools from different countries can be flawed because the conditions of data collection or the populations being compared can vary so widely.

Lack of standardization is like comparing apples and oranges. Too often a researcher may make inferential leaps in analyzing data and make side-by-side comparisons that are inappropriate. Additionally, researchers' inattention to detail or carelessness can produce errors. "Fuzzy" operational variables must be clearly and concretely defined.

LACK OF OBJECTIVITY

When reading a piece of research, it is wise to ask some questions. Who sponsored the study? What are the researcher's credentials? Who has a vested interest in the results? Are the researchers pushing hidden political or social agendas? Does the research project have inherent biases?

LACK OF PEER REVIEW

Be extremely skeptical of research that is distributed solely by mass media (in news releases, television sound bites, and popular magazines). Legitimate research is published in peer-reviewed publications. These professional research journals employ a rigorous and objective process to evaluate the appropriateness of the research design, data analysis, and interpretations. A list of the major education-related research journals is included at the end of this chapter.

The Importance of Statistics

In applying the scientific method, a researcher generates a hypothesis about some observed phenomenon and proceeds to objectively collect data to test that hypothesis. The researcher then analyzes the data to either confirm or refute the hypothesis. This may take the form of an experiment specifically designed to test the hypothesis.

Frequently, the researcher measures the data. Anytime one collects a series of measurements, some variation will occur. Statistical analysis helps a researcher determine whether differences between two (or more) sets of measurements occur purely by chance or if some other variable caused the differences.

Basic Research and Statistics Glossary

correlation   The most commonly used measure of association. It indicates the strength of a linear relationship between two variables. Remember that correlations do not support causality.

correlation coefficient   A measure of the relationship between variables. It is expressed numerically with a value between −1.0 and +1.0. A zero represents no relationship at all. A minus sign before the coefficient indicates an inverse relationship between the variables: as one variable increases, the other decreases. A positive number indicates a positive relationship: as one variable increases, so does the other.

hypothesis   A tentative statement predicting the relationship between variables.

mean, median, and mode   The three mathematical calculations are used to provide a picture of a group of measurements. These three calculations are measures of central tendency. They represent different concepts.

The *mean* is the statistical average of a group of numbers. It is calculated by adding all numbers in a set of numbers and then dividing by the number of observations in the set. Examples would include grade point average, the Dow Jones, or average daily temperature. The mean is the most commonly used measure of central tendency. One disadvantage is that extreme numbers can distort the mean or average. Imagine the effect of including Bill Gates in a calculation of the average annual salary of a group of people.

The *median* is the middle value in an ordered selection of measurements. It is the midpoint: half the cases would be above, and half would be below the median. If a set contains an odd number of figures, the median is the middle number. Typically, the median is a better indicator of central tendency than the mean when there are some extremely small or large measurements.

The *mode* is the most frequent value in a set of observations. The mode is a particularly useful measure when the data are not numbers but categories (for example, shoe sizes, cities). For example, in the set of values 1, 3, 5, 5, 5, 7, the mode would be 5 because this value occurs most frequently in the set. A distribution can have two modes (hence, bimodal).

normal distribution   A bell-shaped graph of data. It is highest in the middle and lowest on the sides, and the right and left halves are symmetrical. Many biological, physical, and social phenomena are normally distributed.

null hypothesis   Generally a hypothesis that no difference or relationship exists between two or more variables. The researcher applies a statistical procedure to either accept or reject the null hypothesis. When the null hypothesis is rejected, the researcher describes the results as statistically significant.

probability   The chance of a particular event occurring. A statistical probability is expressed as a number between one and ten. The closer the number is to one, the greater the probability of occurrence. Flipping a coin for heads or tails would carry a .5 probability of either result.

random sample   A sample in which each member of the population has the same probability of inclusion.

range   The statistical range is the difference between the lowest and highest numbers in an array of numbers. For example, the range of heights of boys on a high school basketball team was from five feet eight inches to six feet seven inches.

replication   An independent verification of a research study's results.

What Works Clearinghouse

The What Works Clearinghouse (WWC) is now online at whatworks.ed.gov/. Created by the U.S. Department of Education's Institute of Education Sciences, the site's purpose is to provide teachers, administrators, policymakers, and the public with reliable and accurate research evidence of what works in education.

Teams of experts in educational research regularly screen research studies to select those of value in making educational decisions. Rigorous selection criteria are applied, with preference given to studies involving randomized control and experimental groups allowing causation to be more readily inferred.

An array of reports, articles, and other WWC publications are already available online, with more being added each month. The initial set of issues examined included:

- *Adult Literacy*
- *Character Education*
- *Delinquent, Disorderly, and Violent Behavior*
- *Dropout Prevention*
- *English Language Learners*
- *Math*
- *Peer-Assisted Learning*
- *Reading*

For each of the above issues, two versions of selected reports are available: a user-friendly, brief, nontechnical summary and detailed technical reports. While some researchers have expressed reservations about the rigidity of the selection criteria, many have heralded the clearinghouse as a potentially valuable resource.

Source: The What Works Clearinghouse at whatworks.ed.gov.

sample   A subset of the total population or universe.

standard deviation   A statistic that describes how tightly all the data are clustered around the mean in an array of data. When the instances are closely bunched together and the bell-shaped curve is steep, the standard deviation is small. When the data are wider apart and the bell curve is flatter, the standard deviation will be large.

validity   The extent to which an instrument measures what it's supposed to be measuring.

variable   A trait or characteristic of a person or an item that can have different values within the population of interest.

For More Information

King, B. M., & Minium, E. W. (2008). *Statistical reasoning in the behavioral sciences* (5th ed.). Hoboken, NJ: Wiley.

Love, N. (Ed.). (2009). *Using data to improve learning for all: A collaborative inquiry approach.* Thousand Oaks, CA: Corwin.

Van Blerkom, M. L. (2009). *Measurement and statistics for teachers.* New York: Routledge.

Checklist to Use in Evaluating Whether an Intervention Is Backed by Rigorous Evidence

Step 1. Is the intervention supported by "strong" evidence of effectiveness?

    A. The quality of evidence needed to establish "strong" evidence: randomized controlled trials that are well designed and implemented. The following are key items to look for in assessing whether a trial is well designed and implemented.

Key items to look for in the study's description of the intervention and the random assignment process:

☐ The study should clearly describe the intervention, including: (i) who administered it, who received it, and what it cost; (ii) how the intervention differed from what the control group received; and (iii) the logic of how the intervention is supposed to affect outcomes.

☐ Be alert to any indication that the random assignment process may have been compromised.

☐ The study should provide data showing that there are no systematic differences between the intervention and control groups prior to the intervention.

Key items to look for in the study's collection of outcome data:

☐ The study should use outcome measures that are "valid"—that is, they accurately measure the true outcomes that the intervention is designed to affect.

☐ The percent of participants of whom the study has lost track while collecting outcome data should be small, and should not differ between the intervention and control groups.

☐ The study should collect and report outcome data even for those members of the intervention group who do not participate in or complete the intervention.

☐ The study should preferably obtain data on long-term outcomes of the intervention, so that you can judge whether the intervention's effects were sustained over time.

Key items to look for in the study's reporting of results:

☐ If the study makes a claim that the intervention is effective, it should report the size of the effect, and statistical tests showing the effect is unlikely to be the result of chance.

☐ Treat with caution a study's claim that the intervention's effect on a subgroup (for example Hispanic students) is different from its effect on the overall population in the study.

☐ The study should report the intervention's effects on all the outcomes that the study measured, not just those for which there is a positive effect.

(Continued)

B. Quantity of evidence needed to establish "strong" evidence of effectiveness.

☐ The intervention should be demonstrated effective, through well-designed randomized controlled trials, in more than one site of implementation.

☐ These sites should be typical school or community settings, such as public school classrooms taught by regular teachers.

☐ The trials should demonstrate the intervention's effectiveness in school settings similar to yours, before you can be confident it will work in your schools or classrooms.

Step 2. If the intervention is not supported by "strong" evidence, is it nevertheless supported by "possible" evidence of effectiveness?

This is a judgment call that depends, for example, on the extent of the flaws in the randomized trials of the intervention and the quality of any nonrandomized studies that have been done. The following are a few factors to consider in making these judgments.

A. Circumstances in which a comparison-group study can constitute "possible" evidence:

☐ The study's intervention and comparison groups should be very closely matched in academic achievement levels, demographics, and other characteristics prior to the intervention.

☐ The comparison group should not be comprised of individuals who had the option to participate in the intervention but declined.

☐ The study should preferably choose the intervention and comparison groups and outcome measures "prospectively"—that is, *before* the intervention is administered.

☐ The study should meet the checklist items listed above for a well-designed randomized controlled trial (other than the item concerning the random assignment process). That is, the study should use valid outcome measures, report tests for statistical significance, and so on.

B. Studies that do not meet the threshold for "possible" evidence of effectiveness include: (1) pre-post studies; (2) comparison-group studies in which the intervention and comparison groups are not well matched; and (3) "meta-analyses" that combine the results of individual studies which do not themselves meet the threshold for "possible" evidence.

Step 3. If the intervention is backed by neither "strong" nor "possible" evidence, one may conclude that it is not supported by meaningful evidence of effectiveness.

Source: Reprinted from Institute of Education Sciences. (2003). *Identifying and implementing educational practices supported by rigorous evidence: A user friendly guide.* Washington, DC: U.S. Department of Education.

LEARNING WHAT WORKS: ACTION RESEARCH

Action or evaluation research is concerned with assessing the effectiveness of a particular treatment or procedure. In the classroom it usually involves teachers gathering and analyzing data about their own practice to improve it. The focus is on resolving practical problems and systematically testing new ideas.

Action research can serve several purposes simultaneously: professional development, curriculum development, school improvement, and self-reflection. It can also give teachers greater confidence in the quality of their classroom decisions.

Because the data analysis is generally qualitative rather than quantitative, an in-depth knowledge of statistics is not required. Often teachers collaborate with colleagues on action research projects. Action research can be an integral part of teachers' mentoring or peer-coaching process. Some teachers work together with university professors on an action research project.

Projects may take from a few weeks to several months. Here are the steps involved:

1. *Identify a research question or classroom problem.* The first step is to select an issue or methodology you would like to research. Usually it is a technique or activity that has potential for improving some aspect of instruction or academic life. It should be something important that is of genuine interest to you.

Sample Research Questions

- How does self-efficacy affect the achievement of students?
- What impact does including the student in parent conferences have?
- How can I get my students to take better notes?
- Has block scheduling improved student learning?
- Does cooperative learning improve students' attitudes toward school?
- What effect does participation in a service project have on classroom civility?
- What strategies will decrease classroom teasing?

2. *Review the research literature.* Do some background reading of previous research related to the issue under study. Why reinvent the wheel? Build on what others have already done. An Internet search can provide useful information, though its credibility must be carefully assessed.

3. *Implement a potential solution.* If feasible, use two comparable groups to test the potential solution. The experimental group receives the proposed treatment; the control group does not.

4. *Collect data.* A wise person once quipped, "Gathering data is like gathering garbage. You'd better know what you are going to do with it before you collect it." Don't accumulate more than you need. Focus precisely on the specific issue under examination. To adequately assess the impact of an innovation, collect data from a variety of sources and from alternative of points of view. Collecting pre- and posttreatment data is helpful in detecting treatment effects.

Potential Data Sources

Anecdotal records	Parent-teacher conference notes
Attendance	Photographs
Audiotapes and videotapes	Portfolios
Case studies	Questionnaires
Cumulative records	Surveys
Grades	Student journals
Interviews	Student work sample
Observations	Test scores

5. *Analyze the data.* Does the project make a difference? Do you see clear patterns in the data?

6. *Take action.* Implement successful solutions. Revise partially successful ones or seek alternative solutions.

7. *Share what you have learned.* Communicate the results to colleagues or parents. This might be done through journal articles, online discussion groups, conferences, or workshops. Include copies of action research projects in your professional portfolio.

For More Information

Cammarota, J., & Fine, M. (Ed.). (2008). *Revolutionizing education: Youth participatory action research in motion.* New York: Routledge.

Hui, M. F., & Grossman, D. L. (2008). *Improving teacher education through action research.* New York: Routledge.

Ross-Fisher, R. (2008). Action research to improve teaching and learning. *Kappa Delta Pi Record, 44*(4), 160–164.

Slavin, R. E. (2007). *Educational research in an age of accountability.* Boston: Pearson.

Stringer, E. T. (2007). *Action research* (3rd ed.). Thousand Oaks, CA: Sage.

PROFESSIONAL ORGANIZATIONS

American Alliance for Health, Physical
  Education, Recreation and Dance
1900 Association Drive
Reston, VA 22091
(800) 213-7193
www.aahperd.org/

American Association of
  Physics Teachers
One Physics Ellipse
College Park, MD 20740-3845
(301) 209-0845
www.aapt.org/

American Council on the Teaching of
   Foreign Languages
1001 North Fairfax Street, Suite 200
Alexandria, VA 22314
(703) 894-2900
www.actfl.org

American Federation of Teachers
555 New Jersey Avenue, NW
Washington, DC 20001
(202) 879-4400
www.aft.org/

American Library Association
50 East Huron Street
Chicago, IL 60611
(800) 545-2433
www.ala.org/

American School Counselor Association
1101 King Street, Suite 625
Alexandria, VA 22314
(800) 306-4722
www.schoolcounselor.org

American Speech-Language-Hearing
   Association
2200 Research Boulevard
Rockville, MD 20852
(800) 638-8255
www.asha.org

Association for Career and Technical
   Education
1410 King Street
Alexandria, VA 22314
(800) 826-9972
www.acteonline.org/

Association for Childhood Education
17904 Georgia Avenue, Suite 215
Olney, MD 20832
(301) 942-2443
www.acei.org/

Association for Educational Communications and Technology
1800 North Stonelake Drive, Suite 2
Bloomington, IN 47404
(800) 423-3563
www.aect.org/

Association for Experiential Education
3775 Iris Avenue, Suite #4
Boulder, CO 80301-2043
(866) 522-8337
www.aee.org/

Association for Supervision and Curriculum
   Development
1703 North Beauregard Street
Alexandria, VA 22311
(800) 933-2723
www.ascd.org

Council for Exceptional Children
1110 North Glebe Road, Suite 300
Arlington, VA 22201
(800) 224-6830
www.cec.sped.org

Council for Learning Disabilities
11184 Antioch Road
Box 405
Overland Park, KS 66210
(913) 491-1011
www.cldinternational.org

International Reading Association
800 Barksdale Road
P.O. Box 8139
Newark, DE 19714-8139
(800) 336-7323
www.reading.org/

International Society for Technology
   in Education
180 West 8th Avenue, Suite 300
Eugene, OR 97401-2916
(800) 336-5191
www.iste.org

Kappa Delta Pi
3707 Woodview Trace
Indianapolis, IN 46268-1158
(800) 284-3167
www.kdp.org/

Learning Disabilities Association of America
4156 Library Road
Pittsburgh, PA 15234-1349
(412) 341-1515
www.ldanatl.org/

Modern Language Association
26 Broadway, Third Floor
New York, NY 10004-1789
(646) 576-5000
www.mla.org/

Music Teachers National Association
441 Vine Street, Suite 3100
3100 Cincinnati, OH 45202-3004
(888) 512-5278
www.mtna.org/

National Art Educators Association
1916 Association Drive
Reston, VA 22091
(703) 860-8000
www.naea-reston.org/

National Association for Bilingual Education
313 L Street, NW, Suite 210
Washington, DC 20005
(202) 898-1829
www.nabe.org/

National Association for Gifted Children
1707 L Street, NW, Suite 550
Washington, DC 20036
(202) 785-4268
www.nagc.org/

National Association for the Education of
    Young Children
1313 L Street, NW, Suite 500
Washington, DC 20005
(800) 424-2460
www.naeyc.org/

National Association of Biology Teachers
12030 Sunrise Valley Drive, Suite 110
Reston, VA 20191
(800) 406-0775
www.nabt.org/

National Association of Elementary School
    Principals
1615 Duke Street
Alexandria, VA 22314
(800) 386-2377
www.naesp.org/

National Association of School
    Psychologists
4340 East West Highway, Suite 402
Bethesda, MD 20814
(301) 657-0270
www.nasponline.org/

National Association of Secondary School
    Principals
1904 Association Drive
Reston, VA 22091-1537
(800) 253-7746
nassp.org/

National Business Education
    Association
1914 Association Drive
Reston, VA 22091-1596
(703) 860-8300
www.nbea.org/

National Catholic Education
    Association
1077 30th Street, NW, Suite 100
Washington, DC 20007
(800) 711-6232
www.ncea.org/

National Council for the Social
    Studies
8555 Sixteenth Street, Suite 500
Silver Spring, MD 20910
(301) 588-1800
www.ncss.org/

National Council of Teachers of
    English
1111 West Kenyon Road
Urbana, IL 61801-1096
(877) 369-6283
www.ncte.org/

National Council of Teachers of
    Mathematics
1906 Association Drive
Reston, VA 22091-1596
(703) 620-9840
www.nctm.org/

National Education Association
1201 16th Street
Washington, DC 20036
(202) 833-4000
www.nea.org/

National Middle School
  Association
4151 Executive Parkway, Suite 300
Westerville, OH 43081
(800) 528-6672
www.nmsa.org/

National Rural Education Association
Beering Hall
100 North University St.
West Lafayette, IN 47907
(765) 494-0086
www.nrea.net/

National Science Teachers
  Association
1840 Wilson Boulevard
Arlington, VA 22201-3000
(703) 243-7100
www.nsta.org

Phi Delta Kappa
408 North Union Street
Bloomington, IN 47405-3800
(800) 766-1156
www.pdkintl.org/

Teachers of English to Speakers of Other
  Languages
700 South Washington Street, Suite 200
Alexandria, VA 22314
(888) 547-3369
www.tesol.edu/

EDUCATION JOURNALS
General Education Periodicals

American Education

American Educator

American Journal of Education

American School Board Journal

American Secondary Education

American Teacher

Changing Schools

Clearing House

Computers and Education

Computers in the Schools

Contemporary Education

Curriculum Inquiry

Curriculum Review

Education

Education, U.S.A.

Education and Urban Society

Education Digest

Educational Forum

Educational Horizons

Educational Leadership

Elementary School Guidance and Counseling

Elementary School Journal

Harvard Educational Review

High School Journal

History of Education

Instructional Science

Instructor

Interchange

International Education

Issues in Education

Journal of Classroom Interaction

Journal of Computer-Based Instruction

Journal of Curriculum and Supervision

Journal of Education

Journal of Education and Psychology

Journal of Educational Thought

Journal of Developmental Education

Journal of Humanistic Education and Development

Journal of Indian Education

Journal of Instructional Development

Journal of Modern Education

Journal of Moral Education

Journal of Negro Education

Journal of Philosophy of Education

Journal of Special Education

Kappa Delta Pi Record

Learning

Lifelong Learning

McGill Journal of Education

Merrill-Palmer Quarterly

Middle School Journal

NASSP Bulletin

NEA Today

New Directions for Teaching and Learning

New Education

Notre Dame Journal of Education

Open Learning: Teaching and Training at a Distance

Peabody Journal of Education

Phi Delta Kappan

Pointer

Progressive Education

Scholastic Education

School Review

Teacher

Theory into Practice

Today's Education

Research Journals

American Educational Research Journal

Educational Record

Educational Research

Elementary School Journal

Human Development

International Journal of Educational Development

International Journal of Educational Research

Journal of Counseling and Development

Journal of Educational Psychology

Journal of Educational Research

Journal of Experimental Education

Journal of Instructional Psychology

Journal of Nonverbal Behavior

Journal of Research and Development in Education

Journal of Research in Science Teaching

Journal of School Psychology

Journal of Teacher Education

Journal of Verbal Learning and Verbal Behavior

Journal of Vocational Education Research

Journal of Youth and Adolescence

Learning and Motivation

Learning Disability Quarterly

National Forum of Applied Educational Research Journal

Oxford Review of Education

Research in Mathematics Education

Research in Science Education

Research in the Schools

Review of Educational Research

Review of Research in Education

Subject Specialty Journals

American Biology Teacher

Arithmetic Teacher

Art Education

Business Education World

Childhood Education

Education and Training of the Mentally Retarded

Educational Theatre Journal

Electronic Learning

Elementary English

Elementary Teachers' Guide to Free Materials

English Education

English Journal

Exceptional Child

Exceptional Children

Focus on Exceptional Children

History and Social Science Teacher

History Teacher

Gifted Child Quarterly

Gifted Child Today

Journal of Business Education

Journal of Chemical Education

Journal of Drug Education

Journal of Economic Education

Journal of Environmental Education

Journal of Industrial Teacher Education

Journal of Nutrition Education

Journal of Physical Education, Recreation and Dance

Journal of Reading

Journal of Reading Behavior

Journal of School Health

Journal of Sex Education and Therapy

Journalism Educator

Language

Language Learning

Language Teaching

Mathematics in School

Mathematics Teacher

Mathematics Teaching

Modern Language Journal

Physical Educator

Physics Education

Psychology in the Schools

Reading

Reading Improvement

Reading Teacher

School Arts Magazine

School Health Review

Science and Children

Science Education

Science Teacher

Scholastic Coach

School Counselor

School Science and Mathematics

Social Education

Social Studies Professional

Social Studies Review

Speech Communication Teacher

Studies in Science Education

Teaching English

Teaching Exceptional Children

Technology Teacher

TESOL Quarterly

Online Education Journals

The number of free, full-text online journals is rapidly increasing, encompassing virtually every academic discipline. A small sampling of open-access journals is included below:

Current Issues in Comparative Education

    www.tc.columbia.edu/cice/

Educational Technology Review

    www.aace.org/pubs/aacej/

Electronic Journal for the Integration of Technology in Education

    http://ejite.isu.edu/

Electronic Magazine of Multicultural Education

    www.eastern.edu/publications/emme/

Journal of Career and Technical Education

    http://scholar.lib.vt.edu/ejournals/JCTE/

Education Week on the Web

    www.edweek.org

Education World

    www.education-world.com

Reading Online

    International Reading Association

    www.readingonline.org

Research and Issues in Music Education

    www.stthomas.edu/rimeonline

Special Education News

    www.specialednews.com

Teacher Magazine

    www.teachermagazine.org

THE Journal

    www.thejournal.com/

For a more comprehensive list of online journals, check the following Web sites:

AERA's Open Access Journals

    http://aera-cr.asu.edu/ejournals/

Library of Congress—News and Periodical Resources on the Web

    www.loc.gov/rr/news/lists.html

Serials in Cyberspace—University of Vermont

    www.uvm.edu/~bmaclenn/

STRESS AND BURNOUT IN THE CLASSROOM

Stress is an inescapable part of any teacher's job. Indeed, Hans Selye, pioneer stress researcher, suggested that the absence of stress is death. Stress is part of the price of living. The greater risk occurs when individuals spend long periods of time under conditions of constant stress or tension.

Researchers have identified some professions, including teaching, as particularly prone to stress. Over a period of time, teachers can begin to experience a condition commonly referred to as burnout. Psychologist Christina Maslach has identified three phases of burnout. The first consists of emotional exhaustion, a loss of energy and enthusiasm, a feeling of being used up with nothing left to give. The second stage is characterized by insensitivity, cynicism, and callousness. The language of this stage is depersonalized, with teachers referring to students as "the animals" or "the beasts." Distrust and even dislike of one's students is evident. Of course, this creates the spiral effect of making students behave in even more distrustful and unacceptable ways.

The final phase embodies a feeling of despair that all one's efforts have been fruitless and the teacher is a failure. In short, burned-out teachers have lost their initial idealism, compassion, zeal, and energy. There is a discrepancy between one's efforts and the perceived rewards one gains from that effort, accompanied by a sense of sadness, hopelessness, helplessness, and lower self-esteem.

Of course, most teachers don't burn out in the classroom. Researchers suggest that approximately 3 to 4 percent of the teachers still in the classroom exhibit chronic symptoms of burnout. Many others leave the profession at the onset of burnout. Some struggle, feeling trapped. Surveys have suggested that about 30 percent of American teachers would prefer to be doing something else.

Various researchers have identified the following symptoms of burnout: physical exhaustion, absenteeism, abuse of alcohol or drugs (some areas have "teacher bars," where teachers congregate after work), chronic fatigue, boredom, depression, cynicism, moodiness, impatience, ulcers, headaches, excessive eating, blaming the students for their own problems, stubbornness, and resistance to change.

The first step in preventing burnout is to recognize its potential sources. It is the cumulative combination of many events over a period of time, not merely one event, that ultimately leads to burnout. Teacher burnout and stress have received a great deal of attention from educational researchers, who have identified the following items as particularly stressful for teachers:

- Angry parents
- Being threatened
- Class interruptions
- Competency testing
- Curriculum changes
- Faculty strikes
- Incompetent administrators
- Involuntary transfers
- Lack of adequate supplies, materials, and books
- Lack of planning time
- Management of disruptive students
- Overcrowded classrooms
- Receiving low evaluations
- School reorganization
- The first week of school
- Unrealistic expectations or standards
- Vandalism and destruction of personal property
- Verbal abuse from students

Stress Management in the Classroom

Teaching will always entail some potentially stressful events. However, teachers can develop strategies to inoculate themselves against the tensions of school life. Here are suggestions for reducing stress and preventing the onset of burnout:

- Avoid the loneliness of teaching. Adult contact can become very rare for some teachers. It is tempting for beginning teachers to isolate themselves, avoiding contact with the more experienced teachers. You can gain much from interacting with your colleagues.

- One of the single best predictors of who will avoid burnout is interaction with a supportive group of colleagues—at least one or two people who understand your frustrations and can listen with empathy. Find one or two people you can eat lunch with each day. Many schools develop support groups that meet periodically to share problems and search for creative solutions.

- At the first sign of burnout, do something different. Change grade levels, plan a new unit, or try teaching a different subject. Experiment with different curricular approaches: cooperative learning, independent study, learning centers, field trips, peer tutoring, teaming, or learning contracts. Continue to seek new challenges and break up old routines. Bring as much variety into your teaching as possible.

- Explore professional rejuvenation through continued education. Take a graduate course, subscribe to professional journals, attend professional workshops, or commit yourself to learning everything you can about a new topic. Learn something novel that you can incorporate into your teaching: some magic tricks, storytelling, drama, graphic design, or public speaking.

- Remember, you can't be all things to all people all the time. You are but a fallible human. The greatest baseball players in the world don't bat one thousand, and you don't have to be perfect either. You won't win them all no matter how hard you try. What counts is that you strive to do your best, to continually improve, and to learn from your mistakes.

- Set priorities. One source of stress for many teachers is overcommitment of their time. Feeling overwhelmed by all the demands on one's time is a cue that it's time to set priorities. Establishing which things are truly both urgent and important helps allocate one's energies and time. The more thought you give to what you value and to your professional and personal goals, the easier it is to set priorities.

> The only difference between a rut and a grave is the depth.
>
> **—Anonymous**

- Learning to say no to unimportant, distracting activities is an essential stress-prevention technique. Learn to judiciously use the phrase "I have a previous commitment" when asked to commit yourself to unimportant activities. You need not elaborate on the exact nature of that commitment (well, you might want to give your spouse more detail!). You must save some reserve of private time to recharge your batteries and renew your enthusiasm. You do no one a favor if you say yes to so many requests that you have little energy left to fulfill those commitments. Learn what your limits are.

- Don't try to do everything yourself. Delegate some tasks to students, aides, volunteers, or colleagues.

- Take care of your body. Substantial research concludes that we are more susceptible to stress and burnout when our bodies are fatigued, out of shape, and deprived of proper nutrition. Make exercise and play a top priority. Get sufficient sleep and eat a healthy balanced diet. Remember, if you take care of your body, your body will take care of you!

- Many schools have incorporated sabbaticals as an option for their teachers. If available, take advantage of one to renew your professional commitment.

Laughter makes good blood.

—Italian proverb

- Learn how and when to ask for help. Most people around you really do want you to succeed. Learn from others' successes and failures. If symptoms of burnout persist for several weeks, consider getting professional help from a qualified counselor.

- Get away. Take advantage of your summers to travel. Take short weekend excursions.

- It is essential to find some time to be alone every week, even if only for a few minutes. Some do it through walking quietly, playing a musical instrument, meditating, praying, or simply resting.

- Monitor your stress level. When you notice yourself becoming more tense, do something about it. Become proactive rather than reactive. Remember, the time to relax is when you can least afford to. Take time for yourself.

- Seek a balance in your life. Develop interests beyond teaching. Save time for social activities, hobbies, and community service. Avoid talking only about school when you are with friends.

- Above all, strive to maintain a healthy sense of humor. It helps keep things in perspective. Remember Henry Ward Beecher's warning that people without humor are like wagons without springs: they are jolted by every pebble in the road.

- Most important, always remember the adage that it is not events in our lives that cause stress but rather what we say to ourselves about those events. Self-defeating, irrational assumptions about the things that happen to us invite feelings of despair, depression, and anger. Challenge that illogical thought pattern. Strive to change "I must . . ." to "I would prefer . . ."

For More Information

Botwinik, R. (2007). Dealing with teacher stress. *Clearing House, 80,* 271–272.

Gates, G. S. (Ed.). (2007). *Emerging thought and research on student, teacher, and administrator stress and coping.* Charlotte, NC: IAP.

Hartney, E. (2008). *Stress management for teachers.* New York: Continuum.

Holmes, E. (2005). *Teacher well-being: Looking after yourself and your career in the classroom.* New York: Routledge.

Leithwood, K., & McAdie, P. (2007). Teacher working conditions that matter. *Education Canada, 47*(2), 42–45.

Stress Busters and Sanity Savers

Take a walk.	Learn a new skill.
Meditate.	Talk to a friend.
Take three slow, deep breaths.	Participate in an aerobic activity.

Read a book.

Avoid unnecessary arguments.

Take a vacation.

Get a massage.

Avoid getting too wrapped up in yourself.

Find some time to be alone.

Stretch.

Ask someone for help.

Get organized.

Challenge your irrational self-talk.

Listen to your favorite music.

Set long-term goals.

Take a nap.

Clean.

Apologize.

Dance.

Pursue a hobby.

Meet new people.

Write a letter.

Have a plan.

Eat a healthy diet.

Just listen.

Decorate your environment.

Try biofeedback training.

Never make important decisions after midnight.

Associate with people from other professions.

Volunteer for a worthy cause.

Problem solve.

Eliminate a self-defeating behavior.

Smile.

Be prepared.

List your strengths and successes.

Take a warm bath.

Keep a journal.

Remember that tomorrow is a new day.

Set priorities.

Join a self-help group.

Do one thing at a time.

Play a musical instrument.

Get professional help.

Try progressive muscle relaxation.

Develop a contract for change.

Look for a new job.

Make a list.

Shop during off-hours.

Take a break.

Maintain a sense of humor.

Visualize a calming scene.

Learn responsible assertiveness.

Distinguish between needs and wants.

Have a good belly laugh.

Relax your jaw.

Monitor your bodily reactions.

Reexamine conflicting goals.

Cultivate new relationships.

Keep a balance in your activities.

Know and accept yourself.

Learn to say no.

Treat others with kindness.

Stop to smell the roses.

Strive for an open mind.

Be an actor, not a reactor.

Unclutter your life.

Make effective planning a habit.

Eliminate needless worry.

Reexamine your shoulds and musts.

Take time for a good lunch.

Allow open time in your schedule.

Clarify your expectations.

Invite someone to lunch.

Live in the present.

Clarify others' expectations.

Avoid catastrophizing.

Get adequate rest.

Avoid perfectionism.

Seek a different perspective.

Help someone.

Try to remain flexible.

Try acupressure.

Hug someone.

Be thankful.

Develop self-affirming habits.

Recall a pleasant experience.

Forgive.

Challenge your assumptions.

Keep things in perspective.

Choose to be happy.

Avoid putting yourself down.

Remember to play.

Cry.

Adopt a pet.

Get up ten minutes earlier.

Sing.

Develop a support network.

Watch a great movie.

Note: Remember that many of the sample templates, letters, handouts for this chapter are available for download from the *Classroom Teacher's Survival Guide* Web site josseybass .com/go/classroomteacher.

Stress Management Contract

Goal: Select one stressor that you would like to eliminate or reduce. It should be one you can reasonably hope to decrease in the next 4–6 weeks. Write this as a goal.

My stress reduction goal is to: _____

_____

_____

Action Plan: Develop a strategy for accomplishing your stress reduction goal.

My strategy for achieving my stress reduction goal is: _____

_____

_____

Obstacles to my success might be: _____

_____

_____

I will need support from: _____

_____

_____

My reward for achieving my goal will be: _____

_____

_____

Each day I will: _____

_____

_____

_____

_____

Stress Symptoms

Physical Symptoms (body)

_____ Increased heart rate

_____ Increased perspiration

_____ Rapid breathing

_____ Headaches

_____ Tense muscles

_____ Dry mouth

_____ Frequent colds

_____ Stomach ache

_____ Colds

_____ Muscle aches

_____ Back pain

_____ Lightheadedness

_____ Sleep difficulties

_____ Trembling or shakiness

_____ Frequent fatigue

Emotional Symptoms (feelings)

_____ Crying

_____ Resentment

_____ Feeling overwhelmed

_____ Irritability

_____ Nightmares

_____ Feeling out of control

_____ Hopelessness

_____ Easily discouraged

_____ Loneliness

_____ Mood swings

_____ Anxiety, panic, nervousness

_____ Tense, edgy

_____ Unexplained sadness

_____ Anger

_____ Boredom

_____ Self-pity

Cognitive Symptoms (thoughts)

_____ Frequent worrying

_____ Confusion, inability to concentrate

_____ Difficulty making decisions

_____ Loss of creativity

_____ Lethargy

_____ Inability to laugh

_____ Forgetfulness

_____ Apathy

_____ Distrust

_____ Negative self-talk

Behavioral Symptoms (actions)

_____ Talking rapidly

_____ Abusing alcohol or drugs

_____ Neglecting responsibilities

_____ Grinding teeth (TMJ)

_____ Laughing nervously

_____ Increasing tobacco use

_____ Losing sex drive

_____ Becoming unable to get things done

_____ Overeating

_____ Being accident prone

FAMOUS AMERICANS WHO ALSO TAUGHT SCHOOL

John Adams, U.S. president

Madeleine Albright, secretary of state

Louisa May Alcott, author

Chester A. Arthur, U.S. president

Clara Barton, founder of the American Red Cross

Alexander Graham Bell, inventor

Dan Brown, author of *The Da Vinci Code*

Sheryl Crow, singer-songwriter

Clarence Darrow, attorney

Amelia Earhart, aviator

Geraldine Ferraro, vice presidential candidate

Roberta Flack, singer

Abigail Fillmore, first lady

Margaret Fuller, transcendentalist author, social reformer

Art Garfunkel, singer

Andy Griffith, actor

John Wesley Hardin, outlaw

Warren G. Harding, U.S. president

Lyndon B. Johnson, U.S. president

Stephen King, author

Eugene McCarthy, U.S. senator, presidential candidate

William McKinley, U.S. president

Herman Melville, author

James Michener, author

Anne Murray, singer

Carry Nation, temperance leader

Pat Nixon, first lady

Thomas Paine, colonial patriot

Gen. John Pershing, World War I leader

Susan Elizabeth Phillips, best-selling author

William Quantrill, Confederate guerilla leader

Dixie Lee Ray, governor of Washington

Eleanor Roosevelt, first lady, author, lecturer

Tim Russert, TV newscaster

Gene Simmons, member of rock group "KISS"

Margaret Chase Smith, U.S. senator from Maine

Mary Church Terrell, social reformer

Strom Thurmond, U.S. senator from South Carolina

John Wooden, UCLA basketball coach

TEN INSPIRATIONAL TEACHER MOVIES

1. *To Sir, with Love* (1967)

A captivating classic, and well worth seeing as its message is as timely as ever. It depicts what teaching should be about.

Sidney Poitier's character, Mr. Thackeray (aka "Sir"), is an aspiring engineer, who accepts a temporary assignment as a new teacher in a London secondary school. He decides he must help his students prepare for life beyond school. The movie's theme song "To Sir with Love," sung by Lulu, became the year's number one hit song.

2. *Dead Poets Society* (1989)

Robin Williams received a nomination for the best actor Academy Award for his role as John Keating, a romantic, idealistic English teacher at a prestigious, staid boarding school. The film is a tribute to all teachers who have inspired their students to do great things with their lives. The theme of standing up for one's own beliefs resonates with many viewers.

An array of memorable lines come from this movie. One of the most cited is "Life is a play and you may contribute one verse. What will it be?" The film also revitalized the mantra of "Carpe Diem" ("seize the day").

Shot on location, the film offers the beautiful scenery of Delaware's St. Andrews Academy as a delightful bonus. Some literature teachers show this movie when discussing transcendentalism.

3. *Stand and Deliver* (1988)

Based on the true story of Jaime Escalante (played by Edward James Olmos), an East L.A. high school math teacher who motivates his "at-risk" students to pass the Advanced Placement Calculus Test.

The film embodies the concept that there are no unteachable students. It also stresses the immense peer pressure faced by ambitious students as they strive to excel in a discouraging academic climate.

This movie depicts what is close to an academic miracle—to achieve such a high-degree of success against such overpowering odds. A movie worth showing to math classes!

4. *Freedom Writers* (2007)

Another take on the inspiring teacher theme, but a fairly accurate account of a touching and inspirational true story. Naive rookie teacher Erin Gruwell (played by Hilary Swank) enters the classroom at Wilson High School in Long Beach, California, filled with enthusiasm and ready to change the world. She faces resistance from both her hardened students, her fellow teachers, and the administration.

Gruwell introduces the writings of Anne Frank and *Zlata's Diary: A Child's Life in Sarajevo* to teach not only English but also compassion and tolerance. She also initiates a project encouraging her students to write about their daily experiences in what is for many a violent, gang-ridden life.

Her students eventually published their journals in a book, *The Freedom Writers Diary*. For more information about the movie and teaching materials, see their Web site (www. freedomwriters.com/).

5. *Front of the Class* (2008)

Based on the true story of Brad Cohen (played by Jimmy Wolk) who passionately wants to become a teacher but faces the immense challenge of having Tourette Syndrome. The production first appeared as a Hallmark Hall of Fame TV movie in December 2008 and is now available on DVD. The movie was based on the book Cohen wrote, *Front of the Class: How Tourette Syndrome Made Me the Teacher I Never Had.*

Not only did Cohen's persistence pay off in a teaching job (after twenty-five interviews); he was awarded the Sallie Mae First Class Teacher of the Year for Georgia. He continues to stress tolerance and acceptance of others among his students. Check out Brad's blog Never Ever Ever Give Up (www.classperformance.com/blog/) for more insights on his teaching career.

6. *Pappr Clips* (2004)

Lauded as one of the best documentaries of 2004, *Paper Clips* depicts the true story of Whitwell, a small Tennessee mountain community. In 1998, Whitwell Middle School students initiated a hands-on project: collecting eleven million paper clips, one for each life exterminated by the Nazis in the Holocaust. The whole community became involved in this powerful lesson on the dangers of racial and social prejudice.

This is a powerful movie to show your students. For more about the film and this inspirational continuing story, see their Web site (www.paperclipsmovie.com).

7. *The Great Debaters* (2007)

Another great movie celebrating the triumph of the underdog. The setting for this real-life saga is Wiley College, a small historically black college, where, in 1935–36, Professor Melvin Tolson (Denzel Washington) coached the debate team to a nearly undefeated season and an invitation to face Harvard University's national champions. (It actually was the University of Southern California.)

James Farmer Jr., the noted civil rights leader, was one of Tolson's students.

8. *Goodbye, Mr. Chips* (1939)

This movie depicts the teacher we hoped for as students and the teacher many of us would like to be. Robert Donat superbly plays the role of Mr. Chipping as he nostalgically recalls his almost sixty-year teaching career at the fictitious Brookfield School. Donat's performance won him the Oscar for best actor. Every teacher should see this original version at least once.

9. *Blackboard Jungle* (1955)

Richard Dadier (Glenn Ford) is an idealistic rookie teacher assigned to a New York inner-city high school. He wrestles with many of the social issues (racism, apathy, violence) faced by too many contemporary teachers. The opening theme song, "Rock Around the Clock," played by Bill Haley and the Comets, helped usher in the rock and roll era.

10. *Music of the Heart* (1999)

Meryl Streep received an Oscar nomination for best actress for her portrayal of violin teacher Roberta Guaspari and her tenacious fight to save the violin music program she had implemented in an East Harlem school. While taking some literary license, the story depicts the true story of Guaspari. Some of her real students even appear in the film.

Professional Development Record

Activity	Goals	Date/Time Spent

Helpful Resources for Teachers

9

SCROUNGING FOR SUPPLIES

Are there activities you would like to try in your class but can't because there aren't funds for the necessary supplies? Cutbacks and tight budgets have led to rationing of paper and books in many schools, with little money available for teaching materials. Yet some teachers have a knack for gathering needed supplies at no or little cost. Since the earliest days of formal education, resourceful teachers have mastered the delicate art of scrounging.

Those teachers who approach their supply shortage creatively realize that much is available for the mere asking and hauling. What a merchant may consider to be useless discards may indeed be treasures in a creative teacher's hands. Here are seven suggestions for improving your skills in scrounging for supplies:

1. *Be specific.* Know exactly what you need and how much. This helps you identify potential donors. Emphasize the specific instructional purpose of the desired item.

2. *Time your request appropriately.* Avoid the rush hours, when merchants will be most preoccupied with their customers. Also try to time your inquiries to miss peak holiday business. Submit your request directly to the owner or manager when possible. A direct request made in person is more likely to be taken seriously.

3. *Emphasize the educational purpose.* Most citizens are aware of schools' strained finances. Your request permits them to help in a small and usually painless way. Mentioning the potential tax deduction for donated items also helps.

4. *Make moderate requests.* Certainly don't ask a donor to deliver merchandise. Any special labor expenses are likely to deter much generosity.

5. *Use your contacts.* Prime prospects are parents of present or past students, previous donors, vocal supporters of schools, as well as relatives and friends. A cousin of the school custodian has a connection with your school that may encourage generosity. A note sent to parents or a brief notice in the local newspaper describing what you need may be successful. Make your needs known!

6. *Don't fear rejection.* There are many legitimate reasons why a request cannot be filled. Usually, it is because the source does not have what you are requesting. For example, if a newspaper office has just discarded all of its old newsprint, you might ask that they hold future waste newsprint for you. Try to pinpoint a specific date to check back.

7. *Show appreciation.* Future donations are more likely if a gift is acknowledged. A special note of thanks from the teacher is a minimum. A large gift warrants a note from the principal or letters from the class or even an acknowledgment in the school or local newspaper. By looking at your local phone directory's Yellow Pages, you can quickly identify a great many potential donors for needed supplies. To stimulate your thinking, consider the following suggestions.

Potential Sources for Teaching Supplies

Airline	Magazines, courtesy kits
Appliance store	Large cartons, cardboard
Bank	Coin wrappers, free maps
Business	Computers, computer software, storage bins, boxes
Carpet store	Carpet remnants, cardboard tubes
Caterer	Leftover crepe paper, party supplies
Computer store	Software, CDs, used computers
Contractor	Scrap lumber, boards, plastic pipe, bricks
Dentist	Toothbrushes, posters, pamphlets, old magazines
Department store	Holiday decorations (after season)
Dry cleaner	Hangers, plastic bags
Electrician	Electrical wire, small pieces of conduit
Farmer	Burlap bags, grains, biological specimens, twine
Florist	Floral wrapping paper, ribbon, plants
Garage sale	Books, magazines, toys, window shades, storage bins, dish pans, books, and so on
Greenhouse	Pots, starter plants, flowers
Greeting card store	Loose colored envelopes, stickers
Hairdresser	Wigs, cosmetics
Hospital	Empty pill bottles, various containers, boxes, health literature, tongue depressors
Insurance company	Note pads, calendars, actuarial tables
Liquor store	Boxes, cartons
Lumber yard	Scrap boards, nail aprons, yardsticks, rulers
Motel/Hotel	Linen, soap, matches, cups
Newspaper office	Newsprint from roll ends, photos, film canisters
Nursing home	Empty pill bottles, boxes
Paint store	Wallpaper sampler books, paint, buckets, stirrers
Parents	Furniture, carpeting, books, cloth material, containers, clothing, greeting card fronts, old shirts for smocks, margarine containers, wallpaper remnants, yarn, and so on
Pizza parlor	Round cardboard plates, pizza boxes for storage

Plasterer .... Five-gallon buckets

Plumber .... Scrap plastic pipe

Post office .... Outdated FBI wanted circulars, stamp posters

Printer .... Paper, card stock, ink, cardboard boxes with lids

Professor .... Books, journals

Radio and TV repair shop ... Magnets, wires, electrical parts, knobs

Radio or TV station............. CDs, DVDs, used equipment, scripts

Real estate company .... Note pads, calendars, local maps

Restaurant .... Bottle corks, party supplies, straws, paper cups, coupons, containers, posters, napkins, empty bottles

Supermarket .... Styrofoam trays, egg crates, berry baskets, shelving

Tailor .... Cloth, empty thread spools

Theater .... Tickets to be used as prizes, movie posters

Tobacco shop .... Empty cigar boxes

Travel agency...................... Travel posters, maps

Upholsterer .... Scrap remnants, thread

Suppliers of Instructional Materials

American Classroom Supply

www.american-classroom-supply.com/

(866) 960-8427

Broad selection of instructional supplies in all subject areas and grade levels

American Educational Products

www.amep.com

(800) 289-9299

Wide array of science education materials, lab supplies, math manipulatives, raised relief maps, posters, games

Carson-Dellosa

www.carsondellosa.com/

(800) 321-0943

Math manipulatives, games, floor puzzles, teacher resources, notes and gift sets, stickers and dots, charts, bulletin board and door decor, free clip art

Continental Press

www.continentalpress.com/

(800) 233-0759

Instructional materials for preK–12; instructional booklets and computer software for reading, literature, language, social studies, and early childhood

Creative Publications

www.creativepublications.com

(800) 624-0822

K–12 math and language arts; manipulatives, overheads, time, counters, money, number concepts, cooperative problem solving, teacher resources, calculators, posters

Creative Teaching Press

www.creativeteaching.com/

(800) 444-4287

K–6 materials; multicultural art activities, books, pocket charts, calendars, charts, bulletin board materials, stickers, rewards, organizers, children's music

Crystal Springs Books

www.crystalsprings.com/

(800) 321-0401

Resources for K–6; whole language, multiage classrooms, developmental education, cooperative learning, inclusion, assessment and evaluation, math and science, discipline, and self-esteem

Curriculum Associates, Inc.

www.curriculumassociates.com/

(800) 225-0248 (U.S. and Canada)

PreK–8; multicultural titles, spelling, writing, phonics, literature, software, plays, DVDs, activities, books (Spanish translations available), study skills and test taking, test prep, ESL-bilingual: language-learning technology

EduMart.com

www.edumart.com/

E-mail: edumart@edumart.com

Over twenty-eight thousand educational items; retail stores across the country

Evan-Moor

www.evan-moor.com/

(800) 777-4362

Books: math, science, geography, writing, art, thematic units, whole language, bulletin board materials, clip art

Gamco Educational Software

www.gamco.com/

(800) 351-1404

Instructional and classroom management software, teacher tools

Lakeshore Learning Materials

www.lakeshorelearning.com/

(800) 421-5354

Arts and crafts supplies, puppets, role-playing supplies and props, classroom furniture, storage and organizer equipment, play equipment, manipulatives

Mari, Inc.

www.mariinc.com/

(800) 955-9494

Reference books, whole language library, math workbooks, sticker books, reading games, graphic organizers, test-preparation materials, library supplies

Marsh Media

www.marshmedia.com/

(800) 821-3303

DVDs, software on health and wellness, guidance, drug education, and consumer education

NIMCO

www.nimcoinc.com/

(800) 962-6662

Drug education and sex education materials, DVDs, games, posters, books, and supplies

Perfection Learning Corporation

www.perfectionlearning.com/

(800) 831-4190

Books for a literature-based classroom including audiobooks, big books, software, books for reluctant readers

Positive Promotions

www.positivepromotions.com/

(800) 635-2666

Safety and health-related promotional materials, calendars, health guides, coloring books, pens, mugs, buttons

Scholastic Professional Books

557 Broadway

New York, NY 10012-3999

http://teacher.scholastic.com/professional/profbooks/

(800) 325-6149

Instructor books in an array of subject areas, classroom management and lesson planning software, technology-based activities

Sunburst

www.sunburst.com/

(800) 431-1934

Creativity tools, audio-video equipment, games, posters, curriculum modules for grades 2–12, staff development

Tom Snyder Productions

www.tomsnyder.com/

(800) 342-0236

K–12 educational software, DVDs, books, time line tools, interactive whiteboard materials

Trend Enterprises

www.trendenterprises.com/

(800) 328-0818

Activity kits, awards, classroom decorations, posters, stickers, bulletin board sets, letters

United Art and Education Supply Co.

www.unitednow.com/

(800) 322-3247

Paints, brushes, crayons, markers, drawing supplies, office supplies, crafts, puzzles, classroom management resources, holiday helpers, signing helpers, musical instruments

Sources of Rubber Stamps

Simon Says Stamp

www.simonsaysstamp.com

Simply Stamps

www.simplystamps.com/

The Stampin' Place

www.stampin.com/online/designs/teacher.htm

TheStampMaker.com

www.thestampmaker.com

THE INTERNET AS A LEARNING RESOURCE

Since 1990, approximately two billion dollars have been spent to put an additional two million computers in America's schools. Virtually all schools are now connected to the Internet. The advent of cyberspace and the explosive expansion of the information superhighway have the potential to profoundly influence American education. Though they will never replace effective teachers, in the coming decade computers will play an increasingly dramatic role in reshaping teaching.

Schools throughout the nation, indeed the world, are plugging into the Internet. The global classroom is fast becoming a reality. The Internet is a worldwide collection of computer networks connecting millions of computers to one another. By the end of 2008, the search engine Google indexed over a trillion URLs or Web sites. The Internet is an enormous learning resource of almost unimaginable potential for enhancing education. By the beginning of 2009, a Pew Foundation survey found that 93 percent of U.S. teens were Internet users. U.S. Department of Labor projections suggest by 2016, one in four jobs will require computer skills. The nation is also adding over one hundred thousand new computer-related jobs each year.

Many teachers and students have already discovered exciting, creative, and productive applications of this technological revolution. Those who do not obtain access to the Internet will surely be at a disadvantage. The Internet holds tremendous promise for all aspects of education: administration, instruction, professional development, and community involvement. Students in the most remote schools in the nation have the world at their fingertips.

Professional development opportunities abound with the Internet. Every day, teachers can interact with others teaching the same subjects and facing the same problems. Collaboration with teachers halfway around the world can be facilitated. Discussion groups already exist for nearly every topic being taught in school. Via e-mail, teachers have direct access to top experts in virtually every field. The potential for using the Internet as a tool to enrich global and cultural awareness is unlimited.

Millions of files are open to your use as teaching resources, including guides and images for use in the classroom. Students can directly communicate with students from other countries and states. Here is just a sampling of what you can find on the Internet:

- NASA's Earth Observatory (earthobservatory.nasa.gov/) provides a massive reference archive, providing numerous up-to-date articles about oceans, the atmosphere, land, and life.

- Middle and high school students can view CNN's Student News (www.cnn.com/studentnews/), a daily commercial-free news broadcast. Teachers can also download free curriculum materials, including news quizzes, learning activities, and discussion questions.

- The Library of Congress (www.loc.gov/index.html) offers photographic and sound collections from both the American Memory Project and the African-American Culture and History online exhibit, as well as access to LOCIS (the Library of Congress Information System).

- Check out the National Weather Service site (nws.noaa.gov/) for just about anything related to climate and weather.

- EdWeb Project (www.edwebproject.org/) is an online tutorial for K–12 educators concerned with the use of telecommunications in teaching. The site provides success stories on computer use in the classroom.

- Opportunities exist for students to engage in cross-cultural language exchanges with French, Russian, Spanish, Japanese, or German students. For example, see Intercultural E-mail Classroom Connections (www.iecc.org/).

- The Educator's Reference Desk (www.eduref.org/) provides a wide assortment of information to educators. The site houses over two thousand lesson plans and more than three thousand links to online education information.

- Thomas (thomas.loc.gov), the Internet link to documents from the House of Representatives and Senate, provides full texts of the *Congressional Record* and information on pending legislation.

- Log into NASA's SpaceLink (spacelink.nasa.gov/), a searchable database of educational materials and information related to NASA Aeronautics and Space Research.

- Images can be downloaded from the National Oceanic and Atmospheric Administration (www.noaa.gov/), U.S. Global Change Research Program (www.usgcrp.gov/usgcrp/default.php), or the National Weather Service (www.nws.noaa.gov/) to study weather patterns. Global weather changes can be observed almost as they are occurring.

- World War II Resources (www.ibiblio.org/pha/) houses hundreds of primary source materials regarding all aspects of the war.

- National Geographic Maps: Tools for Adventure (www.mywonderfulworld.org/toolsforadventure/index.html) offers an extensive collection of maps from every area of the world.

- Daily White House press releases and briefings are available online at www.whitehouse.gov/.

- A computerized cadaver is available through the Visible Human Project at the National Library of Medicine. Magnetic resonance imaging and computerized tomography were used to scan nineteen hundred slices of the corpse of a 205-pound man. Portions of this database may be viewed at www.nlm.nih.gov/research/visible/visible_human.html/.

- An assortment of electronic publications—journals, books, newsletters, newspapers, and digests—is available through the Internet. The full texts of these publications are available for online reading or retrieval as portable document format (PDF) files. Many are listed at the end of this chapter and in Chapter Eight.

E-mail

The most common use of computer networks is exchanging e-mail messages. In 2008, an estimated 1.6 billion e-mail boxes existed worldwide, exchanging over 180 billion e-mail messages per day.

Any Internet user can send text messages to any other computer user with an Internet address. A variety of directories can help locate another user's Internet address (one directory is Switchboard at switchboard.com). Software, such as Eudora or Outlook Express, makes sending and receiving e-mail messages fairly easy.

Here are just a few of e-mail's educational applications:

- Some students practice their new foreign language skills by communicating with native students speaking that language.

- Anyone can send messages to the president or vice president through e-mail (president@whitehouse.gov or vpresident@whitehouse.gov).

- Often the top experts in any field of study can be contacted by e-mail.

- Many schools use electronic pen-pal connections to learn more about other cultures.

Electronic Discussion Groups

Thousands of e-mail discussion groups cover almost every conceivable topic; there are scores of groups related to education. To participate in discussions, a user must first subscribe to the listserv. The process may vary somewhat, but generally one sends an e-mail to the subscription address with the message "subscribe NAME OF GROUP First name Last name." For example: "subscribe MIDDLE-L Janet Smith" (without the quotes) would get Janet Smith subscribed to the Middle-L discussion group.

Several excellent Web sites catalog the thousands of discussion groups. These are among the most comprehensive directories:

Classroom Connect

www.classroom.com/community/email/

The Ezine Directory

www.ezine-dir.com/

USENET Discussion Groups

www.edwebproject.org/usenets.html

Yahoo Groups

http://groups.yahoo.com/

Some Popular Online Education Discussion Groups

TITLE	TOPIC	SUBSCRIPTION E-MAIL ADDRESS
ACSOFT-L	Educational software	listserv@wuvmd.wustl.edu
ADMIN	Educational administration	listproc@bgu.edu
BIOPI-L.	Teaching biology	listserv@ksuvm.ksu.edu
CHATBACK	Special education	listserv@sjuvm.stjohns.edu
ECENET-L	Early childhood education	listserv@postoffice.cso.uiuc.edu
EDNET	Internet use in education	ednet@nic.umass.edu
EDTECH	Educational technology	listserv@msu.edu
EDUTEL	Educational technology	listserv@vm.its.rpi.edu
EFFSCHPRAC	Effective school practices	mailserv@oregon.uoregon.edu
ELED-L	Elementary education	listserv@ksuvm.ksu.edu
FLTEACH	Teaching foreign languages	listserv@ubvm.cc.buffalo.edu
H-HIGH-S	Teaching high school social studies	listserv@msu.edu
K12ADMIN	K–12 educational administration	listserv@suvm.syr.edu
K12ASSESS-L	K–12 educational assessment	mailserv@lists.cua.edu
MIDDLE-L	Middle level education	listserv@postoffice.cso.uiuc.edu
MULT-ED	Multicultural education	listproc@gmu.edu
NCSS-L	Social studies education, K–12	listproc2@bgu.edu
NCTM-L	Math teachers	listproc@scied.fit.edu
NEWEDU-L	New educational methods	newedul@uscvm.bitnet
PHYSHARE	Teaching high school physics	listserv@lists.psu.edu
SPECED-L	Special education	specedl@uga.cc.uga.edu
TAG-L	Talented and gifted education	listserv@vm1.nodak.edu
TEACHEFT	Teacher effectiveness	listserv@wcupa.edu

Online Resources for Beginning Teachers

A to Z Teacher Stuff

www.atozteacherstuff.com/

Access myriad of teaching ideas and resources

ADPRIMA

www.adprima.com/ideamenu.htm

Ideas for new teachers and education students

Education World

www.education-world.com/a_curr/curr152.shtml

Advice for first-year teachers

Inspiring Teachers

www.inspiringteachers.com/

Beginning teacher's toolbox

Teacher Focus

www.teacherfocus.com

Chat and resources for new teachers

Teacher Tap

www.eduscapes.com

ICATS: Integrating Teaching and Technology

U.S. Department of Education

www.teachersfirst.com/whatexpect.pdf

What to expect your first year of teaching

Online Lesson Plan Archives

Cool Teaching Lessons and Units

www.coollessons.org

Emphasizes hands-on learning projects

Daily Lesson Plan Archive (*New York Times*)

www.lessonplanspage.com/

High-quality lessons for grades 6–12

Education Reform

www.digitalequity.edreform.net/resource/1106

A huge treasury of teacher resources and tools

Educator's Network

www.theeducatorsnetwork.com/

Massive guide to online lesson plan archives

Educator's Reference Desk

www.eduref.org/

Over two thousand unique lesson plans submitted by teachers

Federal Resources for Educational Excellence

www.ed.gov/free/

Teaching and learning resources from thirty federal agencies

Gateway to Educational Materials

www.thegateway.org/

Thousands of educational materials, including lesson
  plans, projects, and activities

Hot Chalk Lesson Archive

www.lessonplanspage.com/

Over 3,500 lessons in all subjects, K–12

LanternFish

www.bogglesworld.com

Lessons for teachers of ESL

Lesson Planet

www.lessonplanet.com/

Searchable database of over 150,000 lesson plans;
  a subscription service; Free trial

Library of Congress

lcweb2.loc.gov/ammem/ndlpedu/

Good variety of lesson plans

National Council of Teachers of Mathematics

www.nctm.org/resources/default.aspx?id=230

Math activities to motivate your students

National Endowment for the Humanities

www.edsitement.neh.gov/

Lessons in art, culture, literature, languages, social studies

National Geographic

www.education-world.com/a_lesson/

Excellent lessons in geography, history, and science

Science NetLinks

www.sciencenetlinks.com/matrix.cfm

Outstanding science lessons

Teacher Tube

www.teachertube.com

Online sharing of instructional videos

Thinkfinity

www.thinkfinity.org/

An array of standards-based educational resources

Online Collaborative Learning Resources

Widespread access to the Internet in classrooms has made possible collaborative learning activities with students across town or around the globe. Online collaborative projects engage and motivate students, challenging them to solve hands-on, real-world problems. Here are a few useful Web sites for getting started in online collaborative learning:

EPal Classroom Exchange

www.epals.com/

Claims to be the largest online classroom community. Students from 191 countries participate in ePal programs.

Global SchoolNet Foundation

www.globalschoolnet.org

Lists over 750 online collaborative learning projects.

Online Collaborative Education Projects

www.globalclassroom.org/collaboration/

Projects connect students around the world.

OzProjects

www.ozprojects.edna.edu.au/

This Australian site promotes international online curriculum projects.

Project Harmony

www.projectharmony.org

Projects promoting multicultural awareness, knowledge, and perspective.

Schools Online

www.schoolsonline.org/

Students from around the world collaborate on educational programs and service projects.

Schools Online

www.schoolsonline.org/whatwedo/

Projects emphasize cross-cultural dialogue.

Educational Search Engines

The Internet provides instant access to billions of documents and Web sites; some general search engines access many sources unsuitable for children. Many teachers steer their students to safe, selective education search engines or directories. Here is a sampling of the best:

Ask for Kids

www.askkids.com/

Kid-friendly filtered search engine.

Awesome Library

www.awesomelibrary.org/

Organizes the Web with thirty-six carefully reviewed resources.

B. J. Pinchbeck's Homework Helper

www.bjpinchbeck.com/

Well-organized portal of education sites.

Blue Web'n

www.kn.pacbell.com/wired/bluewebn/

Online library of outstanding Internet sites categorized by subject, grade level, and format. Excellent search engine.

Free-Ed Net

www.free-ed.net/

Access a wide range of free courses and instructional sites in many subjects. Primarily for high school and adult students.

Gateway to 21st Century Skills

www.thegateway.org/

Catalogs over fifty thousand screened educational resources.

INFOMINE

infomine.ucr.edu/

Well-designed site, accessing a multitude of scholarly sources.

Teen Space

www.ipl.org/div/teen/

Internet public library specifically for teens.

Yahoo! Kids

kids.yahoo.com/

Fun educational resources for kids, with games, reference, music, e-cards, movies, news, science.

Useful Online Databases

A vast array of easily accessible databases may be found on the Internet. Creative teachers incorporate online research of these treasures into their lessons.

Smithsonian Institution: The Smithsonian Institution (www.si.edu/) provides an assortment of information and pictures on the Internet. Teachers and students may access hundreds of stimulating online exhibits.

Access to Libraries: Teachers and students can access online library catalogs and databases at virtually every major library in the United States, including the Library of Congress, and many in other nations. Databases such as ERIC, the world's largest collection of information about education, can be accessed. For example, Harvard's libraries can be accessed at lib. harvard.edu/, and Stanford University's libraries at www-sul.stanford.edu/.

Song Lyrics: The Lyrics Connection (www.lyricsconnection.com/index.html) provides a search function to locate song lyrics, biographies, and discographies. The Digital Tradition (www. mudcat.org/) is an Internet archive containing the lyrics and music to thousands of folk songs and children's songs.

Tutorials and Lessons: Workshops and courses are available over the Internet. Thousands of learners can participate simultaneously in a broad and rapidly expanding array of tuto-

rial programs. Its use as a virtual classroom is likely to increase in the coming decade. The paperless classroom is not beyond imagination. The electronic town hall meeting is fast becoming a reality. For example, *Mr. Shakespeare and the Internet* (shakespeare.palomar.edu) organizes anything and everything about the Bard and his works, from full-text files of his plays and sonnets to an assortment of lesson plans. Check out the Shakespeare Biography Quiz.

E-books: Project Gutenberg (promo.net/pg/) is a master depository of over six thousand e-books, full texts available over the Internet.

Facts and Figures: The *CIA World Factbook* (www.cia. gov/index.html) provides current information on the nations of the world. Access it online or download the book as a PDF file. The U.S. Census Bureau (www.census.gov/) offers a mass of data on the decennial census, as well as approximately a hundred surveys and other census analyses conducted each year. View, download, and print a vast library of maps covering virtually any U.S. address.

NASA: NASA (www.nasa.gov/home/index.html) provides the educational community a virtual library of space- and aeronautical-related files and links. Special events, missions, and intriguing NASA Web sites are featured in Spacelink's Hot Topics and Cool Picks areas.

Software and Shareware: Download hundreds of freeware and shareware programs from Pass the Shareware (www.shareware.com) or 5 Star Shareware (www.5star-shareware. com). All programs are scanned for viruses, tested, and rated. Macintosh users can find a large depository of freeware and shareware at Mac Shareware (www.macshareware.com).

Telescopes Online: Harvard's MicroObservatory (mo-www.harvard.edu/MicroObservatory) is a network of five automated telescopes teachers and students can access over the Internet. This site demonstrates desktop astronomy and astrophysics to students. Users of MicroObservatory actually control the telescopes online, focus them, and direct their image photography.

Online Directories

Content on the Internet has grown exponentially in the past decade. Several outstanding online catalogs organize resources, making them more readily accessible. Some of the more helpful ones include the following:

About.com, the Human Internet (www.about.com/)

Owned by the *New York Times*, this site accesses over one million of the finest Internet sites, covering over fifty thousand subjects. A network of expert "Guides," volunteer experts, help others answer almost any question. Data is organized into an array of channels.

Educator's Reference Desk (www.eduref.org/)

The valuable site should be bookmarked by every educator. It provides instant access to thousands of Web sites as well as a searchable lesson plan archive.

Librarians' Internet Index (lii.org/)

Driven by the motto "Information you can trust," this top-notch portal selects the best of the Web, excluding purely commercial sites that offer no information. Updated weekly, this site is a good starting point for scholarly information seeking, and is recognized as one of the best free reference Web sites. Use this in conjunction with a filter product if you are using it with children.

Yahoo (www.yahoo.com/)

Yahoo is one of the oldest and largest Internet directories, offering an extensive master index to much of what is available on the World Wide Web.

Helpful Books on Using the Internet in the Classroom

Green, T. D., Brown, A., & Robinson, L. (2008). *Making the most of the Web in your classroom: A teacher's guide to blogs, podcasts, wikis, pages, and sites.* Thousand Oaks, CA: Corwin.

Nelson, K. (2008). *Teaching in the digital age: Using the Internet to increase student engagement and understanding.* Thousand Oaks, CA: Corwin.

Reich, J., & Daccord, T. (2008). *Best ideas for teaching with technology: A practical guide for teachers, by teachers.* Armonk, NY: M.E. Sharpe.

Richardson, W. (2009). *Blogs, wikis, podcasts, and other powerful Web tools for classrooms* (2nd ed.). Thousand Oaks, CA: Corwin.

Willoughby, T., & Wood, E. (Eds.) (2008). *Children's learning in a digital world.* Malden, MA: Blackwell.

Organizations Supporting Educational Use of the Internet

Association for Educational Communications and Technology (www.aect.org)

An international forum for exchanging ideas on instructional and educational technology. Sponsors an International Student Media Festival, recognizing outstanding student-produced classroom media projects.

Association for the Advancement of Computing in Education (www.aace.org)

Promotes information technology in education and e-learning research, development, learning, and its practical application.

International Society for Technology in Education (ISTE) (www.iste.org)

Seeks to improve teaching and learning through the application of educational technology. Publishes the periodical *Learning & Leading,* featuring practical ideas for applying educational technology in the classroom.

International Technology Education Association (www.iteaconnect.org)

Promotes the development of computer literacy in schools. Publishes *The Technology Teacher,* targeting K–12 technology classroom application. Another ITEA periodical, *Technology and Children,* focuses on K–8 applications of computer technology.

COMPUTER SOFTWARE FOR IMPROVING TEACHER PRODUCTIVITY

A fine selection of computer software packages are available to help teachers with many of the tasks of instruction and recordkeeping. The prices listed here were accurate in the winter of 2009. They may vary with time and by vendor.

Class Action Gradebook

$39 (Macintosh, Windows)

CalEd Software

www.classactiongradebook.com/

Grade book, seating charts, proficiency reports, and more.

Classmaster

$66 (Macintosh, Windows)

William K. Bradford Publishing Co.

www.wkbradford.com/classmast.htm

Computer grade book and attendance software.

Crossword Compiler

$59 (Windows)

WordWeb Software

www.crossword-compiler.com

Make your own crossword puzzles.

Crossword Construction Kit

$25 (Windows)

Insight Software Solutions

www.crosswordkit.com

Design crossword puzzles.

Grade Quick!

$70 (Macintosh, Windows, Palm)

Jackson Software

www.edline.com

Handles a variety of grading options, customized progress reports.

Gradekeeper

$20 (Macintosh, Windows)

www.gradekeeper.com/

Record grades and attendance.

Inspiration

$69 (Macintosh, Windows)

Inspiration Software

www.inspiration.com/

Electronic graphic organizer tool; draws concept maps.

MicroGrade

$90 (Macintosh, Windows)

Chariot Software Group

www.chariot.com/micrograde/index.asp

Scores assignments, calculates grades, generates performance reports. Includes optional e-mail and Internet grade-posting feature.

MicroTest Pro

$89 (Macintosh, Windows)

Chariot Software Group

www.chariot.com

Test bank holds up to fifteen thousand items; customizes tests.

Moodle

moodle.org

Free (accessible via any browser)

Moodle is free open-source software package for developing Internet-based courses and Web sites. Over half a million educators have already registered to use this software. An exciting view of the future applications of open-source software.

Puzzlemaker

$50 (Macintosh, Windows)

Discovery Channel School

puzzlemaker.discoveryeducation.com

Generates ten kinds of word and math puzzles.

School Maestro III

$44 (Windows)

Russ & Ryan EdWare

www.rredware.com

Advanced grade book software. Students and parents can access online progress reports, attendance reports, and homework assignments.

Test Maestro II

$35 (Windows)

Russ & Ryan EdWare

www.rredware.com

Test bank and test generator for teachers.

ThoughtManager for Education

$40 (Macintosh, Windows, Palm)

Hands High Software

www.thoughtmanager.com/html/

Create and organize lesson plans, lectures, and learning activities. Record student learning with standards-based checklists and rubrics. Manage classroom activities.